Pro SQL Server 2012 Integration Services

T0094376

Francis Rodrigues
Michael Coles
David Dye

Apress®

Pro SQL Server 2012 Integration Services

ISBN-13 (pbk): 978-1-4302-3692-4

ISBN-13 (electronic): 978-1-4302-3694-8

President and Publisher: Paul Manning
Lead Editor: Jonathan Gennick
Technical Reviewer: Rodney Landrum
Editorial Board: Steve Anglin, Ewan Buckingham, Gary Cornell, Louise Corrigan, Morgan Ertel, Jonathan Gennick, Jonathan Hassell, Robert Hutchinson, Michelle Lowman, James Markham, Matthew Moodie, Jeff Olson, Jeffrey Pepper, Douglas Pundick, Ben Renow-Clarke, Dominic Shakeshaft, Gwenan Spearing, Matt Wade, Tom Welsh
Coordinating Editor: Anita Castro
Copy Editor: Sharon Wilkey
Compositor: Bytheway Publishing Services
Indexer: Dhaneesh Kumar
Cover Designer: Anna Ishchenko

Distributed to the book trade worldwide by Springer Science+Business Media New York, 233 Spring Street, 6th Floor, New York, NY 10013. Phone 1-800-SPRINGER, fax (201) 348-4505, e-mail orders-ny@springer-sbm.com, or visit www.springeronline.com.

For information on translations, please e-mail rights@apress.com, or visit www.apress.com.

Apress and friends of ED books may be purchased in bulk for academic, corporate, or promotional use. eBook versions and licenses are also available for most titles. For more information, reference our Special Bulk Sales–eBook Licensing web page at www.apress.com/bulk-sales.

Any source code or other supplementary materials referenced by the author in this text is available to readers at http://www.apress.com/9781430236924. For detailed information about how to locate your book's source code, go to www.apress.com/source-code.

This book is dedicated to my family and friends without whose support and encouragement the writing would not have been possible.

–Francis Rodrigues

Contents at a Glance

Contents

About the Authors

 **Francis Rodrigues** is a computer science graduate of the Loyola University in Maryland. He is also an alumnus of Regis High School, a Jesuit school in New York City. He currently works as a business intelligence consultant based out of New York City. He is an expert developer of enterprise business intelligence projects. His specialties include extract, transform, and load (ETL) solutions based on SQL Server and SQL Server Integration Services (SSIS). In his spare time, he can be found mountain biking in various locations in the New York area.

 **Michael Coles** has more than a decade's experience designing and administering SQL Server databases. A prolific writer of articles on all aspects of SQL Server, particularly on the expert use of T-SQL, he holds MCDBA and MCP certifications. He graduated magna cum laude with a bachelor of science degree in information technology from American Intercontinental University in Georgia. A member of the United States Army Reserve, he was activated for two years following 9/11.

 **David Dye** is a Microsoft SQL Server MVP, instructor, and author specializing in relational database management systems, business intelligence systems, reporting solutions, and Microsoft SharePoint. For the past 9 years David's expertise has been focused on Microsoft SQL Server development and administration. His work has earned him recognition as: a Microsoft MVP in 2009 and 2010, a moderator for the Microsoft Developer Network for SQL Server forums, Innovator of the Year runner-up in 2009 by SQL Server Magazine, and in the Training Associates Technical Trainer Spotlight in April 2011. David currently serves as a technical reviewer and co-author with APress Publishing in the SQL Server 2012 series, and as an author with Packt Publishing.

About the Technical Reviewer

 **Rodney Landrum** has worked with SQL Server longer than he can remember. He writes regularly about technologies, including Integration Services, Analysis Services, and Reporting Services. He has authored *SQL Server Tacklebox* and three Reporting Services books. He contributes regularly to SQLServerCentral, SQL Server Magazine, and Simple–Talk. His day job involves overseeing a large SQL Server infrastructure in Orlando. He swears he owns the phrase "Working with Databases on a Day to Day Basis". Anyone who disagrees is itching to lose an arm wrestling match.

CHAPTER 1

Introducing Integration Services

I'm the glue that holds everything together.

—Singer Otis Williams

Your business analysts have finished gathering business requirements. The database architect has designed and built a database that can be described only as a work of art. The BI architects are designing their OLAP cubes and the dimensional data marts that feed them. On the other hand, maybe you're a one-man show and have designed and built everything yourself. Either way, the only piece that's missing is a tool to bring it all together. Enter SQL Server Integration Services (SSIS).

Like Otis Williams, cofounder of the Motown group the Temptations, SSIS is the glue that holds it all together. More than that, SSIS is the circulatory system of your data warehousing and BI solutions. SSIS breathes life into your technical solutions by moving data—the lifeblood of your organization—from disparate sources, along well-known paths, and injecting it directly into the heart of your system. Along the way, SSIS can validate, cleanse, manipulate, transform, and enrich your data for maximum effectiveness.

In this book, we'll take you on a tour of SSIS, from building your very first SSIS package to implementing complex multipackage design patterns seamlessly. This chapter introduces you to SSIS and the concepts behind extract, transform, and load (ETL) processes in general. We begin at the beginning, with a brief history of ETL, Microsoft-style.

A Brief History of Microsoft ETL

Before we dive headfirst into the details of Microsoft's current-generation ETL processing solution, it's important to understand just what ETL is. As we have stated, *ETL* is an acronym for *extract, transform, and load*, which is a very literal description of modern data manipulation and movement processes. When we talk about ETL, we are specifically talking about (1) *extracting* data from a source, such as a database or flat files; (2) *transforming* data, or manipulating and enriching it en route to its destination; and (3) *loading* data into its destination, often a database.

Over the years, business requirements for data processing in nearly any industry you can point to have grown more complex, even as the amount of data that needs to be processed has increased exponentially. Unfortunately, the number of hours in a day has remained fairly constant over the same time period, meaning you're stuck with the same limited processing window each day to transport and manipulate an ever-growing magnitude of data. ETL solutions have become increasingly sophisticated and robust in response to these increased data processing demands of performance, flexibility, and quality.

1

So we'll begin our journey into SSIS by looking at how ETL has evolved in the SQL Server world. Up to SQL Server 6.5, the *bulk copy program (bcp)* was the primary tool for loading data into SQL Server databases. A command-line utility, bcp made loading basic text files into database tables fairly simple. Unfortunately, the flip side of that simplicity was that you could use bcp only to load data from flat files, and you couldn't perform additional validations or transformations on the data during the load. A common database-to-database ETL scenario with bcp might include extracting data from a database server to a delimited text file, importing the file into a SQL Server database, and finally using T-SQL to perform transformations on the data in the database. The bcp utility is still provided with all versions of SQL Server, and is still used for simple one-off data loads from flat files on occasion.

In response to the increasing demands of ETL processing, Data Transformation Services (DTS) made its first appearance in SQL Server 7. With DTS, you could grab data from a variety of sources, transform it on the fly, and load it into the database. Although DTS was a much more sophisticated tool than bcp, it still lacked much of the functionality required to develop enterprise-class ETL solutions.

With the release of SQL Server 2005, Microsoft replaced DTS with SQL Server Integration Services (SSIS). SSIS is a true enterprise ETL solution with several advancements over its predecessors, including built-in logging; support for a wide variety of complex transformation, data validation, and data cleansing components; separation of process control from data flow; support for several types of data sources and destinations; and the ability to create custom components, to name a few.

SSIS in SQL Server 11 represents the first major enhancement to SSIS since its introduction way back in 2005. In this newest release, Microsoft has implemented major improvements in functionality and usability. Some of the new goodness includes the ability to move ETL packages seamlessly between environments, centralized storage and administration of SSIS packages, and a host of usability enhancements. In this book, you'll explore the core functionality you need to get up and running with SSIS and the advanced functionality you need to implement the most complex ETL processing.

ETL: THE LOST YEARS

Although bcp is efficient, many developers and DBAs over the years found the need for solutions that can perform more-complex solutions. During the "lost years" of SQL Server ETL, a large number of home-grown ETL applications began to sprout up in shops all over the world. Many of these solutions were very inefficient, featuring hard-coded sources and destinations and inflexible transformations. Even in the 21st century, there are quite a few of these legacy home-brewed ETL applications running at some of the world's largest corporations. Building and maintaining in-house ETL applications from scratch can be an interesting academic exercise, but it's terribly inefficient. The extra time and money spent trying to maintain and administer the code base for these applications can take a significant chunk of the resources you could otherwise devote to designing, developing, and building out actual ETL solutions with an enterprise ETL platform.

What Can SSIS Do for You?

SSIS provides a wide array of out-of-the-box functionality to accomplish common ETL-related tasks. The major tasks you'll encounter during most ETL processing include the following:

- **Extracting data** from a wide variety of sources including flat files, XML, the Internet, Microsoft Excel spreadsheets, and relational and nonrelational databases. If the stock source adapters don't cover your needs, SSIS's support for .NET gives you the ability to extract data from literally any data source that you have access to.

- **Validating data** according to predefined rules you specify as it moves through your ETL process. You can validate data by using a variety of methods such as ensuring that strings match patterns and that numeric values are within a given range.

- **Performing Data cleansing**, or the process of identifying invalid data values and removing them or modifying them to conform to your predefined constraints. Examples include changing negative numbers to zero or removing extra whitespace characters from strings.

- **Deduplicating data**, which is the elimination of data records that you consider to be duplicates. For a given process, you may consider entire records that are value-for-value matches to be duplicates; for other processes, you may determine that a value match on a single field (or set of fields), such as Telephone Number, identifies a duplicate record.

- **Loading data** into files, databases such as SQL Server, or other destinations. SSIS provides a wide range of stock destination adapters that allow you to output data to several well-defined destinations. As with data extraction, if you have a special destination in mind that's not supported by the SSIS stock adapters, the built-in .NET support lets you output to nearly any destination you can access.

Nearly any process that you can define in terms of ETL steps can be performed with SSIS. And it's not just limited to databases (though that is our primary focus in this book). As an example, you can use Windows Management Instrumentation (WMI) to retrieve data about a computer system, format it to your liking, and store it in an Excel spreadsheet; or you can grab data from a comma-delimited file, transform it a bit, and write it back out to a new comma-delimited file. Not to put too fine a point on it, but you can perform just about any task that requires data movement and manipulation with SSIS.

What Is Enterprise ETL?

You've seen us refer to SSIS as an *enterprise ETL solution* in this chapter, and you may have asked yourself, "What is the difference between an enterprise ETL solution and any other ETL solution?" Don't worry, it's a common question that we asked once and that has since been asked of us several times. It has a very simple answer: enterprise ETL solutions have the ability to help you meet your nonfunctional requirements in addition to the standard functional requirements of extract, transform, and load.

So what is a *nonfunctional requirement* and what does it have to do with ETL? If you've ever been on a development project for an application or business system, you're probably familiar with the term. In the previous section, we discussed how SSIS helps you meet your ETL *functional requirements*—those requirements of a system that describe what it does. In the case of ETL, the functional requirements are generally pretty simple: (1) get data from one or more sources, (2) manipulate the data according to some predefined business logic, and (3) store the data somewhere.

Nonfunctional requirements, on the other hand, deal more with the qualities of the system. These types of requirements deal in aspects such as robustness, performance and efficiency, maintainability, security, scalability, reliability, and overall quality of an ETL solution. We like to think of nonfunctional requirements as the aspects of the system that do not necessarily have a direct effect on the end result or output of the system; instead they work behind the scenes in support of the result generation.

Here are some of the ways SSIS can help you meet your nonfunctional requirements:

- **Robustness** is provided in SSIS primarily through built-in error-handling to capture and deal with bad data and execution exceptions as they occur, transactions that ensure consistency of your data should a process enter an unrecoverable processing exception, and checkpoints that allow some ability to restart packages.

- **Performance and efficiency** are closely related, but not entirely synonymous, concepts. You can think of performance as the raw speed with which your ETL processes accomplish their tasks. Efficiency digs a bit deeper and includes minimizing resource (memory, CPU, and persistent storage) contention and usage. SSIS has many optimizations baked directly into its data flow components and data flow engine—for instance, to tweak the raw performance and resource efficiency of the data flow. Chapter 14 covers the things you can do to get the most out of the built-in optimizations.

- **Maintainability** can be boiled down to the ongoing cost of managing and administering your ETL solution after it's in production. Maintainability is also one of the easiest items to measure, because you can ask questions such as, "How many hours each month do I have to spend fixing issues in ETL processes?" or "How many hours of manual intervention are required each week to deal with, or to avoid, errors in my ETL process?" SSIS provides a new project deployment model to make it easier to move ETL projects from one environment to the next; and BIDS provides built-in support for source control systems such as Team Foundation Server (TFS) to help minimize the maintenance costs of your solutions.

- **Security** is provided in SSIS through a variety of methods and interactions with other systems, including Windows NT File System (NTFS) and SQL Server 11. Package and project deployment to SQL Server is a powerful method of securing your packages. In this case, SQL Server uses its robust security model to control access to, and encryption of, SSIS package contents.

- **Scalability** can be defined as how well your ETL solution can handle increasing quantities of data. SSIS provides the ability to scale predictably with your increased demands, providing of course that you create your packages to maximize SSIS's throughput. We discuss scalable ETL design patterns in Chapter 15.

▪ **TIP:** For in-depth coverage of SSIS design patterns, we highly recommend picking up a copy of *SSIS Design Patterns* by Andy Leonard, Matt Masson, Tim Mitchell, Jessica Moss, and Michelle Ufford (Apress, 2012).

- **Reliability**, put simply, can be defined as how resistant your ETL solution is to failure—and if failure does occur, how well your solution handles the situation. SSIS provides extensive logging capabilities that, when combined with BIDS's built-in debugging capabilities, can help you quickly track down and fix the root cause of failure. SSIS can also notify you in the event of a failure situation.

All these individual nonfunctional requirements, when taken together, help define the overall quality of your ETL solution. Although it's relatively simple to put together a package or program that shuttles data from point A to point B, the nonfunctional requirements provide a layer on top of this basic functionality that allows you to meet your service-level agreements (SLAs) and other processing requirements.

SSIS Architecture

One of the major improvements that SSIS introduced over DTS was the separation of the concepts of *control flow* and *data flow*. The control flow manages the order of execution for packages and manages communication with support elements such as event handlers. The data flow engine is exposed as a component within the control flow and it provides high-performance data extraction, transformation, and loading services.

As you can see in Figure 1-1, the relationship between control flows, data flows, and their respective components is straightforward.

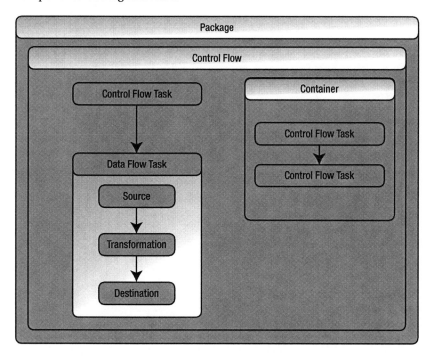

Figure 1-1. Relationship between control flow and data flow

Simply speaking, a package contains the control flow. The control flow contains control flow *tasks* and *containers*, both of which are discussed in detail in Chapter 4. The *Data Flow task* is a special type of task that contains the data flow. The data flow contains *data flow components*, which move and manipulate your data. There are three types of data flow components:

- **Sources** can pull data from any of a variety of data stores, and feed that data into the data flow.

- **Transformations** allow you to manipulate and modify data within the data flow one row at a time.

- **Destinations** provide a means for the data flow to output and persist data after it moves through the final stage of the data flow.

Although the simplified diagram in Figure 1-1 shows only a single data flow in the control flow, any given control flow can contain many data flows. As the diagram also illustrates, both control flows and data flows are found within the confines of SSIS packages that you can design, build, and test with Microsoft Business Intelligence Development Studio (BIDS). BIDS is a shell of the Visual Studio integrated development environment (IDE) that .NET programmers are familiar with. Figure 1-2 shows the data flow for a very simple SSIS package in the BIDS designer.

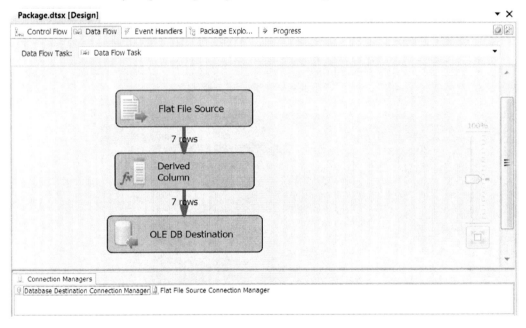

Figure 1-2. *Simple SSIS package data flow in BIDS*

Since the introduction of SSIS, Microsoft has made significant investments in the infrastructure required to support package execution and enterprise ETL management. In addition to data movement and manipulation, the SSIS infrastructure supports logging, event handling, connection management, and enumeration activities. Figure 1-3 is a simplified pyramid showing the major components of the SSIS infrastructure.

■ **NOTE:** We introduce BIDS and discuss the new designer features in Chapter 2.

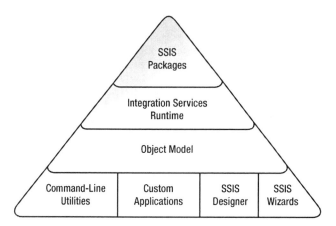

Figure 1-3. SSIS architectural components (simplified)

At the base of the pyramid lie the command-line utilities, custom applications, the SSIS designer, and wizards such as the import/export wizard that provide interaction with SSIS. These applications and utilities are developed in either managed or unmanaged code. The object model layer exposes interfaces that allow these utilities and applications to interact with the Integration Services runtime. The Integration Services runtime, in turn, executes packages and provides support for logging, breakpoints and debugging, connection management and configuration, and transaction control. At the very top of the pyramid is the SSIS package itself, which you design and build in the BIDS environment, to contain the control flow and data flows discussed earlier in this chapter.

BYE-BYE, DATA TRANSFORMATION SERVICES

Back in SQL Server 2005, Microsoft announced the deprecation of Data Transformation Services (DTS). DTS was supported as a legacy application in SQL Server 2005, 2008, and 2008 R2. But because SSIS is a full-fledged enterprise-class replacement for DTS, it should come as no surprise that DTS is no longer supported with this newest release of SQL Server. This means that the Execute DTS 2000 Package task, the DTS runtime and API, and Package Migration Wizard are all going away. Fortunately, the learning curve to convert DTS packages to SSIS is not too steep, and the process is relatively simple in most cases. If you have legacy DTS packages lying around, now's the time to plan to migrate them to SSIS.

Additionally, the ActiveX Script task, which was provided strictly for DTS support, will be removed. Many of the tasks that ActiveX Script tasks were used for can be handled with precedence constraints, while more-complex tasks can be rewritten as Script tasks. We explore precedence constraints and Script tasks in detail in Chapters 4 and 5.

New SSIS Features

There are a number of improvements in the SQL Server 11 release of SSIS. We discuss these new features and enhancements throughout the book. Before we dig into the details in later chapters, we are summarizing the new features here for your convenience:

- **Project deployment model**: The new project deployment model is new to SQL Server 11 SSIS. The key features of this new deployment model are the Integration Services catalog, environments, and parameters. The new deployment model is designed to make deployment and administration of SSIS packages and ETL systems easier across multiple environments. We discuss the project deployment model in Chapter 17.

- **T-SQL views and stored procedures**: The new project deployment model includes several new SSIS-specific views and stored procedures for SQL Server. We present these views and stored procedures in Chapter 17, during the discussion of the project deployment model.

- **BIDS usability enhancements**: BIDS has been improved to make package development and editing simpler. The BIDS designers are now more flexible, and UI enhancements such as the Integration Services toolbox make it easier to use. We present the new features in BIDS and SQL Server Management Studio (SSMS) in Chapter 3.

- **Object impact and data lineage analysis**: The object impact and data lineage analysis feature provides metadata for locating object dependencies—for instance, which tables a package depends on. This new tool provides useful information for troubleshooting performance problems or dependency issues, or when taking a proactive approach to locating dependencies. We demonstrate impact and data lineage analysis in Chapter 12.

- **Improved Merge and Merge Join transformations**: The Merge and Merge Join transformations have been improved in SQL Server 11 SSIS by providing better internal controls on memory usage. We cover the new features of the Merge and Merge Join transformations in Chapter 6.

- **Data correction component**: The Data Correction transformation provides a tool to help improve data quality. We discuss this new transformation in Chapter 7.

- **Custom data flow component improvements**: SQL Server 11 SSIS includes improvements that allow developers to more easily create custom data flow components that support multiple inputs. We explore these new features in the discussion of custom data flow components in Chapter 21.

- **Source and Destination Assistants**: The new Source and Destination Assistants are designed to guide you through the steps to create a source or destination. We talk about the new assistants in Chapter 6.

- **Simplified data viewer**: The data viewer has been simplified in SQL Server 11 SSIS to make it easier to use. We demonstrate the data viewer in Chapter 8.

Our Favorite People and Places

There are a number of SSIS experts and resources that have been out there since the introduction of SSIS. Here are some of our recommendations, a "best of" list for SSIS on the Web:

Andy Leonard is an SSIS guru and SQL Server Most Valuable Professional (MVP) who has been a head-down, hands-on SSIS developer from day 1. In fact, Andy was a contributing author on the original *Professional SQL Server 2005 Integration Services* (Wrox, 2006) book, the gold standard for SQL Server 2005 SSIS. Andy's blog is located at http://sqlblog.com/blogs/andy_leonard/default.aspx.

Jamie Thomson may well be one of the most prolific SSIS experts. Having blogged on hundreds of SSIS topics, Jamie is a SQL Server MVP and the original *SSIS Junkie*. You can read his newest material at http://sqlblog.com/blogs/jamie_thomson/ or catch up on your SSIS Junkie classic reading at http://consultingblogs.emc.com/jamiethomson.

Brian Knight, founder of Pragmatic Works and a SQL Server MVP, is a well-known writer and trainer on all things BI and all things SSIS. Catch up with Brian at www.bidn.com/blogs/BrianKnight.

Books Online (BOL) is the holy book for all things SQL Server, and that includes SSIS. When you need an answer to a specific SQL Server or SSIS question, there's a very high probability your search will end at BOL. With that in mind, we like to cut out the middleman and start our searches at http://msdn.microsoft.com/en-us/library/ms130214(v=SQL.110).aspx.

SQLServerCentral.com (SSC) was founded by a roving gang of hard-core DBAs, including the infamous Hawaiian-shirt- and cowboy-hat-wearing Steve Jones, a SQL Server MVP. Steve keeps SSC updated with lots of community-based content covering a wide range of topics including SSIS. When you want to check out the best in community-generated content, go to www.sqlservercentral.com.

SSIS Team Blog, maintained by Microsoft's own Matt Masson, is located at http://blogs.msdn.com/b/mattm. Check out this blog for the latest and greatest in SSIS updates, patches, and insider tips and tricks.

Allan Mitchell and **Darren Green**, SSIS experts and SQL MVPs from across the pond, share their expertise at www.sqlis.com.

CodePlex is a Microsoft site hosting open source projects. From www.codeplex.com, you can download a variety of open source projects that include the AdventureWorks family of sample databases, open source SSIS custom components, complete SSIS-based ETL frameworks, ssisUnit (the SSIS unit testing framework), and BIDS Helper. This is one site you want to check out.

Professional Association for SQL Server (PASS) is a professional organization for all SQL Server developers, DBAs, and BI pros. Membership is free, and the benefits include access to the *SQL Server Standard* magazine. Visit PASS at www.sqlpass.org for more information.

We highly recommend visiting these sites as you learn SSIS or encounter questions about best practices or need guidance on how to accomplish very specific tasks in your packages.

Summary

SSIS is a powerful and flexible enterprise ETL solution, designed to meet your most demanding data movement and manipulation needs. This chapter introduced some of the basic concepts of ETL and how SSIS fits into the SQL Server ETL world. We presented some of the core concepts of the SSIS architecture and talked about the newest features in SQL Server 11 SSIS. We wrapped up with a listing of a few of our favorite people and resource sites. In Chapter 2 we introduce BIDS and SSMS, with an emphasis on the newest features designed to make your ETL package design, build, and testing easier than ever.

CHAPTER 2

BIDS and SSMS

At each increase of knowledge, as well as on the contrivance of every new tool, human labour becomes abridged.

—Inventor Charles Babbage

After gathering the requirements and specifications for the new processes, it is time to design the ETL flow. This includes deciding the tools to use, the time frames for data processing,the criteria for success and failure, and so forth. One of the integral parts of deciding which tools to use is determining the sources for the data and the capability of the tools to gain access to it with ease and to extract it efficiently. As we discussed in Chapter 1, efficiently describes the taxing of the network, hardware, and overall resources optimally. One of the best characteristics of SSIS is its ease of development and maintenance (when best practices and standards are followed), the widerange of sources it can access, the transformations that it can handle inflight, and most important, cost, as it comes out of the box with SQL Server 11.

When installing SQL Server 11, you have options to install three toolsets essential for developing ETL processes: Business Intelligence Development Studio (BIDS), SQL Server Management Studio (SSMS)—Basic, and Management Studio—Complete. BIDS uses the Visual Studio 2010 platform for the development of SSIS packages as well as the creation of projects that cater to the components of the SQL Server 11 suite. Management tools include SSMS, the SQL Server command-line utility (SQLCMD), and a few other features. With these core components, developers can issue Data Definition Language (DDL) statements to create and alter database objects. They can also issue Data Manipulation Language (DML) statements to query the database objects using Microsoft's flavor of the Standard Query Language (SQL), Transact-SQL (T-SQL). Data Control Language (DCL) allows users to configure access to the database objects.

This chapter covers the project templates that BIDS supports.It also provides a brief overview of the elements of the SQL Server 11 suite.

SQL Server Business Intelligence Development Studio

BIDS, which utilizes Visual Studio 2008 as the development platform, supports a few project templates whose sole purpose is to provide insight into data. This insight can come from moving pertinent data from a source to a database (ETL processes using SSIS projects), from developing cubes that can provide optimal high-level summaries of data (cubes developed using SQL Server Analysis Services, SSAS projects), and from creating reports that can be run directly against databases or cubes (reports designed using SQL Server Reporting Services, SSRS projects). Figure 2-1 shows the business intelligence projects that are available within Visual Studio.

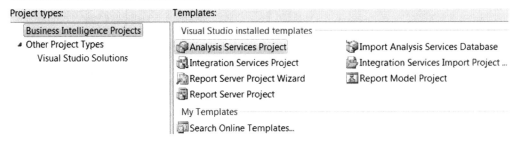

Figure 2-1. *Projects available with BIDS*

For SQL Server 11, the projects require the installation of .NET Framework 3.5. Visual Studio solutions can maintain multiple projects that address the different disciplines within the SQL Server suite. A few elements carry across multiple projects. These elements are listed next, and logically tie together at a solution level:

- **Data sources** are the disparate sources that have the data that will be imported by the members. These sources can be created by using a wizard and edited through the designer. Various components within the project can access these connections.

- **Data source views** (DSVs) are essentially ad hoc queries that can be used to extract data from the source. Their main purpose is to store the metadata of the source. As part of the metadata, key information is also stored to help create the appropriate relationships within the Analysis Services database.

- **Miscellaneous** is a category including all files that serve a support function but are not integral. This includes configuration files for Integration Services.

Analysis Services Project

The *Analysis Services project* is used to design, develop, and deploy a SQL Server 11 Analysis Services database. More often than not, the purpose of ETL projects is to consolidate several systems into one report-friendly form in order to summarize activity at a high level. Analysis Services cubes perform roll-up calculations against dimensions for quick and efficient reporting. This project template provides a folder structure depicted in Figure 2-2 that is needed to develop an Analysis Services database. After development, the cube can be deployed directly to Analysis Services.

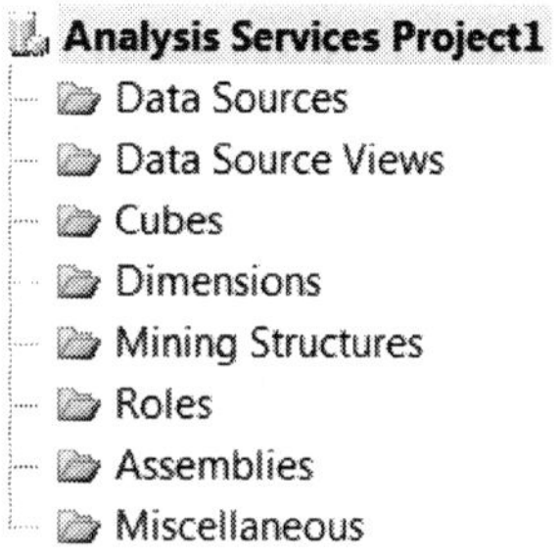

⚁ Analysis Services Project1
- ▱ Data Sources
- ▱ Data Source Views
- ▱ Cubes
- ▱ Dimensions
- ▱ Mining Structures
- ▱ Roles
- ▱ Assemblies
- ▱ Miscellaneous

Figure 2-2.*Folder structure for an Analysis Services project*

These folders organize the files in a developer-friendly format. This format also helps with building and deploying projects. A partial list of the folders is listed below:

- **Cubes**contains all the cubes that are part of the Analysis Services database. The dimensions can be created using a wizard, utilizing the metadata stored within the DSVs.

- **Mining Structures** apply data-mining algorithms on the data from the DSVs. They can help create a level of predictive analysis depending on the quality of the data and the usage of the appropriate algorithm. You can use the Mining Model Wizard to help create these as well as the Mining Model Designer to edit them.

- **Roles**contains all the database roles for the Analysis Services database. These roles can vary from administrative permissions to restrictions based on the dimensional data.

- **Assemblies** holds all the references to Component Object Model,COM, libraries and Microsoft .NET assemblies.

░ **TIP:** SSIS packages can be used to process cubes. These packages can be executed at the end of a successful ETL process.

The Analysis Services database, like Integration Services, can source data from a variety of locations and physical storage formats. The DSVs use the same drivers and are not necessarily limited to the SQL Server database engine. Prior versions of SQL Server as well as other relational database management systems (RDBMSs) are available as sources. The languages for querying SQL Server cubes arecalled Multidimensional Expressions (MDX) and Data Mining Extensions (DMX). Some of the objects that can be defined in a cube for analytic purposes are measures, measure groups, attributes, dimensions, and hierarchies. These objects are critical in organizing and defining the metrics and the descriptions of those metrics that the end user is most interested in.Another important feature that Analysis Services provides is the concept ofkey performance indicators (KPIs).KPIscontain calculations related to a measure group. These calculations are vital in evaluating the performance of a business.

Integration Services Project

The *Integration Services project* template enables the developer to create SSIS packages. The package is the executable work unit within SSIS. It consists of smaller components that can be executed individually during development, but Integration Services executes at the package level. The debugging option in Visual Studio will execute the package as a whole, but the control flow executables can also be individually tested. Figure 2-3 shows a sample Integration Services project. This project will automatically be added to your current solution if you have one open. Otherwise, a temporary solution will be created.

NOTE: Even though Visual Studio has the ability to execute packages, we recommend using the command line to execute them when testing. Visual Studio debugging mode should be used during development. We discuss more options on running SSIS packages in Chapter 20.

Figure 2-3. *Folder structure for an Integration Services project*

The following list describes the objects and folders that will appear in your project:

- **SSIS Packages** contains all the packages associated with the project. These work units are the actual components that will execute the ETL. All the packages are added to the .dtproj file. This XML-based file lists all the packages and configurations that are part of the project.

- **Miscellaneous** contains all the file types other than the .dtsx files. This folder is essential for storing configuration files and will be useful for consolidating connections, especially when utilizing a source control application. Team Foundation Server is introduced later in this chapter.

NOTE: With SQL Server 11, data sources and data source views cannot be added to a project. Instead, these connections can be added to the individual packages. In prior versions, data sources could be added as connection managers and were allowed to refer to the included DSVs as the tables in source components. Using this methodology to access data on SQL Server was not the optimal way to extract data.

The debugging option in Visual Studio executes the current package. This feature is useful for watching the behavior of the package (how quickly rows pass through the components in the Data Flow tasks, how quickly executables complete, the successful matches of Lookups and Merge Joins, and so forth). During the execution, three colors indicate the status of the executable and data flow components: yellow—in progress, red—failure, and green—success. This use of different colors is helpful during development because it shows how the precedence constraints and the Data Flow tasks move the data through.

⬛ **NOTE:** Unless a package calls another package as an executable, the current package is the only one that will run in Debug mode, not all the packages in the project. Visual Studio will open every package that is called in a parent-child configuration and execute them. If there are too many packages, certain ones may open with a Memory Overflow error displayed, but the package may execute in the background and continue onto the subsequent packages.

TO UNDO OR REDO, THAT IS THE QUESTION

From its introduction in SQL Server 2005, SSIS did not have native undo or redo ability. The buttons for these operations existed on the toolbar but were permanently grayed out regardless of the changes made in the SSIS Designer. The most common method to undo changes was to close the package without saving those changes. Even with source control, this was always a tricky operation to perform. With SQL Server 2011, SSIS developers now enjoy undo functionality that other Visual Studio developers have enjoyed for many iterations of the software. With SSIS, clicking the OK button commits the changes. To leave the code unchanged, you should make it a habit to click the Cancel or Close button if you are only reviewing the code. The undo and redo ability extends to a certain level to the editing of components.

Report Server Project Wizard

The *Report Server Project Wizard* allows you to automatically create a Report Server project. You have to specify the connections to data sources, including security information if necessary, queries for the reports, and so forth. After the project has been created, the Report Designer can be used to make all the modifications.

Report Server Project

The *Report Server project* allows the developer to create all the objects necessary for reports. The reports can be deployed on a portal, where end users can access them. The portal can utilize SharePoint, where users can even save their own reports that they frequently utilize. Usually a web browser is used to access the reports. Reports should use a cube if they summarize data (that is, perform counts, sums, and averages). If the reports display detail-level information, querying a database is most likely the more efficient route. Including too much detail on a report can impact the load time on the end user's browser as well as the query time on the server. Figure 2-4 demonstrates the folder structure that is available for Report Server projects.

Figure 2-4. Folder structure for a Report Server project

The folders contain objects that perform the following tasks:

- **Shared Data Sources** contains necessary components of the Report Server project. These components allow the reports to connect to the data sources that will be the basis for the reports.

- **Shared Datasets** contains multiple reports used to source common datasets.

- **Reports** stores all the `.rdl` files that are the actual reports. You can modify the reports by using the designer.

When you are creating reports, the Design view enables you to modify the visual layout of the page and the code for the data that goes into each element. Depending on the source for the data, you will have to use the appropriate variant of SQL or MDX. Sources for reports can include RDBMSs, report models, and XML. In addition to the Design view, there is a Preview view that can be used to run the report to make sure that the data renders as desired. Using this view caches the data locally on the developer's machine, so clearing the cache often is recommended.

Import Analysis Services Database

The *Import Analysis Services Database project* template automatically generates all the items of an Analysis Services project. The wizard asks you to point to an Analysis Services database. The wizard will reverse-engineer all the project items based on the existing database. The project can be used to modify the objects and redeploy them to the server to update the database.

Integration Services Project Wizard

The *Integration Services Project Wizard* will automatically generate all the items of an Integration Services project. The wizard will ask for the source of an existing project (either the `.dtproj` file or a package deployed on a SQL Server instance). This wizard will import all the objects from the existing project.

Report Model Project

The *Report Model project* utilizes SQL Server databases to generate reports. By definition, a report model stores the metadata of its sources and their relationships. The data sources allow you to access the DDL of the specified source and utilize it for the report models. The DSVs allow you to store the metadata from the sources and generate models for reporting. The Model Designer can create report models by using the SQL Server or Oracle 9.2.0.3 and later versions of the RDBMSs. While models based on an RDBMS can be modified, those based on Analysis Services cannot. All the data within a data source is automatically included in the model. Figure 2-5 demonstrates all the objects and folders available to a Report Model project.

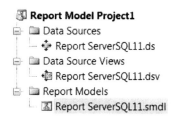

Figure 2-5. *Folder structure for a ReportModel project*

■ **NOTE:** An `.smdl` file can refer to only one data source (`.ds`) and one data source view (`.dsv`). This limitation will prevent you from performing cross-database joins.

There are three parts to the report model: the Semantic model, which assigns business-friendly names to the data objects; the Physical model, which represents the objects in data source views and outputs metadata of queries contained within; and the mapping, which aligns the Semantic and Physical models. The Semantic Model Definition Language (`.smdl`) contains only one Semantic and Physical model, and mapping. As Figure 2-6 demonstrates, the DDL can be read by the designer and used to generate a model that describes the objects of the data source view.

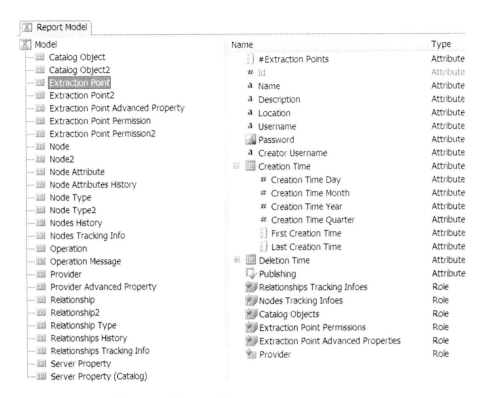

Figure 2-6. *Model for import from a DSV*

Deploying the Report Model project allows end users access to the data that is present in the underlying databases. The project needs to be deployed to a report server, where the users have access to it.

Integration Services

The basis forenterprise ETL processes in SQL Server 11 is the SSIS package.The Development Studio has undergone some radical changes since SQL Server 2008 in terms of the interface and some performance enhancements in the components. Developing packages begins with a Visual Studio 2008 BIDS project. The project file (`.dtproj`) will be the manager of the packages. It enumerates the packages that will be built and deployed; we discuss this process in greater length later in Chapter 19. The project file also assists with development within Team Foundation Server (TFS), a Visual Studio code repository system. Setting up TFS and working within this framework of source control is covered in Chapter 20. During the build process, all the configuration files (`.dtsxConfig`) will be created as listed in each of the packages included in the project.

One of the biggest changes that will get developers excited is the ability to undo and redo changes. In prior versions of the toolset, you had to close the package without saving changes and reopen the package. This meant that if you wanted to maintain a change but had made an unwanted one after it, your *only option* was to close the package without saving. The other alternative was to disable tasks, which often lead to packages that were swamped with disabled executables or containers. Figure 2-7 shows the history of changes that the Undo and Redo functionality now provides.

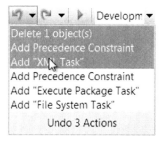

Figure 2-7. Undo and Redo functionality

Project Files

Some of the changes in SSIS 2012 are the properties available for project files. The properties of the project file allow for the configuration of build process— namely, the folder path of the packages. The folder path property also allows the user to directly deploy the project onto a SQL Server database, an Integration Services catalog. The Integration Services catalog is discussed in further detail in Chapter 18. Manually adding or deleting package (.dtsx) files in the file system will not modify or update the project file. In fact, deleting packages from the file system will actually corrupt the project. Listing 2-1 demonstrates the XML tags that can be modified to add or remove packages from the project.

■ **NOTE:** We recommend adding existing packages within Visual Studio. However, if a package already exists in the project folder, a copy of the original package will be created and the copy will be added to the project by Visual Studio. Usually the copy package name will be appended with "(1)".

Listing 2-1. Sample from a Project File

```
<Database>
<Name>Integration Services Project1.database</Name>
<FullPath>Integration Services Project1.database</FullPath>
</Database>
<DataSources />
<DataSourceViews />
<DeploymentModelSpecificContent>
<Manifest>

<SSIS:Project SSIS:ProtectionLevel="DontSaveSensitive"
xmlns:SSIS="www.microsoft.com/SqlServer/SSIS">

<SSIS:Properties>
<SSIS:Property SSIS:Name="ID">{bf2a36bf-0b7c-471d-95c7-3ee9a0d74794}
               </SSIS:Property>
```

```
<SSIS:Property SSIS:Name="Name">Integration Services Project1</SSIS:Property>
<SSIS:Property SSIS:Name="VersionMajor">1</SSIS:Property>
<SSIS:Property SSIS:Name="VersionMinor">0</SSIS:Property>
<SSIS:Property SSIS:Name="VersionBuild">0</SSIS:Property>
<SSIS:Property SSIS:Name="VersionComments">
</SSIS:Property>
<SSIS:Property SSIS:Name="CreationDate">
        2011-02-14T22:44:55.5341796-05:00</SSIS:Property>
<SSIS:Property SSIS:Name="CreatorName">SQL11</SSIS:Property>
<SSIS:Property SSIS:Name="CreatorComputerName">SQL11</SSIS:Property>
<SSIS:Property SSIS:Name="OfflineMode">0</SSIS:Property>
<SSIS:Property SSIS:Name="Description">
</SSIS:Property>
</SSIS:Properties>

<SSIS:Packages>
<SSIS:Package SSIS:Name="Package.dtsx" SSIS:EntryPoint="1" />
</SSIS:Packages>
<SSIS:Parameters />

<SSIS:DeploymentInfo>
<SSIS:PackageInfo>
<SSIS:PackageMetaData SSIS:Name="Package.dtsx">
<SSIS:Properties>
<SSIS:Property SSIS:Name="ID">{A41A08A6-7C50-4DEC-B283-D76337E73505}</SSIS:Property>
<SSIS:Property SSIS:Name="Name">Package</SSIS:Property>
<SSIS:Property SSIS:Name="VersionMajor">1</SSIS:Property>
<SSIS:Property SSIS:Name="VersionMinor">0</SSIS:Property>
<SSIS:Property SSIS:Name="VersionBuild">1</SSIS:Property>
<SSIS:Property SSIS:Name="VersionComments">
</SSIS:Property>
<SSIS:Property SSIS:Name=
        "VersionGUID">{9181C329-7E44-4B3D-B125-14D94639BF03}</SSIS:Property>
<SSIS:Property SSIS:Name="PackageFormatVersion">6</SSIS:Property>
<SSIS:Property SSIS:Name="Description">
</SSIS:Property>

<SSIS:Property SSIS:Name="ProtectionLevel">0</SSIS:Property>

</SSIS:Properties>

<SSIS:Parameters />

</SSIS:PackageMetaData>
</SSIS:PackageInfo>
</SSIS:DeploymentInfo>
</SSIS:Project>
</Manifest>
</DeploymentModelSpecificContent>
<Miscellaneous />
<Configurations>

<Configuration>

<Name>Development</Name>
```

```
<Options>
```

```
<OutputPath>bin</OutputPath>
```

```
<ConnectionMappings />
<ConnectionProviderMappings />
<ConnectionSecurityMappings />
<DatabaseStorageLocations />
<ParameterConfigurationValues />
</Options>
</Configuration>
</Configurations>
```

This portion of a simple project file contains all the essential elements to developing and using an SSIS ETL process. As you may have guessed, this information is stored as Extensible Markup Language (XML). This makes it feasible to modify the project directly by editing the XML.

We would like to highlight the following key tags/properties (further details are discussed in later chapters):

> `ProtectionLevel` allows you to secure sensitive information such as credentials. This property can be set at the project level as well as the package level. However, both settings should be the same. All the packages within a project need to have the same protection level set as the project file when building the project. We discuss this property at greater length in Chapter 19.

> `Packages` contains all the packages that are associated with the project. Copying and pasting this tag and modifying the name to reflect a package that exists in the working directory will forcibly add the package to the project. When the project is opened in Visual Studio, the package will be listed in the packages folder. Modifying the project file directly can sometimes help avoid the hassle of creating clean file names as opposed to using the Visual Studio wizard to add existing packages.

> `Parameters` can be used at runtime to set values in the package. This property allows for certain components of the package to change values. The most notable place for this is in the OLE DB source component that can parameterize a SQL statement. Parameterizing a package is covered in greater detail in Chapter 16.

> `Configuration` determines whether you build or deploy the project. By default, the property is set to build the project. Different settings can be used for the various configurations that you create, depending on the purpose for each configuration. The configuration manager on the Project Settings allows you to create different configurations.

> `OutputPath` sets the folder path to the objects that will be built for the project. By default, it is set to the bin directory. When the deployment utility needs to be created, a different path can be defined. In 2005 and 2008, creating the deployment utility used the default folder path of `bin\Deployment`.

Tool Windows

The BIDS environment provides tools that organize all the components into easy-to-find sections. To begin, a Start page contains some important reference items. The Recent Projects panel contains a history of some of the projects that were opened. At the bottom of this pane are links to open existing projects anda link to create BIDS projects and other Visual Studio projects. The Getting Started pane contains links to BOL topics that can help developers learn the toolsets. If the Team Foundation Server Team Explorer utility is installed, a Source Control page is available. This page allows the developer to quickly access the projects assigned to him or her and refresh the copies of the code with specific versions stored on the repository.

The Tool window within BIDS assists with the development, as shown in Figure 2-8. The middle section is the actual designer for SSIS packages. An addition to the designer comes in the form of a Zoom tool that is clear when it is inactive, but when the mouse hovers over it, it becomes opaque. Right below the Zoom scale is a Zoom-to-Fit button that will automatically determine the best zoom level to show the contents while maintaining the current arrangement.

Below the designer are the connection managers. These are the sources and destinations for the ETL process. They contain the connection information such as server name, database name, and depending on the protection level that is defined, security credentials. Drivers might be needed for certain connections to be created. Only certain drivers come by default. Others can be obtained from Microsoft. Most of the drivers are free to download from Microsoft; other companies may charge for them. Certain practices should be followed when using or naming connection managers; we discuss them in Part 2 of the book.

■ **NOTE:** If the BIDS tools are installed on a 32-bit operating system, only the 32-bit version of the drivers will be installed. On a 64-bit operating system, both 32-bit and 64-bit tools will be installed. It is also important to note that not all 32-bit tools are available in 64-bit. The Microsoft OLE DB Provider for Jet (Office Access and Excel engine) and the SQL Server Compact Provider (SQL Server Compact) are not available in 64-bit. In a 64-bit environment, the default execution of the packages in Visual Studio utilizes the 64-bit tools. If these are unavailable, the package will either hang or fail. The Run64BitRuntime project property controls this execution. When set to True, all the packages associated with the project will be run in 64-bit mode. False results in 32-bit execution.

Figure 2-8. *Tool window for SSIS 2011*

Designer Window

The tabs across the top of the designer show the controls for the ETL process. The control flow consists of the three distinct types of components: containers that can logically group tasks together, tasks for the package's functional requirements, and the precedence constraints that control and order the flow between the executables, containers, and tasks. We cover the control flow in detail in Chapters 5 and 6.

The Data Flow tab is the designer that allows the developer to take control of the actual dataprocessing. The Data Flow task is the component that moves data from the sources to the destinations, while allowing for transformations to occur inflight.

The Event Handlers tab allows for actions to be designedfor runtime events according to the triggers that are activated (OnError, OnExecStatusChanged, and so forth). The triggers can be attached to all the executables and tasks in the package. We give an in-depth walk-through of event handling in Chapter 10.

The Package Explorer tab provides a quick glance at the entire package. It shows all the contents of the package in tree view, as shown earlier in Figure 2-8. As you can see in the figure, the variables appear in different places; this is due to thedefined scope of the variable. Variables are discussed in Chapter 11.

One of the new features that has been added with regards to variables is the addition of a variable property, RaiseChangedEvent. This allows for certain change criteria to trigger events that can be captured by the event handlers. It also allows for SSIS logging to capture this event through the log provider you use. Figure 2-9 shows the tree diagram view of the objects in a package.

■ **NOTE:** When developing SSIS packages, the concept of focus plays an important role. Focus basically means which component is currently selected. This is critical to keep in mind when creating variables. Having a container or an executable accidentally selected when creating a variable will limit it to that particular object. BIDS allows you to "move" variables between scopes. However, all Visual Studio does is create a new variable in the new scope with the name of the original variable having a 1 appended, and then Visual Studio deletes the original variable.

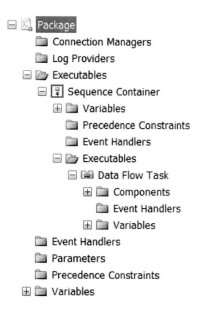

Figure 2-9. *The Package Explorer*

During the execution of the package, a Progress tab appears to the right of the Package Explorer tab. This tab continuously updates with the current state of the execution process until the end with either a success or failure. This tab will show which executable(s) is currently running, the number of rows that lookup components have cached, and more. It also captures the progress of the pre-execute processing as well as the post-execute processing. After the execution, it renames itself to the Execution Results tab. The Execution Results tab contains the same output as the very end of the Progress tab. One of the most critical pieces of information stored in the Execution Results tab is the number of rows committed to the destinations.

At the top-right corner of the Designer window, there are two buttons. These buttons are shortcuts to the Parameters and Variableswindow pane and the SSIS Toolbox window pane. They come in handy when trying to quickly look at the parameters and variables and the tools available for the selected context.

Resolve References

An exciting new feature for the data flow is the Resolve References utility. This is available by right-clicking on a data flow path between two components and selecting Resolve References. This is a powerful tool because it allows mappings to be generated and maintained in an Excel spreadsheet and then simply be added as the mapping between the source and the input of the destination. This is a vast improvement on the previous version's Restore Invalid Column References Editor that usually caused worry among developers when it was used. Figure 2-10 displays the Resolve References utility as it appears in Visual Studio.

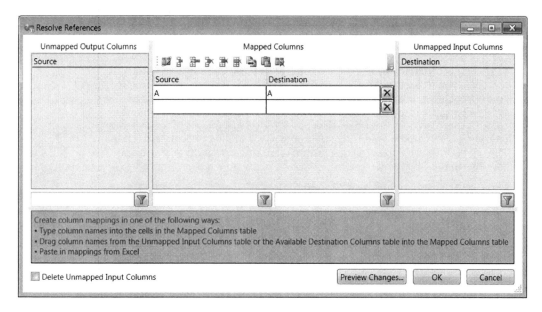

Figure 2-10. Resolve References utility

This tool can quickly update the metadata due to DDL changes or source/destination changes. Its usefulness comes in the ability to see all the columns in the pipeline at once as opposed to seeing them in a drop-down list, one column mapping at a time. In the Mapped Columns pane of the utility, the buttons perform the following functions from left to right:

Automap Columns attempts to best match the columns in the source and the columns in the destination based on the name. This feature has been present in SSIS in previous versions, usually generating the mappings in destination components.

Insert Cell allows you to stagger present mappings without losing all the mapped columns currently present. It will shift the cells down from the currently selected cell in either the Source or the Destination column.

Insert Row inserts a whole row so that entirely new mappings can be constructed. As in set theory, order is not important. The order that the mappings present themselves does not matter, just as long as the mappings exist.

Delete Cell shifts the cells up to the current highlighted cell. This can be used to shift the mappings from their correct position.

Delete Row deletes an entire row of unwanted mappings. Use this to remove columnmappings—for example, if the Automap feature created a relationship between unrelated columns.

Eliminate Blank Rows deletes all the rows that do not contain both sides of the mapping. It will not delete a row if there is a Source or a Destination columnpopulated.

Copy Mappings to Clipboard copies the contents of the entire mapping table in Excel format. This can be used to store the mappings in a spreadsheet for documentation purposes.

Paste from Clipboard pastes the contents of the Clipboard into the utility. It will allow you to paste columns that don't exist in the metadata, but after the grid is populated, it will validate the mappings. If the columns do not exist, error messages will appear at the bottom of the pane informing you that the column specified does not exist. Also, pasting always appends to the existing mappings; you cannot overwrite a mapping if it is already present in the table. The only prerequisite to using this button is making sure that there are only two columns in the Clipboard.

Clear All Mappings wipes away the contents of the mapping table and moves the columns back to their respective panes, Unmapped Output Columns and Unmapped Input Columns.

■ **NOTE:** If columns are removed from the source of a data flow, they will be recognized as still existing upstreamin the pipeline when a component downstream is still using it in its mapping.After the dependencies are removed, the column will be removed from the pipeline.

In order to keep the packages organized and readable, a menu item named Format allows you to line up the elements of the control flow and the data flow according to your desires. For simple flows, the Auto Layout should suffice to make the package presentable. For more-complex packages, there are options to align the components, to modify the distance between them, and to make them the same size. For these options, the components to which the formatting is to be applied need to be selected prior to applying these changes. The first component selected will be the reference for the rest of the components. For example, the other components will have their alignment determined with respect to the first selected component.

SSIS Toolbox

To the left of the Designer window is the SSIS Toolbox. This is a name change from prior versions of BIDS, where it was known as justToolbox. There is a Toolbox still present in Visual Studio, but it does not have any components for the SSIS Designer.The SSIS Toolbox changes to show only the components that are pertinent to the current view of the designer.

At the bottom of the SSIS Toolbox, there is a brief description of the selected component that can be helpful for first-time developers. Right-clicking the description shows the option to Show Type Information. This option gives detailed information about the selected tool, such as the assembly name and the location of the .dll. With this description, there are two reference points, a Help button in the top-right corner of this section and the Find Samples hyperlink, which takes you to CodePlex with a prepopulated search.

The SSIS Toolbox is organized in a completely different way than previous versions. The new organization of the Control Flow components is organized into four groups: Favorites, Common, Containers, and Other Tasks. The Favorites by default include the workhorses of the SSIS world, the Data Flow task and the Execute SQL task.

■ **TIP:** By default, SSIS 11 has its own grouping of components, but this grouping can be changed according to your needs. Tasks can be moved to the other groupings by right-clicking the component and moving it to the desired grouping. Containers are the exception; they can be moved only to Favorites or Common.

The SSIS Toolbox for the data low is organized in a similar fashion to the control flow. The components are divided into categories: Favorites, Common, Other Transforms, Other Sources, and Other Destinations. Just as with the control flow tasks, this grouping is modifiable to a degree for personal preferences. The default favorites for the data flow are new to SSIS:the Destination Assistant and Source Assistant. These assistants organize the connection managers defined in the package by their storage type, as shown in Figure 2-11. By default, they show only the data storage applications that have drivers installed on the machine. The assistants can be used to create new connection managers if the desired ones do not already exist.

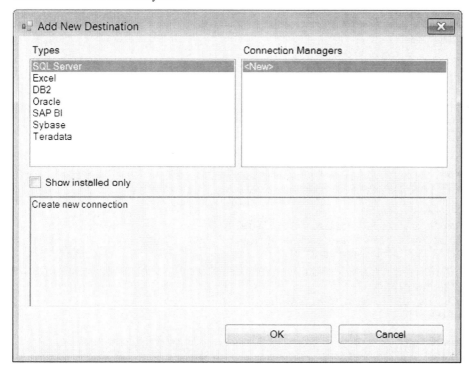

Figure 2-11. Destination Assistant

Package Code View

The actual code behind SSIS packages is stored as `.dtsx`files thatare XML based. The XMLis available either by opening the package file in a text editor or by clicking the View menu in Visual Studio and selecting View Code when the package is open. The differences between the XMLcontainedin the `.dtsx` files in SQL Server 2008 and in SQL Server 11 are vast. The attributes for each of the tags is given on a new line, making the code much more human readable. This feature also makes the packages modifiable using diff tools. In TFS, the Compare Files tool now becomes a viable option for identifying differences between package versions. It also makes the Merge tool in TFS easier to operate to combine two versions of a package. Listing 2-2 shows a sample from an SSIS 11 package's data flow source component.

Listing 2-2. Data Flow Task Component

```
<component

    refId="Package\Data Flow Task\OLE DB Source"
componentClassID="{165A526D-D5DE-47FF-96A6-F8274C19826B}"
contactInfo="OLE DB Source;Microsoft Corporation;
       Microsoft SQL Server; (C) Microsoft Corporation; All Rights Reserved;
       http://www.microsoft.com/sql/support;7"
    description="OLE DB Source"
    name="OLE DB Source"
    usesDispositions="true"
    version="7">
<properties>
<property
        dataType="System.Int32"
        description="The number of seconds before a
    command times out.  A value of 0 indicates an infinite time-out."
        name="CommandTimeout">0</property>
<property
        dataType="System.String"
        description="Specifies the name of the database object used to open a rowset."
        name="OpenRowset"></property>
<property
        dataType="System.String"
        description="Specifies the variable that contains the
    name of the database object used to open a rowset."
        name="OpenRowsetVariable"></property>

<property
        dataType="System.String"
        description="The SQL command to be executed."
        name="SqlCommand"

UITypeEditor="Microsoft.DataTransformationServices.Controls.ModalMultilineStringEditor,
        Microsoft.DataTransformationServices.Controls, Version=11.0.0.0, Culture=neutral,
                PublicKeyToken=89845dcd8080cc91">SELECT 1 AS A
WHERE 1 = 1;</property>

<property
        dataType="System.String"
        description="The variable that contains the SQL command to be executed."
        name="SqlCommandVariable"></property>
<property
        dataType="System.Int32"
```

```
         description="Specifies the column code page to use
      when code page information is unavailable from the data source."
         name="DefaultCodePage">1252</property>
<property
         dataType="System.Boolean"
         description="Forces the use of the DefaultCodePage
      property value when describing character data."
         name="AlwaysUseDefaultCodePage">false</property>
<property
         dataType="System.Int32"
         description="Specifies the mode used to access the database."
         name="AccessMode"
         typeConverter="AccessMode">2</property>
<property
         dataType="System.String"
         description="The mappings between the parameters in the SQL command and variables."
         name="ParameterMapping">"0",{F05D0A62-4900-482A-88D9-DE0166CB4CB9};</property>
</properties>
<connections>

<connection
         refId="Package\Data Flow Task\OLE DB Source.Connections[OleDbConnection]"
         connectionManagerID="Package.ConnectionManagers[FRANKIE-VM\SQL11.SSISDB]"
         description="The OLE DB runtime connection used to access the database."
         name="OleDbConnection" />

</connections>
<outputs>
<output
         refId="Package\Data Flow Task\OLE DB Source.Outputs[OLE DB Source Output]"
         name="OLE DB Source Output">

<outputColumns>
<outputColumn
            refId="Package\Data Flow Task\
      OLE DB Source.Outputs[OLE DB Source Output].Columns[A]"
            dataType="i4"
            errorOrTruncationOperation="Conversion"
            errorRowDisposition="FailComponent"
            externalMetadataColumnId=
      "Package\Data Flow Task\OLE DB Source.Outputs
      [OLE DB Source Output].ExternalColumns[A]"
            lineageId="Package\Data Flow Task\OLE DB Source.Outputs
      [OLE DB Source Output].Columns[A]"
            name="A"
            truncationRowDisposition="FailComponent" />
</outputColumns>
<externalMetadataColumns
         isUsed="True">
<externalMetadataColumn
            refId="Package\Data Flow Task\OLE DB Source.Outputs
      [OLE DB Source Output].ExternalColumns[A]"
```

```
dataType="i4"
            name="A" />
</externalMetadataColumns>

</output>
<output
        refId="Package\Data Flow Task\OLE DB Source.Outputs[OLE DB Source Error Output]"
        isErrorOut="true"
        name="OLE DB Source Error Output">
<outputColumns>
<outputColumn
            refId="Package\Data Flow Task\OLE DB Source.Outputs
        [OLE DB Source Error Output].Columns[A]"
            dataType="i4"
            lineageId="Package\Data Flow Task\OLE DB Source.Outputs
        [OLE DB Source Error Output].Columns[A]"
            name="A" />
<outputColumn
            refId="Package\Data Flow Task\OLE DB Source.Outputs
        [OLE DB Source Error Output].Columns[ErrorCode]"
            dataType="i4"
            lineageId="Package\Data Flow Task\OLE DB Source.Outputs
        [OLE DB Source Error Output].Columns[ErrorCode]"
            name="ErrorCode"
            specialFlags="1" />
<outputColumn
            refId="Package\Data Flow Task\OLE DB Source.Outputs
        [OLE DB Source Error Output].Columns[ErrorColumn]"
            dataType="i4"
            lineageId="Package\Data Flow Task\OLE DB Source.Outputs
            [OLE DB Source Error Output].Columns[ErrorColumn]"
            name="ErrorColumn"
            specialFlags="2" />
</outputColumns>
<externalMetadataColumns />
</output>
</outputs>
</component>
```

Some key points to highlight when looking through the XML of an extremely simple source component includethe simplicity of the package in comparison to that of prior versions of SSIS, and some changes in how the objects are now tracked by the package. One of the key reasons for the readability improvement of the XML is that some default settings are not generated. If, for example, the IsSorted property of a source component is left at the default value of False, as was done in Listing 2-2, no extra XMLwill be generated to store that metadata. In prior versions of SSIS, all the gritty details are stored in the XML of a package. The following list highlights some of the more important properties:

refId indicates the path to the object within the package. This property uniquely identifies the component within the package.

SqlCommand is a property that usually contains the exact query that will execute against the RBDMS.

Connections contains all the connection information stored within the package for the data source component. It is possible to save login credentials for the package, but it is not recommended. Even the connection managers have refId.

Output Columns the metadata about the output of the package is important to make sure that the data is inserted properly. If there is a failure simply with converting the data into something SQL Server can process, the package can be set to fail as a result.

Another change that is noticeable just by looking at the XML is the way the lineageId is tracked in the XML. A lineageId is used by SSIS to track all columns within data flows, including the error columns that get added to the pipeline by components. Instead of hard-coding an integer value as was done in previous versions, SSIS now uses the names of the objects to essentially create a path to an object, and because objects have to have unique names within SSIS, the path itself creates the unique identifier for the columns.Another great improvement in the readability of the XML was made by replacing the < and > entity encodings with their appropriate special characters.

A new addition to the XML of the package is a section called CDATA, which captures the visual layout of the components in a package. Listing 2-3 demonstrates this section of the package code. It captures not only the size and location coordinates of the package, but also the shape of the data flow path between data flow components and the precedence constraints in the control flow. This metadata is noncritical to the package itself and will be regenerated if corrupt or missing when the package is opened in Visual Studio.

Listing 2-3. CDATA *Section of a Simple Package*

```
<![CDATA[<?xml version="1.0"?>
<!--This CDATA section contains the layout information of the package.
        The section includes information such as (x,y) coordinates, width, and height.-->
<!--If you manually edit this section and make a mistake, you can delete it. -->
<!--The package will still be able to load normally but the previous layout
        information will be lost and the designer will automatically
        re-arrange the elements on the design surface.-->
<Objects
  Version="sql11">
<!--Each node below will contain properties that do not affect runtime behavior.-->
<Package
    design-time-name="Package">
<LayoutInfo>
<GraphLayout
        Capacity="4" xmlns="clr-
namespace:Microsoft.SqlServer.IntegrationServices.Designer.Model.Serialization;assembly=
        Microsoft.SqlServer.IntegrationServices.Graph">
<NodeLayout
        Size="152.276666666667,42"
        Id="Package\Data Flow Task"
        TopLeft="5.49999999999999,5.49999999999989" />
</GraphLayout>
</LayoutInfo>
</Package>
<TaskHost
```

```
        design-time-name="Package\Data Flow Task">
<LayoutInfo>
<GraphLayout
        Capacity="4" xmlns="clr-
namespace:Microsoft.SqlServer.IntegrationServices.Designer.Mode
        l.Serialization;assembly=Microsoft.SqlServer.IntegrationServices.Graph"
        xmlns:mssgle="clr-namespace:Microsoft.SqlServer.Graph.LayoutEngine;assembly=
        Microsoft.SqlServer.Graph" xmlns:x="http://schemas.microsoft.com/winfx/2006/xaml">
<NodeLayout
        Size="151.083333333334,42"
        Id="Package\Data Flow Task\OLE DB Source"
        TopLeft="15.918333333333,5.5" />
<NodeLayout
        Size="171.920000000001,42"
        Id="Package\Data Flow Task\OLE DB Destination"
        TopLeft="5.50000000000001,107.5" />
<EdgeLayout
        Id="Package\Data Flow Task.Paths[OLE DB Source Output]"
        TopLeft="91.46,47.5">

<EdgeLayout.Curve>
<mssgle:Curve
            StartConnector="{x:Null}"
            EndConnector="0,60"
            Start="0,0"
            End="0,52.5">
<mssgle:Curve.Segments>
<mssgle:SegmentCollection
                Capacity="5">
<mssgle:LineSegment
                End="0,52.5" />
</mssgle:SegmentCollection>
</mssgle:Curve.Segments>
</mssgle:Curve>
</EdgeLayout.Curve>
<EdgeLayout.Labels>
<EdgeLabelCollection />
</EdgeLayout.Labels>
</EdgeLayout>

</GraphLayout>
</LayoutInfo>
</TaskHost>
<PipelineComponentMetadata
    design-time-name="Package\Data Flow Task\OLE DB Source">
<Properties>
<Property>
<Name>DataSourceViewID</Name>
</Property>
</Properties>
</PipelineComponentMetadata>
<PipelineComponentMetadata
```

```
        design-time-name="Package\Data Flow Task\OLE DB Destination">
<Properties>
<Property>
<Name>DataSourceViewID</Name>
</Property>
<Property>
<Name>TableInfoObjectType</Name>
<Value
        type="q2:string">Table</Value>
</Property>
</Properties>
</PipelineComponentMetadata>
</Objects>]]>
```

As the default comment explains, this data is stored using (x,y) Cartesian plane coordinates and width and height pairings, in that pairing order.The highlighted section shows the capturing of the data flow paths' lines.

SQL Server Management Studio

SQL Server 11's built-in tool for access and maintenance is the Management Studio. It allows you to configure, administer, and develop components of SQL Server. Connecting to the database engine allows you to use T-SQL as well as the SQL Command utility by using SQLCMD mode for operating-system commands. The database engine allows the use of DDL to create the objects, DML to access the data in the objects, and DCL to define user access to the objects for DDL and DML.Management Studio allows you to create and modify T-SQL, MDX, DMX, XML,and XML for Analysis(XMLA) scripts, and even plain-text files.

Management Studio is critical in developing SQL queries for SSIS. These queries can be used by the source component, Execute SQL task,lookup component, and the OLE DB command component. The most efficient way to retrieve data from a database for SSIS Data Flow tasks is to specify only the columns that are required. This allows the buffers to fill with rows rather than columns, which will be disregarded. This is especially important for lookup components as well, because by default they cache the result set and thus only the key columns and the output columns should be specified in the select statement rather than the whole dataset.

■ **NOTE:** Cascading lookup components will stack the buffers created during runtime. Each lookup will create a copy of the buffer preceding it and add the new lookup result columns to the copy of the buffer. The buffers are not released until the batch of rows is committed or reaches the end of the data flow. Stacking multiple lookups in the data flow may lead to memory overflows and poor performance. Only the necessary columns should be brought into the pipeline by components.

Tool Windows

The query window for accessing the database engine is shown in Figure 2-12. With the addition of IntelliSense in SQL Server 2008, query development became easier because of the quick reference information that is returned on functions and the AutoFill on database objects. With SQL Server 11, Management Studio has been built around the Visual Studio framework. This is most evident with the startup screen that declares this fact.

By default, three windows compose the Management Studio environment.On the left is the Object Explorer window; it allows you to see all the objects that are defined through a tree view with the server as the root node. In addition to displaying the objects, it provides wizards and options to perform management and administration tasks. The Object Explorer can be used to connect to multiple instances as well as the different engines of SQL Server. With the database engine, the query window is the primary mode of access. The query window by default sits in the middle, but can be dragged anywhere on the screen. It is not limited to the Management Studio window. If multiple screens are used, the query window can be moved to a different screen from the one with Management Studio.

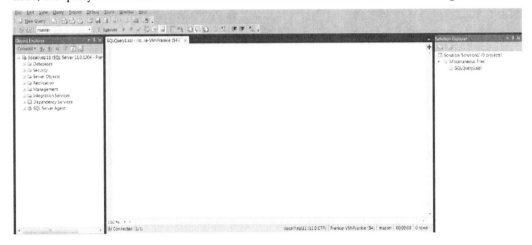

Figure 2-12. Tool windows for SQL Server Management Studio

By default, the setup of Management Studio has three bars at the top: the menu bar, the toolbar, and the context menu. These bars can help you quickly access the objects and data that you need without having to hunt around for options. The following list highlights the populartoolbar buttons:

New Queryopens a new query window based on the context of the Object Explorer. If the selected object is a member of a database engine, the query will be a SQL query. Ifthe object is an Analysis Services database, the query will be an MDX query. The query will automatically be connected to the service that the selected object belongs to, or it will use the connection information of the current query window.

Database Engine Query opens a new query window and asks for connection information needed to access the database. The connection is necessary to execute and parse queries.

Analysis Services MDX Query creates a new query window that can query cube data. For those who are not Analysis Services developers, using the Browse Cube option through the Object Explorer may suffice.

Analysis Services DMX Query creates a new query window for data-mining expressions. These queries are used to access the data-mining models that are present on a cube.

Analysis Services XMLA Query creates a new query window for defining Analysis Services database objects. This query is usually developed using BIDS, and they run against Analysis Services to create a cube.

Activity Monitor opens a window that shows the state of the server. The refresh rate can be modified to show the information at a desired pace. Figure 2-13 demonstrates the various statistics that are tracked by the monitor.

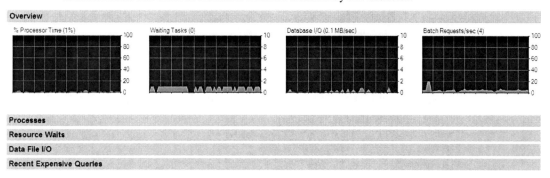

Figure 2-13. Management Studio Activity Monitor

The context menu is specific to the query window that is currently selected. The MDX and DMX queries have the same menu, whereas the database engine and XMLA queries have a slightly different one. The main differences between the cube queries and the T-SQL queries are the result display and the execution plan options that are present with the T-SQL queries but not with the cube queries. Because the XMLA does not query the data but rather defines the objects that perform the analysis, it has a completely different toolset. Cube and T-SQL queries both have the following tools:

Connect connects a disconnected query to a database that is appropriate for the query type.

Change Connection prompts you with the connection information to allow you to change the instance being queried.

Available Databases is a drop-down list of all the available databases on the current instance.

Execute, which is by far the most commonly used, executes the query in the current window. If a section of code is highlighted, it will execute only the code that is highlighted.

■ **NOTE:** Errors in execution usually will display a line number where the error is most likely to be found. This line number is in respect to the start of the batch where the statement began. Line 10 might actually be line 30 in the query window. To help locate errors, we recommend you turn on Line Numbers through the Options menu and selecting Text Editor.

Parse, which is another popular function, will parse the query to verify that it is syntactically correct. It will not verify that the objects exists. Usually IntelliSense will provide some error highlighting if a connection is made to a SQL Server 2008 or later instance.

CommentOutthe Selected Lines adds a single-line commentwith two hyphens (--) at the beginning of each of the current or selected lines.

Uncomment Out the Selected Lines removes any single-line comments, marked by two hyphens (--), from the beginning of each of the current or selected lines.

Decrease Indent removes any present indentation from the beginning of the current or selected lines of code.

Increase Indent adds indentation to the selected or current line of code. By default, the indentation is a tab, but this can be changed in the Options menu.

Specify Values for Template Parameterspops up a window that will replace the parameters in a query template with the values specified. The utility automatically reads in the parameters defined in the template, as shown in Figure 2-14. There are a wide range of templates available for both SQL Server and Analysis Services. Figure 2-15 displays the templates for both.

T-SQL queries have a few extra context options that the other query types do not. These involve outputting the results and query plan explorers. The buttons associated with the SQL queries are as follows:

Display Estimated Execution Plan shows the estimated query plan for the queries in the query window. The plan is displayed graphically at the bottom in the output screen with its own tab, Execution Plan. This utility is essential when you are performance-tuning your queries.

Query Options opens a Query Options window that allows you to set certain options for query execution and the result set.

IntelliSense Enabled toggles IntelliSense on and off.

Include Actual Execution Plan includes the query plan with the results. This plan differs from the estimated plan in that it displays the actual actions taken by the query optimizer. The plan is displayed in a tab called Execution Plan.

Include Client Statistics displays the client statistics in a tab called Client
Statistics. This utility will actually record the statistics from different executions
of the queries, showing changes from each execution as well as averages for
each statistic.

Results to Text outputs the results from the queries as text output. The output
is space delimited and can be hard to read, but in the absence of a spreadsheet
program, it is the easiest way to transmit the results of a query.

Results to Grid displays the results in a grid format that can be easily copied to
Excel or another spreadsheet editor. The result set can be copied entirely,
specific columns or specific records at a time.

Results to File outputs the results directly to a specified file. The file needs to
be defined with each execution of the query. The default format for the result
set is a report file (`.rpt`).

For the XMLA query, the context menu is mainly composed of XML editor options. These are meant
to help close the current tags and give information about the current attribute of the object.

SQL Server Management Studio Project

Just as in BIDS, SSMS supports projects. These projects, however, are limited to three types: SQL Server
scripts, consisting of T-SQL scripts; Analysis Services scripts, consisting of MDX, DMX, and XMLA
scripts; and SQL Server Compact Edition scripts. The projects consist of three parts: Connections,
Queries, and Miscellaneous. The following list provides a brief description of these parts:

Connections stores all the connections related to the project. After the
connection has been created, queries can be created with the connection set
without having to use the Object Explorer. If a connection isn't created
independently, connections made for a query in the projectare automatically
added.

Queries contains all the queries associated with the project. Depending on the
type of the project, only the supported files can be added to this folder (for
example, `.sql` for SQL Server).

The connection information of the queries is stored within the project file (`.ssmssqlproj`
or`.ssmsasproj`) itself. Just as with BIDS, the project files contain vital information. For Management
Studio projects, they contain information such as time-out periods, the queries contained, and the
connection information for the queries. Opening a query included in a project will open it with the
connection to the server it was originally connected to.

Templates

SQL Server Management Studio provides many templates to store common DDL and DCL statements.
These statements exist for both SQL Server and Analysis Services; the templates are shown in Figure 2-
14. The templates contain parameters that are easily replaceable using a utility known as Specify Values
for Template Parameters, shown in Figure 2-15. This utility performs similar functionality to Search and
Replace, but is built specifically to identify all the parameters and to display them all in one place. The
templates are stored in a treestructure with the template type at the root. To access the Template
Explorer, you can select View from the toolbar and click Template Window. At the top-left corner of the

window, you will see two buttons that will allow you to open either SQL Server templates or Analysis Services templates. The templates open as new query windows.

Figure 2-14. Code templates in Management Studio

After expanding to the tree that you desire, you can add the template to a query window by simply double-clicking it. After the template is open, the Specify Values for Template Parameters button on the context menu can be used to prompt the utility. The real power behind the templates is that you can create your own set of templates that are specific to your needs. You can add comment blocks at the top of the scripts that provide details about the script and its contents, and all of this can be parameterized. The parameters have the following format:`<parameter_name, data_type, value>`. The `parameter_name` specifies the name of the parameter, the `data_type` specifies the data type of the parameter, and the `value` specifies the value that will replace every instance of the parameter.

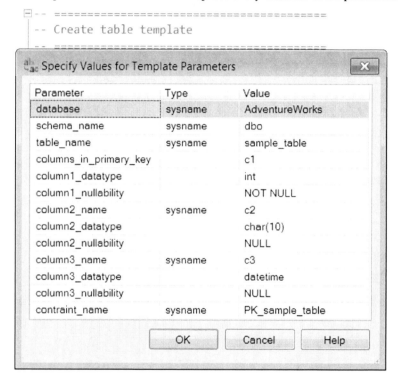

Figure 2-15. Specify Values for Template Parameters

You can also add your templates to the folder of your choosing. Becausemost objects have folders for their templates, you are likely to create a template in an existing folder rather than creating your own template folder.

Code Snippets

Code snippets have been present in the Visual Studio environment for a few iterations. With SQL Server 11, they are now available with Management Studio. They work in a similar fashion as the templates, but unlike the templates, they can be inserted directly into the current query window. Ctrl+K, Ctrl+X brings up the snippet inserter with a drop-down of available snippets. The best part of the snippets is the ability to add your own custom snippets for code packets you utilize most often. This feature has been extremely helpful with Visual Studio development and is a welcome feature in SQL Server 11. Listing 2-4 displays a custom snippet that we created to script a drop and a create statement for a table.

■ **NOTE:** The default set of snippets consist mainly of DDL and DCL object create scripts. This is extremely useful because SSMS stores the actual syntax that we developers most likely would use to reference Microsoft Developers Network, MSDN, or Book Online, BOL. With the ability to create your own snippets, it is likely that 90 percent of your everyday syntax can be coded for this purpose. Aside from syntax, common blocks for your queries (joins you perform on a majority of your queries, where clauses that are crucial to the business logic, and so forth) can all be scripted so that they can be added to your code with a few keystrokes rather than typing them out over and over again.

Listing 2-4. Snippet for Drop and Create Table

```xml
<?xml version="1.0" encoding="utf-8" ?>
<CodeSnippets xmlns="http://schemas.microsoft.com/VisualStudio/2005/CodeSnippet">

<_locDefinition xmlns="urn:locstudio">
<_locDefault _loc="locNone" />

<_locTag _loc="locData">Title</_locTag>

<_locTag _loc="locData">Description</_locTag>
<_locTag _loc="locData">Author</_locTag>
<_locTag _loc="locData">ToolTip</_locTag>
</_locDefinition>
<CodeSnippet Format="1.0.0">
<Header>

<Title>Drop and Create Table</Title>

<Shortcut></Shortcut>
<Description>Drops a table if it exists, then creates a table.</Description>
<Author>Rodrigues, Coles</Author>
<SnippetTypes>
<SnippetType>Expansion</SnippetType>
</SnippetTypes>
</Header>
<Snippet>
<Declarations>

<Literal>
<ID>SchemaName</ID>
<ToolTip>Name of the schema</ToolTip>
<Default><![CDATA[<schema_name, sysname, dbo>]]></Default>
</Literal>

<Literal>
```

```
<ID>Tablename</ID>
<ToolTip>Name of the table</ToolTip>
<Default>Sample_Table</Default>
</Literal>
<Literal>
<ID>column1</ID>
<ToolTip>Name of the column</ToolTip>
<Default>ID</Default>
</Literal>
<Literal>
<ID>datatype1</ID>
<ToolTip>Data type of the column</ToolTip>
<Default>INT IDENTITY(1,1) NOT NULL</Default>
</Literal>
<Literal>
<ID>column2</ID>
<ToolTip>Name of the column</ToolTip>
<Default>Desc</Default>
</Literal>
<Literal>
<ID>datatype2</ID>
<ToolTip>Data type of the column</ToolTip>
<Default>NVARCHAR(50) NULL</Default>
</Literal>
</Declarations>

<Code Language="SQL">
<![CDATA[
IF  EXISTS
(
SELECT *
FROM sys.objects
WHERE object_id = OBJECT_ID(N'[$SchemaName$].[$Tablename$]')
AND type in (N'U')
)
DROP TABLE [$SchemaName$].[$Tablename$];
GO
CREATE TABLE $SchemaName$.$Tablename$
(
    $column1$ $datatype1$,
    $column2$ $datatype2$
);
GO
$end$]]>
</Code>

</Snippet>
</CodeSnippet>
</CodeSnippets>
```

Some of the key components of the snippets are highlighted in Listing 2-4 and detailed here:.

Title is the name that Management Studio will use to uniquely identify your custom snippet. The wizard that adds snippets to the collection will forcibly rename the snippet if it detects a collision with an existing snippet in the same folder path.

Literal defines the components of the snippet that can be replaced quickly. Using the Tab key traverses through the literals in the code. The literal can be defined as a default value that can be set as a parameter. Using parameters as the default values for literals is the key to repurposing the Specify Values for Template Parameters utility for code snippets.

Codecontains the actual code that is to be inserted in the script. The code block will be inserted as it is in the CDATA block. It will preserve the whitespace and replace the literals with their specified defaults.

After a code snippet has been inserted using the snippet inserter, you can use the Tab key to navigate the query by automatically highlighting the replacement points and replacing them with your own strings. For more-complex snippets that reuse code, it may be a better idea to utilize parameters, as we have shown in Listing 2-4. This allows you to take advantage of the Specify Values for Template Parameters feature within Management Studio.

Queries for SSIS

The queries that are created in Management Studio can be saved on the file system to be easily incorporated into SSIS. For example, an OLE DB source component has a Browse button in the editor that will allow you to import the query saved on the file system as the SQL command for the source component. This option becomes available only if SQL Command is used as the data access mode. Queries can also be imported by lookup components if they are set to use the results of a SQL query. With this functionality, it becomes easier for developers to write the SQL that they will be using to extract the data and to import it directly to their SSIS packages as needed. Combining this with the code snippet functionality of Management Studio, convoluted joins and where clauses can be stored for easy access to any script.

Summary

SQL Server 11 offers the capabilities of an entire business intelligence endeavor through its Business Intelligence Development Studio. This chapter introduced all the new features of and enhancements to an important tool in the arsenal, Integration Services. We also introduced a crucial component of maintaining and administering the SQL Server suite, Management Studio. We concluded by describing how all of these components come together to build an end-to-end solution as well as some enhancements made for the developers' code reusability. Chapter 3 will walk you through developing your very first package and introduce you to some of the best practices you should get in the habit of using from the start.

Hello World—Your First SSIS 2012 Package

Take the first step in faith. You don't have to see the whole staircase, just take the first step.

—Civil Rights Movement leader Martin Luther King Jr.

In the previous chapter, we introduced you to SQL Server 11's development tools, BIDS and SSMS. Before we start discussing the in-depth details, we will walk you through some example packages to demonstrate the capabilities of this powerful toolset. As a developer, it is much easier for you to gain an understanding after you've tried out the tools for yourself. This chapter teaches you how to start with the simplest package, consisting of a Data Flow task that will have only a source and a destination. After walking you through creating the easy package, we will guide you through a more complex, real-life example of a package. This package's goal will be to emulate some of the potential requirements that may become a part of your ETL process, and as such is a relatively complex example to be introduced in the third chapter.

The reason we are not covering all the details before we lead you to the first package is that SSIS has a vast set of tools, a majority of which will not be used together at the same time. Most projects will utilize only a few of the connection managers, for example, while SSIS has a much larger number available. Depending on the requirements of the project, the processes handled by SSIS might have to be divided with other tools. This chapter provides a quick glance at some of the capabilities of SSIS.

For this chapter, we took our data from the US Census Bureau web site, `http://2010.census.gov/2010census/data/`. We use the Apportionment and Population Density datasets in this chapter. The only change we made to this data is to remove some header and footer records to keep the introduction to developing SSIS 11 packages simple. The actual data itself was not modified. *Apportionment* refers to the dividing of the total seats in the House of the Representatives among the 50 states, depending on their population. *Population Density* reports the average population per square mile of the state.

Integration Services Project

As we discussed in the previous chapter, the key to SSIS development is the Integration Services pin BIDS. The project file can organize all the files that are related to an ETL process. When you first create a project, Visual Studio will automatically create the first package for the project and name it

`Package.dtsx`. The first package will be completely empty, and the initial designer will show the control flow. You have the ability to rename the package as soon as it is generated.

Key Package Properties

The package has properties that are organized according to the function they provide. These properties carry out the functional and nonfunctional requirements of the ETL process. Functional requirements comprise the principles of extract, transform, and load (ETL), whereas nonfunctional requirements take care of the robustness, performance and efficiency, maintainability, security, scalability, reliability, and overall quality of the ETL process. There are a few properties that we recommend you look over when creating new packages in the project:

> `Name` can be modified through Visual Studio's Solution Explorer. The benefits of modifying through Visual Studio's Solution Explorer as opposed to modifying through the file system or the property field in the package include the automatic recognition by the project file and the automatic renaming of the package name property. Upon creation, this value is defaulted to the name assigned by Visual Studio.

> `DelayValidation` determines whether the package objects will validate when the package is opened for editing. By default, this property is set to `False`, meaning that all the objects will validate when the package is opened. By setting this property to `False`, you will validate only during runtime. This can be dangerous to do during the development phase if there are Data Definition Language, DDL, changes or structural changes to either the sources or the destinations. It may be useful when developing large packages, by allowing the packages to open/load faster, but we recommend keeping the SSIS packages as modular as possible. We discuss the different options for modularity in Section 2 of this book.

> `ID` provides a unique identifier for the package. This property becomes important when considering logging options. This ID will distinguish the packages that are run for a particular execution. A new identifier is generated when a new package is added to the project, but when an existing package is added or a package is copied and pasted in Solution Explorer, the identifier of the original package is carried over. This value is not directly modifiable, but there is an option to generate a new ID.

> `ProtectionLevel` manages the sensitive data stored in the package. By default, this property is set to `EncryptSensitiveWithUserKey`. This option encrypts the whole package with a key that will identify it with the current user. Only the current user will be able to load the package with all the information. Other users will see only blanks for usernames, passwords, and other sensitive data. We recommend using the `DontSaveSensitive` option, especially if multiple developers will be working on the same set of packages. Sensitive data can be stored in configuration files. We discuss the security aspects of developing and deploying packages in Chapter 19.

Package Annotations

After taking a look at the properties set on the new package, one of the first things we recommend is adding an annotation to the package. This can be done by right-clicking on the background of the current designer view and selecting Add Annotation. Annotations can be used to document the package so that fellow developers can easily identify the purpose of the package without having to open and read through all the tasks. Thoroughly examining the packages can be saved for debugging time. The kind of information the annotations should contain is identified in Figure 3-1.

```
Name: HelloWorld.dtsx
Modified: 3/22/2011
Purpose: Move data from a .csv file to a SQL Server 11 database
Parameters: None
Variables: None
```

Figure 3-1. *Recommended annotation to control flow*

The name represents the name of the current package. This is displayed in several places in Visual Studio, but with the vast improvements to the XML behind the SSIS packages, don't be surprised if you have to look there for certain information. The annotation string itself is stored in the `CDATA` at the bottom of the package XML.

The modified date simply dates the last set of changes made to the package. This piece will help in the absence of a code repository. The file system modified date is not always accurate in capturing actual changes to SSIS packages. Clicking the OK button on many of the designers as well as moving objects around in the designer tabs will cause Visual Studio to recognize changes even if there aren't any functional changes. This can cause the file system to inaccurately represent functional changes to the packages.

The purpose simply identifies the objectives of the package. Modular programming is characterized by having separate, interchangeable code blocks or modules. We cover some design patterns that will enable you to maintain this practice with SSIS 11 in Section 2 of this book. The purpose covers the end state after the execution of the package—which data elements have been moved, which items have been moved around on the file system, the execution of stored procedures, and so forth. This is meant to be a high-level description rather than a detailed description but essentially will depend on your design of the ETL process.

Parameters and variables are related in that they can be used to pass values between packages. *Parameters* are external values that can be set prior to the execution of the package. *Variables* are internal mechanisms to pass information between packages. In prior versions of SQL Server Integration Services, variables served both purposes through configurations either by using configuration files to assign values or by inheriting values through parent variables. It is important to identify parameters because they are accessible to all the packages in a project; this construct becomes extremely useful when utilizing the parent-child package design. The parent package can automatically detect the parameters defined in the child package as well as assign which variables or parameters to pass along to it.

Variables can now be used for the sole purpose of passing values among packages without modification from external processes. When assigning parameters and variables, they are available in the same drop-down list along with the system variables. You also have the option to write expressions to assign parameter values to variables. Variables are passed to a child package by reference rather than by value. Any modification made to the value will require a Script task in the child package to propagate the change back up to the parent package. There is an alternative to using the Script task to modify the parent package, which allows you to directly access the variable. However, this method also causes the executables accessing the variables within the child package to error during the runtime, when the child package is executed on its own. We discuss these options in Chapter 16.

Variable listing is sensitive to the scope of the variables. The scope of a variable can be from the package as a whole or within a specific container, task, or event handler. With multiple variables, you can easily lose track of them all, so the annotation can save a lot of digging around. The Package Explorer tab and the Show Variables of All Scopes option in the Parameters and Variables toolbar allow the same functionality, but with the annotation, you can document the role they play in the process.

■ **NOTE:** Parameters, variables, and system variables are listed in the same drop-down list when they are being assigned. We recommend that you use namespaces to avoid any confusion. We discuss parameters and variables in complete detail in Chapter 10.

Package Property Categories

The package properties are divided into categories to group them by the function they provide. These categories are generally broad and contain a lot more configurable properties than the main ones outlined in the preceding section. These categories and their properties address some of the nonfunctional capabilities of SSIS 11. We briefly introduce the categories here and provide more in-depth analysis in the later chapters:

Checkpoint properties control the restart ability of SSIS package execution. You have to define a file path and name for the progress to be stored during execution. In the event of a failure, this file will be used to restart the process at the task at which it previously failed. This functionality by itself will not handle the rollback of committed data. After a successful execution, this file is automatically deleted.

Execution properties define the runtime aspects of the package. These include the number of failures that the package can tolerate and how to treat the failures of nested containers with respect to the success of the parent container. Performance tuning can also start with the properties in this section. If memory overflows become an issue, the number of concurrent executables can be limited.

Identification properties are used to uniquely recognize packages. These properties include some of the ones listed previously (specifically, `Name` and `ID`). Other information that the package can capture is the machine that it was created on and the user who created it. Another important property that is categorized here is `Description`, which is free-form text.

Misc properties are a mixture of those that cannot be cleanly classified in the other categories. This category includes disparate properties that vary in function from logging behavior of the package execution to listing configurations created for the package.

Security properties handle the sensitive information that may be stored in a package. The main property in this segment, `ProtectionLevel`, was listed earlier. These properties can be configured depending on the different environments used for development, testing, and production. Some settings will allow you to move the packages between environments without causing authentication issues.

■ **TIP:** One option that can help speed up development of SSIS 11 packages is the `OfflineMode` property in the Misc category. This property prevents the package from opening connections to validate metadata. This property is read-only and can be modified by using the SSIS menu on the menu bar. Another option for modifying this property is handled through a file, `<project_name>.dtproj.user.` This XML-based file includes the property `OfflineMode`. This directly corresponds to the package property, but affects all the packages within that project. If you modify this file, you should close the project, modify the file, and then reopen the project. Modifying this file will allow you to avoid having to change it every time you need to make a project change, but there are obvious dangers associated with that. Once development is complete or if the structure of the source or destination has changed, we highly recommend that you set this property to `False`. It is a best practice to validate metadata whenever a package is modified; it will help to ensure that the proper source and destination are being used for development along with many other issues that will start to mysteriously arise during runtime.

Hello World

With a brief introduction to SSIS 11 package properties under your belt, let us dive right into creating a package. The first step in developing a package in Visual Studio requires a project. For this particular chapter, we created a project aptly titled `Chap3_HelloWorld`. Figure 3-2 demonstrates how to create a new Integration Services project within Visual Studio. You access the dialog box by going to the File menu on the toolbar and choosing New ä Project. An alternative to this is to use the Recent Projects pane on the Start page. There is hyperlink to create a Project at the bottom.

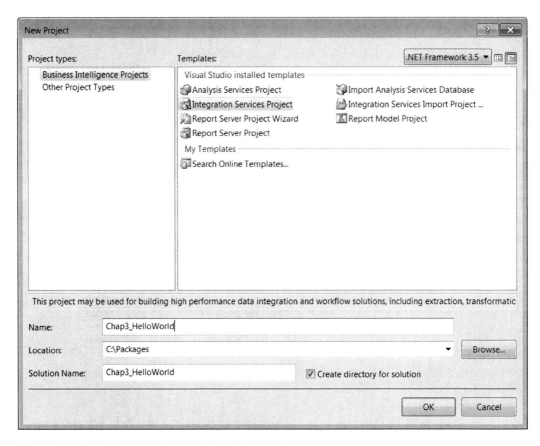

Figure 3-2. Creating a new Integration Services project

Following are some of the elements within the dialog box, and a brief description of their purpose:

- The Name text field in the dialog box assigns the name to the project file. This name should be sufficiently broad to cover the various packages that will be stored. Because we are trying to demonstrate only a simple package, the project name refers to a simple process.

- The Location field indicates the directory where the project will be stored on the file system during development. For simplicity, we created a short folder path to store our packages.

- The Solution Name field is automatically populated with the same value as is provided in the Name field, but it can be changed if the name does not suit the solution.

- The Create Directory for Solution check box is extremely useful for keeping the projects organized. It will create a subfolder within the defined Location and place all the files (`.database`, `.dtproj`, `.dtproj.user`, `.dtsx`, and so forth) and subfolders required for building and deploying within it.

After the project is created, Visual Studio will automatically generate a package and name it `Package.dtsx`. One of the first steps we recommend that you perform is to modify this name to a more appropriate and descriptive name. If you change it directly through Solution Explorer, you will get a dialog box asking you to confirm a change to the `Name` property of the package. If you change the name of the package through the Properties window, you will not get a dialog box to confirm a change to the file name. This behavior allows the two to be out of sync, but there is no reason to have such a scenario. We recommend that you keep them in sync.

Because we are not creating a complex package with large amounts of metadata, we are going to leave the `DelayValidation` property to `False`. This package will simply take data from a flat file and move it to a SQL Server 11 database without any transformations. This is the simplest ETL task SSIS can perform, taking data from a source storage platform and placing it in a destination storage platform. We will also skip over the ID generation because we did not copy this package from an existing one.

We will set `ProtectionLevel` to `DontSaveSensitive`. This will allow us to work on the package without having to remember a password or having to use the same machine through a common user account. It will also force us to store any required connection information in a different file other than the package. We encourage you to store sensitive information in configuration files for both the security of storing the information only once and the ability to limit access to this file.

After all the desired properties are set, we can start the actual development of the package. We recommend that you add an annotation like the one shown in Figure 3-1 that outlines the basic design we are going to implement for the ETL process. With the annotation in place, we know the function of all the objects in the package. The first step toward the ETL process is identifying the data you want to extract, the location of the data, and some rudimentary data (metadata) about the data. When handling flat files, metadata becomes crucial because a low estimation of column lengths will result in truncation.

■ **NOTE:** The `ProtectionLevel` setting needs to be the same on all the packages associated to a project as the project's `ProtectionLevel` property.

Flat File Source Connection

The first object we will add to the package is a flat file connection. We do this by right-clicking in the Connection Managers pane at the bottom of the designer and selecting New Flat File Connection. This opens the Flat File Connection Manager Editor, depicted in Figure 3-3. We recommend that you replace the default name of the connection with one that will enable you to easily identify the data to which the manager is providing access. The name of the connection must be unique. In addition, we also recommend writing a short description of the manager in the Description field. These two fields will reappear in all of the pages listed in the left panel of the editor.

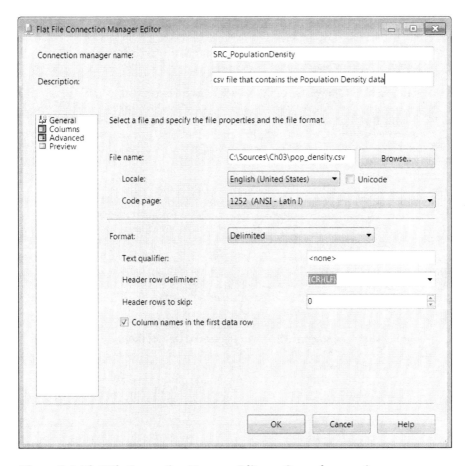

Figure 3-3. *Flat File Connection Manager Editor —General properties*

The File Name field stores the folder path and the file name that will be associated with this particular data set. The Browse button allows you to use Windows Explorer to locate the file and automatically populate the path into the field. When using the Browse option, it is important to note that the default file type selected is `.txt`. In our case, we are using a `.csv` file for our data, so we had to change the file type to be able to view it in Windows Explorer. The Locale drop-down provides a list of regions for language-specific ordering of time formats. The Unicode check box defines the dataset to use Unicode and will disable the Code Page ability. The Code Page option enables you to define non-Unicode code pages for the flat file.

The Format section of the Flat File Connection Manager Editor's General page allows you to define how SSIS will read in the file. There are three formats to choose from: Delimited, Fixed Width, and Ragged Right. Delimited, the default format, enables you to define the delimiter in the Columns tab. For `.csv` (comma-separated values) files, the delimiter is a comma. Fixed Width defines the columns in the flat file as having a determined column length for each of the columns. The length is measured in characters. A ruler helps you define the individual characters for each column. You can choose from various fonts in order to accurately display the characters. Ragged Right follows the same rules as Fixed Width except for the last column. The last column has a row delimiter rather than a fixed width.

The Text Qualifier text box allows you to specify the qualifiers that denote text data. The most common way to qualify text is by using quotes. The Header Row Delimiter list defines the characters that mark the first row of data. Usually, this is the same as the row delimiter. For `.csv` files, the row delimiter is a carriage return immediately followed by a line feed. When we downloaded the data from the Census Bureau's web site, we cleaned up some of the header records so that only the column names and the actual data remained. The check box labeled Column Names in the First Data Row allows SSIS to easily read in the file and capture the column names defined in the `.csv` file, as demonstrated by Figure 3-4. This cleans up the names so that you don't see names such as Column1, Column2, and so forth. and replaces those generic names with the actual column headers defined in the `.csv` file.

■ **NOTE:** We will not create a configuration file this early in the book, but this folder path will be a critical piece of information that is stored within the connection string property of the connection. When looping through a list of files with the same metadata, it is also possible to change the connection string during runtime.

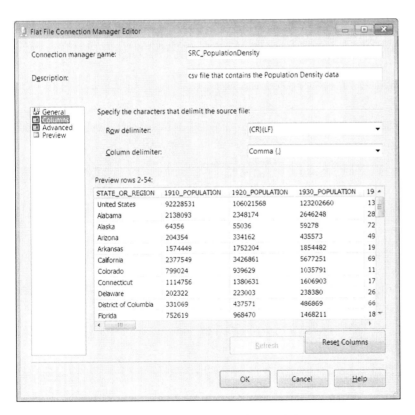

Figure 3-4. Flat File Connection Manager Editor—Columns page

The Columns page of the Flat File Connection Manager Editor allows you to define the row delimiter and the column delimiter. With `.csv` files, the rows are delimited with carriage returns and line feeds, and the columns are delimited with commas. After setting these values, you can preview a sample of the rows using the delimiter values defined. If you need to make any changes to the delimiter, you can refresh the Preview pane to see how the changes will impact the connection manager's reading of the file. The Reset Columns button will remove all the columns except the original columns.

With the Fixed Width option, the Preview pane has a ruler at the top. In this mode, the preview will ignore the new line characters in the actual file. The marks along the ruler will demarcate the columns' widths. Each column can have its width defined using the ruler. The Preview pane will visually assist with how the connection manager will read in the data. The Ragged Right option will have an extra field that will allow you to define the row delimiters.

The Advanced page of the Flat File Connection Manager Editor, shown in Figure 3-5, allows you to modify the metadata of each column. The columns represented here are dependent on the columns defined through the Columns page. In the Advanced page, you can modify each of the columns' names, column delimiter, data type, output column width, and text qualified. For the last column in the flat file, the column delimiter will be the row delimiter. Depending on the data type chosen (numeric data), data precision and data scale become available. The column type determines these options, and for the delimited formats these are the columns available. For the other two formats, you can define the input column widths individually. Changes here will be reflected in the Preview pane on the Columns page.

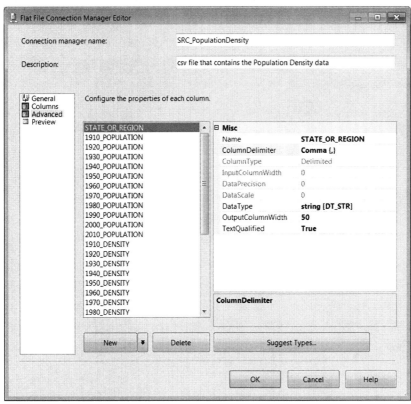

Figure 3-5. *Flat File Connection Manager Editor—Advanced page*

The Preview page displays a sample dataset from the source according to the metadata defined in the other pages. Figure 3-6 demonstrates this page of the Flat File Connection Manager Editor. It also has the option to skip data rows in the source. This is a different option than the one on the General page. The General page option allows header rows to be ignored so that the appropriate row can be used as the source for the column names. This Preview page option will ignore rows that immediately follow the row containing the column headers.

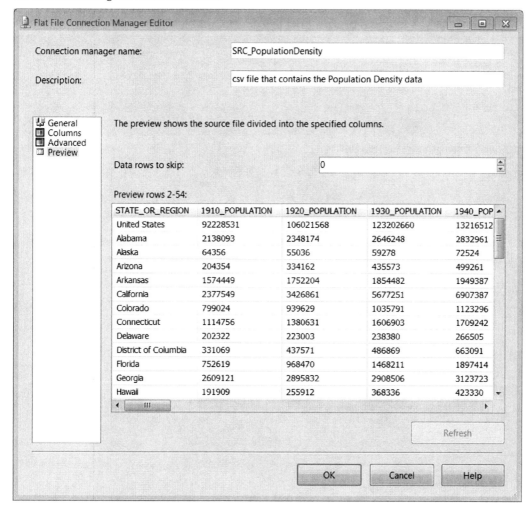

Figure 3-6. *Flat File Connection Manager Editor—Preview page*

OLE DB Destination Connection

With the source of our data ready for extraction, we need to set up the destination for loading. For this example, we will be using a SQL Server 11 database as the destination. We will create a table that will fit the metadata of the source, essentially taking the data from a file system flat file and storing it in a relational database management system (RDBMS). The first step in creating an Object Linking and Embedding Database, OLE DB, Connection Manager is to right-click in the Connection Managers pane in the designer window. Here you will have to add a data connection to a server, using the dialog box shown in Figure 3-7, if you do not already have one. You will need the login information ready when you are creating the data connection. If you do not have the server name, you can put in the IP address of the server, or if you want to load the data in a local instance on your machine, you can call it by using the `(local)\instance` name.

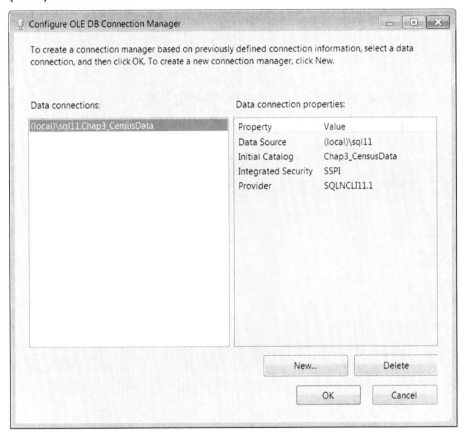

Figure 3-7. *Configuring the OLE DB Connection Manager*

This manager allows you to store data connections that you use in SSIS. This is not limited to connections used within a particular project. You can configure the new connections by using the wizard shown in Figure 3-8. By default, the connections stored within the connection manager will have names in the following format: `DataSource.InitialCatalog.` The Data Connection Properties pane will show the connection string information and the default values for that particular connection. Clicking the New button will prompt the Connection Manager Wizard depicted in Figure 3-8. Connection managers are not limited to extract or load duties; they can perform both tasks, although doing both simultaneously may risk contention issues.

The Data Connection Properties pane shows all the information needed to extract—or in our case, load—data into a SQL Server 11 database. The Data Source refers to the server and the name of the instance on the RDBMS on the server. The IP address can be just as easily used, but we recommend using the name of the machine wherever possible. The Initial Catalog is the database in which the data will be extracted from or loaded to. The Integrated Security property determines how the database is accessed: whether a username and password are used or Windows Authentication passes on the credentials. For our example, we will be using Windows Authentication. The Provider is the driver that is used to connect to the database. SQLNCLI1.1 is the driver required to connect to a SQL Server 11 database.

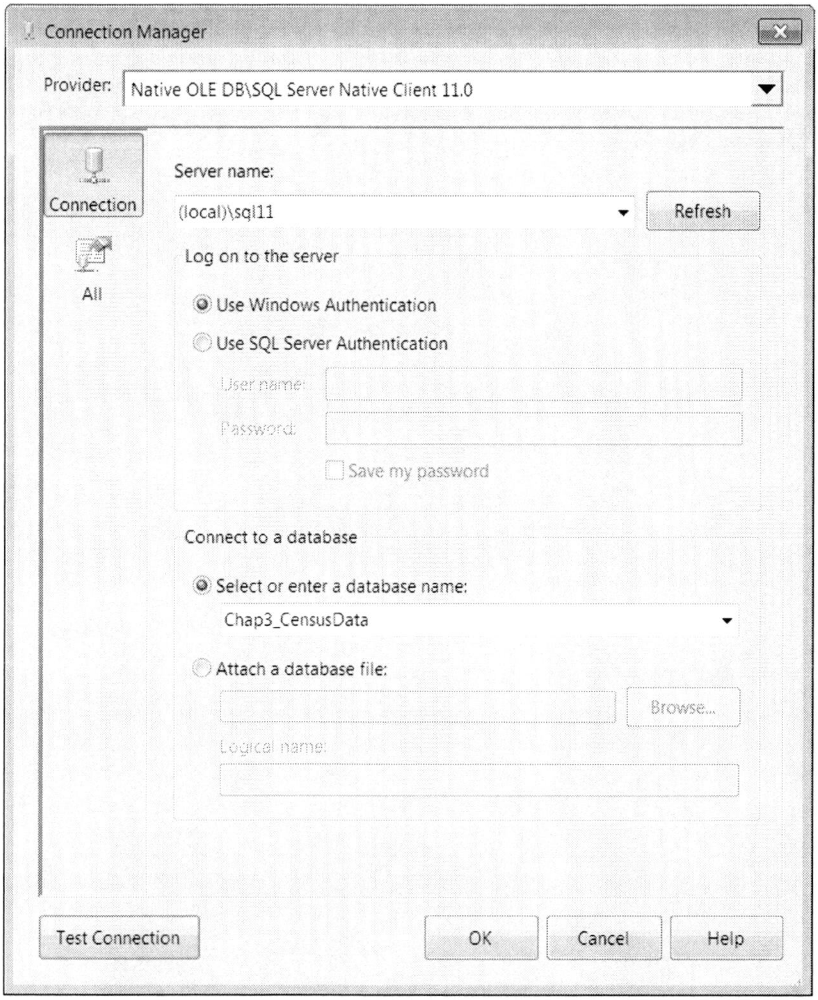

Figure 3-8. Connection Manager—Connection page

On the Connection page, you are asked to provide all the details needed to connect to a particular database. In this case, we want the database in which we will be storing the Population Density data. This information can be easily referenced in the Data Connection Properties pane on the Configure OLE DB Connection Manager wizard after the connection has been created. The wizard allows you to easily review all the previously created connections for reusability. The Server Name of the connection manager must also include the instance name. The radio buttons below that field indicate the access mode to use. When using Windows Authentication, make sure you have the proper credentials to access the server and database. Without access, you will not be able to gather or validate the required metadata. For each connection, you have to specify the database you intend to use. Utilizing configuration files will allow you to store the connection information in a separate file. This allows changes to propagate across multiple packages that are configured to use the file rather than manually opening and updating each instance of the connection manager. The Test Connection button uses the information provided to ping the server and database. It is a quick way to test your credentials and validate access to the selected database. The All page of the Connection Manager dialog box, shown in Figure 3-9, gives you access to all the available properties of the connection.

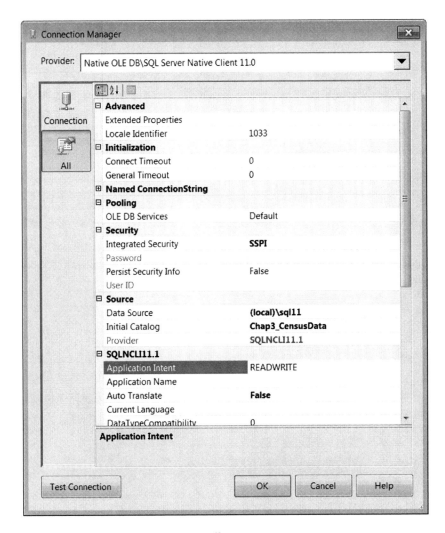

Figure 3-9. Connection Manager—All page

Utilizing the All page provides properties beyond those in the Connection page. This page allows you to fully modify the connection manager to meet your needs. You can define connection timeouts to provide a maximum limit in how long a query can run. We would not recommend tweaking these properties unless you need to for very specific reasons. By default, these settings should provide the optimal performance that you require. After you add the connection manager, we recommend that you rename it immediately so that when you try to access it later, you can easily identify it.

Data Flow Task

After adding the connection managers for the source and destinations of our dataset, we can move on to adding the executable that will extract and load the Population Density data. The Data Flow task can be found in the Favorites subsection of the SSIS Toolbox. It is here by default and can be moved around if you do not use it too often. Figure 3-10 illustrates the control flow pane with a single Data Flow Task.

■ **TIP:** One of our favorite people, Jamie Thomson, has a blog entirely devoted to naming conventions for SSIS objects. These conventions can be found on his EMC Consulting site at
`http://consultingblogs.emc.com/jamiethomson/archive/2006/01/05/ssis_3a00_-suggested-best-practices-and-naming-conventions.aspx`. We will be adding to this list the naming conventions for the new components.

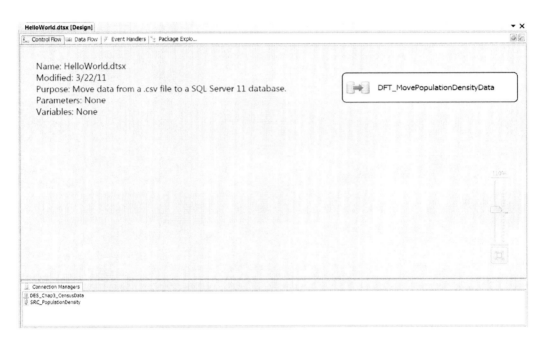

Figure 3-10. `HelloWorld.dtsx`—*control flow*

Using the naming convention introduced by Jamie Thomson, we named the preceding executable `DFT_MovePopulationDensityData`. The `DFT` indicates that it is a Data Flow task. The rest of the name describes the function of the Data Flow task. Each of the control flow components has its own symbol, allowing you to readily recognize the object. The data flow symbol has two cylinders with an arrow from one pointing to the other.

▓ **TIP:** The Format menu on the menu bar has two options that will keep the Control Flow and the Data Flow windows orderly. The first option, Autosize, automatically changes the size of the selected objects to allow the names to fit. The second option, Auto Layout Diagram, changes the orientation of objects in the current window so that the objects' middles (height) and centers (width) line up evenly. In the Control Flow window, the executables or containers that are designed to execute simultaneously will have their middles lined up, while those designed to be sequential will have their centers lined up. The execution order in the control flow is determined by the precedence constraints that are defined. For the Data Flow window, the pipeline is used to organize the objects. Usually the components in the Data Flow window will not have multiple objects lining up their middles unless there are multiple streams.

You can add the connection managers in a different order than we have done in this package. We approached creating this package from a step-by-step manner in which identifying the source and destinations was the first agenda. As you will see in the sections with the assistants, you can add connection managers as you are adding the components to Data Flow. We see this as providing a chance to create ad hoc managers rather than creating the sources and destinations through a planned process.

Source Component

With the connection manager in place for the Population Density file and the Data Flow task to extract the data, we can add the source component that will open the connection and read in the data. In SSIS 11, the addition of the Source Assistant greatly helps organize the different connection managers we created. Figure 3-11 demonstrates how the Source Assistant enables you to quickly add a source component for your desired connection. In this example, the source we are looking for is `SRC_PopulationDensity`. If you choose to, you can add a new connection manager here for your source data by selecting `<New>` and clicking the OK button.

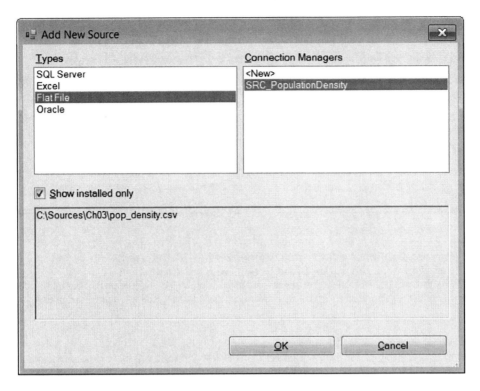

Figure 3-11. *Source Assistant*

The Types pane contains all the connection managers that are currently supported by your machine. Drivers for other connection managers such as DB2 can be downloaded from Microsoft's web site. For our package, we are concerned with only the Flat File source, and in the Connection Managers pane, all the managers of that type are listed. In this package, `HelloWorld.dtsx`, there is only one such manager. The bottom pane shows the connection information for this particular flat file, so you can even see the file name and path. In previous versions of SSIS, you had to know the connection information for each manager before you added the source component. The Source Assistant did not exist to show you the connection string for the different managers. The naming convention used for the connection managers is important in this regard. After clicking the OK button, you will automatically add the component to `DFT_MovePopulationDensityData`. By default, the name of the component is Flat File Source, but by using the defined naming conventions, we changed the name to `FF_SRC_PopulationDensity`. The component automatically resizes when you type in the name so that you get a clear idea of how much space the component will use up in the window.

Destination Component

With our source component in place, we can now add the destination for our data. The other new assistant that has been added to SSIS 11 is the Destination Assistant. This assistant offers the same organizational help that the Source Assistant provides. One of the key features of the assistant is the connection information that is displayed in the bottom of the pane, as depicted in Figure 3-12. The option to add a new connection manager is available through the assistant. Naming the connection managers appropriately will make identifying the proper connection much easier.

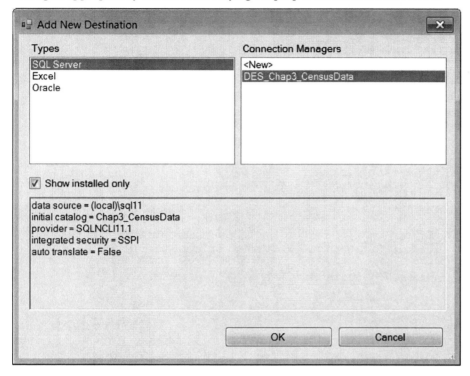

Figure 3-12. Destination Assistant

After we select the connection manager we want, DES_Chap3_CensusData, we can add it to the data flow by clicking the OK button. The component will be added with the default name of OLE DB Destination. We will adhere to the naming convention and rename it OLE_DST_CensusData. Just as was the case with the source component, it will automatically resize to fit the name provided.

Data Flow Path

After we have both the source and the destination components in the Data Flow task, we need to instruct SSIS to move the data from the source to the destination. This is done by defining a path for the data flow. To add the path, you have to click the source component. You will see two arrows appear at the bottom of the component. The green arrow represents the flow of data after a successful read, and the red redirects rows that fail during the read. The green arrow is recognized by SSIS as the Flat File Source output, and the red arrow is referred to as the Flat File Source Error Output. These two arrows are shown in Figure 3-13.

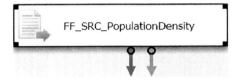

Figure 3-13. Source component—outputs

The data flow path can simply be created by clicking and dragging the green arrow from the source component to the destination component. The other option is to use the wizard to Add Path in the Data Flow. This wizard can be accessed by right-clicking the source component and selecting Add Path. This opens a dialog box enabling you to choose the components and the direction of the path, as shown in Figure 3-14.

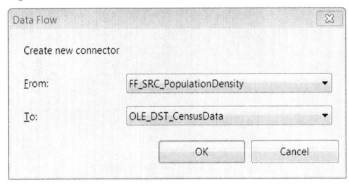

Figure 3-14. Data FlowCreate New Connector

With this connector wizard, we can define the direction of the data flow. This connector wizard will affect the settings of the wizard that appears after this one, as depicted in Figure 3-15.

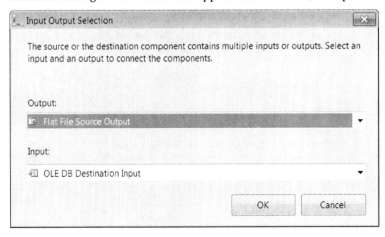

Figure 3-15. Input Output Selection

This wizard allows you to match the inputs and the outputs of the source and destination components. For the output, you have two options: the Flat File Source Output and the Flat File Source Error Output. Because we want the actual data from the file, we selected the Flat File Source Output. The OLE DB destination component can accept only one input. After you click OK, the data path will be created between these two components using the outputs and inputs that were defined. But creating the data path is not the final step; we need to map the columns between the source and the destination.

Mapping

As you recall, we had to define all the columns that we were expecting from the source. The same process is required when moving the data to a destination. After we create the data path between the source and the destination, Visual Studio provides a small reminder of this fact through a small red x on the destination component, as can be seen in Figure 3-16. The error will propagate to the control-flow-level executable, so you will see the x on DFT_MovePopulationDensityData as well.

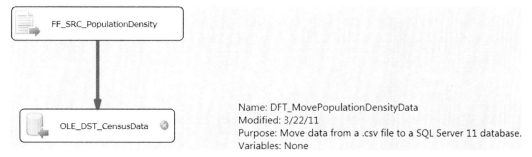

Figure 3-16. *Data Flow task—mapping error OLE DB destination*

You can identify the reason behind the errors by holding your cursor on top of the x mark. In our case, we did not define the destination table for our data. To fix this issue, we have to double-click the destination component to open the OLE DB Destination Editor. The editor, shown in Figure 3-17, allows you to modify the connection manager to be used as well as some options regarding the actual insertion of data into the database.

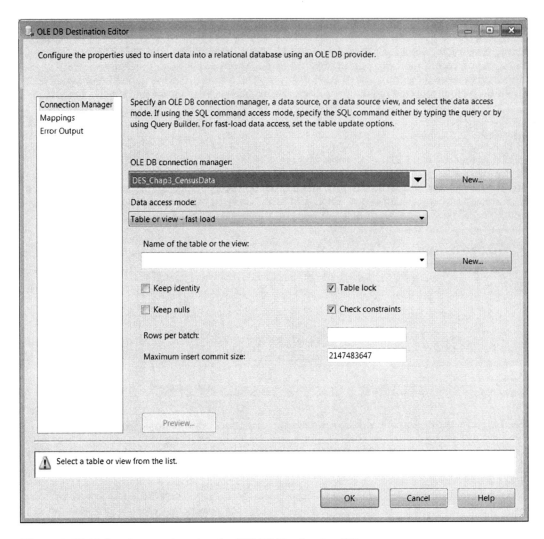

Figure 3-17. *Fixing the error by using the OLE DB Destination Editor*

The OLE DB Connection Manager drop-down list allows you to change the connection manager from the one selected when the Destination Assistant was used. The Data Access Mode list provides you with a few options on how to load the data. The Table or View option loads data into a table or view defined in the destination database. This option fires insert statements for each individual row. For small datasets, these transactions may seem fast, but as soon as the data volumes start increasing, you will experience a bottleneck using this option. The Table or View – Fast Load option is optimized for bulk inserts. This option is the default when setting up the destination component. The Table Name or View Name Variable option uses a variable whose value is the name of the destination table. This option also uses only row-by-row insert statements to load the data. Table Name or View Name Variable – Fast Load also utilizes the value of a variable to determine the destination table but it is optimized for bulk insert.

The SQL Command option utilizes a SQL query to load the data. This query will execute for each record that appears in the input of the destination component.

We do not have a table ready to load the data from the source, but the OLE DB Destination Editor has the ability to generate a CREATE TABLE script based on the metadata passed to its input. The table script it generates for this particular dataset is shown in Listing 3-1. If we had removed columns from the pipeline prior to passing them to the destination component, they would not have been added to this create script. The bold code denotes the changes we made to the script to conform to our naming standards. By default, the table name was OLE_DST_CensusData, the name given to the component. The editor does not specify table schema when it generates the create table script. If the table you want to load the data into is already created, it is available in the drop-down list.

Listing 3-1. *Create Table Script for Population Density Data*

```
CREATE TABLE dbo.PopulationDensity (
    [STATE_OR_REGION] varchar(50),
    [1910_POPULATION] varchar(50),
    [1920_POPULATION] varchar(50),
    [1930_POPULATION] varchar(50),
    [1940_POPULATION] varchar(50),
    [1950_POPULATION] varchar(50),
    [1960_POPULATION] varchar(50),
    [1970_POPULATION] varchar(50),
    [1980_POPULATION] varchar(50),
    [1990_POPULATION] varchar(50),
    [2000_POPULATION] varchar(50),
    [2010_POPULATION] varchar(50),
    [1910_DENSITY] varchar(50),
    [1920_DENSITY] varchar(50),
    [1930_DENSITY] varchar(50),
    [1940_DENSITY] varchar(50),
    [1950_DENSITY] varchar(50),
    [1960_DENSITY] varchar(50),
    [1970_DENSITY] varchar(50),
    [1980_DENSITY] varchar(50),
    [1990_DENSITY] varchar(50),
    [2000_DENSITY] varchar(50),
    [2010_DENSITY] varchar(50),
    [1910_RANK] varchar(50),
    [1920_RANK] varchar(50),
    [1930_RANK] varchar(50),
    [1940_RANK] varchar(50),
    [1950_RANK] varchar(50),
    [1960_RANK] varchar(50),
    [1970_RANK] varchar(50),
    [1980_RANK] varchar(50),
    [1990_RANK] varchar(50),
    [2000_RANK] varchar(50),
    [2010_RANK] varchar(50)
);
GO
```

The column names and lengths were defined based on the metadata defined in the Flat File Connection Manager. Because we did not define the columns as Unicode, the default data types for all the columns are varchar. This create script is made available through an editable text box that opens when you click the New button for the destination table selection. With the script modified to meet our needs, we need to execute it on the destination database to create the table.

After we create the table on the database, it will appear in the drop-down list of destination tables. Because the column names and data types match exactly for the columns in the destination input, the mapping is automatically created by SSIS, as shown in Figure 3-18. In order to see the mapping, you need to click the Mappings option in the left pane of the editor.

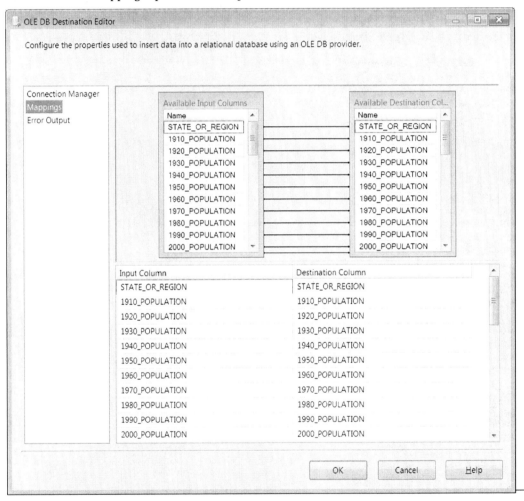

Figure 3-18. *OLE DB Destination EditorMappings page*

To create mappings from the input columns to the destination, you have two options. You can use the UI on the top half of the editor, which allows you to click and drag the input column to its matching destination column. Alternatively, you can use the bottom half of the screen, where the input columns are shown in drop-down lists next to each destination column. You can map an input column to only one destination column. If you want to map the same column to multiple destinations, you will have to use a component in the pipeline that will add the duplicate column.

Before we run this package in Visual Studio, we have to make sure that the project `ProtectionLevel` property matches the value set in the package, `DontSaveSensitive`. Without changing this property, Visual Studio will report build errors and will not allow us to execute the package. After all the components have been created and the properties set, we can take a quick look at the Package Explorer window to quickly review the objects in the package. The Package Explorer for `HelloWorld.dtsx` is shown in Figure 3-19.

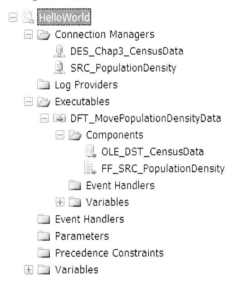

Figure 3-19. `HelloWorld.dtsx`—Package Explorer

The Variables folder in Figure 3-19 is expandable because there are default system variables that are created for all the packages. They are created with Package scope, so all defined executables and containers will have access to them. Because this package is designed to be as simple as possible, a majority of the objects have been skipped. We have only one executable, `DFT_MovePopulationDensityData`, on the control flow so we do not see any precedence constraints.

Aside from offering an organized view of the package's object, the Package Explorer design window also allows you to quickly navigate to the object that requires modification. Double-clicking the individual connection manager will open its editor. Double-clicking the Data Flow task will open that particular Data Flow task's design window.

Execution

We have finally arrived at the fruits of our labor. We have set up the package, and all the objects are in place to allow us to move data from the flat file to the SQL Server 11 database. Using Visual Studio to execute the package requires opening the package as a part of a project. Visual Studio performs build operations before each debugging operation by default. This allows you to see the progress of each component and executable. Figure 3-20 displays the Standard toolbar with the Start Debugging button highlighted. Another option to execute a package in Visual Studio is to right-click the package and select Execute Package. The solution file also starts the debug mode; to use this method, you have to right-click the solution name in Solution Explorer, going to the Debug Group and then selecting Start New Instance.

Figure 3-20. Visual Studio Standard toolbar

There are three colors associated with the Visual Studio debug mode for SSIS 11: green denoting success, yellow denoting in progress, and red denoting failure. Figure 3-21 shows the output of the debug operation of this package. Visual Studio provides a row count for each data path; for this simple package, there is only one. This output informs us that 53 rows were extracted from the flat file and successfully inserted into the destination table.

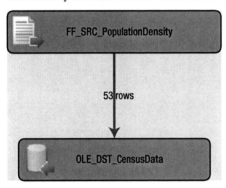

Figure 3-21. `DFT_MovePopulationDensityData`*—execution visuals*

Another option to execute the package is to use the Start Without Debugging option in the Debug menu on the menu bar. This will prompt Visual Studio to call `dtexec.exe` and provide it with the proper parameters to execute the package. One downside to this option is that Visual Studio does not provide the parameter that limits reporting to errors only. Executing the package without a limit on reporting will result in a massive output that will most likely overrun the screen buffer for the command prompt. We recommend using the command prompt to call `dtexec.exe` yourself with the proper parameters you desire. You can even store the output to a file to review the execution details. We cover this option fully in Chapter 26.

To validate that the data has been loaded into the database, you can run queries to test the ETL process results. Listing 3-2 shows a quick way to verify that the data loaded properly. The first query performs a row count to show the number of records in the table. The second query will output all the records that are stored in the table.

■ **NOTE:** Because we do not truncate the table as a part of the package, you will load the data multiple times unless you execute a truncate statement on the table. The more times you execute the package without deleting the data, the more duplicate records you will find.

Listing 3-2. *Queries to Verify Successful Data Loads*

```
SELECT COUNT(*)
FROM dbo.PopulationDensity;

SELECT STATE_OR_REGION
      ,1910_POPULATION
      ,1920_POPULATION
      ,1930_POPULATION
      ,1940_POPULATION
      ,1950_POPULATION
      ,1960_POPULATION
      ,1970_POPULATION
      ,1980_POPULATION
      ,1990_POPULATION
      ,2000_POPULATION
      ,2010_POPULATION
      ,1910_DENSITY
      ,1920_DENSITY
      ,1930_DENSITY
      ,1940_DENSITY
      ,1950_DENSITY
      ,1960_DENSITY
      ,1970_DENSITY
      ,1980_DENSITY
      ,1990_DENSITY
      ,2000_DENSITY
      ,2010_DENSITY
      ,1910_RANK
      ,1920_RANK
      ,1930_RANK
      ,1940_RANK
      ,1950_RANK
      ,1960_RANK
      ,1970_RANK
      ,1980_RANK
      ,1990_RANK
      ,2000_RANK
      ,2010_RANK
FROM dbo.PopulationDensity;
```

By querying the data, you are inadvertently enjoying one of the benefits of having data in an RDBMS as opposed to a flat file. This particular dataset uses the column name to delineate the data that it contains. This is a relatively denormalized dataset forcing you to select a particular year and statistic combination to view the data. In 2020, the only way to update this data would be to add new columns to support the new data. With data normalization, we tend to prefer loading data rather than modifying existing table structures. For a more complex and real-world example, the next package will illustrate how we might go about normalizing the data on the fly by using SSIS 11.

Real World

The simple package example quickly exposed you to SSIS 11 development. However, in everyday situations, the requirements will not be as simple. This next example shows you some functional requirements you might face in the workplace. In this package, we will combine the Population Density data with the Apportionment data and store it as a query-friendly dataset in the database. To do this, we will build on the work we did for the Hello World example.

In order to leverage the development on `HelloWorld.dtsx`, we simply added the package to a new solution, `Chap3_RealWorld`. After we created the new solution, we deleted the default `Package.dtsx` and then right-clicked the solution file and selected Add Existing Package in the Add Group. After it was added, we renamed it in Visual Studio to `RealWorld.dtsx`. Adding it to the new project simply creates a copy of the file. If you create all your solutions in one folder, you will create a copy named `RealWorld (1).dtsx`. Figure 3-22 shows the executables that we created to allow the package multiple runs without having to externally delete previous data.

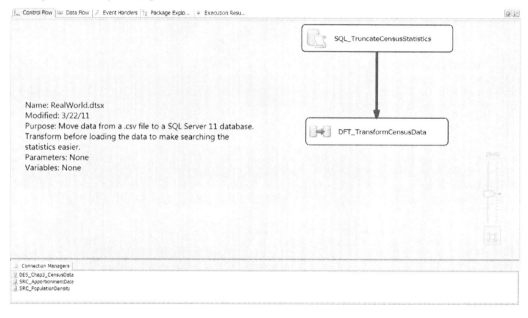

Figure 3-22. `RealWorld package added to new Chap3_RealWorld solution`

Control Flow

In addition to the two connection managers we had for the first package, we added a third connection manager, SRC_ApportionmentData, so that we may be able to extract the Apportionment dataset. We also added an Execute SQL task executable, SQL_TruncateCensusStatistics, in order to run the package without having to truncate the table between executions of the package. The Data Flow task, DFT_TransformCensusData, is more complex in comparison to DFT_MovePopulationDensityData because of the components we had to use to meet the requirements. The transformation components we will introduce to you are the Derived Column, Sort, Merge Join, and Unpivot components.

■ **CAUTION:** The Sort component can be an extremely memory-intensive component, depending on the data volumes. If you are using large flat files, we recommend that you store the data in properly indexed staging tables and use the database to perform the necessary joins. Because our US Census flat files are relatively small, we can use a Sort component for our example.

Execute SQL Task

SQL_TruncateCensusStatistics requires an OLE DB connection for it to execute the SQL statement contained within it. This executable can be used for many purposes, from extracting data from a database and storing it as an object for the SSIS package to access to executing update statements. For our purposes, we will use it to truncate the table every time we run the package. The green arrow, a precedence constraint, ensures that the Execute SQL task completes execution before the Data Flow task starts executing. DFT_TransformCensusData will execute only on the successful completion of SQL_TruncateCensusStatistics. Figure 3-22 shows the configuration of the Execute SQL task. There are some key attributes of the task that we modified before we placed the executable:

Name is a unique identifier for the task in the control flow. No two tasks of the same type can have the same name. This name is the label that is displayed in the control flow designer.

Description is a text field that provides a short explanation of the task's function in the package. It is not required to modify this attribute but it can help those who are new to the package understand the process more easily.

Connection, a required attribute, is blank by default. Because we want to truncate the destination table, we use the same connection manager as the OLE DB destination component. There is no need to create a new connection manager just for the Execute SQL task.

SQL Statement contains the DDL, Data Manipulation Language(DML), or Data Access Language, DAL, statements that need to be executed. As you can see in Figure 3-23, we put in one statement followed by a batch terminator and GO. When you modify the statement, a text editor opens and you can type the statement. Without the text editor, you cannot place GO on a new line and thus will have an error when you execute the package.

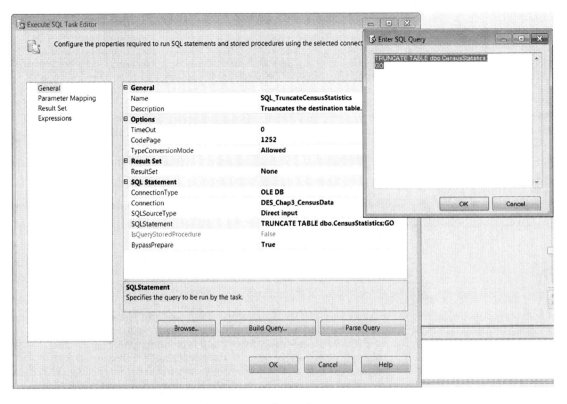

Figure 3-23. SQL_TruncateCensusStatistics—configuration

Data Flow Task

The Data Flow task executable is the workhorse of `RealWorld.dtsx`. It extracts data from the flat files, joins the data in the two files, and outputs the data in a normalized format. This process can be done by pulling the data directly into SQL Server in a staging table and then using SQL to convert the data into the desired form. Strictly in terms of I/O, this second approach is usually inefficient because it requires two passes of the data. The first read extracts it from the flat file source, and the second one extracts it from the staging table. The process we implemented takes one pass of the file, and because SSIS is optimized for row-by-row operations, it does add extra overhead to transform the data on the fly. The only risk in this method is the use of the Sort component to sort the data from the flat files. The workflow of `DFT_TransformCensusData` is shown in Figure 3-24. The left stream represents the Population Density data, and the right stream represents the Apportionment data.

■ **CAUTION:** Even though some implementations perform multiple passes on the data, the methods we described might yield better execution times and memory utilizations than using some of the blocking components in SSIS. Even Microsoft does not recommend using the Sort component on large data flows. The *large* descriptor is directly dependent on the hardware that is available to help process the data.

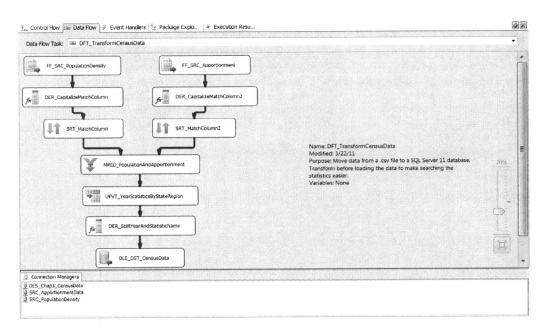

Figure 3-24. DFT_TransformCensusData

FF_SRC_PopulationDensity and FF_SRC_Apportionment, flat file sources, use the same properties as the source components of the HelloWorld package with the exception of the source file. Because the files contain different census data about the same states, we want to combine them into one dataset. The only option to handle this requirement during the extraction is to use a Merge Join component. In order to use this component, the data needs to be sorted by the key values (join columns). SSIS is case and space sensitive, so we have to prepare the join columns before we can sort them. The Derived Column components take care of this for each of the data streams. The Derived Column component creates a new column by evaluating an expression for every row that is passed through the data flow path. The newly created column can be added as a new column, or you can replace an existing column of the same data type in the data flow path.

As shown in Figure 3-25, the Derived Column component uses string functions in order to ensure that the columns from the different flat files match. To add it to the Data Flow, you can double-click the object in the SSIS Toolbox or click and drag it onto the flow. The first thing we suggest that you do after adding it is renaming it using the standards. After adding it to the flow, you must connect the data path to it. After you connect the data path, you can double-click it to open the editor. In the editor, we added the expression UPPER(TRIM(STATE_OR_REGION)) and used the Add as New Column option. We also renamed the column to MatchColumn to capture the purpose of the column.

The top panes allow you to easily reference the available inputs for the derived column as well as the functions that can perform the derivations. The Variables tree displays all the variables that are available to the scope of the data flow that the component belongs to. Because we did not define any variables for this example, the only variables available are the system variables that are a part of all packages. The Columns tree allows you to quickly click and drag the available columns into the expression. The functions are categorized by the different data types they return. With these two reference panes, you can easily start to modify the input with ease.

The TRIM() function removes the leading and trailing spaces of the included string object. Because SSIS will not ignore trailing spaces as SQL Server can be set to do, we need to take extra precautions when joining or looking up with SSIS. The UPPER() function will change the case of the included string object to uppercase. SSIS is also case sensitive, whereas SQL Server has options that can disable this feature. By forcing the column to be in uppercase and generating a new column to hold this uppercase string, we are not actually modifying the original. This will allow us to insert the data into the database as is without alteration. Because this is a Unicode string column, only the Length column is populated; for numeric data types, the precision and scale come into play, and for string data, the code page can be specified. The data will tie together based on the STATE_OR_REGION value, so we have to use this column as the key value later in the pipeline.

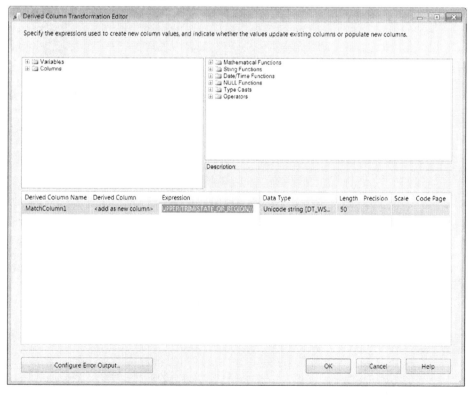

Figure 3-25. *Derived column—modifying the match column*

The Sort component performs the exact task that the name suggests: it sorts columns in ascending and descending orders. You should rename it as soon as you add it to the data flow. After the data flow path is connected to it from `DER_CapitalizeMatchColumn`, it can sort multiple columns, each marked by its position in the sort order, as Figure 3-26 demonstrates. There are also options available for the string comparisons performed for the sorting. Because we handled the case and empty space issues through the expression in the derived column, we do not need to worry about the comparison flags. The output alias allows you to rename the sorted column. The columns that are not being sorted are simply marked to be passed through. By checking off columns in this component, we can actually trim the pipeline, but for this particular example, we are looking for all the data present. There is a check box at the bottom that will remove rows with duplicate sort values. This functionality will arbitrarily remove the duplicate record. There is no reason to allow this nondeterministic behavior unless all the columns in the pipeline are being included in the sort; then this feature will allow you to effectively remove your duplicates.

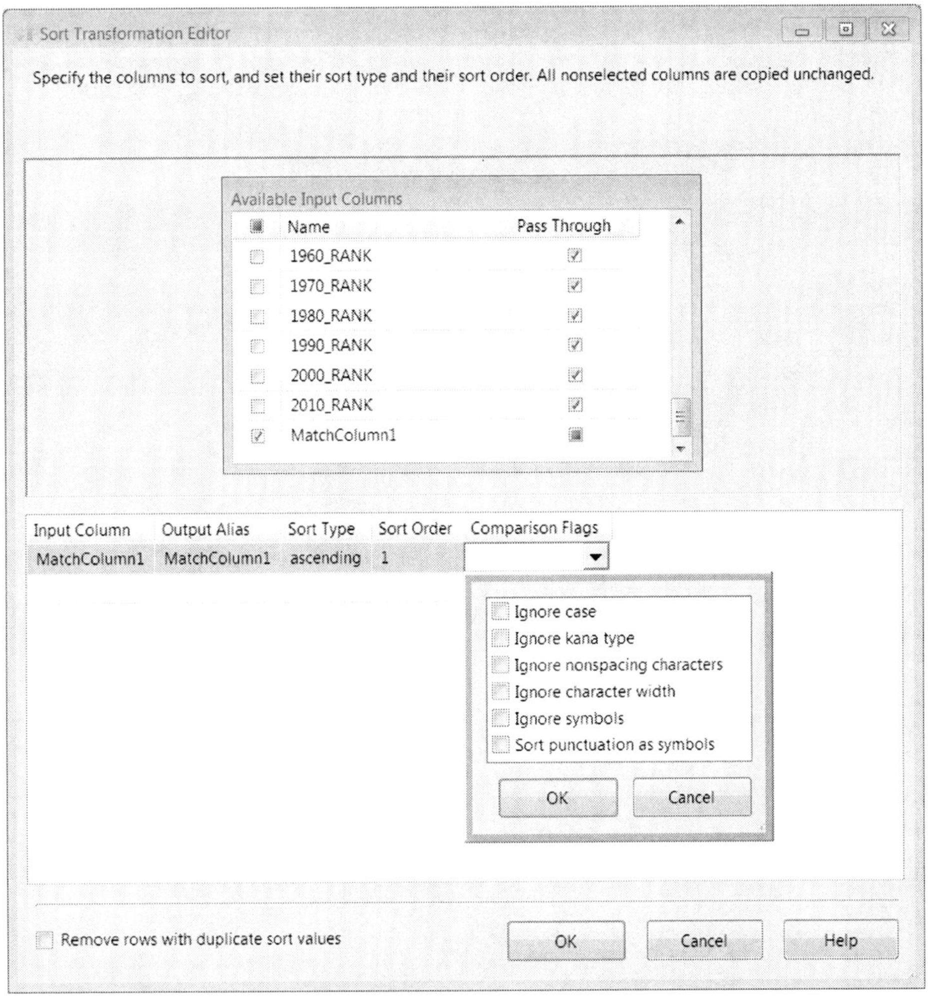

Figure 3-26. Sort Transformation Editor

The Merge Join component in Figure 3-27 brings all the data together. It will utilize the metadata to automatically detect which columns are being sorted and use their sort order to join them. We want to perform an inner join so that only states that are represented in both flat files are passed through. The component supports inner, left, and full outer joins. There is a Swap Inputs button that can add the right join functionality by swapping the outputs pointing to its inputs. The tables in the top half visually represent the left and right inputs. The name of their source is present as the name of the table.

We want only one state name column to pass through, and because we are performing an inner join, it does not matter which input's state name we use as long as we pick only one of them. We checked off all the columns that are present in the pipeline with the exception of the `MatchColumns` from both inputs and the right input's `STATE_OR_REGION`.

We highly recommend that you trim your pipeline as high up in the data flow as possible. This allows you to use your buffer space on required data only. The output alias allows you to rename each of the columns that the component includes in its output after the join. The Merge Join component has an important property that needs to be set when you include the component in a data flow. The property name is `TreatNullsAsEqual`. By default it is set to `True`, but we recommend that you set it to `False`. There are implications when leaving this property with the default value, mainly the possibility of creating cross join like datasets.

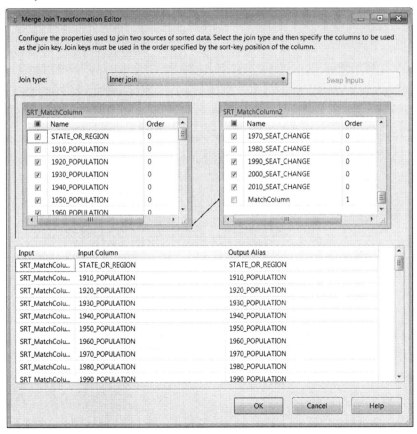

Figure 3-27. Merge Join Transformation Editor

The Unpivot component, whose editor is shown in Figure 3-28, is designed to make denormalized datasets into more-normalized datasets. It works similarly to the UNPIVOT operator in T-SQL. The STATE_OR_REGION column contains the data around which we want to unpivot the rest of the columns as rows. In order make sure that the component ignores the column, we set it to be simply passed through the component. The rest of the columns are passed as inputs to the component. These columns will be unpivoted into rows directly in the data flow path. The Destination Column creates a column to store the statistic that is reported in each column and maintain it as a part of the column as it is turned into a row value. The Pivot Key Value represents the string that will be a part of the dataset to show what the statistic represents. In the text field for Pivot Key Value Column Name, you can name the column that will store the pivot key values. With our dataset, the pivot key represents the combination of the year and the statistic's name, so we named it YearAndStatisticName.

■ **NOTE:** With the Unpivot transformation task, you will see your record count increase. This count can be mathematically calculated based on the distinct record count of the unpivoted columns (n) and the number of columns that will be pivoted (m). The resulting record count will be $n \times m$. In our example, there are 51 distinct records for the states (this includes a row for the United States as a whole), and we have 66 columns that need to be unpivoted. The resulting row count will be 3,366.

When you are choosing the columns to pass as inputs to the component, the Pivot Key Value is automatically populated. This default value it takes is the column name itself. You can also define the specific column each pivot key will populate; for our purpose, we require only that all the statistics are populated into one column. A column name is required for the pivot key column.

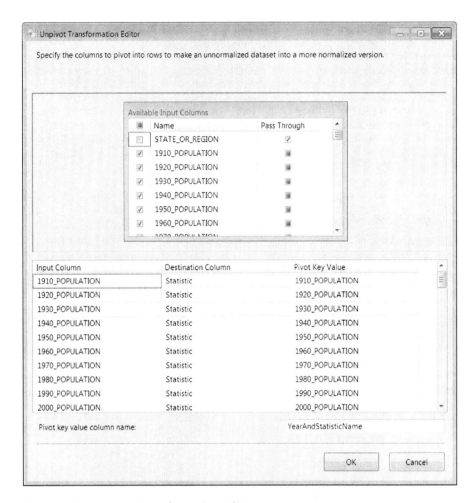

Figure 3-28. *Unpivot Transformation Editor*

Because the Pivot Key combines two values, `Year` and `Statistic Name`, we utilize a derived column to split that data into two columns. Figure 3-29 demonstrates how we split the column. We add two columns based on the data stored in the `YearAndStatisticName` column. We use the following expressions to generate the `Year` and the `StatisticName` columns, respectively:
`LEFT(YearAndStatisticName,4)` and `SUBSTRING(YearAndStatisticName,6,LEN(YearAndStatisticName))`.

Because we know that the first four characters of the column value have to be the year, we can use the `LEFT()` string function to extract the year and store it in a new column named `Year`. For the statistic name, we have to use the whole string with the exception of the first five characters. The `SUBSTRING()` string function allows us to define start and end positions of the string. The sixth position is the first character after the underscore, and we want to get the rest of the string, so we use the `LEN()` string function to define the position of the last character of the string.

Derived Column Name	Derived Column	Expression	Data Type	Length	Precision	Scale	Code Page
Year	<add as new column>	LEFT(YearAndStatisticName,4)	Unicode string [DT_WS...	4			
StatisticName	<add as new column>	SUBSTRING(YearAndStatisticName,6,LEN(YearAndStatisticName))	Unicode string [DT_WS...	250			

Figure 3-29. DER_SplitYearAndStatistics

With the original column split into more-granular data, we can insert this data into a table with the structure defined in Listing 3-3. We used the functionality of the OLE DB destination component to generate create table scripts based on the inputs to generate this script. We removed the column `YearAndStatisticName` from the create script because it was no longer required. In the mapping of the OLE DB destination component, we ignore the YearAndStatisticName column. The data types of the derived columns are Unicode, but the columns that are sourced from the flat file maintain their code page.

Listing 3-3. Create Table Script for Census Data

```
CREATE TABLE dbo.CensusStatistics
(
    [STATE_OR_REGION] varchar(50),
    [Year] nvarchar(4),
    [StatisticName] nvarchar(250),
    [Statistic] varchar(50)
);
GO
```

The results of the execution are shown in Figure 3-30. As we discussed earlier, the row count of the output of the Unpivot operator is directly related to the number of distinct records of the ignored columns in relation to the number of columns unpivoted. The Merge Join also omits two records from the left input stream because they are not contained in the Apportionment dataset. The data for the District of Columbia and Puerto Rico is not included in the Apportionment data because these two territories do not have representation in the US Congress. Because we performed an inner join, only data that is common to both sets is allowed to flow further down the pipeline.

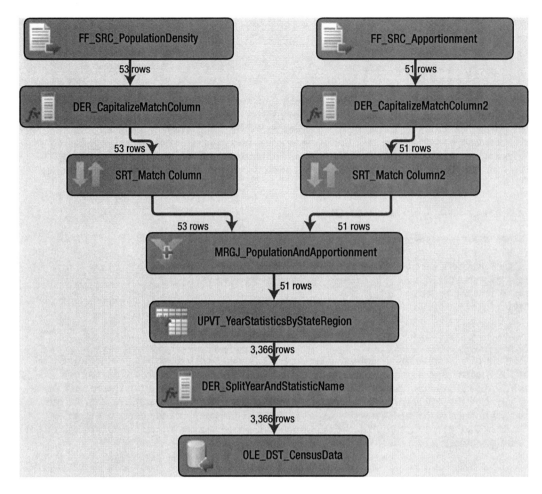

Figure 3-30. *RealWorld.dtsxexecution*

The query in Listing 3-4 shows us the benefits of transforming the data in such a way. Without the Unpivot component, we would have to include all the columns we required in the SELECT clause. With this component, we simply define the proper WHERE clause to see only the data that we require. The denormalized form allows us to include more statistics and more years without having to worry about modifying the table structure to accommodate the new columns.

Listing 3-4. *Query for Denormalized Data*

```
SELECT cs.STATE_OR_REGION,
       cs.Year,
       cs.StatisticName,
       cs.Statistic
FROM dbo.CensusStatistics cs
```

```
WHERE cs.Year = '2010'
        AND cs.STATE_OR_REGION = 'New York';
```

The query in Listing 3-4 shows us all the statistics for the state of New York in the year 2010. Without the denormalization, we would have to include six columns to account for the year and the different statistics. If we wanted to see all the data for New York since the data collection started, we would have to include 66 columns rather than simply omitting the WHERE clause limiting the year.

Summary

SSIS 11 enables you to extract data from a variety of sources and load them into a variety of destinations. In this chapter, we introduced you to a simple package that extracted the data and loaded it without any transformations. This demonstrated the simplest ETL task that an SSIS 11 package can perform. We then upped the ante and introduced you to a slightly more complex package that transformed the data as it was being extracted. This package demonstrated some of the demands of the real world on ETL processes. We walked you through the process of adding the executables and the components to the package designers. In the next chapter, we will show you all the connection managers available to you in SSIS 11.

CHAPTER 4

Connection Managers

Eventually everything connects—people, ideas, objects.
The quality of the connections is the key to quality per se.

-American designer Charles Eames

SSIS uses *connection managers* to encapsulate, manage, and abstract away physical data stores. Connection managers allow you to read from, and write to, nearly any data store for which you have drivers and access. You can use connection managers to pull data from flat files, databases, or Excel spreadsheets and push data to databases, custom file formats, or web sites, for instance. In this chapter, you'll start by looking at some of the most commonly used connection managers and move on to the more advanced, and less commonly used, connection managers SSIS supports. Some of the infrequently used connection managers can be used to connect to web servers, FTP servers, and even Windows events, to name a few examples.

Commonly Used Connection Managers

SSIS first introduced the concept of connection managers as a means of encapsulating and managing connection information for nearly any type of data store, provided of course that you have adequate drivers for your data store. You can create connection managers that define connections to fixed-width and delimited flat files, binary files, Excel spreadsheets, web sites, and SQL Server Analysis Services cubes, among others. You can also connect to a wide variety of database servers including SQL Server, Oracle, Teradata, DB2, MySQL, and any other database management system (DBMS) for which you can find Open Database Connectivity, ODBC, or OLE DB drivers. Each connection manager can be used by multiple tasks as well as data sources and destinations. After you create a connection manager, regardless of the creation method, they are all centrally located at the bottom of the Control Flow and Data Flow designer windows in the Connection Managers pane. This section introduces some of the most commonly used connection managers.

NOTE: For some DBMSs, such as Oracle, Teradata, and MySQL, you'll need to download and install appropriate ODBC or OLE DB drivers from the DBMS vendor or a third-party vendor on your development machines and servers.

The Connection Managers section of the BIDS designer is always at the bottom of the Control Flow and Data Flow designer windows. In this section, you can see all of the connection managers that are available to your SSIS package. You can also create new connection managers by right-clicking in this section, as shown in Figure 4-1.

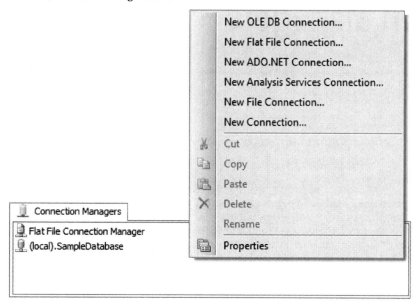

Figure 4-1. Connection Managers section of the BIDS designer window, with pop-up context menu

The pop-up context menu of the Connection Managers section is accessed by right-clicking in the area. The context menu has options for creating commonly used connection managers, including OLE DB connections to databases, flat file connections to delimited and fixed-width files, ADO.NET managed database connections, and others. Selecting the New Connection option shows the complete list of connection managers supported by SSIS, as shown in Figure 4-2.

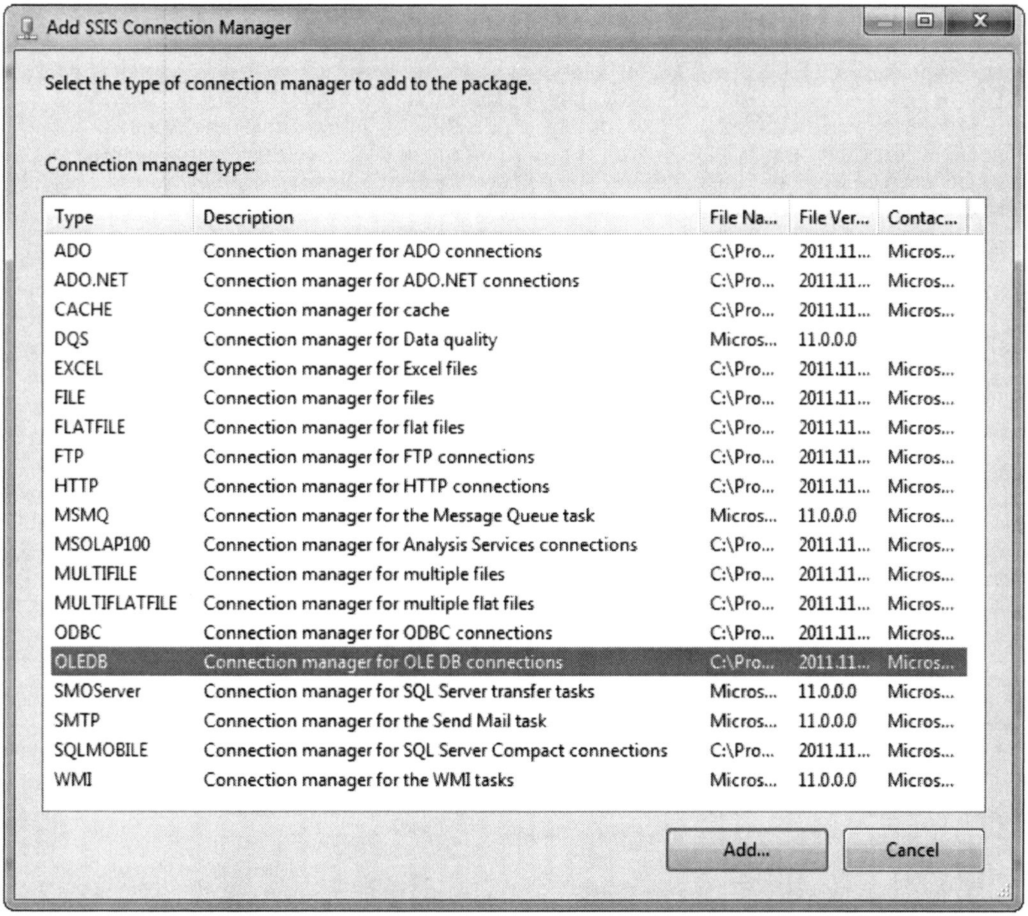

Figure 4-2. *Add SSIS Connection Manager dialog box listing all available connection managers*

The following sections describe the connection managers and the connectivity functionality they provide. The Type of the connection manager may not clearly describe the connectivity capabilities. To get a much clearer description, refer to the Description column of the Add SSIS Connection Manager. In the following sections, the connection managers are categorized by type because that is how they will be referred to by Visual Studio and the debugger.

OLE DB Connection Managers

OLE DB stands for *Object Linking and Embedding, Database.* It is essentially an API based on the Component Object Model (COM), providing support for a wide variety of data sources. OLE DB was designed as a successor to the older *Open Database Connectivity (ODBC).* OLEDB is a component-based specification that supports connections to relational and nonrelational data sources. Using OLE DB, you can connect to databases such as SQL Server and Oracle, Microsoft Access databases, e-mail servers, file systems, hierarchical databases, and more.

Generally speaking, OLE DB providers for relational databases come in two flavors: native and OLE DB for ODBC versions. The native OLE DB providers are faster than the OLE DB for ODBC versions, because they communicate with the low-level database APIs directly for maximum performance. The OLEDB for ODBC providers are OLE DB providers that sit on top of ODBC, so there's another layer of abstraction between OLE DB and the database. The performance with these types of providers is usually not quite as good as with native OLE DB providers.

▪ **NOTE:** Some people spell *OLE DB* as *OLEDB*, and still others use *OLE-DB*. As you can tell by looking at the images in this section, Microsoft chooses to use multiple spellings. Any of these are considered correct. We'll stick with OLE DB throughout this book..

When you create a new OLE DB Connection Manager, you will choose an OLE DB provider from the list at the top of the dialog box shown in Figure 4-3.

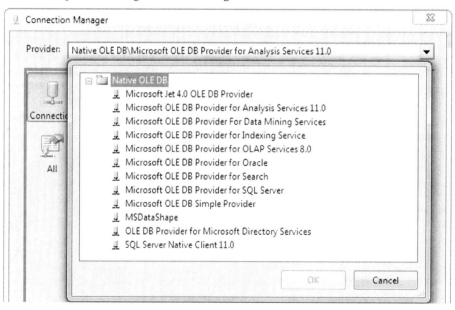

Figure 4-3. Selecting a provider in the OLE DB Connection Manager dialog box

Like us, you may find yourself choosing the Microsoft OLE DB Provider for SQL Server more often than any of the other providers, but when you need to connect to an Access database (Jet OLE DB provider), an Oracle RDBMS server, or even Microsoft Directory Services, SSIS can do that too.

OLE DB VS. ODBC

We mentioned previously that native OLE DB providers tend to be faster than ODBC providers. There are other differences as well.

OLE DB is a component-based specification, providing a set of object-oriented interfaces that abstract away the source of the data. You can create an OLE DB provider to retrieve data from nearly any data source in tabular format.

ODBC, on the other hand, is an older procedural API that defines a handful of actions you can perform against a database. Because of its lineage, ODBC is strongly tied to relational databases, whereas OLE DB is more abstract in its definition of a data source. ODBC also tends to be more "plain vanilla" in its functionality, while OLE DB offers flexibility for vendor-specific extensions such as performance-enhancing functionality. Most of the time, you'll probably use OLE DB or one of the managed providers for data access.

File Connection Managers

Files of various formats are often used to feed ETL processes. Whether you're pulling data from delimited or fixed-width flat files, binary files, Excel spreadsheet files, or combinations of files, SSIS has got you covered. Here's a quick breakdown of the types of files that SSIS supports natively:

> **FLATFILE**: Flat files are text files structured as delimited files, fixed-width files, or ragged-right files. Flat files can be delimited by using commas (.csv), Tab or pipe (|) characters (.txt), or any other delimiter you decide to use.

> **FILE**: The File Connection Manager lets you choose any file as input or output, including text files, binary files, XML files, or any other format you prefer. Note that if you choose a structured file for input, such as a delimited text file or XML file, you are responsible for recognizing and managing the structured data in your data flow.

> **EXCEL**: The Excel File Connection Manager connects your data flow to an Excel workbook.

> **MULTIFILE**: The Multifile Connection Manager is useful if you have several files that are of the same format. It's a little trickier, requiring some data flow gymnastics, if you want to use it with several files of differing formats.

> **MULTIFLATFILE**: The Multiflat File Connection Manager can connect to several flat files of the same format. If your files are of differing formats, your data flow can easily be consumed with trying to process the files by using different business logic.

With this variety of File Connection Managers, you can retrieve data from literally any file in any format. For file formats whose structure is not natively supported by the SSIS data flow, such as binary files, you will have to write custom code to handle the file format. The General page of the Flat File Connection Manager Editor, shown in Figure 4-4, allows you to choose the name, format, and code page for the source file. You can also choose the locale for the source data, whether or not the source data is Unicode, and other options including the number of header rows to skip (if any).

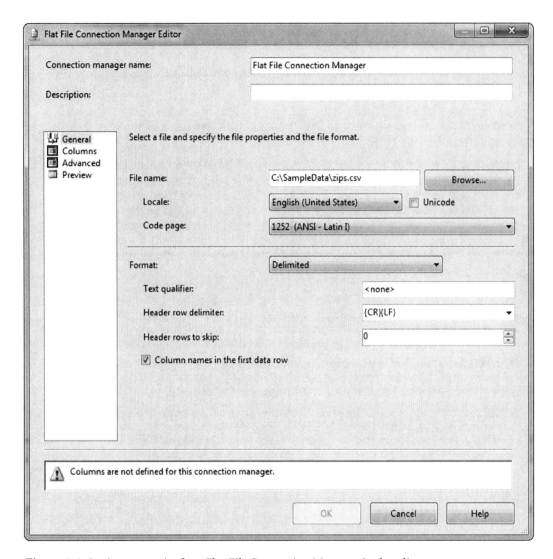

Figure 4-4. *Setting properties for a Flat File Connection Manager in the editor*

The Flat File Connection Manager Editor allows you to see the columns in the source file, with options to choose the end-of-row delimiter and the column delimiter. As you can see in Figure 4-5, the editor also shows a preview of the data in your source file.

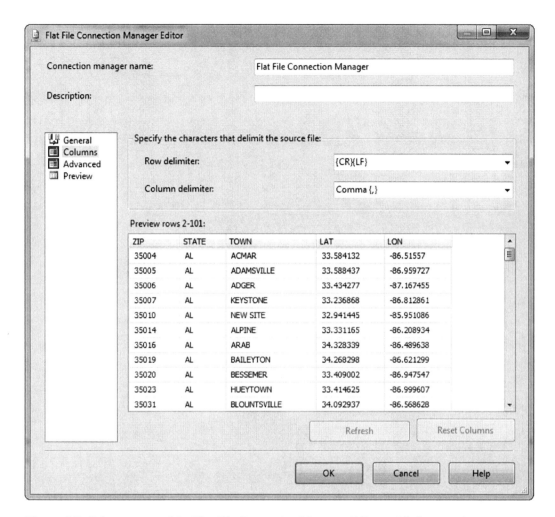

Figure 4-5. *Columns page of the Flat File Connection Manager Editor, with data preview*

The Advanced page of the Flat File Connection Manager Editor gives you an opportunity to change column-level properties, such as the data type and size of the column. Figure 4-6 shows the column properties on the Advanced page.

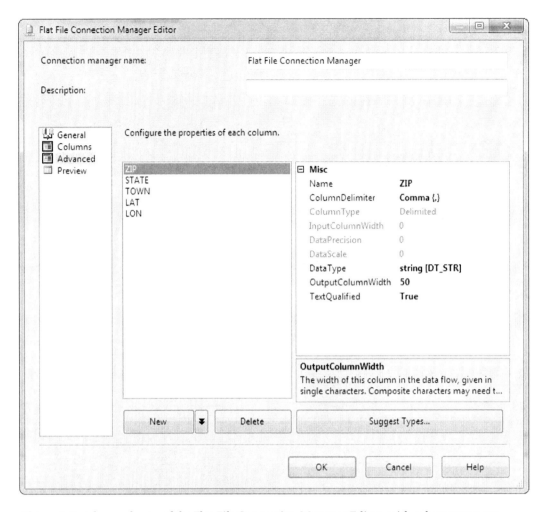

Figure 4-6. *Advanced page of the Flat File Connection Manager Editor, with column property configurations*

ADO.NET Connection Manager

The ADO.NET Connection Manager uses a managed .NET provider to give you access to your data. One of the biggest benefits of the managed connection managers is that you can easily access this type of connection manager from within managed code, such as in a Script task in the control flow or script component in the data flow. One of the most commonly used .NET providers is the SqlClient data provider, which is specific to SQL Server. Other managed provider options include the OracleClient, Odbc, and SQL Server Compact Edition.

The .NET Providers for OleDb options give you the choice to access several OLE DB providers via managed code. When using these providers, SSIS uses .NET COM interop to create a managed wrapper around your OLE DB provider. This makes these connection managers easier to access in .NET code, but can affect performance because there's an extra layer of communication between the managed wrapper and the unmanaged OLE DB provider. Figure 4-7 shows the providers available to the ADO.NET Connection Manager.

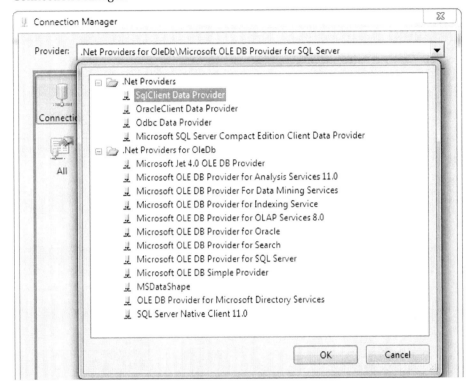

Figure 4-7. Choosing a .NET Provider in the ADO.NET Connection Manager Editor

The ADO.NET Connection Manager Editor enables you to edit the properties of the connection. For the commonly used SqlClient provider, the options are simple: a server name, a database to connect to, and authentication credentials. On the All page, you can set advanced features including encryption and replication support. Figure 4-8 shows the connection editor properties for the SqlClient provider.

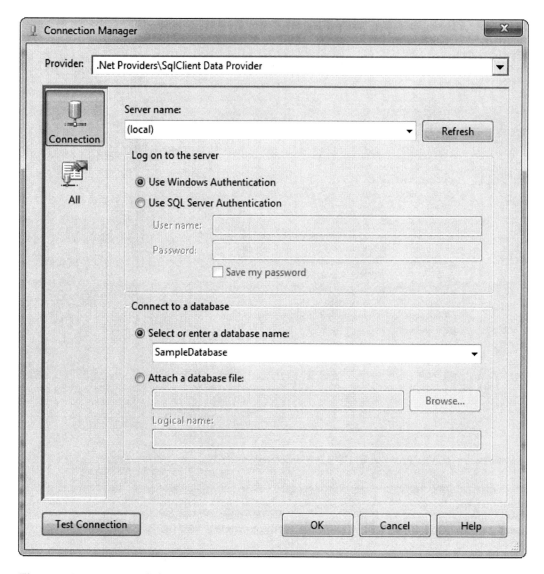

Figure 4-8. ADO.NET SqlClient Connection Manager Editor

Cache Connection Manager

The Cache Connection Manager was introduced in SQL Server 2008. This type of connection manager allows you to cache lookup data in memory in advance. Consider a scenario like this: you have two lookup components, and both are reading the same large number of rows from the same table. You can use a Cache Connection Manager to cache the lookup data in advance and connect both lookup components to use the same Cache Connection Manager. This means you have to read the data in only once, and it will consume less memory than two separate lookups caching the same data.

The Cache Connection Manager can be populated with a cache file (.caw) or by a Cache transformation, which we cover later in this chapter. Figure 4-9 shows the Cache Connection Manager Editor's General tab. This tab lets you set the name of the connection manager and select a cache file as the source for the connection manager if you choose.

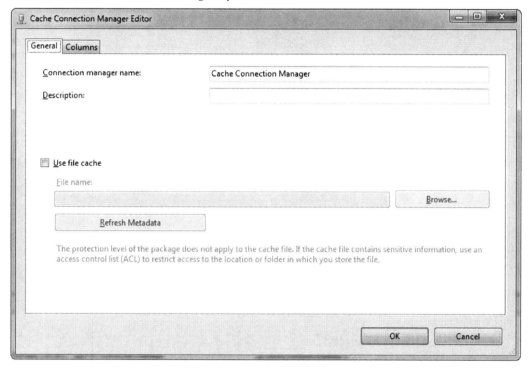

Figure 4-9. *Cache Connection Manager Editor General tab options*

The Columns tab of the Cache Connection Manager Editor lets you set properties of the individual columns of the Cache Connection Manager. You can set each column's data type, length, precision/scale, or code page, for instance. Figure 4-10 shows the Columns tab properties.

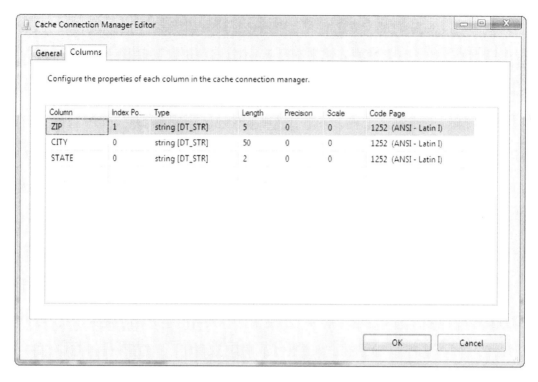

Figure 4-10. Cache Connection Manager Editor Columns tab properties

Other Connection Managers

In the previous section, you looked at some of the most commonly used connection managers. SSIS supplies several others (for example, the FTP and HTTP Connection Managers, Analysis Services Connection Manager, and Data Quality Services Connection Manager) in order to access systems that do not necessarily lend themselves to direct data access. For example, FTP servers usually don't contain raw data, but they may store files that in turn may have the required data. These connection managers allow you to access these different storage systems so that you can retrieve data.

FTP Connection Manager

The FTP Connection Manager allows you to connect to File Transfer Protocol (FTP) servers. The connection editor allows you to define time-outs, ports, and several other properties, as shown in Figure 4-11.

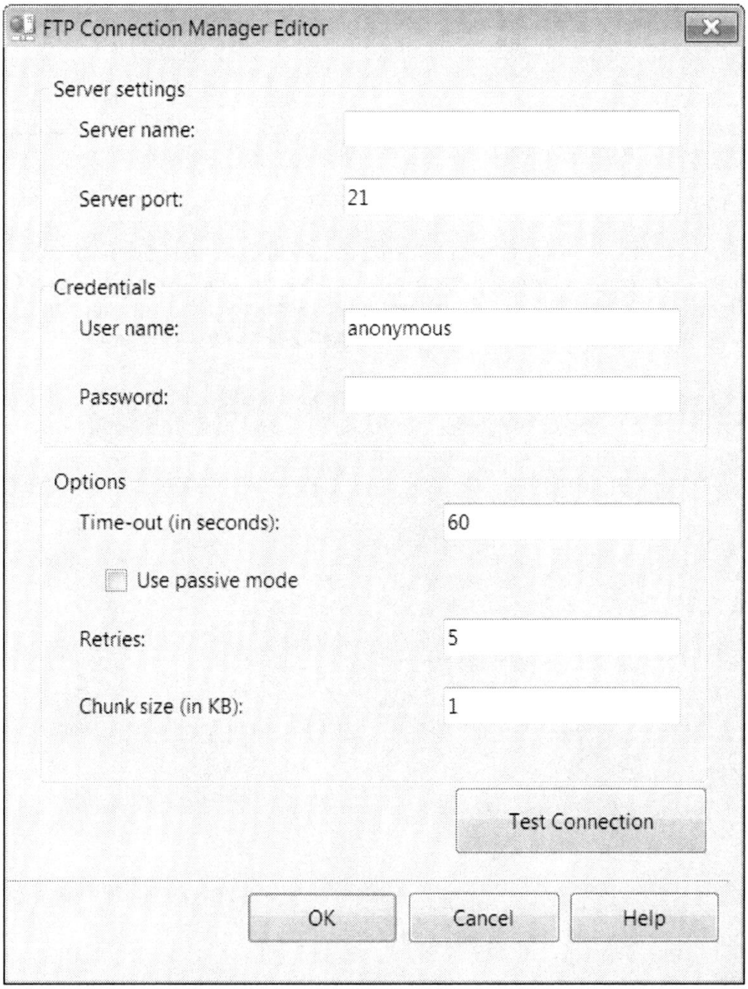

Figure 4-11. *FTP Connection Manager Editor*

The Server Name and the Server Port fields allow you to define the FTP server that the connection should be made to and the port that the server will be listening to. The Credentials section stores the authentication information. By default, the value is Anonymous. The Time-Out field defines, in seconds, the period of time that a task may take before timing out. The value 0 signifies that the connection will not time out. The check box that enables passive mode indicates that the package will start the connection. By default, active mode has the server initiate the connection. The Retries field sets the number of retries; 0 indicates unlimited retries. The Chunk Size denotes the size for chunks when transmitting data. The Test Connection button allows you to test the connection parameters.

■ **NOTE:** The FTP Connection Manager supports only anonymous and simple authentication. Windows authentication is not supported.

HTTP Connection Manager

Just as FTP can be used to store files, Hypertext Transfer Protocol (HTTP) can be used to store data. The HTTP connection allows you to connect to a web server to perform tasks. This connection enables you to upload and download files to and from a web server. This connection manager works in conjunction with a Web Service task. Figure 4-12 shows the options that are used to configure this connection manager.

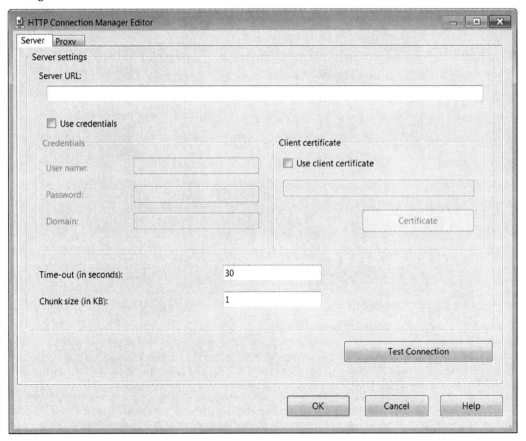

Figure 4-12. HTTP Connection Manager Editor—Server page

The Server URL stores the URL to the desired web server. If you intend to use Web Services Description Language (WSDL) on the Web Services task, the URL should end with ?wsdl. The Use

Credentials option allows you to specify the login information necessary to connect to the web server. The User Name, Password, and Domain are the key elements for the credentials to be recognized by the server. The Use Client Certificate option allows you to specify a certificate to authenticate the connection. Once enabled, the Certificate button allows you to select a certificate to use. The Time-Out setting allows you to define the time allotted to connect to a web server. The Chunk Size option determines the size of data to be written. The Test Connection button allows you to test your current configuration of the connection manager as illustrated in Figure 4-13.

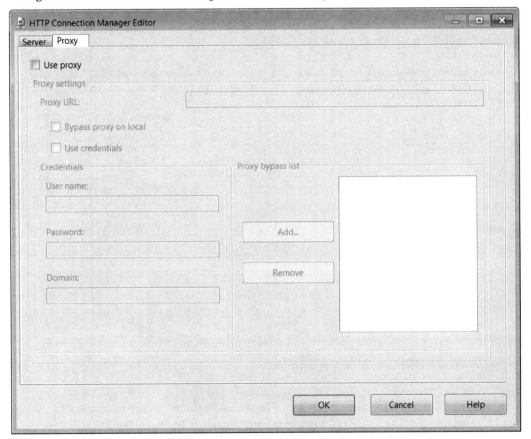

Figure 4-13. *HTTP Connection Manager Editor—Proxy page*

The Proxy page allows you to use a proxy server to connect to the defined URL. The Proxy URL requires the URL for the proxy server being used. The Bypass Proxy on Local option allows you to bypass using the proxy server for local addresses. The Use Credentials check box allows you to provide the authentication information that might be needed to connect to the proxy server. The User Name, Password, and Domain are the key components necessary for access to the proxy server. The Add and Remove buttons allow you to modify a list of addresses defined to bypass the proxy server.

MSOLAP100 Connection Manager

The Analysis Services Connection Manager, MSOLAP100, allows you to connect to an Analysis Services engine and during design time connect to an Analysis Services project. At runtime, the connection will connect to only the server and the database with the deployed Analysis Services project. Figure 4-14 shows how to add an Analysis Services Connection Manager.

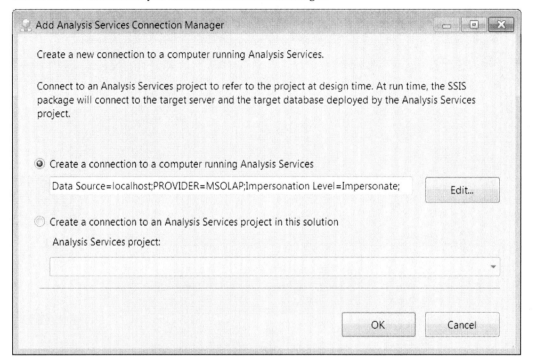

Figure 4-14. *Add Analysis Services Connection Manager*

Creating a connection to an Analysis Services instance is as simple as providing the server name. By default, the provider for this connection manager is set to Microsoft Online Analytical Processing (MSOLAP), defining the OLAP engine as the Analysis Services engine. The Impersonation Level allows you to define the authentication to use. The different Impersonation Levels are defined in the following list. The Analysis Services Execute DDL task and Analysis Services Processing task utilize this connection to access the Analysis Services database. The Data Mining Model Training destination component can utilize this connection to apply models to the data. The option to create the connection to an Analysis Services project in this solution utilizes the project only for metadata. At runtime, the tasks will need to utilize this connection to connect to an existing database.

> **Anonymous**: The server does not see any information about the client during access.
>
> **Identify**: The server knows the client's identity and can use the client's access control list.

Impersonate: The server can impersonate the client with dependencies on the location of the server and the client. If the server and the client are on the same machine, the server can access the network resources of the client. If they reside on different machines, the server has access to only the resources available on its own machine.

Delegate: The server can impersonate the client regardless of the machine.

DQS Connection Manager

The Data Quality Services (DQS) Connection Manager allows you to connect to a Data Quality Services server and database. The Data Correction transformation task utilizes this connection to access a set of data correction rules before applying them to the pipeline.

MSMQ Connection Manager

The Microsoft Message Queuing, MSMQ, Connection Manager allows you to connect to a message queue that utilizes message queuing. The connection manager will connect a Message Queue task to the specified queue in order to trigger the message service. Figure 4-15 demonstrates how to set up the manager.

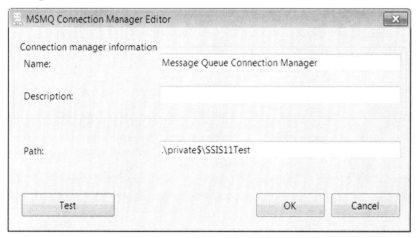

Figure 4-15. MSMQ Connection Manager Editor

There are two ways to define the path, depending on the type of message queue. For private queues, the format is `<computername>\Private$\<queuename>`. A period can also be used to represent the local machine, as shown in Figure 4-15. For public queues, the format simply eliminates the private path: `<computername>\<queuename>`.

■ **NOTE:** By default, message queuing is turned off on Windows installations. You will have to enable the service and create your own queue so that SSIS can utilize it.

SMO Connection Manager

SQL Server Management Object (SMO) Connection Manager enables the package to establish a connection with a SQL Management Object server. This connection manager is utilized by the transfer tasks that are present by default in SSIS 11. Figure 4-16 shows you the editor for this connection manager.

Figure 4-16. *SMO Connection Manager Editor*

The SMO Connection Manager Editor requires only the server name and the authentication mode to access the server. The Refresh button reloads the list of available servers. The Test Connection button will check the current configuration provided in the editor. The different transfer executables allow you to perform Data Access Language (DAL), moving and copying databases, and other functions. Depending on the task you use, you will have to define the database, but transfer tasks will all utilize this connection to connect to a server.

SMTP Connection Manager

The SMTP Connection Manager allows you to connect to a Simple Mail Transfer Protocol (SMTP) server. The Send Mail task utilizes this connection manager to send e-mails when certain conditions are met in the execution of the package. Figure 4-17 demonstrates the options available in the connection manager's editor.

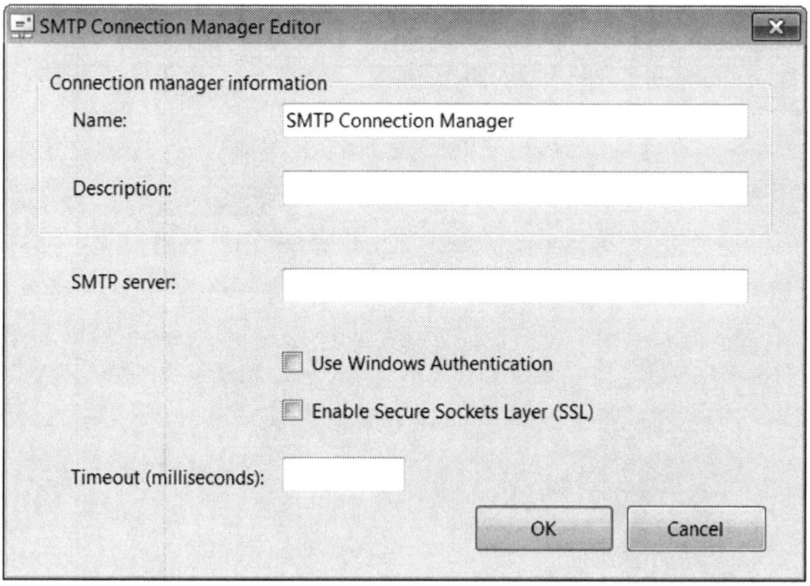

Figure 4-17. *SMTP Connection Manager Editor*

The Name uniquely identifies the connection. The Description should be filled in to help fellow developers understand the role of this connection. The SMTP Server field is used to indicate the server name. By default, the connection manager utilizes Anonymous authentication but it does allow you to choose Windows Authentication via a check box. Selecting the Enable Secure Sockets Layer (SSL) option allows you to encrypt the data when you are sending e-mails. The Timeout field defines in milliseconds the amount of time you have to connect to the server.

■ **CAUTION:** When connecting to Microsoft Exchange, use Windows Authentication, because the exchange servers can deny unathenticated SMTP connections.

SQLMOBILE Connection Manager

The SQLMOBILE Connection Manager allows you to connect to a SQL Server Compact database. The SQL Server Compact destination uses this connection manager to load data into the SQL Server Compact database. Figures 4-18 and 4-19 demonstrate the configuration of the connection manager.

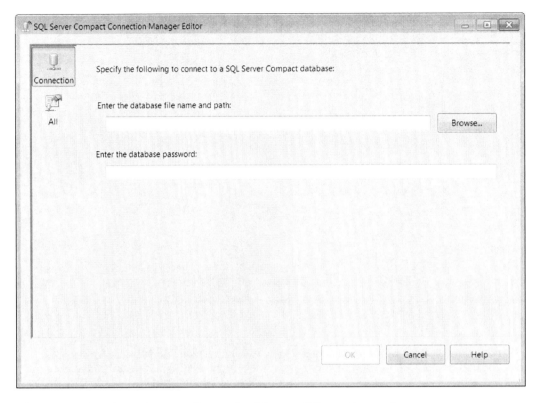

Figure 4-18. SQL Server Compact Connection Manager Editor—Connection page

---

■ **NOTE:** The provider that enables you to connect to a SQL Server Compact database is available in only 32-bit mode. If you are developing or executing on a 64-bit machine, you will have to use 32-bit mode.

The database file name and path indicates the location of the SQL Server Compact database. The Browse button opens Windows Explorer to help look for the file location. The password to the database can be stored in the Enter the Database Password field. The All page in Figure 4-19 shows all the options available when using this connection manager.

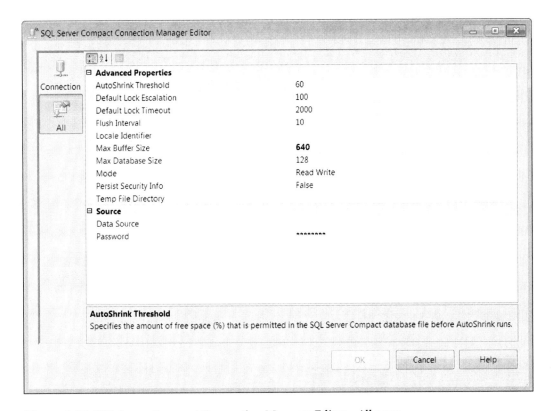

Figure 4-19. SQL Server Compact Connection Manager Editor—All page

The properties exposed by the All page allow you to configure the minute details of the connection manager. Some of these properties include the growth size and time-out settings. All of the properties are as follows:

AutoShrink Threshold: The percent of free space allowed before autoshrink is allowed to execute.

Default Lock Escalation: The number of locks SQL Server Compact is allowed before it escalates the locks.

Default Lock Timeout: The interval during which a transaction will wait for a lock. This is measured in milliseconds.

Flush Interval: The interval during which committed transactions are flushed to disk. This is measured in seconds.

Locale Identifier: Specifies the Locale ID of the SQL Server Compact database.

Max Buffer Size: Specifies the amount of memory SQL Server Compact uses before flushing data to disk. This is measured in kilobytes (KB).

Max Database Size: Defines the maximum size of the SQL Server Compact database. This is measured in megabytes (MB).

Mode: Specifies the access mode for the SQL Server Compact database. By default, it is set to Read Write. Read Write gives you permission to both read from and write to the database. Read Only specifies that you can only read from the database. Exclusive provides exclusive access to the database. Shared Read allows multiple users to read from the database simultaneously.

Persist Security Info: Allows the connection information to be stored as part of the connection's string.

Temp File Directory: Specifies the location of the temporary database file for the SQL Server Compact database.

Datasource: Specifies the name of the SQL Server Compact database to access.

Password: Specifies the password of the SQL Server Compact.

WMI Connection Manager

The WMI Connection Manager enables access to Windows Management Instrumentation. The Web Services task utilizes this connection manager. Figure 4-20 displays the configuration of the WMI Connection Manager Editor.

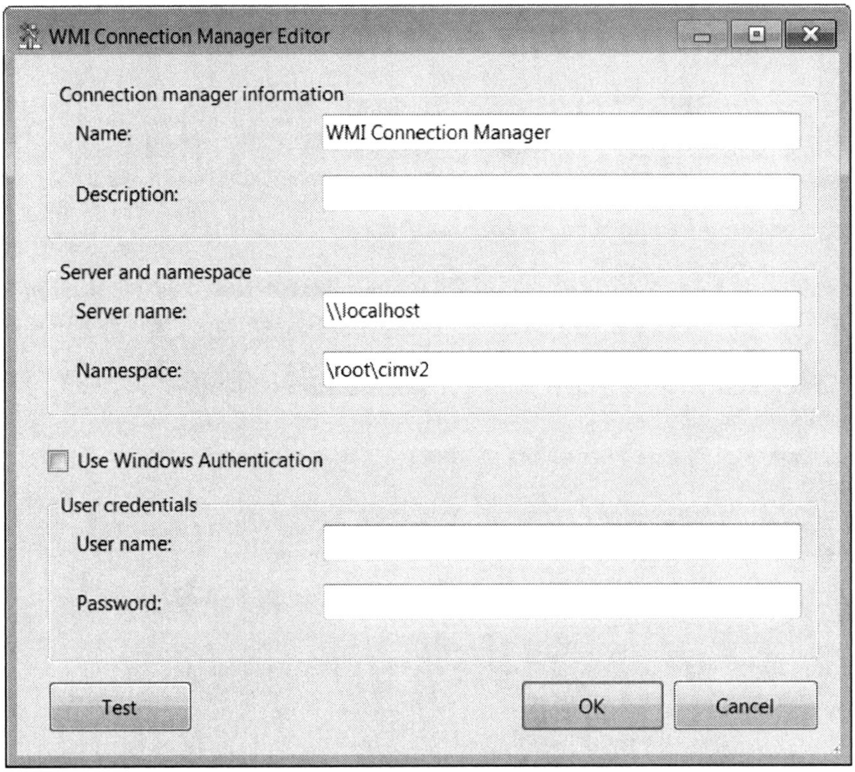

Figure 4-20. WMI Connection Manager Editor

The Name field uniquely defines the connection manager. The Description should be used so that other developers will know the exact purpose of the connection manager. The Server Name denotes the location of the management instrument. The Namespace defines the WMI namespace to use. The check box will enable the usage of Windows Authentication. If you use this option, you do not need to provide the user name and password. The Test button will test the current configurations set in the editor.

Summary

The connection managers that SSIS can access are the backbone of the ETL process that the packages carry out. They allow both the extraction of data as well as its insertion. Certain connection managers have a rather simple configuration, while others have a much more complex set of properties. In this chapter, you looked in great detail at the most frequently used connections. You also were introduced to some of the more sparingly used connection managers. The next chapter will guide you through the basic executables, containers, and precedence constraints available for the control flow.

CHAPTER 5

Control Flow Basics

You cannot always control what goes on outside. But you can always control what goes on inside.

—Self-help advocate Wayne Dyer

The previous chapter introduced you to SQL Server 11's connection managers. The purpose of this chapter is to introduce some of the basic control flow items that will enable you to utilize those connection managers. The control flow has its own designer page in the Designer window in Visual Studio. In this chapter, we detail the control flow tasks that you are most likely to use on a daily basis. Chapter 6 covers the less frequently used executables. The control flow defines the operations that a package performs, and the order and conditions required to execute them.

What Is a Control Flow?

The *control flow* is the backbone of any SQL Server Integration Services 11 package. It consists of executables, containers, and precedence constraints. *Executables* are the most versatile component of an SSIS package. They include such tasks as the Execute SQL task, Data Flow task, and Script task. These tasks can be used to start stored procedures, extract and load data, and change the states of variables. *Containers* are used to logically organize the tasks. The containers can be used to simply organize or to loop through the tasks. *Precedence constraints* determine the execution path or flow. They allow you to determine the order of the tasks' execution. By not defining certain constraints, you can take advantage of concurrent task execution.

The control flow designer pane has a zoom tool that allows you to zoom in and out to see all the components. The SSIS Toolbox also changes to allow you to access only the context-specific items. The data flow components are not available in the control flow. When adding items to the control flow, you have two choices: you can either click and drag the item from the SSIS Toolbox onto the control flow, or you can double-click the item.

Depending on the item being added to the control flow, we recommend having the referencing objects in place before adding the item. For example, if you are adding an Execute SQL task, create a connection manager to the database, or if you are adding a loop container, create the variable that it may depend on first. Having the requirements of the process are essential in developing SSIS packages efficiently. Creating objects in the reverse order on the fly is as close as you can get to spaghetti code in SSIS. With the autoformatting options, convoluted precedence constraint flows can be minimized.

■ **NOTE:** Because the control flow represents the package itself, the package properties are available by right-clicking on the control flow designer background. Each of the components within the control flow has its own set of properties distinct to itself, but the control flow's properties are the package properties.

SSIS Toolbox for Control Flow

The components for the control flow are contained within a collapsible/closable window in Visual Studio known as the *SSIS Toolbox*. This window gives you access to all the components available for the control flow. We should note that this window is context specific, so when you are using the different designer windows, it will show tools available for that designer. The different components are categorized in the groups shown in Figure 5-1.

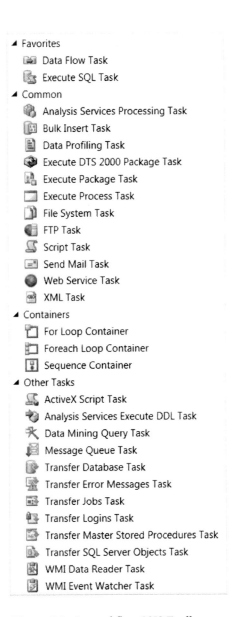

▲ Favorites

▶ Data Flow Task

▶ Execute SQL Task

▲ Common

▶ Analysis Services Processing Task

▶ Bulk Insert Task

▶ Data Profiling Task

▶ Execute DTS 2000 Package Task

▶ Execute Package Task

▶ Execute Process Task

▶ File System Task

▶ FTP Task

▶ Script Task

▶ Send Mail Task

▶ Web Service Task

▶ XML Task

▲ Containers

▶ For Loop Container

▶ Foreach Loop Container

▶ Sequence Container

▲ Other Tasks

▶ ActiveX Script Task

▶ Analysis Services Execute DDL Task

▶ Data Mining Query Task

▶ Message Queue Task

▶ Transfer Database Task

▶ Transfer Error Messages Task

▶ Transfer Jobs Task

▶ Transfer Logins Task

▶ Transfer Master Stored Procedures Task

▶ Transfer SQL Server Objects Task

▶ WMI Data Reader Task

▶ WMI Event Watcher Task

Figure 5-1. Control flow SSIS Toolbox

These groupings, which allow you to organize your SSIS Toolbox in a way that will give you quick access to the components you use most frequently, are as follows:

Favorites represents the most frequently used components. This category organizes the components in an easy-to-find place at the top of the SSIS Toolbox. By default, the Data Flow task and the Execute SQL task are placed in this category.

Common organizes the commonly used components utilized in SSIS development. These components are useful for the non-ETL aspects of the ETL process. These components allow you to manipulate the source or destination of the data so that it can be extracted or loaded more easily.

Containers groups together the different task containers. These containers execute tasks as defined by precedence constraints.

Other Tasks holds the tasks that are not usually used. These tasks are related more to database administration and nonfunctional requirements than they are to ETL.

Your customizations to the SSIS Toolbox will carry forward for all projects and can be modified at any time. If you want to revert to the default setup, you can right-click and select the Restore Toolbox Defaults option. One of the key features that makes the SSIS Toolbox effective in development is the unique icon for each of the components. The icons represent the purpose of each task in a meaningful way. These icons also appear on the component itself after it has been placed in the control flow.

■ **NOTE:** In prior versions of BIDS, the name of the window pane was *Toolbox*. With SQL Server Integration Services 11, the name has changed to *SSIS Toolbox*. If you create your own custom component for the control flow, you have to add it to the assembly folder of the machine as well as the appropriate components folder for the SQL Server Installation. Chapter 21 covers custom components further.

The SSIS Toolbox contains many components that assist with ETL requirements. In this book, we are dividing the list into basic and advanced components. This chapter covers the basic tasks that will likely be part of most solutions you design. Some of these tasks will have their own chapters, so we will not describe them in full detail in this chapter.

Favorite Tasks

The default list of tasks in the Favorites group is the Execute SQL task and the Data Flow task. You can modify this group to include tasks that you use frequently. This section details the default listing. This group is conveniently shown at the very top of the SSIS Toolbox for the control flow.

Data Flow Task

The *Data Flow task* can be described as the heart and soul of the ETL process. This executable contains components that extract data from the disparate sources, transformational components that can clean and modify the data inside the data stream, and destination components where the data can be committed. The data stream within SSIS is known as the pipeline. The Data Flow task has its own designer window so that you can customize the process as much as you need. We discuss the Data Flow task and all of its components further in Chapters 7 and 8. Figure 5-2 shows the executable as it will appear when added to the control flow.

Figure 5-2. Data Flow task

The icon of this executable shows two cylinders with a green arrow pointing from one to the other. The first cylinder represents the source of the data, the green arrow represents the transformations, and the second cylinder represents the destination of the data. The icon may suggest that data can originate from one source, but the Data Flow task can extract data from multiple sources concurrently. Likewise, it supports outputting the data to multiple destinations simultaneously.

This component is covered in much greater detail in later chapters, as mentioned earlier. Some of its properties include the following:

DelayValidation delays the validation of the metadata until runtime.

Disable prevents the execution of the Data Flow task during runtime.

MaximumErrorCount defines the number of errors the Data Flow task can tolerate.

Description provides a short description of the Data Flow task.

Name shows the distinct name of the Data Flow task.

DefaultBufferMaxRows defines the maximum number of rows that a buffer can hold. This property goes hand in hand with the DefaultBufferSize property. Together they can solve some of the issues with a poorly performing Data Flow task.

DefaultBufferSize defines the size in bytes of a buffer in the Data Flow task. Certain transformations within a Data Flow task create copies of existing buffers. This is covered in greater detail in Chapters 7 and 8.

RunInOptimizedMode optimizes the data flow path by not allocating space for unused columns. Even though this property may be set to True, it will still give warnings about removing the columns from the Data Flow path.

TransactionOption allows you to define whether the executable supports transactions. If the executable is called by a parent and transactions are enabled, the executable will be a part of the parent transaction. Mostly for performance reasons, we recommend that you leave this option set to the default.

Execute SQL Task

The *Execute SQL task* allows you to run SQL statements or execute stored procedures against an RDBMS by using various connection managers. The connection managers that the Execute SQL task can utilize are the Excel Connection Manager, OLE DB Connection Manager, ODBC Connection Manager, ADO Connection Manager, ADO.NET Connection Manager, and SQL Server Compact Edition Connection Manager. Figure 5-3 shows the executable as it appears in the control flow. The icon shows a cylinder with a scroll overlapping its bottom right. The cylinder represents a database system, while the scroll represents scripts. In this particular case, the script is a SQL script.

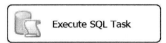

Figure 5-3. *Execute SQL task*

Execute SQL Task Editor—General Page

The Execute SQL task can be used to truncate tables before being loaded or to create constraints after the data has been loaded, to verify data integrity (DDL statements). The Execute SQL task can also be used to retrieve data and store it in SSIS variables (DML statements). The data retrieved can be a single row or a tabular data set. The Execute SQL Task Editor allows you to set up the executable to perform different functions. Figure 5-4 shows the General page of the Execute SQL Task Editor.

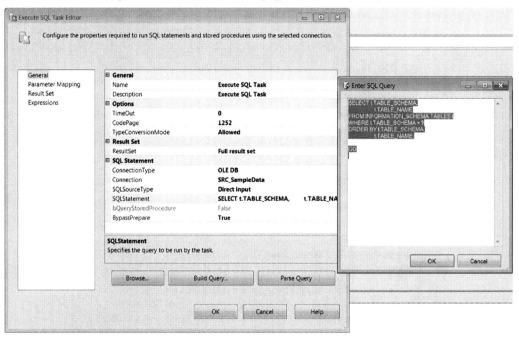

Figure 5-4. *Execute SQL Task Editor—General page*

The following list discusses some of the key properties on the General page:

Name is a unique identifier for the task in the control flow. No two tasks of the same type can have the same name. This name is the label that is displayed in the control flow designer.

Description is a text field that provides a short explanation of the task's function in the package. Modifying this attribute is not required but can help those who are new to the package understand the process more easily.

Connection is a required attribute that, by default, is blank . This value should indicate the name of the connection manager against which the SQL statement should be executed.

ResultSet allows you to define the type of the result that the query will return. There are four types of result sets: Single row, Full result set, XML, or none. Single row can be used for singular scalar values or for tabular datasets that return only one row. The Full result set option allows you to store tabular data in an SSIS object type variable. If an ORDER BY clause is defined in the SQL statement, the variable will maintain the data in a sorted list. XML result sets allow you to store XML data in a variable. None indicates that there is no result set returned. Successful executions of the SQL statements return values that indicate such. Mapping the result set to the appropriate variables can be performed in the Result Set page of the editor.

ConnectionType represents the type of connection manager that you will use to connect to the database.

Connection **Manager** is the name of the connection manager that will allow you to connect to the database.

SQLSourceType defines the method used to pass the SQL statement to the Execute SQL task. The choices are Direct input, File connection, and Variable. Direct input allows you to type the SQL statement directly into the text field SQL statement. The File connection option allows you to specify a particular file that contains the query to execute. Variable allows you to assign a query to a string variable and pass it to the task.

SQLStatement contains the SQL statements to execute on the indicated database. This field appears only if Direct input is selected as the source type of the query.

FileConnection allows you to select a connection manager to source the SQL statements. This option is available only if File connection is used as the source type.

SourceVariable is a list of variables that can store the SQL statements. This drop-down is available only if Variable is selected as the source type.

SQLStatement contains the DDL, DML, or DAL statements that need to be executed. When you modify the statement, a text editor opens in which you can type the statement. Without the text editor, you cannot place the GO on a new line and thus will have an error when you execute the package.

■ **NOTE:** In order to execute DDL and Data Control Language, DCL, statements, you need to ensure that the credentials used have appropriate permissions. If you have multiple statements, only the first statement is allowed to return a result set.

■ **NOTE:** We recommend using the semicolon (;) statement terminator if you intend on executing multiple statements within a singular Execute SQL task. At the end of the statements, you can add the GO batch directive on a new line in the text editor. When setting up a result set, ensure that the query that returns the result set is the final query in the SQLStatement field.

The Browse button at the bottom allows you to import a query from a file into the SQLStatement field. It will open a Windows Explorer window to help navigate to the desired file. The Build Query button opens a graphical tool that assists you in constructing a query. This option is available only for the Direct input source type. The Parse Query button validates the syntax of the defined SQL query.

Execute SQL Task Editor—Parameter Mapping Page

Parameters allow you to pass variables to the SQL query that is to be executed. Depending on the SQL connection, the parameters use different markers and names for mapping. Table 5-1 shows the different markers, the associated names to use with the markers, and a sample query for each connection. The Parameter Mapping page in Figure 5-5 demonstrates parameterizing the SQL statement.

Table 5-1. Parameter Markers and Names

Connection	Parameter Marker	Parameter Name	Sample
ADO	?	Param1, Param2, …	SELECT t.TABLE_SCHEMA, t.TABLE_NAME FROM INFORMATION_SCHEMA.TABLES t WHERE t.TABLE_SCHEMA = ? ORDER BY t.TABLE_SCHEMA, t.TABLE_NAME;

Connection	Parameter Marker	Parameter Name	Sample

ADO.NET	@<ParamName>	@<ParamName>	SELECT t.TABLE_SCHEMA,
			        t.TABLE_NAME
			FROM INFORMATION_SCHEMA.TABLES t
			WHERE t.TABLE_SCHEMA = @tableSchema
			ORDER BY t.TABLE_SCHEMA,
			        t.TABLE_NAME;

ODBC	?	1, 2, 3, 4, …	SELECT t.TABLE_SCHEMA,
			        t.TABLE_NAME
			FROM INFORMATION_SCHEMA.TABLES t
			WHERE t.TABLE_SCHEMA = ?
			ORDER BY t.TABLE_SCHEMA,
			        t.TABLE_NAME;

Excel, OLE DB	?	0, 1, 2, 3, …	SELECT t.TABLE_SCHEMA,
			        t.TABLE_NAME
			FROM INFORMATION_SCHEMA.TABLES t
			WHERE t.TABLE_SCHEMA = ?
			ORDER BY t.TABLE_SCHEMA,
			        t.TABLE_NAME;

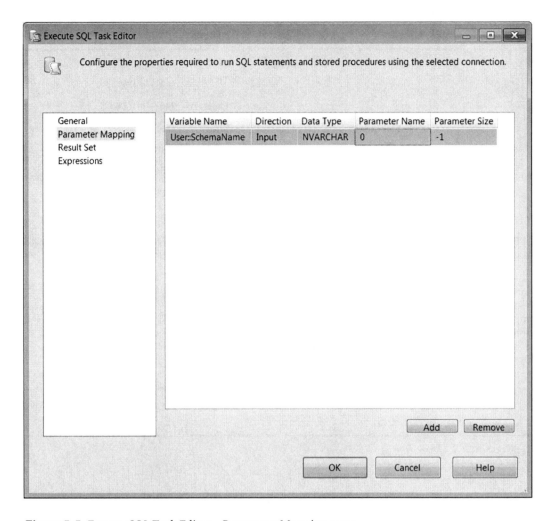

Figure 5-5. *Execute SQL Task Editor—Parameter Mapping page*

Multiple markers can be used throughout the query. The marker for ADO, ODBC, Excel, and OLE DB connections is a question mark (?). The enumerator for ADO and ODBC begins at 1. However, the parameter must be named with Param prefacing the ordinal position. The enumerator for Excel and OLE DB connections begins at 0. The ADO.NET connection is the only one that uses a qualifier (@) and name combination for the parameter mapping. The same variable can be passed to the same SQL statement multiple times.

To add a mapping for a parameter in the SQL statement, you need to click the Add button on the Parameter Mapping page. The columns on the mapping page specify all the details for each of the mappings. The Remove button simply removes the selected mapping. The properties are as follows:

Variable Name provides the particular variable that will be passed to the parameter in the SQL statement. The namespace of the variable is important because it allows for multiple variables to have the same name.

Direction indicates whether the variable is an input parameter, an output parameter, or a return code.

Data Type assigns a data type to the parameter. It does not automatically use the data type defined for the SSIS variable. The drop-down lists all the data types that are available to SSIS.

Parameter Name gives a name to the parameter. Depending on the connection type, you must name the parameter appropriately and make sure that the ordinal position of the marker in the query coincides with the name. The ordinal position plays an important role for this column when using some of the connection types.

Parameter Size defines the size of the variable length data types. This allows the provider to allocate the appropriate space for the parameter value.

Execute SQL Task Editor—Result Set Page

For SQL statements whose results need to be accessed by SSIS, we can assign those result sets to SSIS variables. One of the most frequently used result set types is the Full result set. This allows you to store the whole result, with a sort order if specified in the SQL statement, directly in a variable whose data type is defined as object. This object can be accessed by a Foreach Loop container to be used as the enumerator, by Script tasks in the control flow, or by a Data Flow task, depending on the scope of the variable. Figure 5-6 demonstrates defining the mapping for a result set of a query.

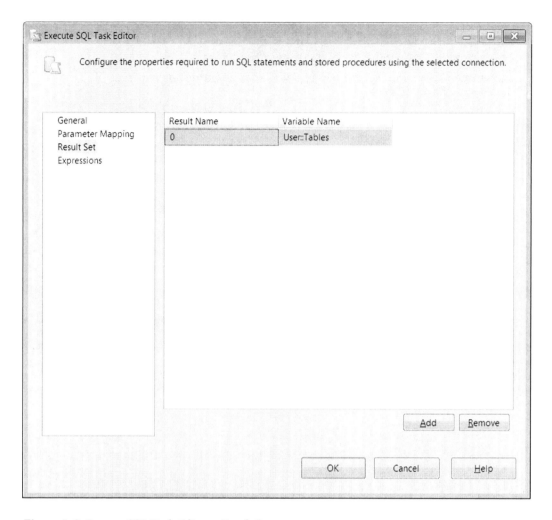

Figure 5-6. *Execute SQL Task Editor—Result Set page*

To assign values from the query to variables, you need to know the ordinal position or name of each column if the result set is a Single row; otherwise set the Result Name to 0. To add this assignment, you need to use the Add button. The results for a Full result set will automatically define the columns in the object. For Single row results, you need to make sure that the data type for each column is compatible with the mapped SSIS variable.

Execute SQL Task Editor—Expressions Page

The Expressions page allows you to define expressions that can change the value of the component's properties. Multiple expressions can be defined for each component. Chapter 9 covers expressions further. Figure 5-7 demonstrates the Expressions page of the Execute SQL Task Editor.

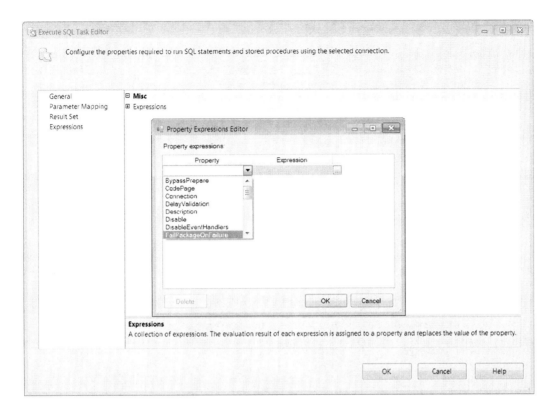

Figure 5-7. Execute SQL Task Editor—Expressions page

■ **NOTE:** Henceforth, we will not display the Expressions page of task editors. Each of the properties that are accessible to the expressions may be unique to the particular task type, but there will be some overlap including `Name` and `Description`.

Common Tasks

The Common grouping in the SSIS Toolbox contains some of the more commonly used tasks. These tasks perform operations that mainly support the ETL nonfunctional requirements. They can vary in operations such as preparing files for the ETL process to sending e-mails as a part of the package execution.

Analysis Services Processing Task

The *Analysis Services Processing task* allows you to process SQL Server Analysis Services (SSAS) objects. The objects include cubes, dimensions, and data-mining models. Figure 5-8 demonstrates the object as it appears in the control flow. This particular example shows the error message returned when a task is not connected to a cube. When you create an Analysis Services Processing task, you must point it to an SSAS database and add the objects you need to process. Without the objects added to the list, you will receive an error message.

Figure 5-8. *Analysis Services Processing task*

The icon for this task is a stack of cubes, with one cube alone on the outside. The cubes represent the SSAS database objects, specifically cubes. The single cube represents the measures as they can be sliced and diced by the different dimensions.

The objects added will be executed in a batch. The batch itself can be processed sequentially or in parallel. Generally, parallel processing will speed up the overall processing time. You have the option to define the number of objects that can be processed simultaneously, or you can let the task determine the objects. The dimensions are usually processed prior to the facts in order to prevent any missing key errors. The workaround for this is to allow processing to continue even with errors. It is a best practice to not ignore errors when processing a cube.

Analysis Services Processing Task Editor—General Page

The General page of the Analysis Services Processing task, shown in Figure 5-9, is extremely straightforward. It allows you to rename the executable and provide a short description of the task. The Name and Description properties will automatically reflect the values that are provided in the designer or the properties window. Only the Name property is modifiable in the designer window.

CHAPTER 5 ■ CONTROL FLOW BASICS

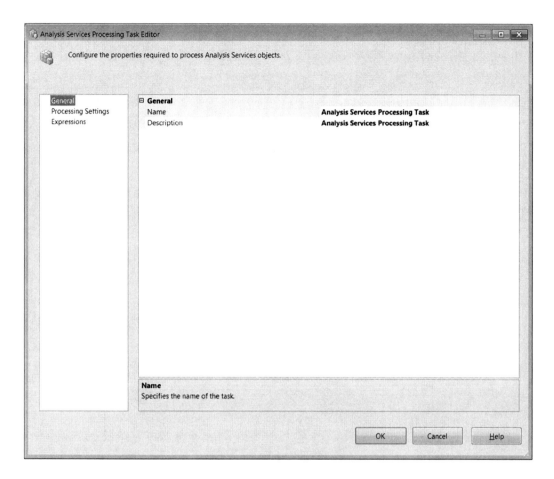

Figure 5-9. Analysis Services Processing Task Editor—General page

---

■ **NOTE:** Henceforth, we will not show the General page of task editors unless the accessible properties include others besides simply `Name` and `Description`.

Analysis Services Processing Task Editor—Processing Settings Page

The Processing Settings page of the Analysis Services Processing task, shown in Figure 5-10, allows you to specify your connection manager to the Analysis Services database and the objects you need to process. It also enables you to configure exactly how each of the objects can be processed.

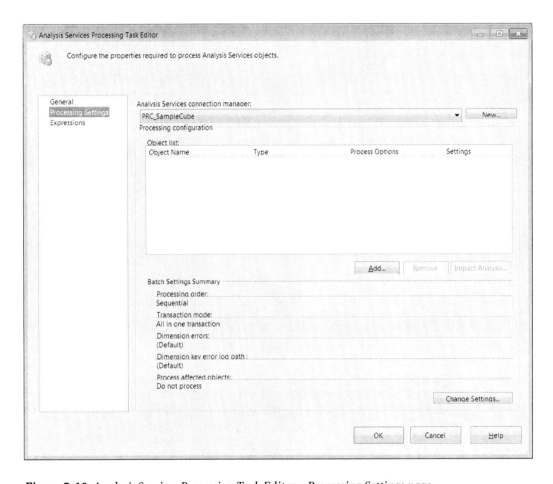

Figure 5-10. Analysis Services Processing Task Editor—Processing Settings page

The Analysis Services Connection Manager drop-down list provides all the existing Analysis Services connection managers in the package. The New button allows you to create one if it does not exist in the package already. The Object List section displays all the objects that are set to be processed by the task. These are examples:

Object Name specifies the name of the object to be processed.

Type displays the type of the object.

Process Options contains a drop-down of the processing options, which include Process Default, Process Full, Unprocess, Process Data, Process Index, and Process Update. Process Default, Process Full, and Unprocess are the only options available to all the object types. Process Default performs only the necessary tasks to initialize the object. The engine analyzes the state of the object to determine the best option to use. Process Full drops and rebuilds the object, updating the metadata as the object is being processed. Unprocess all the data that the object contains. Dimensions, cubes, measure groups, and partitions are the only objects with access to the Process Data and Process Index options. Process Data loads data into the objects without building indexes or aggregations. Process Index rebuilds only the indexes and aggregations without modifying the existing data. Process Update is available only to dimensions. It performs inserts, updates, and deletes on the dimensional data.

Settings provides the processing settings for the object.

The Add button allows you to add the objects in the database to the Object list. The Remove button deletes them from the list. The Impact Analysis button displays all the objects affected by processing the selected object. When the task performs the analysis, it takes into account the processing option that is selected. The impact analysis provides its own Object list of affected objects, which are as follows:

Object Name identifies the object that is affected by the defined object's processing.

Type displays the affected object's type.

Impact Type shows the effects of processing the selected object. The following impacts are shown: Object Will Be Cleared (Unprocessed), Object Would Be Invalid, Aggregation Would Be Dropped, Flexible Aggregation Would Be Dropped, Indexes Will Be Dropped, and Nonchild Object Will Be Processed. All except Object Will Be Invalid will provide an error message. The rest are simply warnings.

Process Object is a check box that allows you to add this object to the process object list.

The Change Settings button opens the dialog box displayed in Figure 5-11. It allows you to change all the settings displayed on the Processing Settings page.

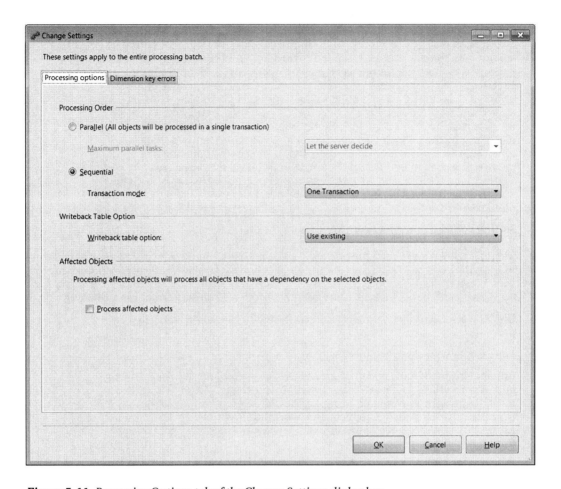

Figure 5-11. Processing Options tab of the Change Settings dialog box

In this dialog box, the radio buttons for Processing Order allow you to choose between processing the objects together or sequentially. When you are processing the objects together, you can either let the server decide the number of objects it can concurrently process or you can pick a number from the drop-down list. The numbers range from 1 to 128, doubling at each interval. When you process sequentially, you can choose to process the data as one transaction or many transactions, even the dependent objects.

The Writeback Table Option list allows you to choose the handling of the writeback table. This option is meant to record changes that occur to the data in the cube as it is being processed. There are three options available for writeback tables:

Create creates a writeback table if it does not already exist, throwing an error if it already exists.

Create Always creates a writeback table if it does not exist, or overwrites it if it does exist.

Use Existing uses the writeback table that already exists, throwing an error if it does not exist.

The Affected Objects section allows you to process the affected objects through a check box. This goes hand in hand with the Object list displayed by the Impact Analysis button.

The Dimension Key Errors tab, shown in Figure 5-12, allows you to change the processing operation's error configuration. This Use Default Error Configuration option will use the server's error configuration while processing. We recommend that you do not configure your own settings for processing unless there is a specific need to do so. Modifying this property may result in different outcomes than from processing a cube using an SSIS package than processing a cube through management studio.

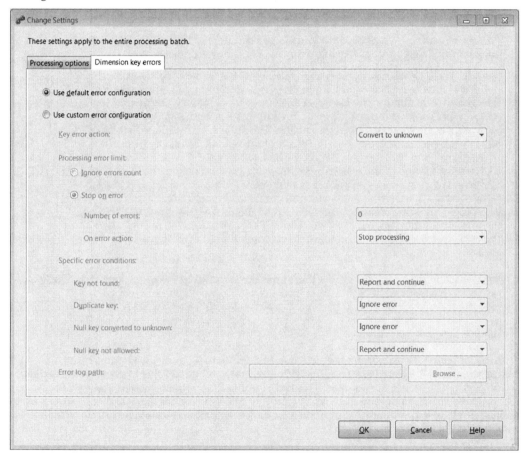

Figure 5-12. Dimension Key Errors tab of the Change Settings dialog box

The custom error configurations are divided into sections of possible errors and options for handling them. The different sections are as follows:

Key Error Action allows you to handle a new key that cannot be referenced in from the appropriate dimension. The two options to handle this error are Convert to Unknown and Discard Record. Convert to Unknown attributes all the data associated with this key to the unknown grouping. This functionality is similar to COALESCE() or ISNULL() in SQL. The second option, Discard Record, completely eliminates all data associated with this record in the object.

Ignore Error Count enables you to ignore errors entirely while processing.

Stop on Error allows you to define the number of errors that the task can tolerate as well as the action to take after the tolerance is reached. The Number of Errors field specifies the number of errors that the task will support. On Error Action gives you two options in case the number of errors is exceeded, Stop Processing and Stop Logging. Stop Processing terminates the processing of the objects. Stop Logging stops logging errors but continues to process the data.

Specific Error Conditions gives you the flexibility to handle certain errors. The options to handle each scenario are Ignore Error, Report and Continue, and Report and Stop. Ignore Error simply continues without taking any action. Report and Continue reports the error but continues processing. Report and Stop reports the error and stops processing. The different conditions that cause errors while processing are Key Not Found, Duplicate Key, Null Key Converted to Unknown, and Null Key Not Allowed. The Key Not Found error indicates that a key was not found in the referenced data, usually a dimension. The Duplicate Key error is thrown when the same key references multiple attributes. Null Key Converted to Unknown occurs when null data is set into the unknown grouping. This is an error because null does not equal null and thus may break the integrity of the data. Null Key Not Allowed is a condition that occurs when the DDL does not allow null keys, but one is encountered when processing the data.

The Error Log Path option defines the file that stores the error log of the processing task. The Browse button allows you to navigate to the file location by using a Windows Explorer window.

Bulk Insert Task

The *Bulk Insert task* provides an extremely efficient option for EL processing. By circumventing the transform capabilities of the Data Flow task, the Bulk Insert task can quickly load vast amounts of data from a flat file source into a SQL Server table. This task supplies functionality similar to the BCP command available in SQL Server but imports data only into SQL Server. Figure 5-13 demonstrates what the component looks like in the control flow. The icon shows the database cylinder with some binary data overlapping it.

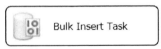

Figure 5-13. Bulk Insert task

Considerations Before Using the Bulk Insert Task

The source data file must exist on a server accessible by the host server, because it is the host server that will execute the Bulk Insert task. When accessing a remote server, Universal Naming Convention (UNC) must be used to indicate the file path and name. The task will use only the file's connection manager for the location of the file. The delimiter information and the header row information needs to be specified to the task. A format file can be used in conjunction with the Bulk Insert task, but that file must exist on the server. Only an OLE DB Connection Manager can be used to connect to the destination database. The account used to execute the Bulk Insert task needs to have , system administrater, sysadmin, rights to the server. The Bulk Insert task will "map" the columns based on the order of appearance in the source file and the ordinal position in the table definition.

Bulk Insert Task Editor—Connection Page

The Connection page of the Bulk Insert Task Editor allows you to define the source and destination of the data, as well as the format of the source data file. The connection for the destination must be an OLE DB Connection Manager. To specify the format information, you can either define it directly in the task itself or you can point the task to a format file stored on the file system. The Format list enables you to choose the formatting options. RowDelimiter provides the character combination that marks the end of a data row. ColumnDelimiter allows the task to identify the character combination that signifies the end of a column. Even though you may have defined the format information on the file connection manager, it will be ignored by the Bulk Insert task, as Figure 5-14 demonstrates. The File is a drop-down list of all the file connection managers that exist in the package.

Figure 5-14. *Bulk Insert Task Editor—Connection page*

Bulk Insert Task Editor—Options Page

The Options page of the Bulk Insert Task Editor allows you to define the properties of the actual process itself. The configuration enables you to specify properties of the source as well as the destination. As Figure 5-15 shows, the options are divided into two groups: Advanced Options and Options.

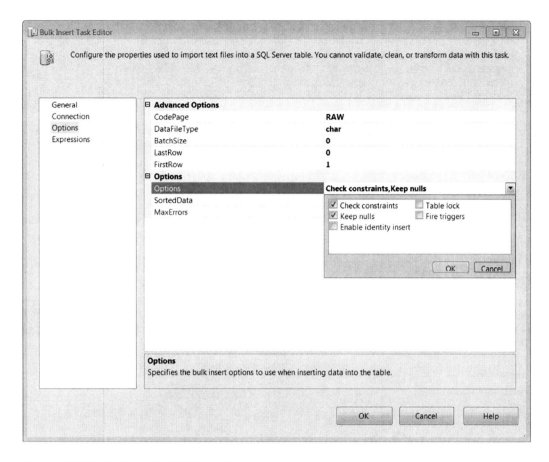

Figure 5-15. Bulk Insert Task Editor—Options page

Following are the options and what they control:

CodePage identifies the code page of the source data in the file.

DataFileType defines the data type to use during the load into the destination.

BatchSize defines the number of rows per batch. The default value, 0, indicates that the entire load operation should be part of one batch.

LastRow points to the last row to import into the destination. The default value, 0, indicates that the end of file (EOF) should determine the last row.

FirstRow points to the first row to import into the destination. This value will allow you to ignore header rows. It is important to skip the first row if it contains the names of the columns.

Options defines some of the integrity checks that can be performed during the bulk insert. Check Constraints ensures that all the constraints defined on the table are not violated. Keep Nulls inserts nulls into the table columns as they appear in the source, despite any default values defined on the table. Enable Identity Insert allows you to insert values into an identity column. Table Lock performs locking operations on the table as it is being loaded by the bulk insert. Fire Triggers allows any triggers defined on the table to be executed.

SortedData provides a comma-separated ORDER'ed BY clause of column names as they appear in the destination table. This specifies that the values are sorted in the source.

MaxErrors defines the error tolerance of the Bulk Insert task. The value 0 indicates that an infinite number of errors are allowed to occur. Any row that cannot be imported is considered an error.

Data Profiling Task

The *Data Profiling task* allows you to quickly get statistically significant information on tables or views in a database. This task can be used to determine foreign-key relationships, candidate keys, or even null ratios of columns. The information about the data can then be loaded into a flat file in XML format or an SSIS variable. Figure 5-16 shows the component as it appears in the control flow. The icon of bar charts indicates statistical information. The Data-Profiling task contains statistical information such as ratio of uniqueness for a possible candidate key or ratio of null data in a column.

Figure 5-16. Data Profiling task

Data Profiling Task Editor—General Page

The General page of the Data Profiling Task Editor asks you to determine the destination for the data profile information. In Figure 5-17, we chose to store the information in a flat file that will be overwritten each time the task is executed. We would like to point out that unlike the General pages of some other tasks, this one does not allow you to provide a Name and a Description.

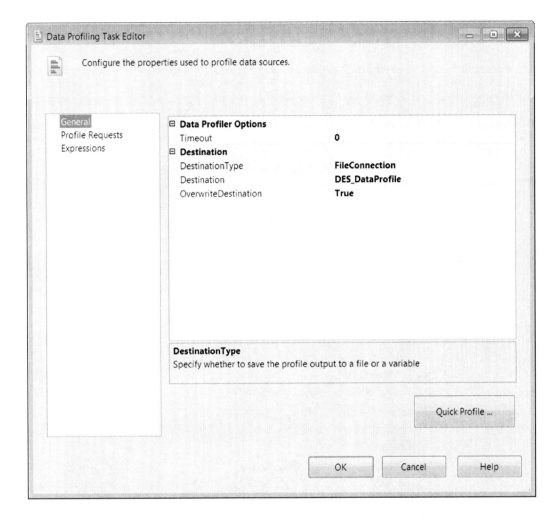

Figure 5-17. Data Profiling Task Editor—General page

Instead of allowing you to modify the Name and Description properties, the General page of the Data Profiling Task Editor provides the following properties for modification:

Timeout allows you to define the amount of time for the task to stop running.

DestinationType provides a drop-down list that allows you to input the data-profiling information in either a variable or a flat file.

Destination lists all the Flat File Connection Managers that are defined in the package. If none have been created or the specific destination isn't connected to, you can create a new one.

OverwriteDestination allows you to overwrite the file if it already exists. The
default value is False, appending the information to the file.

The Quick Profile button opens the dialog box shown in Figure 5-18. It allows you to quickly define
the information you need to collect on a given database. The Quick Profile Dialog windowallows only
one table or view per. After you select all the information that needs to be computed, the selections are
imported to the Profile Requests list. The Data Profiling task connects to the database by using an
ADO.NET connection. After selecting the connection, you can specify the table or view to profile.
The check boxes allow you to profile specific information. We discuss the details of each option in
Chapter 12.

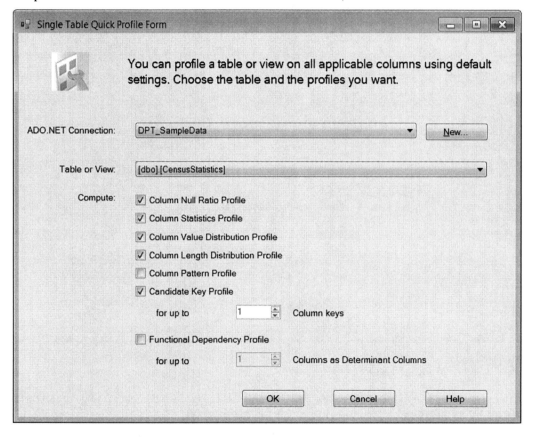

Figure 5-18. *Single Table Quick Profile Form dialog box*

Data Profiling Task Editor—Profile Requests Page

The Profile Requests page of the Data Profiling Task Editor, shown in Figure 5-19, allows you to
configure the options for each of the profile requests. The All Requests list shows the Profile Type and
the Request ID of each request. The View drop-down allows you to filter the requests by profile type.

Information such as the ConnectionManager and the TableOrView values are imported from the Single Table Quick Profile Form. The RequestID is automatically generated but can be modified after it has been added to the Profile Requests page. The ThresholdSetting option allows you to set the type of threshold you want as the success criteria of your profile. Using this field will allow you to discover keys that are nearly unique. The MaxNumberOfViolations property can define the number of duplicates or failures of the key you want to tolerate.

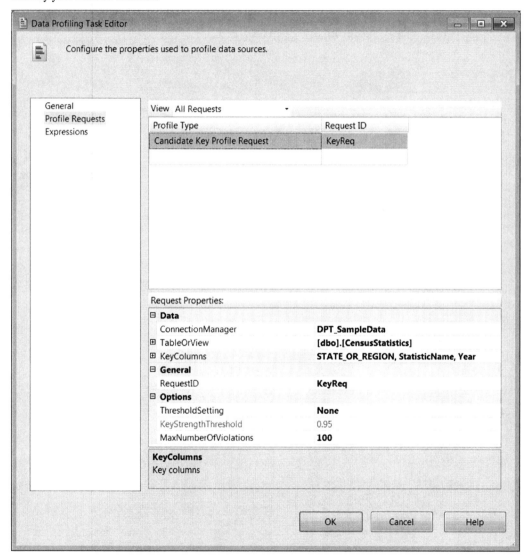

Figure 5-19. Data Profiling Task Editor—Profile Requests page

Execute Package Task

One of the most flexible ETL design patterns uses one package to call other packages. This design requires the use of the *Execute Package task*, an executable that allows a package to call another package as a part of its execution. The original package's variables can be accessed by the called package. The original package can also pass along any parameters that have access to it. Figure 5-20 shows the component in a control flow. Its icon is a file with blue squares—three on the file, and one outside it. The three blue squares represent executables contained within the file itself, and a single square outside the file indicates access to executables outside the immediate package.

Figure 5-20. Execute Package task

Execute Package Task Editor—Package Page

The Package page of the Execute Package Task Editor allows you to specify the location and name of the package. The location of the package can be indicated by accessing the project that the current package belongs to. This will populate the `PackageNameFromProjectReference` list with all the packages contained within the current project. Figure 5-21 shows the task utilizing the project to reference the package. This ETL design pattern is called *parent-child design*. We cover it in more detail in Chapter 16.

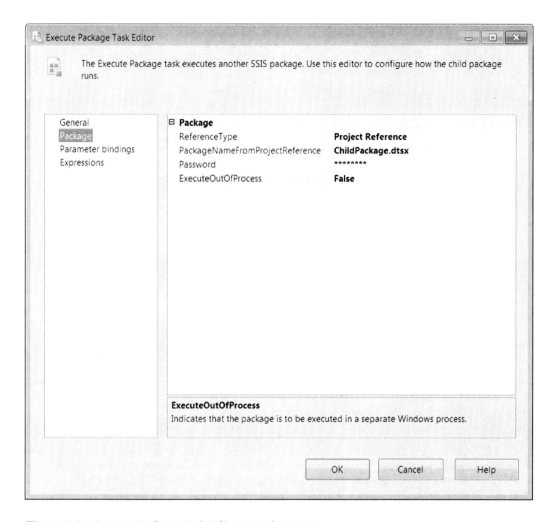

Figure 5-21. *Execute Package Task Editor—Package page*

Depending on the ReferenceType required, the properties that appear on the Package page will vary, with the exception of ExecuteOutOfProcess and Password. The properties are as follows:

> ReferenceType allows you to select the location of the package. Project Reference indicates that the child package exists as an object within the current project. External Reference allows you to access a package on the file system or SQL Server.

> PackageNameFromProjectReference lists all the packages that are a part of the current project. This property is available only with the Project Reference type.

Password is the password that is used to encrypt the child package. Even though in Figure 5-21 it appears that there is a password, the package is not encrypted. By default, SSIS fills in this field. Clicking the field opens a dialog box that asks you to specify and verify the password.

ExecuteOutOfProcess specifies that the package can be executed as a new Windows process.

Location defines whether the package exists on the file system or SQL Server. This property is available only for the External Reference type.

Connection specifies the connection manager to use to access the package. For the file system location, the connection lists all the file connection managers defined in the package. The SQL Server location lists all the OLE DB Connection Managers created in the package.

PackageName appears only for packages stored on SQL Server. It opens a dialog box that allows you to pick a package that exists on the server.

PackageNameReadOnly imports the value from the file connection manager used to connect to the package.

Execute Package Task Editor—Parameter Bindings Page

To facilitate the new deployment model, parameters are allowed to be passed between the parent and child packages. Figure 5-22 shows the Parameter Bindings page that allows you to specify the parameters to pass on to the child package. The Add button adds bindings to the task. The parent package will connect to the specified package and read in all the defined parameters. For the example in Figure 5-22, we created two parameters, ParentCreatorName and ParentStartTime, in ChildPackage.dtsx. The parameters can be added in the Parameters and Variables window. As with the variables, you have to specify a name and data type for the parameter. The parameter does not have a namespace as variables do.

This is a new functionality added to this version of SSIS. In the prior versions, configurations had to be added to the child package to pass variable values by reference. The parameters allow you to pass values from the parent to the child packages without adding explicit configurations to the child packages. The parameters are a part of the execution of the child packages. This is useful when you deploy packages to different environments and each environment requires a different set of values of the variables or connection strings of the connection managers.

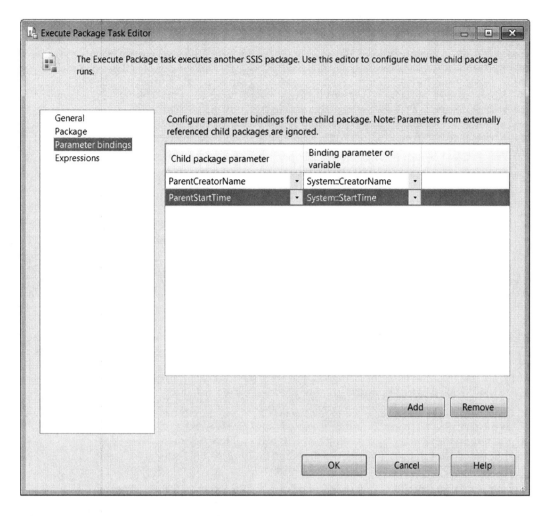

Figure 5-22. Execute Package Task EditorParameter Bindings page

---

■ **TIP:** If the Execute Package Task Editor does not automatically detect the parameters defined in the child package, we recommend saving your changes, closing Visual Studio, and reopening the parent package. This lack of automatic detection can occur if you add new parameters to the child package while the parent package is open.

Execute Process Task

One of the most useful functionalities of SSIS is its ability to perform tasks that are not strictly ETL. One of the tasks that allow this functionality is the *Execute Process task*. This executable allows you to call batch files or applications from within the package. This task can also run command-line utilities or other applications. It even provides properties that will accept parameters that should be used when calling the process. Figure 5-23 demonstrates this task in the control flow. The icon for this task is an application window, showing that the purpose of this task is to run other programs. This task can be used to run dtexec.exe to call another package, but those packages will not be run in the Visual Studio Debug mode.

Figure 5-23. Execute Process task

■ **NOTE:** If user input is required when the package is executed through SQL Server Agent, the package will fail.

The Execute Process Task Editor's Process page, shown in Figure 5-24, allows you to pass in all the relevant information necessary to run the external process. It also allows you to pass outputs from the execution to SSIS variables. In the sample shown in Figure 5-24, we simply use the findstr utility in Windows to pull the lines that have the string New and store the results in the User::ProcessOutput variable. The modifiable properties for the Execute Process task are as follows:

RequireFullFileName allows you to fail the task if the executable does not exist in the specified file path. We strongly recommend that you define the path and not rely on the Windows path being set. This will avoid deployment issues in different environments. The path itself can be set through the Expressions page by modifying variables according to your needs.

Executable specifies the process you need to run. You can specify the complete path in this field.

Arguments are passed to the executable.

WorkingDirectory defines the folder path to the executable. The Browse button will open a Windows Explorer dialog box to assist you in defining the path. If there is a chance the path may vary from environment to environment, we recommend using an expression to set this property.

StandardInputVariable uses a variable to provide an input to the executable.

StandardOutputVariable specifies a variable to store the output of the process.

StandardErrorVariable specifies a variable to store the error output of the process.

FailTaskIfReturnCodeIsNotSuccessValue specifies whether to fail the task if the return value of the process does not match the SuccessValue property.

SuccessValue is the value that the process will return to indicate a successful execution.

TimeOut represents the number of seconds tolerated for the execution of the process. The default value, 0, indicates that the process can no limit defined.

TerminateProcessAfterTimeOut is available only if a TimeOut value is specified. If set to True, the process will terminate if the TimeOut value is reached.

WindowStyle represents the style of the window during the execution. The choices for the style are Normal, Maximized, Minimized, and Hidden.

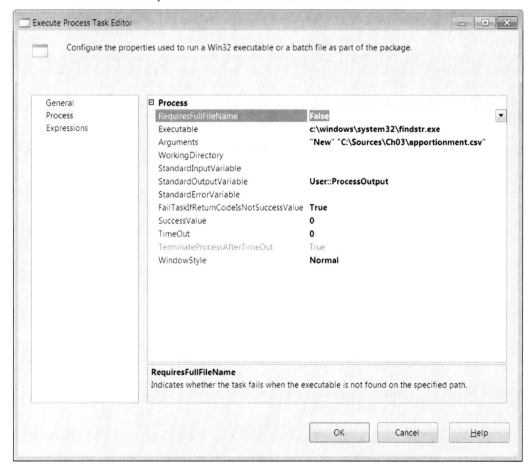

Figure 5-24. Execute Process Task Editor—Process page

File System Task

For certain ETL projects, files from the file system are used for data sources or as controllers of a project. To allow for manipulating the file system in order to handle these files appropriately, SSIS has the *File System task*. This task, shown in Figure 5-25, performs manipulations on files and directories. The icon for this task shows two files demonstrating the elements of this task's operations.

Figure 5-25. *File System task*

The File System Task Editor's General page, displayed in Figure 5-26, allows you to configure the operations you need the task to perform. The task will dynamically change the properties available for editing, depending on the operation selected. In the sample that we demonstrate, we simply copy one file to another location.

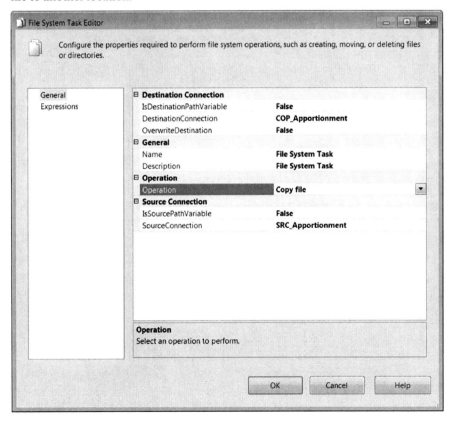

Figure 5-26. *File System Task Editor—General page*

The available properties for the File System task are as follows:

IsDestinationPathVariable specifies whether the path for the destination of the operation is static or in an SSIS variable.

DestinationConnection uses a file connection manager's connection string to specify the location of the destination. This property is available in the editor only if IsDestinationPathVariable is set to False.

DestinationVariable uses an SSIS variable to specify the location of the destination. This property is available in the editor only if the IsDestinationPathVariable is set to True.

OverwriteDestination defines whether the operation will overwrite existing files in the destination directory.

UseDirectoryIfExists defines whether the operation will fail when the specified directory already exists. This property is available in the editor only when the selected operation is Create directory.

IsSourcePathVariable specifies whether the path for the source of the operation is static or in an SSIS variable.

Name defines the name of the specific task.

Description is a text field that briefly summarizes the task's objective.

Operation lists the file system processes the task can perform. Copy directory copies the whole source directory to the destination path. Copy file copies the source file to the specified destination path. Create directory creates a directory in the specified location. Delete directory deletes the specified directory. Delete directory content deletes all the contents of the specified location. Delete file deletes the specified file. Move directory moves the source directory to the destination specified. Move file moves the source file to the destination path. Rename file renames the source file to the specified destination name.

Set attributes allows you to modify the attributes of the specified source file. Hidden allows you to specify whether the source file should be set to hidden. ReadOnly allows you to set the ReadOnly property of the specified file. Archive allows the specified file to be archivable. System allows you to set the file as a system file.

FTP Task

The *FTP task* allows you to connect to an FTP server to download or upload files that you require for your ETL processes. In addition, it allows you to perform some of the same operations as with the File System task, but on the server instead of the file system. Figure 5-27 shows the task as it appears in the control flow. The icon for this task is a globe with a server tower in front of it, indicating a file system that can be accessed remotely.

Figure 5-27. *FTP task*

FTP Task Editor—General Page

The FTP task uses an FTP Connection Manager or a variable containing the server information to connect to the FTP server. For more information about the FTP connection, refer to Chapter 4. The task will connect to the server at runtime and carry out the specified operation. Figure 5-28 shows the FTP Task Editor General page.

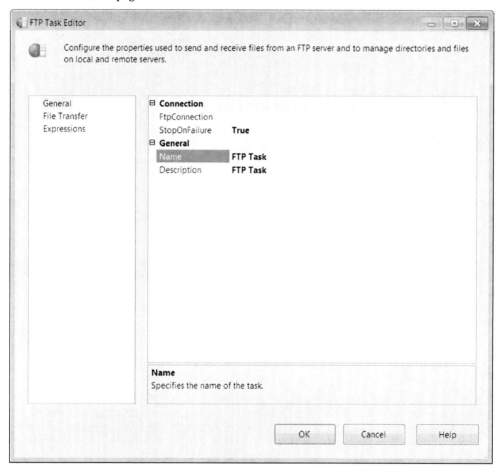

Figure 5-28. *FTP Task Editor—General page*

The following list describes all the properties available on the General page:

FtpConnection lists all the FTP Connection Managers defined in the package. This manager will be used to connect to the server.

StopOnFailure allows the task to fail if the FTP process fails.

Name allows you to specify the name of the FTP task so that it may be uniquely defined.

Description allows you to provide a brief summary of the task's objective.

FTP Task Editor—File Transfer Page

The File Transfer page of the FTP Task Editor, shown in Figure 5-29, allows you to define the properties necessary to carry out the selected operation. This page, which is very similar to the General page of the File System Task Editor, dynamically changes the properties available for editing depending on the operation selected.

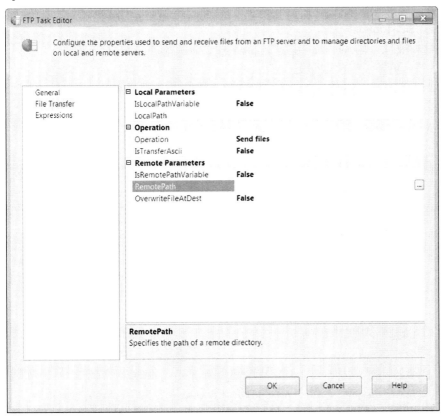

Figure 5-29. FTP Task Editor—File Transfer page

Following is the full list of possible properties:

IsLocalPathVariable defines whether the location of the local file is stored in a variable or can be accessed by using aa defined File Connection Manager.

LocalPath lists all the file connection managers created in the package.

LocalVariable lists variables that store the file path.

Operation lists the operations that can be performed by the FTP task. Send files sends the file specified in the local location to the remote location. Receive files downloads the file specified in the remote location to the local location. Create local directory creates a directory in the path specified in the local location. Create remote directory creates a directory in the path specified in the remote location. Remove local directory deletes the directory specified in the local location. Remove remote directory deletes the directory specified in the remote location. Delete local directory deletes the specified file in the local location. Delete remote directory deletes the specified file in the remote location.

IsTransferAscii specifies whether the transfer between the local and remote locations is in ASCII mode.

IsRemotePathVariable specifies whether the remote file path is defined in a variable or FTP Connection Manager.

RemotePath lists all the FTP Connection Managers created in the package.

RemoteVariable lists variables that store the remote location.

Script Task

One of the best ways to manipulate the objects in the package is a *Script task*. The Script task can use Visual Basic or C# in order to extend the functionality of the SSIS package beyond the provided tasks and connection managers. The Script task in the control flow is different from the Script task in the Data Flow task in that it modifies package-level objects, whereas the data flow Script task handles the data at the row level. Figure 5-30 shows the Script task as it appears in the control flow. Its icon looks like the Execute SQL task's icon, but without the cylinder representing a database. The scroll icon indicates that the purpose of the task is to process a script. We have a whole chapter dedicated to scripting, Chapter 9.

Figure 5-30. Script task

As we mentioned, the Script task allows you to extend the processes that SSIS components have natively. One of those advantages is the ability to access the .NET libraries. Certain libraries can give you access to the file system and perform tasks that are beyond the functionality of the File System task or the Execute Process task. Figure 5-31 demonstrates the Script page of the Script Task Editor. In this particular example, we simply open a message box displaying the value of a variable at runtime. This technique is helpful when you are tracing an issue and are unsure of a variable's value.

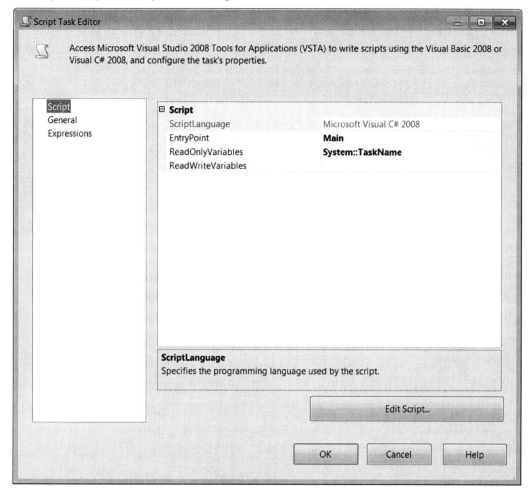

Figure 5-31. *Script Task Editor—Script page*

The following properties are configurable on the Script page:

ScriptLanguage allows you to choose between Visual Basic and C# as your scripting language. Chapter 9 weighs the pros and cons of using each language.

EntryPoint defines the initial method SSIS calls at runtime. By default, it is the main() method inside the ScriptMain class. Because the major code blocks are automatically generated when you initially create the task, you don't need to worry about the basic references.

ReadOnlyVariables is a comma-separated list of all the variables to which you want the script to have read-only access. Without all the variables specified, you will run into an error when you try to refer to its properties in the script. By clicking the ellipsis, you can open a dialog box that will display all the variables available to the scope of the Script task. After you select the variables you want to access in the script, you can import them into this property.

ReadWriteVariables is a comma-separated list of all the variables to which you want the script to have read/write access. You can populate this field in the same way as for ReadOnlyVariables.

The Edit Script button opens a script editor. The first time you open the script, it will automatically include the proper assemblies and create some default classes and methods. The script editor is based on the Visual Studio Tools for Applications (VSTA). Figure 5-32 shows the script editor with some of the prepopulated code and comments. The initial code block provides access to all the necessary assemblies. The only modification we made to this code is in the main() method. We added a line of code that pops up a message box showing you the value of a specific variable. The line of code is MessageBox.Show(Dts.Variables["System::TaskName"].Value.ToString());. The MessageBox.Show() method creates the message box. The method's parameter, Dts.Variables["System::TaskName"].Value.ToString(), accesses the Variables collection of the package. It is important to make sure that the variable is in scope for the Script task and that it is at least provided as a ReadOnly variable, as shown earlier in Figure 5-31.

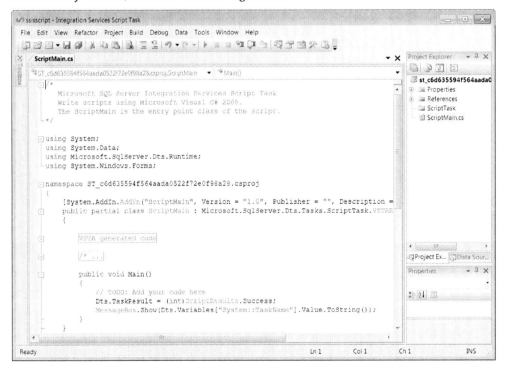

Figure 5-32. *Visual Studio Tools for Applications—script editor*

When we execute this package using the Visual Studio Debug mode, we receive a message box displaying the original value of the variable because there was no change performed on it. The System::TaskName variable contains the name of the current task. We can assign values to ReadWrite variables by using C# or Visual Basic assignment operations. We discuss scripting in great detail in Chapter 9.

Send Mail Task

It is often the case that managers and database administrators would like to know when a process fails unexpectedly. ETL processes are not exempt from this requirement. SSIS provides a task that can send e-mails by using a mail service. It requires an SMTP Connection Manager in order to connect to a mail server. SSIS allows only Windows Authentication and anonymous authentication. For more about the connection manager, refer to Chapter 4. In Figure 5-33, we demonstrate the task as it appears in the control flow. The icon is a stamped envelope with a return address and mailing address, indicating all the necessary components for the task.

Figure 5-33. Send Mail task

The Mail page of the Send Mail Task Editor, shown in Figure 5-34, allows you to configure all the properties you need to send an e-mail. One of the key features of this task is the ability to attach files. You can output your logging to a file to attach to an e-mail before you send it off to provide context for the failure.

147

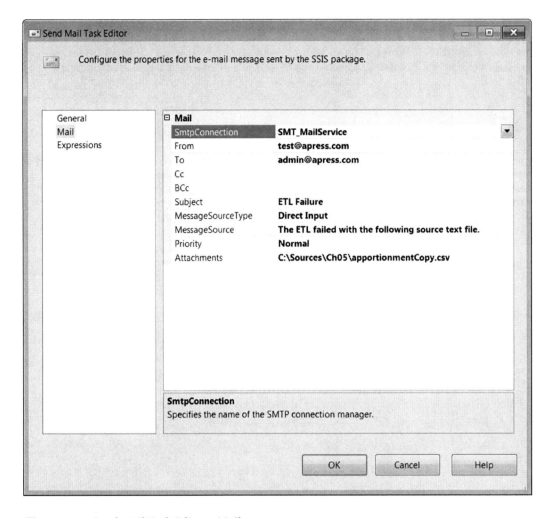

Figure 5-34. Send Mail Task Editor—Mail page

The following list describes all the properties that can be configured:

SMTPConnection specifies the SMTP Connection Manager to use in order to send out the e-mail.

From defines the sender's e-mail address.

To lists the recipients of the e-mail, using semicolons to separate the different e-mails.

Cc defines the carbon-copy recipients of the e-mail. This list separates each e-mail address with a semicolon.

Bcc lists the blind-carbon-copy recipients of the e-mail. This list is separated by using semicolons as well.

Subject provides the subject of the e-mail that is to be sent out.

MessageSourceType lists the options for the body of the e-mail message. The three options are Direct input, File connection, and Variable. Direct input allows you to type in the message directly. The File connection option lets you choose a file connection manager to the file that will contain the body of the e-mail. The Variable option allows you to select an SSIS variable containing the body of the e-mail.

MessageSource is populated based on the source type that is selected. The File connection and Variable options open a dialog box that lets you select the connection manager or variable you wish to include as the message body. With Direct input, you can directly type in a message.

Priority defines the priority of the e-mail message. The options are Low, Medium, and High.

Attachments lists the different files to attach to the e-mail. The files are separated by the pipe character. This field, unlike other instances, does not utilize a file connection manager but rather a file path as it exists on the file system of the executing machine.

Web Service Task

Another key point of versatility of SSIS is its ability to connect to a web server and execute methods against using web services. The *Web Service task* utilizes the HTTP Connection Manager to accomplish such requirements. Figure 5-35 shows the task in the control flow. The task's icon is similar to that of the FTP task, except that the Web Service task icon does not have an image of a server overlapping the globe. The globe icon indicates that the task's operations are done against a remote service.

Figure 5-35. *Web Service task*

Web Service Task Editor—General Page

The General page of the Web Service task allows you to define the connection information necessary to connect to the web server. This is done mainly through the HTTP Connection Manager that needs to be defined before the rest of the properties of the task can be set. Figure 5-36 displays the General page of the task's editor.

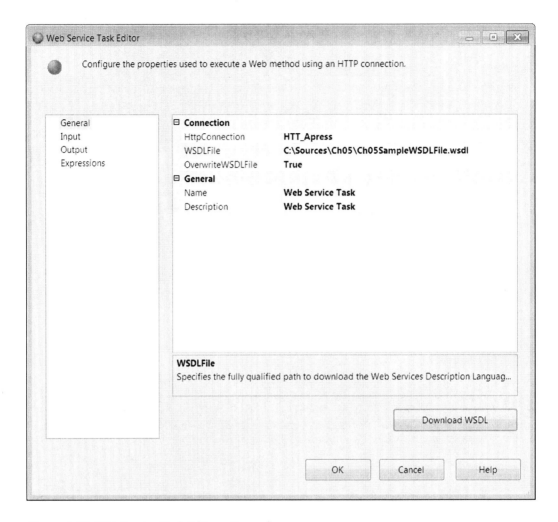

Figure 5-36. *Web Service Task Editor—General page*

The available properties are as follows:

> HTTPConnection lists all the HTTP Connection Managers defined in the package. Just like the FTP connections, the HTTP connections support only Windows authentication and anonymous authentication.

> WSDLFile provides the full path for the Web Services Description Language file that you need to use in order to execute methods against the web server. The file contains the methods available to the web service and their parameters. The file must exist in the defined path at runtime. At design time, you can create a new file with the .wsdl extension and use the overwrite property to download it from the web services.

OverwriteWSDLFile specifies whether you should overwrite the file from the web server. This option allows you to download the latest file from the web server and overwrite the local copy of it.

Name specifies the name of the Web Service task.

Description provides a short explanation of the task's objective.

Download WSDL uses the HTTP Connection Manager to download the WSDL file from the web server. This button is enabled only when a local file path is provided.

Web Service Task Editor—Input Page

The Input page of the Web Service task allows you to specify the method on the web server and its parameters. The task will use the specified HTTP Connection Manager to call the method. It will use the WSDL file in order to populate the drop-down lists shown in Figure 5-37.

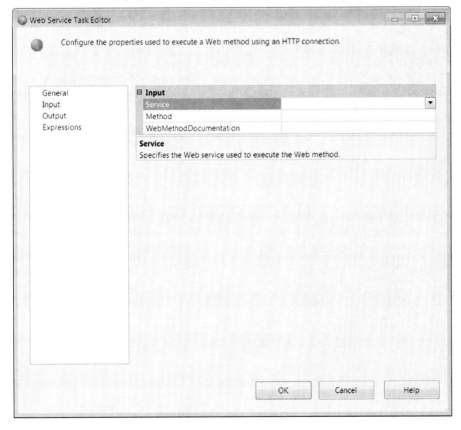

Figure 5-37. Web Service Task Editor—Input page

The following properties can be configured on the Input page:

> Service is a drop-down list of the web services available. Select the one required to execute the method.

> Method picks a method from a list that the web service can execute.

> WebMethodDocumentation provides a description of the web service method that is being called. The ellipsis button allows you to type a multiline description.

> Name lists the names of the method's parameters.

> Type lists the data type of the method's parameters. The Web Service task supports primitive data types such as integers and strings.

> Variable lists the variables that will store the values for the input parameters.

> Value allows you to type in the value directly.

XML Task

SSIS can be used in various operations on Extensible Markup Language (XML) data. The data can be stored in the form of variables or files, or even directly inputted. The task that is provided to handle these operations is the *XML task*. The results of the operations can be outputted into a file for review or further processing. Figure 5-38 shows the task as it appears in the control flow. The icon is a globe contained within tags denoting the markup format of the language.

Figure 5-38. *XML task*

The General page of the XML task, shown in Figure 5-39, allows you to configure all the necessary properties. Depending on the type of operation, the editor will dynamically change to allow for only the necessary properties to appear. One necessary component of the task is the XML input.

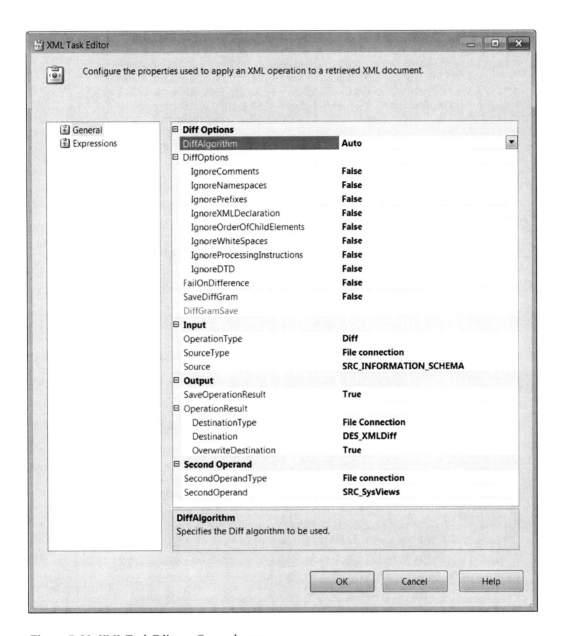

Figure 5-39. XML Task Editor—General page

The available properties are as follows:

OperationType defines the type of operation that the task will perform. The choices are Validate, XLST, XPATH, Merge, Diff, and Patch. Validate can compare a source input against Document Type Definition (DTD) or an XML schema definition. XLST will perform Extensible Stylesheet Language transformations on the sources. XPATH will perform XPath queries on the sources. Merge will compare two inputs, taking the first input and then adding the content of the second to the first. Diff compares the two inputs and writes their differences to an XML diffgram file. Patch takes an XML Diffgram and applies it to a source input and generates a new document that has the contents of the Diffgram.

SourceType defines whether the XML is retrieved by Direct input, File connection, or Variable.

Source enables you to input XML directly into the text field if the SourceType was set as Direct input. For file connection or variable sources, this option is a drop-down list of connections or variables that can be used.

SaveOperationResult allows you to save the results of the operation on the XML source.

DestinationType allows you to save the results of the operation in either a file pointed to by a connection manager or a variable.

Destination lists all the available file connections or variables to store the output, depending on the destination type selected.

OverwriteDestination specifies whether you want to overwrite the existing value of the destination with the new output.

SecondOperandType defines whether the second XML input is Direct input, File connection, or a Variable.

SecondOperand lists all the available connections or variables, depending on the operand type selected.

ValidationType lets you select between DTD and XSD. DTD will use a Document Type Definition, whereas the XSD will allow you to use an XML Schema definition as the second operand. This property is available only with the Validate operation.

FailOnValidationFail will fail the task if the execution returns a failure. This property is available only with the Validate operation.

PutResultSetInOneNode allows you to place the results of the XPath operation into one node. This property is available only with the XPATH operation.

XPathOperation allows you to select the XPath result set type. The different result set types are Evaluation, Node list, and Values. Evaluation returns the results of an XPath function. Node list returns certain nodes as XML. Values returns only the values of the selected nodes as one concatenated string.

XPathStringSourceType defines the type of source that will identify the merge location in the first XML input. The choices are Direct input, File connection, and Variable. This property is available only with the Merge operation.

XPathStringSource points to the string that will identify the merge location of the XML input. This property is available only with the Merge operation.

DiffAlogrithm lists the types of algorithms available for the generation of the Diffgram. The Auto option allows the XML task to determine the best algorithm for the operation. Fast allows for a quick but less-accurate comparison. The Precise option allows for more-accurate results at the cost of performance. This property is available only with the Diff operation.

DiffOptions represents the options available when attempting to perform the Diff operation. IgnoreXMLDeclaration allows you to ignore the XML declaration. IgnoreDTD allows you to ignore the DTD. IgnoreWhiteSpaces ignores the amount of whitespaces when comparing documents. IgnoreNamespaces allows you to ignore the Uniform Resource Identifier (URI) of the XML. IgnoreProcessingInstructions allows you to compare multiple processing commands. IgnoreOrderOfChildElements allows you to compare the order of the child elements. IgnoreComments defines whether the task will ignore comment nodes. IgnorePrefixes defines whether or not you compare the prefixes of the elements and attribute names.

FailOnDifference defines whether the task will fail if it encounters a difference between the XML inputs.

SaveDiffGram allows you to save the Diffgram that is generated as a result of the comparison operation.

DiffGramDestinationType allows you to choose the method of saving the generated Diffgram through either a file connection or a variable.

DiffGramDestination allows you to pick between defined file connection managers or variables in the package to store the Diffgram.

Precedence Constraints

After you add executables to the control flow, you have the option to define the order of execution. The order of execution is dictated by the *precedence constraints* that you define. When you don't define any constraints, the executables will execute at the same time, as is the case with the Execute Process task and the Data Profiling task. To add a precedence constraint, click the task and then click and drag the arrow to the task that should execute next. After you have an arrow connecting the tasks, you can right-click the arrow and select a type from the menu; the default constraint is Success. Constraints can be defined on tasks, containers, and event handlers.

There are three types of precedence constraints. The first constraint, denoted by a green arrow, is the *Success constraint*. It allows the constrained executable to run only if the preceding executable completed successfully. The second constraint, denoted by a blue arrow, is the *Completion constraint*. The Completion constraint allows the constrained executable to run only if the precedence executable completed its execution. The Completion constraint does not distinguish between a successful execution and one that returns an error. The third constraint, denoted by a red arrow, is the *Failure constraint*. The Failure constraint will run the constrained executable only if the preceding executable returns an error. The precedence constraint can be configured to use expressions as well. Figure 5-40 shows the Precedence Constraint Editor.

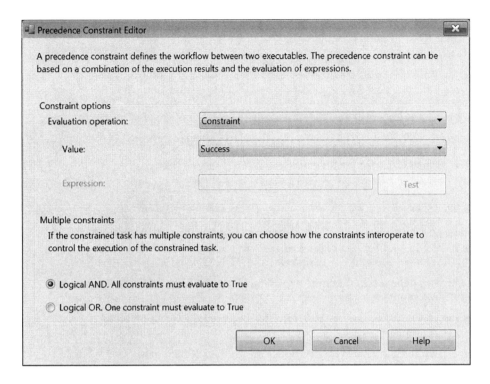

Figure 5-40. *Precedence Constraint Editor*

The Precedence Constraint Editor allows you to configure properties specifically regarding the execution of the constrained executable. The following are the configurable properties:

> **Evaluation Operation** specifies the constraining element of the constrained executable. The options for this property are Expression, Constraint, ExpressionAndConstraint, and ExpressionOrConstraint. Expression indicates that the constrained executable will execute only when the expression evaluates to True. The Constraint option will allow the executable to be constrained only by the constraint's value. ExpressionAndConstraint will require the results of the constraint and the evaluation of the expression to allow the execution of the executable. The ExpressionOrConstraint option will require either the constraint or the expression and expression to evaluate to True or FALSE.

> **Value** defines the constraining element of the executable. The prior executable's execution has to evaluate to this value in order for the constrained executable to execute. The options for this property are Completion, Success, and Failure.

> **Multiple Constraints** specifies the conditions of the executable's execution if it is constrained multiple times. The two options are Logical AND and Logical OR. These options will either perform a logical AND or logical OR between all the constraints specified in order to execute the constrained executable.

For the sample shown in Figure 5-41, the Execute Process task and the Data Profiling task will execute at the same time. The Script task will execute only if the Execute Process task executes successfully. The Bulk Insert task will execute after the Execute Process task completes its operations. The Send Mail task will execute only if the Execute Process task fails in its execution. At any given execution, you will have the combination of the Script task and the Bulk Insert task, or the combination of the Send Mail task and the Bulk Insert task, executing at the same time because those tasks are constrained by only the Execute Process task.

■ **NOTE:** An executable can constrain multiple executables as well as be constrained by multiple executables. The type of constraints can vary as well. This will allow an executable to run only if certain execution results are achieved. An executable cannot constrain or precede itself.

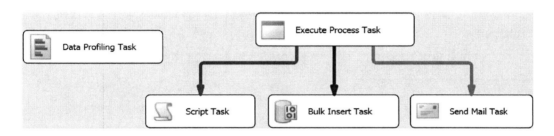

Figure 5-41. *Precedence constraints and parallel tasks*

Basic Containers

Adding many tasks to the control flow can make reading the SSIS Package difficult. One of the ways that we can avoid cluttering the control flow is by utilizing the containers. The *containers* allow you to group together multiple tasks and even other containers. There are three types of containers that SSIS provides: For Loop container, Foreach Loop container, and Sequence container. This section introduces the Sequence Container. The other two, we leave for Chapter 6. There is one other method of organizing that is present within SSIS, and that is grouping. It is not a container in the strictest sense, but it allows for the package to be visually readable.

Containers

All three containers are organized in the SSIS Toolbox in the Containers folder by default. They can be moved to the Favorites and Common groups. Containers modularize SSIS packages. They can be used to limit the scope of variables so that you can define variables for access only by tasks and containers contained within the parent container. The scope of a variable is a part of the variable definition and exists in a column in the list of variables in the Parameters and Variables window. The executables within a container create a subroutine within the package. The tasks defined within a container cannot initiate the execution of a task or container outside the container. The arrow at the right of the container's name allows you to collapse the contents of the container for configuration.

■ **TIP:** Using containers frequently within your packages gives you the ability to execute all the objects within the container in Visual Studio's Debug mode. You cannot execute the entire package but rather just the executables within the container. To do this, you can simply right-click the container and select Execute Container. In order to access Debug mode, the package needs to be opened as a part of a project.

Figure 5-42 demonstrates a potential use of a Sequence container. The icon for the container is a blue square outline containing a solid blue square and a blue arrow. The icon shows several potential executables being contained by the container. The Execute Process task is the first task to execute, and then the constrained Script task will execute only if the first task executes successfully.

■ **NOTE:** The sequence containers support the Transaction property, allowing Execute SQL tasks to execute as a single transaction.

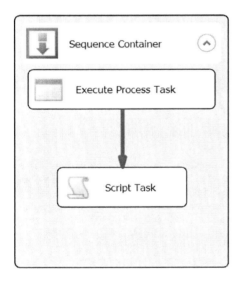

Figure 5-42. Sequence container

Groups

Groups in the SSIS control flow are not containers, but they offer some of the organizing advantages that containers offer. We do not recommend using groups because they can lead to SSIS spaghetti code. Unlike containers, groups do not isolate the executables within them. They allow precedence constraints to be created between objects inside and outside the group, as shown in Figure 5-43. In this example, we have an Execute SQL task preceding a Data Flow task. It appears as if the Data Flow task and File System task should execute together, but in reality the Execute SQL task and the File System task will execute at the same time. Just like containers, groups can collapse the objects they contain.

NOTE: Groups do not allow you to execute the objects they contain. They merely allow you to visually organize the objects.

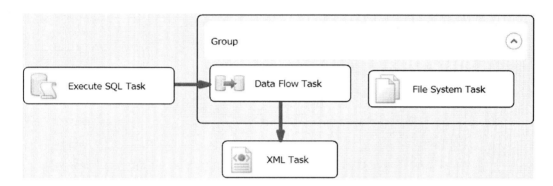

Figure 5-43. Groups

Breakpoints

During the execution of the objects in a package, each executable fires events. Visual Studio's Debug mode allows you to create *breakpoints* that will listen for these events and suspend the execution. Breakpoints can be defined on tasks, containers, and the package as a whole in the control flow. To create breakpoints, you have to right-click the object and select Edit Breakpoints. This selection opens the dialog box shown in Figure 5-44.

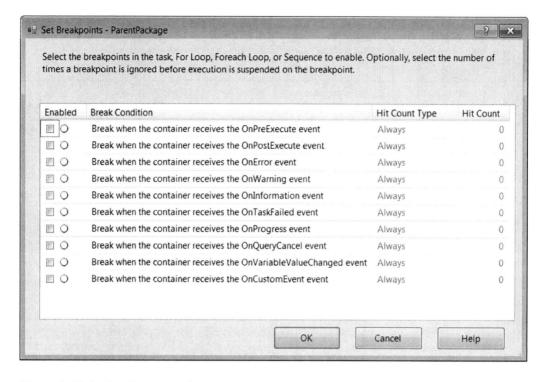

Figure 5-44. *Set Breakpoints options*

This dialog box allows you to specify the Break Condition, the occurrence of the condition that will increment the count, and the count that will be tolerated before the execution is suspended. This section introduces the events that SSIS issues. We discuss them in greater detail in Chapter 11. The events are as follows:

> OnPreExecute creates an event right before the target object starts execution.
>
> OnPostExecute creates an event right after the target object completes execution.
>
> OnError creates an event when the target object causes an error during execution.
>
> OnWarning creates an event when the target object is not in a state to error but it is not designed optimally.
>
> OnInformation creates an event when the target object issues information about the execution.
>
> OnTaskFailed creates an event when the target object fails execution.
>
> OnProgress creates an event when the target object is in the middle of executing.

OnQueryCancel creates an event when the target object is stopped in the middle of executing.

OnVariableValueChanged creates an event when a variable value changes during the execution of the target object.

OnCustomEvent creates an event when there are custom events that the target object raises during execution.

The Hit Count Type column in the Set Breakpoints dialog box defines the criteria that causes the target object to suspend its execution. The options are Always, Hit Count Equals, Hit Count Greater Than or Equal To, and Hit Count Multiple. The Always hit count will always suspend the execution of the target, every time the enabled break condition event is raised. This option disables the Hit Count column. The Hit Count Equals option will suspend the target only if the condition event is raised enough times to match the defined hit count. The Hit Count Greater Than or Equal To option will suspend the execution every time the condition event is raised, starting when the number of event occurrences matches the hit count. The Hit Count Multiple option will cause the target to suspend its execution every time the break condition event is raised enough to be a multiple of the defined hit count.

Summary

This chapter introduced the basic control flow items that will enable you to utilize some the connection managers introduced in Chapter 4. The control flow designer window uses the SSIS Toolbox to add executables. These executables and containers are organized in groups that can be customized for your development habits. This chapter introduced the Favorites and the Common groups. Precedence constraints define the order and conditions in which the objects execute. Containers can be used to modularize the packages. This chapter presented the sequence container. Breakpoints can be used in the Debug mode, depending on the events the target objects raise. Chapter 6 covers the remaining tasks and containers.

Advanced Control Flow Tasks

It is not worthwhile to try to keep history from repeating itself, for man's character will always make the preventing of the repetitions impossible.

—Author Mark Twain

Chapter 5 introduced you to SQL Server 11's most widely used executables, containers, and precedence constraints. The executables and containers are organized in the SSIS Toolbox in configurable groups. We already introduced the Favorites and Common groups as well as one of the containers. This chapter presents the remaining tasks in the Other Tasks group and the remaining containers. These tasks and containers generally perform administrative tasks for database objects. The containers are designed to repeatedly execute the contained processes. As the preceding quote suggests, executing certain processes multiple times might be a necessary component of the ETL design. The containers discussed in this chapter support controlled, repetitive executions of certain processes.

Advanced Tasks

The tasks detailed in the previous chapter assist us in preparing our sources and destinations for the ETL process. The remaining group, Other Tasks, consists of tasks that carry out administrative objectives. A majority of the tasks handle transferring database objects between databases.

NOTE: Because DTS packages will no longer be supported in future versions of SQL Server, the ActiveX Script task and Execute DTS 2000 Package task are deprecated.

Analysis Services Execute DDL Task

The *Analysis Services Execute DDL task* allows you to execute DDL statements against a SQL Server Analysis Services (SSAS) database. This task is capable of creating, dropping, and altering data-mining objects as well as multidimensional objects on an Analysis Services database. Figure 6-1 demonstrates how this task appears in the control flow designer window. The icon, a cube with a green arrow pointing at it, shows the SSIS task's ability to access Analysis Services objects.

Figure 6-1. *Analysis Services Execute DDL task*

Modifying this task is mainly handled on the DDL page of the Analysis Services Execute DDL Task Editor, shown in Figure 6-2. A connection manager pointing to an SSAS database is required to utilize this task. The connection manager can be specified in the Connection drop-down list. The SourceType allows you to select between Direct input, File connection, and Variable. This field specifies the location of the DDL to be executed.Direct input allows you fill in the DDL directly to the task. File connection specifies a file connection to a file that contains the DDL. The Variable option stores the DDL in an SSIS string variable. With the Direct input option, the field SourceDirect allows you to type in the DDL. The File connection and Variable options change the field name to Source and allow you to select a defined file connection or SSIS variable from a drop-down list. The General page allows you to modify the Name and Description of the task. The Expressions page allows you to define expressions that can modify the task's property values.

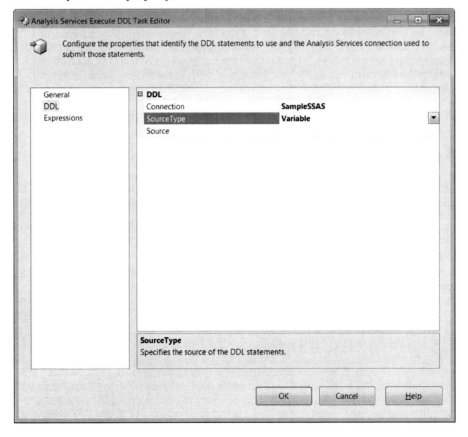

Figure 6-2. *Analysis Services Execute DDL Task Editor—DDL page*

The DDL for the task is written in Analysis Services Scripting Language (ASSL). The ASSL contains information defining the Analysis Services database and database objects. This includes login information and other sensitive information. The ASSL is stored inside an XML of Analysis (XMLA) command. The XMLA commands are used to create, drop, and alter objects on the server.

■ **TIP:** If you place the DDL directly into the package, you may want to consider using the `EncryptAllWithUserKey` or `EncryptAllWithPassword` protection levels. Because the XMLA may contain sensitive information, encrypting it is advisable.

Data Mining Query Task

The *Data Mining Query task* allows you to run Data Mining Extensions (DMX) statements based on data-mining models defined on an Analysis Services database. The output for these queries usually is a predictive analysis based on the provided data. The DMX statement can reference multiple models, each using its own predictive algorithm. Figure 6-3 shows the task as it appears in the control flow designer window. The icon, a pickax with some files behind it, shows the basic idea behind data mining, which is digging through the data that is available to find the meaningful pieces. This task utilizes the ADO.NET Connection Manager to connect to the Analysis Services database.

Figure 6-3. Data Mining Query task

Data Mining Query Task Editor—Mining Model Tab

The Mining Model tab of the Data Mining Task Editor allows you to specify the database and the mining model to use for a specific query. Figure 6-4 shows the options that are available on this page of the editor. The UI for this particular task's editor is different from the rest you have encountered so far. Instead of having the pages listed to the left side of the field options, the pages are shown as tabs.

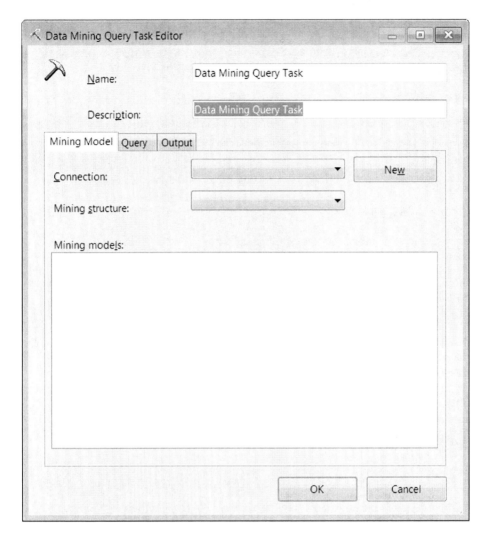

Figure 6-4. Data Mining Task Editor—Mining Model tab

The following are properties that are modifiable in the Mining Model tab:

> **Name** uniquely defines the Data Mining task.
>
> **Description** provides a brief summary of the task's purpose.
>
> **Connection** allows you to select a defined connection to an Analysis Services database.
>
> **New** creates a new SQL Server Analysis connection.

Mining Structure lists all the mining structures defined on the Analysis Services database.

Mining Model lists all the mining models created on the selected mining structure.

Data Mining Query Task Editor—Query Tab

The Query tab of the Data Mining Task Editor allows you to either manually type a query or use a graphical tool to create the desired query. The query accepts SSIS variables as parameters. It can also store the results from the query into SSIS variables. The parameter mapping rules shown in Chapter 5 apply to this task as well. The naming convention of the parameter is dependent on the connection manager type that is used, in this case the ADO.NET connection manager for Analysis Services. Each of these modifications has its own tab within the Query tab, as shown in Figure 6-5.

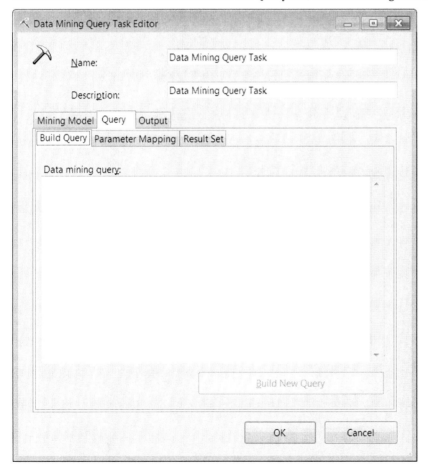

Figure 6-5. *Data Mining Query Task Editor—Query tab*

These properties are configurable in the Query tab:

Build Query contains a text field that allows you to type the data-mining query.

Build New Query button opens a graphical tool that will assist you with generating the data-mining query. After the query has been generated, it will be imported from the tool into the text field. You can further modify it after it is in the field.

Parameter Name lists the parameters used by the data-mining query.

Variable Name lists the SSIS variable that is mapped to the particular parameter.

Add button adds a mapping to the parameter list.

Remove button removes the selected mapping from the parameter list.

Result Name is the name of the result from the data-mining query. It can be changed to be the real result name provided by the query.

Variable Name specifies the variable for storing the result set.

Result Type allows you to define the result as either a single row or a dataset.

Add button allows you to add a mapping for a result value.

Remove button allows you to remove an existing mapping from the list of results.

Data Mining Query Task Editor—Output Tab

The Output tab of the Data Mining Query Task Editor allows you to store the output of the data-mining query. The storage is handled by ADO.NET and OLE DB connections only. Figure 6-6 shows the Output tab of the Data Mining Query Task Editor. The data can be inserted into SQL Server tables for further querying.

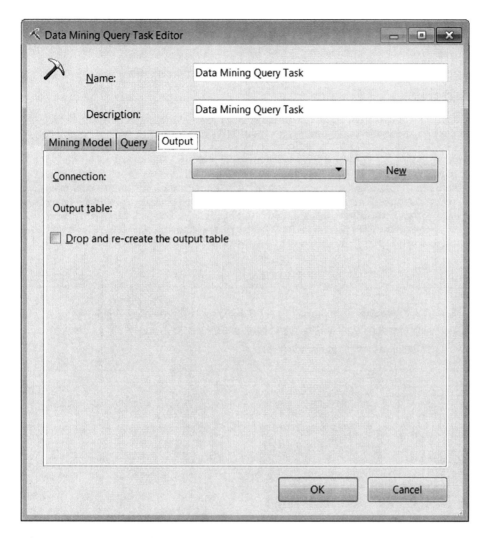

Figure 6-6. Data Mining Query Task Editor—Output tab

The Output tab supports the configuration of the following properties:

>**Connection** lists all the ADO.NET and OLE DB connections that have been defined in the package.

>**New** button creates a new ADO.NET or OLE DB connection if the desired one does not already exist.

>**Output Table** provides the name of the table to store the results of the data-mining query.

Drop and Re-create the Output Table allows you to clear prior data by dropping and rebuilding the table. This enables metadata updates to be loaded without issues.

Message Queue Task

The *Message Queue task* uses Microsoft Message Queuing (MSMQ) to send messages between SSIS packages or between custom applications. The messages themselves can be composed of text and can carry data files or SSIS variable values. There are some primary reasons for using the Message Queue task in your ETL solutions. One way to utilize the message queuing is to suspend a package's execution until the package receives a certain message. This allows external, non-ETL processes to complete and then immediately initiate the ETL. Along with suspension of the SSIS packages, this task can be used to transmit files as a part of its message. This file can be the output of the ETL process or external processes that indicate to the package that data source files are ready for SSIS access. The task can also be used to transfer files across the system. Figure 6-7 shows the task as it appears in the control flow. The icon contains two envelopes, one overlapping the other, with a downward blue arrow specifying an ordered transmission.

■ **NOTE:** By default, the Microsoft Message Queuing service is not started on older versions of Microsoft operating systems. On the newer operating systems (Vista and later, and Server 2008 and later), you need to install the appropriateWindows features in order to use the service.

Figure 6-7. Message Queue task

Message Queue Task Editor—General Page

The General page of the Message Queue Task Editor allows you to define whether the task is responsible for sending or receiving messages. Depending on the role of the task, the pages available are automatically modified to allow for Send or Receive options. Figure 6-8 shows the Message Queue Task Editor's General page.

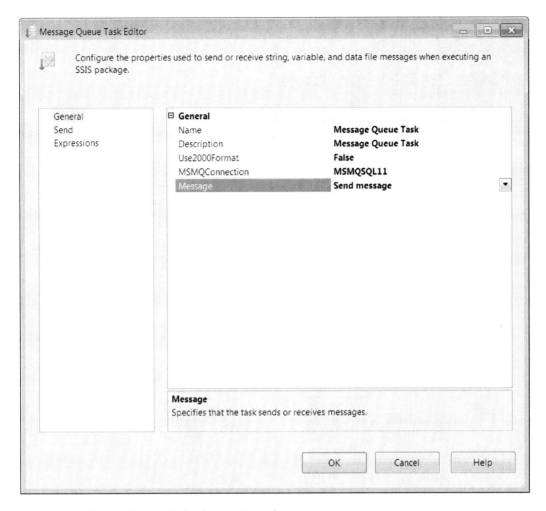

Figure 6-8. Message Queue Task Editor—General page

The following properties are configurable on the General page:

Name provides a unique name for the Message Queue task.

Descriptionprovides a brief statement about the object of the particular Message Queue task.

Use2000Format specifies whether to use the 2000 version of Message Queuing.

MSMQConnection lists all the defined Microsoft Message Queuing Connection Managers. This field also allows you to create a connection manager if one does not exist.

Message allows you to choose whether the task sends or receives a message. This option will modify the pages available in the editor.

Message Queue Task Editor—Send Page

The Send page of the Message Queue Task Editor becomes available only when the Send option is selected for the Message property. This particular page allows you to modify the properties associated with sending messages to other applications or packages. Figure 6-9 shows you all the properties that are available for modification.

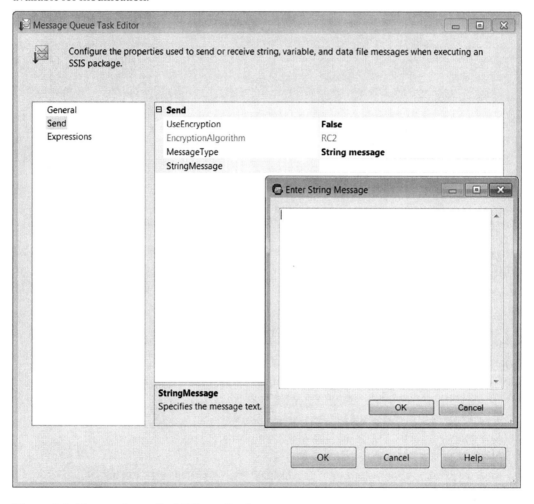

Figure 6-9. Message Queue Task Editor—Send page

The Message Queue task's properties are as follows:

> UseEncryption specifies whether the message is encrypted.

> EncryptionAlgorithm specifies the name of the encryption algorithm to use. This property becomes available only if the UseEncryption property is set to True. The only encryption algorithms supported by MSMQ are the RC2 and RC4 algorithms. These are relatively weak compared to newer ones and therefore will require some scrutiny before implementing the Message Queue task.

> MessageTypedefines the type of message the task will transmit. The options are Data file message, Variable message, and String message. Choosing the different options will automatically alter the succeeding property displayed in the editor.

> DataFileMessage transmits the message stored within a file. The ellipsis button allows you to navigate to the desired file.

> VariableMessage indicates that the message is stored in an SSIS variable.

> StringMessage indicates that the message is stored within a string that is provided directly. As Figure 6-9 demonstrates, a text box can be used to type in longer messages.

Message Queue Task Editor—Receive Page

The Receive page of the Message Queue Task Editor is available only when the Receive option is selected for the Message property. This page allows for the modification of the properties that can be set when the package receives a message from MSMQ. Certain configurations will allow the package to receive only very specific messages. Figure 6-10 shows the Receive page of the Message Queue task. The Expressions page allows you to define expressions that can modify the task's properties' values.

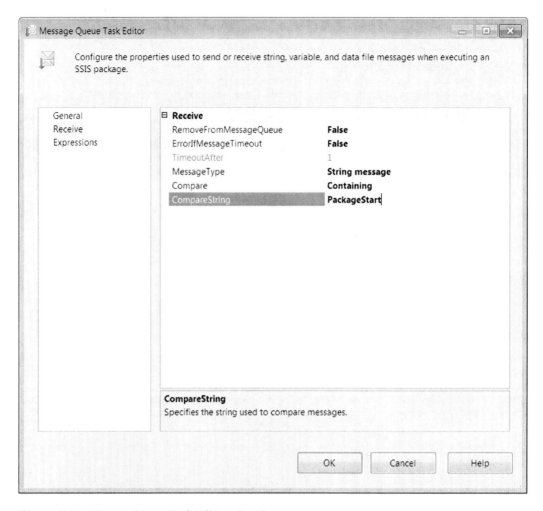

Figure 6-10. Message Queue Task Editor—Receive page

The properties of the Message Queue task are as follows:

RemoveFromMessageQueue indicates whether the message should be removed from the MSMQ service after it is received by the package.

ErrorIfMessageTimeOut specifies whether the task should fail when it is timed out.

TimeoutAfter defines the length of time, in seconds, after which the task will time out.

MessageType lists the types of messages the task can anticipate. Selecting the options will dynamically modify the properties that are available for modification in the editor. The options are Data file message, Variable message, String message, and String message to variable.

SaveFileAs defines the name and location of the file to which the message will be stored. This property is available only with the Data file message option selected as the message type.

Overwrite allows the previous contents of the file to be deleted before the new message is stored. This property is available only with the Data file message option selected as the message type.

Filter identifies whether the package receives a message from a particular package. There are two options for this property, No filter and From package. No filter indicates that the task does not filter out messages. TheFrom package option receives messages from a specific package. This property is available only for Data file messages and Variable messages.

IdentifierReadOnly can contain theGUID of the package from which the message may originate. This option is available only with theFilter property set to No filter. It is read-only. This property is available only for Data file messages and Variable messages.

Identifier contains the GUID of the package from which the task will receive messages. The name of the package can also be specified by using the ellipsis button to locate the package.This property is available only for Data file messages and Variable messages.

Compare defines the match criteria used to compare and filter the message. The options available are None, Exact match, Ignore case, and Containing. Depending on the option chosen, the CompareString property becomes modifiable. The None option does not allow for any comparison of the message that is received. Exact match filters messages based on the exact match of the provided string. Ignore case filters out messages based on a case-insensitive match. Containing matches will filter messages based on the messages containing the provided string. This property is available only for String messages and String messages to variables.

CompareString defines the string that will be used for the comparison criteria. This property is available only for String messages and String messages to variables.

Variable specifies the variable that will receive the message. The ellipsis button allows you to create a new variable, if one isn't defined, that will receive the message. This option is available only when the Variable message option is selected for the message type. This property is available only with String message to variable selected.

Transfer Database Task

A crucial nonfunctional task of an ETL process might be to move source databases to different servers with appropriate hardware that can support the ETL queries. The *Transfer Database task* allows you to move or copy databases between servers or even on the same server. The copy and move processes can operate on databases in offline and online mode. The task utilizes the SQL Management Object Connection Manager to move the databases. Figure 6-11 shows the task as it appears in the control flow designer window. The icon is a yellow cylinder with a bent arrow indicating that the database is being transmitted.

Figure 6-11. *Transfer Database task*

The Databases page of the Transfer Database Task Editor, shown in Figure 6-12, contains the properties that will configure the transfer of the database. In this particular example, we are simply copying a database, its .mdf(master data file), and its .ldf(log data file) files. In addition to the location of these files, we need to specify the network file-share location of the files as well. The General page allows you to modify the Name and Description of the task. The Expressions page allows you to define expressions that can modify the values of the task's properties.

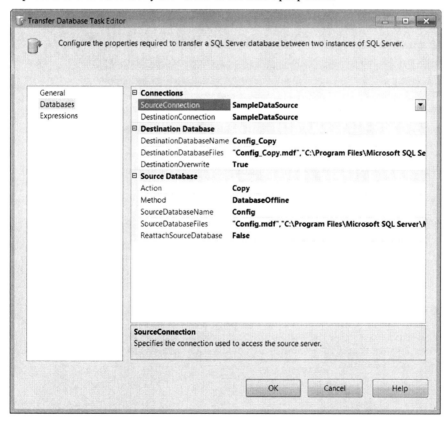

Figure 6-12. *Transfer Database Task Editor—Databases page*

The configurable properties are as follows:

SourceConnection lists all the SMO Connection Managers defined in the package. Select the connection that contains the database you require to be copied or moved. It allows a new connection to be created if the desired one does not exist.

DestinationConnection specifies the SMO connection to the server to which the source database should be copied or moved.

DestinationDatabaseName specifies the name of the database after it is moved or copied to the destination server.

DestinationDatabaseFiles specifies the file names of the .mdf and .ldf files for the destination database. The ellipsis button allows you to use a dialog box to specify the location of these files. The network file share for each of the file locations can also be specified. The dialog box will automatically use the server settings to populate the folder paths for the .mdf and the .ldf files. You will have to specify the network file share.

DestinationOverwrite specifies whether the destination database should be overwritten if it exists on the server.

Action defines the task's operation as either a copy or a move of the source database.

Method defines whether the Database Transfer task will source a database that is in online or offline mode. For offline mode, the user who executes the package must have sysadmin authority to the server. This authority is required because this mode will create a copy of the present .mdf, .ldf, and .ndf files. For online mode, the user who executes the package must be either a system administrator or the database owner of source database. It will leave the database operational and will use the .NET SMO namespace.

SourceDatabaseName specifies the name of the database that is to be copied or moved from the source server.

SourceDatabaseFiles specifies the files associated with the specified source database. The ellipsis button opens a dialog box that allows you to locate the files. The dialog box will automatically populate the information for the files based on the database settings for the file locations. You need to specify the network file share.

ReattachSourceDatabase specifies whether the task should reattach the source database if an error occurs during the execution.

Transfer Error Messages Task

A set of database objects that may be crucial for an ETL process are the user-defined error messages. The *Transfer Error Messages task* can be used to transfer these messages across servers. The task uniquely identifies the user-defined error message with the combination of the identifier and the language of the error message. Based on this combination, the task can manage existing error messages by overwriting existing error messages, failing the task when an existing error message is found, or by ignoring the existing error message. Figure 6-13 shows the task as it appears in the control flow. The icon shows a brief message with a caution sign and an arrow. The arrow indicates the transfer of such messages.

Figure 6-13. *Transfer Error Messages task*

■ **NOTE:** The Transfer Error Messages task will not copy system error messages, that is, messages with identifier values below 50,000.

The Messages page of the Transfer Error Messages Task Editor allows you to modify the properties of the task in order to perform the transfer on the required server and objects. The task uses a SQL Management Object Connection Manager to connect to the required server as the source of the user-defined error messages. The General page allows you to modify the Name and Description of the task. The Expressions page, shown in Figure 6-14, allows you to define expressions that can modify the values of the task's properties.

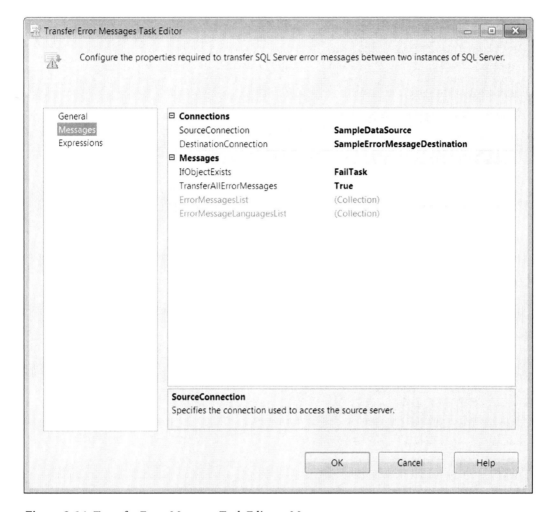

Figure 6-14. *Transfer Error Messages Task Editor—Messages page*

The Transfer Error Messages task's modifiable properties are as follows:

SourceConnection lists the SMO Connection Managers available to be used as the source of the user-defined error messages.

DestinationConnectionlists the SMO Connection Managers available to be used as the destination of the user-defined error messages. The user that executes the package must have sysadmin or serveradmin authority to the server in order to create user-defined error messages.

IfObjectExistslists the options that are available if the transferred error message exists on the destination server. The options are FailTask, Overwrite, and Skip. The FailTask option causes the task to error when a duplicate message is encountered. The Overwrite option overwrites the error message on the destination server. The Skip option ignores the duplicate error message on the destination server.

TransferAllErrorMessages defines whether the task will copy all user-defined error messages or just a specified list of error messages. The two options for this property are True and False.

ErrorMessageListallows you to create a list of user-defined error messages to copy.

ErrorMessageLanguageListallows you to create a list of the languages for which to create copies of the error messages. A message must have the us_english error message version before storing in other languages. The code page for us_english is 1033.

Transfer Jobs Task

Another set of objects that can be vital to an ETL process and that need to be moved between SQL Server instances are SQL Agent jobs. The *Transfer Jobs task* serves this exact requirement. It utilizes the SQL Management Object Connection Manager to transfer these objects. In order to use this task, the user executing the package needs to have sysadmin access or a SQL Agent role on the msdb database on both the source and destination instances. Figure 6-15 demonstrates the Transfer Jobs task as it appears in the control flow. The task's icon shows a process flow controlled by an application. The icon is indicative of SQL Server Agent jobs thatrun processes in a given order.

Figure 6-15. Transfer Jobs task

The Jobs page of the Transfer Jobs Task Editor allows you to configure all the properties necessary to copy SQL Server Agent jobs between two instances of SQL Server. Figure 6-16 shows all the properties that are available on this page. Just like the previous transfer tasks, the Transfer Jobs task uses the SMO Connection Manager. The General page allows you to modify the Name and Description of the task. The Expressions page allows you to define expressions that can modify the values of the task's properties.

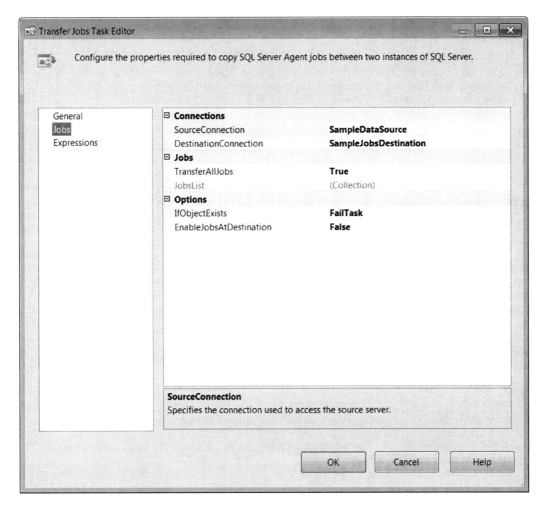

Figure 6-16. Transfer Jobs Task Editor—Jobs page

The Jobs page enables you to configure the following properties:

SourceConnection lists the SMO Connection Managers that are defined in the package. Select the connection that points to the instance you need to use as your source of the SQL Server Agent jobs.

DestinationConnection identifies the SMO Connection Manager that points to the instance you need to use as the destination for the SQL Server Agent jobs.

TransferAllJobs allows you to choose either transferring all the SQL Server Agent jobs that exist on the source instance or those on a defined list. Selecting False allows the JobsList property to become definable.

JobsList enumerates the specific SQL Server Agent jobs to copy to the destination instance.

IfObjectExists allows you to determine the action to perform if the SQL Server Agent job already exists on the destination instance. The choices are FailTask, Overwrite, and Skip. FailTask causes the task to error when it encounters the same job on the destination instance. Overwrite re-creates the duplicate job on the destination instance with the definition found in the source instance.Skip ignores the duplicate job altogether.

EnableJobsAtDestination allows you to enable the copied jobs to be enabled on the destination instance. The two options are True and False.

Transfer Logins Task

Logins are vital for access to data within a database. They can restrict access to different objects within a database. The Transfer Logins task provides for a quick way to copy logins between SQL Server instances. This task can copy all logins, specified logins, or specified logins for a particular database. The task uses SMO Connection Managers to transfer the logins. The user who executes the packages must have sysadmin access to both servers for the transfer of the logins. Figure 6-17 demonstrates the task as it appears in the control flow. The icon shows a picture of a person with a lock and an arrow. The lock and the picture denote the security information that will be transferred.

Figure 6-17. Transfer Logins task

The Logins page, shown in Figure 6-18, allows you to configure all the necessary properties in order to transfer SQL Server logins between two SQL Server instances. The General page allows you to modify the Name and Description of the task. The Expressions page allows you to define expressions that can modify the values of the task's properties.

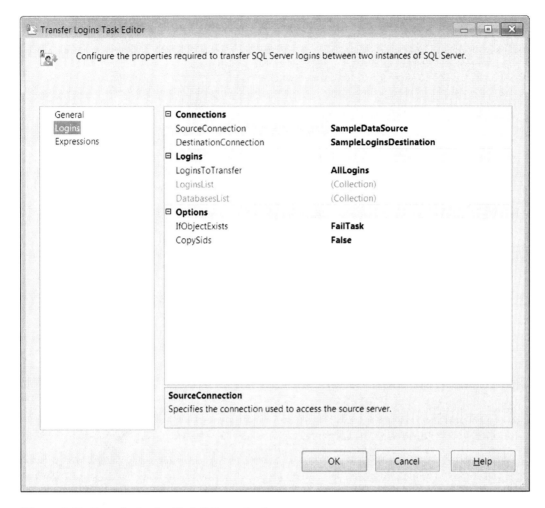

Figure 6-18. *Transfer Logins Task Editor—Logins page*

The Logins page allows the configuration of the following properties:

SourceConnection lists the SMO Connection Managers that can be used as the source for the SQL Server logins.

DestinationConnection lists the SMO Connection Managers that can be used as the destination for the SQL Server logins.

LoginsToTransfer allows you to define the logins to transfer to the destination. The AllLoginsoption will copy all the logins defined on the source SQL Server instance to the destination server SQL Server instance.SelectedLogins allows you to enumerate specific logins to transfer to the destination. AllLoginsFromSelectedDatabase requires you to specify the logins to transfer to the destination; however, the logins are further limited by the DatabaseList property.

LoginsList enumerates the specific logins to transfer to the destination, depending on the option chosen for LoginsToTransfer. The ellipsis button provides you with a list of all the logins on the server to select from. This list is limited if a database list is specified.

DatabasesList enumerates only the databases whose logins you need to transfer.

IfObjectExists defines how the task handles duplicates. The options for this property are FailTask, Overwrite, and Skip. FailTask causes the task to error when it encounters the existing login on the destination.Overwrite re-creates the login with the definition from the source.Skip leaves the login as is on the destination server.

CopySids specifies whether the copy operation should include the security identifiers with the logins. It is vital for this property to be set to True when transferring databases because otherwise the logins will not be recognized by the destination database.

Transfer Master Stored Procedures Task

The user-defined stored procedures on the master database of a SQL Server instance are often required when generating a new SQL Server instance. The *Transfer Master Stored Procedures task* allows you to perform this operation by using the SMO Connection Manager. The user executing the package needs to have read access to the master stored procedures on the source SQL Server instance and sysadmin authority on the destination in order to create them. Figure 6-19 shows the task as it appears in the control flow. The icon, an application window with an arrow, resembles stored procedures in the sense that procedures contain a few statements.

Figure 6-19. *Transfer Master Stored Procedures task*

The Stored Procedures page of the Transfer Master Stored Procedures Task Editor, shown in Figure 6-20, allows you to configure all the necessary properties in order to copy master stored procedures between the master databases of two SQL Server instances. The task will uniquely identify the master stored procedures based only on their names. The General page allows you to modify the Name and Description of the task. The Expressions page allows you to define expressions that can modify the values of the task's properties.

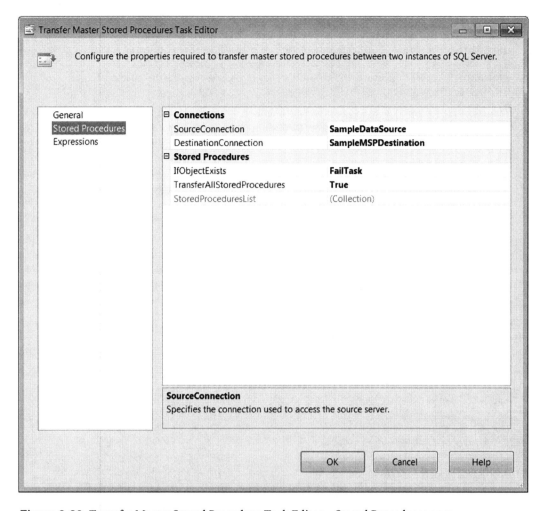

Figure 6-20. *Transfer Master Stored Procedure Task Editor—Stored Procedures page*

The Stored Procedures page provides these properties to be configured:

SourceConnection identifies the SMO Connection Manager to use as the source for the master stored procedures.

DestinationConnection identifies the SMO Connection Manager to use as the destination for the master stored procedures.

IfObjectExists allows you to manage the existence of the master stored procedure on the destination SQL Server instance. The FailTask option causes the task to error when a duplicate master stored procedure is encountered on the destination server. Selecting Overwrite re-creates the master stored procedure with the definition on the source server. Skip leaves the definition of the master stored procedure on the destination server as it is.

TransferAllStoredProcedures allows you to choose between copying all of the user-defined stored procedures on the source master database or a specified set. Setting this property to True enables the StoredProcedureList property for edit.

StoredProcedureList specifies the list of the user-defined stored procedures you need to copy to the destination server. The ellipsis button opens a dialog box that lists all the available stored procedures available for transfer.

Transfer SQL Server Objects Task

One way to transfer select data and objects from a SQL Server database is to use the *Transfer SQL Server Objects task*. By combining a few of these tasks, you can copy objects from several SQL Server databases and create them in one SQL Server database. This functionality is extremely useful, especially if you intend on using a staging database to store your data in a similar system as a preprocess of your ETL process. We discuss more options on preprocessing your data in Chapter 14. Figure 6-21 shows the task as it appears in the control flow designer window. The icon, acylinder on a script with an arrow indicating the transfer, represents the scripts of the various database objects that will be used during the transfer.

Figure 6-21. Transfer SQL Server Objects task

The Objects page of the Transfer SQL Server Objects task, shown in Figure 6-22, allows you to configure all the necessary properties for transferring the required objects between databases. The actual transfer will utilize SMO Connection Managers. The General page allows you to modify the Name and Description of the task. The Expressions page allows you to define expressions that can modify the values of the task's properties.

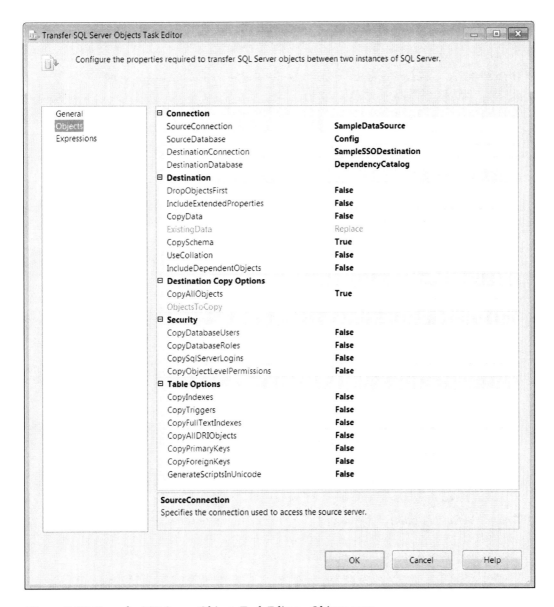

Figure 6-22. Transfer SQL Server Objects Task Editor—Objects page

The Objects page allows you to modify the following context-specific properties:

> SourceConnectionselects the SMO Connection Manager that will be the source of the database objects.

SourceDatabase lists all the databases that exist on the SQL Server instance to source the database objects. Select the databasethat has the objects you need to copy.

DestinationConnection selects the SMO Connection Manager that points to the destination server.

DestinationDatabasenames the database that you need to contain the new objects. The database must exist on the server before you can assign this field.

DropObjectsFirst determines whether the existing objects that are being transferred should be dropped before the transfer.

IncludeExtendedProperties specifies whether the defined extended properties of the objects should be copied to the destination as well.

CopyData specifies whether the data should be copied along with the objects.

ExistingData defines whether the data should replace or append the existing data in the destination database. This option is available for edit only when the CopyData property is set to True.

CopySchema defines whether the schema should be copied over along with the object.

UseCollation defines whether the default collation of the destination server should be used or copied from the source database.

IncludeDependentObjects specifies whether the selected objects should cascade to the objects on which they depend.

CopyAllObjects defines whether all the defined objects on the source database should be copied to the destination. If this option is set to False, all the required objects need to be manually set.

ObjectsToCopy expands to show all the types of objects that can be copied. With each of the types, there is a property to copy every object of that type. The types of objects are Assemblies, Partition Functions, Partition Schemas, Schemas, User-Defined Aggregates, User-Defined Types, and XML Schema Collections. There are a set of properties for each of these object types.

CopyAllTables determines whether all the tables in the source database are to be copied.

TablesList specifies the tables that should be copied from the source database.

CopyAllViewsdetermines whether all the views in the source database are to be copied.

ViewsList specifies the views that should be copied from the source database.

CopyAllStoredProcedures determines whether all the stored procedures in the source database are to be copied.

StoredProceduresList specifies the stored procedures that should be copied from the source database.

CopyAllUserDefinedFunctions determines whether all the user-defined functions in the source database are to be copied.

UserDefinedFunctionsList specifies the user-defined functions that should be copied from the source database.

CopyAllDefaults determines whether all the default definitions in the source database are to be copied.

DefaultsList specifies the defaults that should be copied from the source database.

CopyAllUserDefinedDataTypes determines whether all the user-defined data types in the source database are to be copied.

UserDefinedDataTypesList specifies the user-defined data types that should be copied from the source database.

CopyAllPartitionFunctions determines whether all the partition functions defined on the source database should be copied.

PartitionFunctionsList specifies the partition functions that should be copied from the source database.

CopyAllPartitionSchemas determines whether all the partition schemas defined on the source database should be copied.

PartitionSchemasList specifies the partition schemas that should be copied from the source database.

CopyAllSchemas determines whether all the schemas in the source database should be copied.

SchemasList specifies the schemas that should be copied from the source database.

CopyAllSqlAssemblies determines whether all the SQL assemblies in the source database should be copied.

SqlAssemblies specifies the SQL assemblies that should be copied from the source database.

CopyAllUserDefinedAggregates determines whether all the user-defined aggregates in the source database should be copied.

UserDefinedAggregatesList specifies the user-defined aggregates that should be copied from the source database.

CopyAllUserDefinedTypes determines whether all the user-defined types in the source database should be copied.

UserDefinedTypes specifies the user-defined types that should be copied from the source database.

CopyAllXmlSchemaCollections determines whether all the XML Schema collections defined in the source database should be copied.

XmlSchemaCollections specifies the XML Schema collections that should be copied from the source database.

CopyDatabaseUsers specifies whether the defined database userson the source database should be transferred.

CopyDatabaseRoles specifies whether the defined database roleson the source database should be transferred.

CopySqlServerLogins specifies whether the logins from the SQL Server instance should be transferred.

CopyObjectLevelPermissions specifies whether the object-level permissions on the source database should be transferred.

CopyIndexes determines whether all the indexeson the source database should be transferred.

CopyTriggersdetermines whether all the triggers on the source database should be transferred.

CopyFullTextIndexesdetermines whether all the full-text indexes on the source database should be transferred.

CopyPrimaryKeys determines whether all the primary keys on the source database should be transferred.

CopyForeignKeys determines whether all the foreign keys on the source database should be transferred.

GenerateScriptsInUnicode determines whether all the scripts used in the transfer should be generated in Unicode.

WMI Data Reader Task

An extremely useful functionality of SQL Server Integration Services is the ability to query the Windows log of the host computer or another computer. The *WMI Data Reader task*uses the Windows Management Instrumentation Query Language (WQL) to return data from the WMI about a machine. The queries can return information about the machine's Windows event log, the machine's hardware, and the applications installed on the machine. Figure 6-23 shows the task as it appears in the control flow. The icon, a clipboard with some tools on it, indicates a diagnostic or checklist.

 WMI Data Reader Task

Figure 6-23. *WMI Data Reader task*

The WMI Options page of the WMI Data Reader task, shown in Figure 6-24, allows you to configure all the necessary properties to query and store the relevant machine information. As the page demonstrates, WQL queries are very similar to SQL queries. The General page allows you to modify the Name and Description of the task. The Expressions page allows you to define expressions that can modify the values of the task's properties.

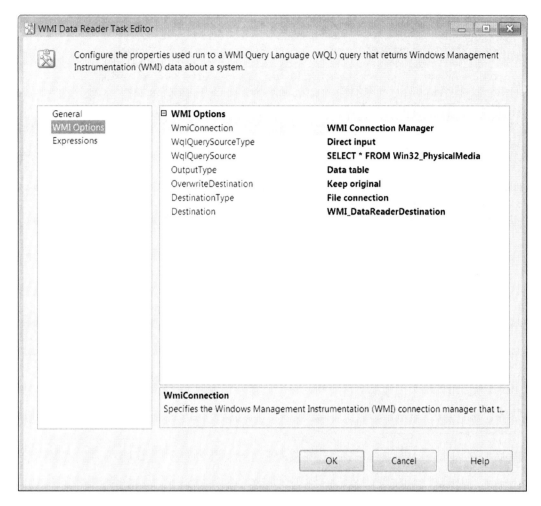

Figure 6-24. WMI Data Reader Task Editor—WMI Options page

The WMI Options page provides for the configuration of the following properties:

WMIConnectionName lists the WMI Connection Manager that points to the Windows machine you need to query.

WQLQuerySourceType defines the method of passing the query to the task. The Direct input option allows you to type the WQL query into the WQLQuerySource field. File connection indicates that the query is stored within a file that can be accessed through a file connection manager. The Variable option allows the query to be stored in an SSIS variable.

WQLQuerySource identifies the access method for the query. With Direct input, you can type the query into this field.

OutputType defines the result set of the query. There are three options for this property:Data table, Property name and value, and Property value. These options show different ways to output the same dataset. The Data tableoption outputs the data in a relational format, with the first row as the column names and the subsequent tuples as the actual information. Property name and value shows the information in a more denormalized format. The properties are listed as the rows, with a comma and whitespace separating them from their values. Each of the rows of data will have their own set of data. The Property value has the same format as the Property name and value, but there is no property name to identify the value.

OverwriteDestination defines whether the data contained within the destination should be overwritten, appended, or kept.

DestinationType defines the destination of the query result. The results can be sent to a flat file by using the File connection option or to an SSIS variable using the Variable option.

WMI Event Watcher Task

An important ability enabling an application to run is determining whether the conditions on the host machine are suitable for its execution. The SSIS *WMI Event Watcher task* allows for this functionality. It utilizes WQL queries directed at WMI event classes to listen to the system's events. The task can be used to wait until a certain event occurs to continue the execution, to delete files to create space if the amount of free space goes below a threshold, or even to await the installation of an application. Figure 6-25 demonstrates the task as it appears in the control flow. The icon is a clipboard with a yellow lightning bolt on it. It shows that the task is watching and waiting for firing of very specific events.

Figure 6-25. WMI Event Watcher task

The WMI Options page of the WMI Event Watcher Task Editor, shown in Figure 6-26, allows you to configure all the necessary properties to watch for and respond to WMI events. This page defines the actions to take after the required event takes place.

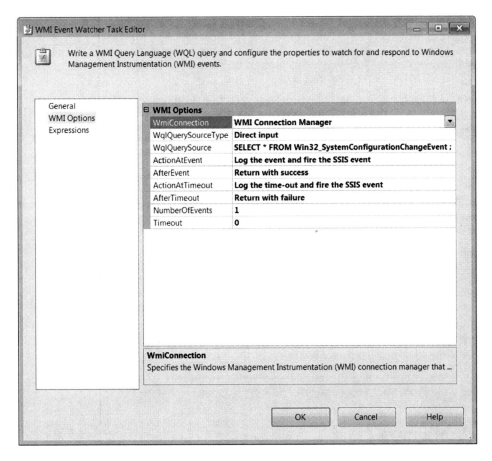

Figure 6-26. *WMI Event Watcher Task Editor—WMI Options page*

The WMI Options page of the WMI Event Watcher task allows the modification of the following properties:

> WMIConnectionName lists all the WMI Connection Managers defined in the package. Select the one the pointing to the target machine.

> WQLQuerySourceType defines the method of passing the query to the task. The Direct input option allows you to type the WQL query into the WQLQuerySource field. File connection indicates that the query is stored within a file that can be accessed through a file connection manager. The Variable option allows the query to be stored in an SSIS variable.

> WQLQuerySourceidentifies the access method for the query. With Direct input, you can type the query into this field.

ActionAtEvent defines the action to take when the WQL query returns a result set indicative of the target event. The options are Log the event, and Log the event and fire the SSIS event. The Log the event option causes the event to be logged without causing SSIS to issue its own event. The second option logs the event as well as have SSIS issue an event as a result.

AfterEvent defines the action the task takes after detecting the required event. The Return with failure option causes the task to error when it receives the result from the WQL query. The Return with success option results in the task completing with success after the required event occurs. Watch for the event again continues listening for the event for the number of times specified in the NumberOfEvents field.

ActionAtTimeout defines the action to take when the WQL query times out. The Log the time-out option causes the event to be logged without causing SSIS to issue its own event. The Log the time-out and fire the SSIS event option logs the time-out as well as has SSIS issue an event as a result.

AfterTimeout defines the action the task takes after reaching the time-out period. The Return with failureoption causes the task to error when the time-out is reached. The Return with successoption causes the task to complete with success even if the required event does not occur. The Watch for the event again option restarts the time-out counter, and the task will continue to wait for the event.

NumberOfEvents defines the number of times the event the task watches for the event occurence before the task completes.

Time-out, a nonzero value, sets the number of seconds without the WQL query returning a result set, after which the task will stop listening for that iteration.

Advanced Containers

The previous chapter introduced the Sequence container as a way of organizing your control flow to make it easier to read. This chapter introduces the other two default containers: the For Loop container and the Foreach Loop container. As their names suggest, these two containers are used to run a set of executables repeatedly. The For Loop container executes a predetermined number of times, whereas the Foreach Loop container relies on an enumerator to dictate its iterations. The containers limit precedence constraints from crossing multiple containers. The iteration commences when the last executable or concurrent executables within the container complete execution. In order to add executables to a container, you need to click and drag them from the SSIS Toolbox onto the space inside the container. The Task Host container cannot be directly accessed, but it keeps the control flow executables organized.

For Loop Container

The For Loop container, which should be used when the number of executions is predetermined, does not rely on objects to determine the number of iterations. The For Loop container utilizes expressions to set, evaluate, and increment the iterator. Figure 6-27 shows the container as it appears in the control flow without any executables. The task's icon is a square with an arrow forming a loop around it. The square represents the process being continuously executed. This loop can also behave as while or a do while loop, depending on the expressions provided. The arrow on the right side of the name tag allows you to collapse the container to minimize the space used in the control flow.

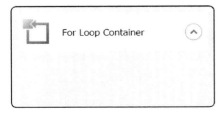

Figure 6-27. For Loop container

The For Loop page of the For Loop Editor, shown in Figure 6-28, allows you to configure the For loop's control. The configuration consists of defining expressions that will initialize, evaluate, and increment the iterator.

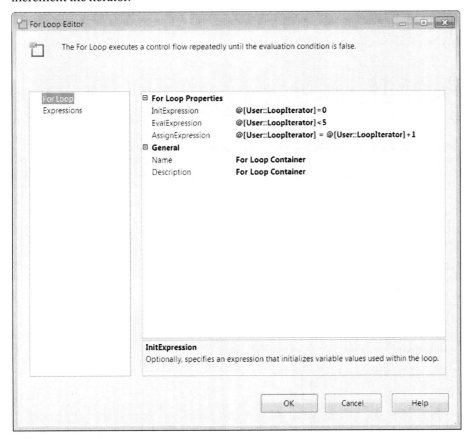

Figure 6-28. For Loop Editor—For Loop page

The For Loop page of the Editor allows you to modify the following properties:

InitExpression provides the expression that will set the initial value of the loop iterator. The expression does not need an assignment value; providing a numeric variable will automatically evaluate to its value. This property is optional for some types of loops.

EvalExpression provides a logical expression whose evaluation determines the continuation of the loop.

AssignExpression provides an expression that will increment the iterator. This field is optional.

Name provides a unique name for the For Loop container.

Descriptionprovides a brief explanation of the looping executables.

■ **NOTE:** Because the For Loop container can be implemented as a while ordo while loop, take extra precautions with the expressions and SSIS variable values used. It is possible for this loop to continue indefinitely.

Foreach Loop Container

The *Foreach Loop container* utilizes enumerators to control its looping behavior. The enumerator itself can consist of various types of objects. Unlike the For Loop container, this loop cannot run indefinitely. The loop will iterate for every member of the enumerator. However, if there are no members, the container will not execute. Figure 6-29 shows the container as it appears in the control flow. The icon consists of three squares stacked on top of each other, with an arrow leading from the square on the bottom to the square on top. This shows that the container loops through a defined list of items.For all types of enumerators, you have the ability to retrieve data from each element as you traverse through the list. This is useful, for example, if you intend to truncate a set of tables on a database. An Execute SQL task inside a Foreach Loop container can generate a SQL statement using values derived from the enumerator.

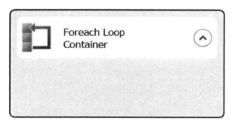

Figure 6-29. Foreach Loop container

Foreach Loop Editor—Collection Page

The Collection page of the Foreach Loop Editor, shown in Figure 6-30, allows you to configure many of the properties that will determine the looping structure of the container. The page will dynamically modify the properties that are available, depending on the type of enumerator you need to use. The enumerator types are Foreach File enumerator, Foreach Item enumerator, Foreach ADO enumerator, Foreach ADO.NET Schema Rowset enumerator, Foreach From Variable enumerator, Foreach Nodelist enumerator, and Foreach SMO enumerator.

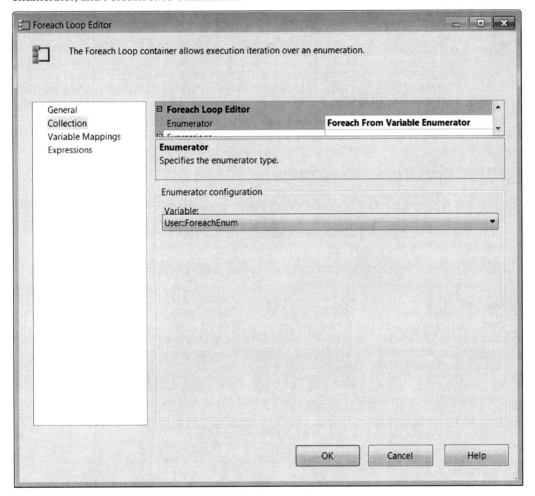

Figure 6-30. *Foreach Loop Editor—Collection page*

The Collection page allows you to configure the following context-specific properties:

Enumerator lists all the types of enumerators available for the Foreach Loop container to traverse.

Foreach File Enumerator allows the container to traverse a list of files.

Folder specifies the working folder within which the files to be enumerated are located.

Browse allows you to navigate the file system to easily find the file folder.

Files lists the files to be used as the enumerator in a comma-separated format. Wildcards can be used to identify files by extension or common naming standards.

Fully Qualified retrieves the folder path, file name, and file extension as thecontainer traverses the file list. This value can be assigned to a variable to be used by an executable within the container.

Name and Extension retrieves the file name and the file extension as the container traverses the file list. This value can be assigned to a variable to be used by an executable within the container.

NameOnly retrieves the file name as the container traverses the file list. This value can be assigned to a variable to be used by an executable within the container.

TraverseSubfolders allows you to include files inside subfolders for the file list.

Foreach Item Enumerator allows you to define a custom list of items for the container to loop through. A window on the Collection page allows you to identify the different elements of the list. The Column button is used to add columns to the enumerator. A new row is added to the list after the last row is populated with values.

Columns button opens a dialog box that allows you to add columns to the enumerator and define their data types.

Remove deletes an element from the enumerator.

Foreach ADO Enumeratorallows the usage of ADO or ADO.NET objects as the enumerators of the container. The ADO objects will enumerate the rows of a singular data table, whereas the ADO.NET objects may enumerate rows in multiple data tables or the data tables themselves.

ADO Object Source lists all the user-created variables within the scope of the container. This variable will be traversed as a data table or a set of data tables.

Rows in First Tabletraverses the rows that appear in the first data table only. This option can be applied to both ADO and ADO.NET objects.

Rows in All Tables (ADO.NET Dataset Only) traverses all the rows in all the data tables.

All Tables (ADO.NET Dataset Only) traverses the data tables themselves.

Foreach ADO.NET Schema Rowset Enumeratoruses a .NET provider for OLEDB to connect to SQL Server and enumerate certain database objects.

Connection lists the .NET provider for OLEDB connections to SQL Server defined in the package.

Schema defines the scheme to be used as the enumerator.

Set Restrictions creates restrictions for each of the schema's properties. A dialog box allows you to define the restriction based on a string value or a variable value.

Foreach From Variable Enumeratorallows you to enumerate the data in an object variable.

Variable lists all the user-created variables.

Foreach Nodelist Enumeratorallows you to enumerate specific nodes of an XML statement resulting from an XPath expression.

DocumentSourceType defines the input method of the XML statement. The `FileConnection` option allows you to specify a connection manager that points to the XML file with the nodes you need. The `Variable` option indicates that the XML is stored within an SSIS variable. The `DirectInput` option requires you to type the XML directly into the editor.

DocumentSource specifies the XML source depending on its type. For the `FileConnection` and `Variable` options, you get a drop-down list that either contains file connections or SSIS variables, respectively. For `DirectInput`, the editor provides a text field to type in the XML.

EnumerationType defines the type of enumeration of the XML nodes. The `Navigator` option utilizes the `XPathNavigator` to enumerate the XML. The `Node` option uses XPath expressions to retrieve the XML nodes. The `NodeText` option uses XPath expressions to retrieve text nodes. The `ElementCollection` option uses XPath expressions to retrieveelement nodes. The first three options require the use of the outer XPath expression that is applied to the XML. The last option uses an outer XPath expression and can applyan inner XPath expression to the element collection.

OuterXPathStringSourceType provides the source type for the XPath expression that is applied to the XML statement. The `FileConnection` option allows you to specify a connection manager that points to the XPath expression. The `Variable` option indicates that the XPath expression is stored within an SSIS variable. The `DirectInput` option requires you to type the XPath expression directly into the editor.

OuterXPathString specifies the XPath expression source depending on its type. For the `FileConnection` and `Variable` options, you get a drop-down list that either contains file connections or SSIS variables, respectively. For `DirectInput`, the editor provides a text field to type in the XPath expression.

InnerElementType specifies the type of inner element in the list. The options for the types are `Navigator`, `Node`, and `NodeText`.

InnerXPathSourceType provides the source type for the XPath expression that is applied to the element collection. The `FileConnection` option allows you to specify a connection manager that points to the XPath expression. The `Variable` option indicates that the XPath expression is stored within an SSIS variable. The `DirectInput` option requires you to type the XPath expression directly into the editor.

InnerXPathString specifies the XPath expression source depending on its type. For the FileConnection and Variable option, you get a drop-down list that either contains file connections or SSIS variables, respectively. For DirectInput, the editor provides a text field to type in the XPath expression.

Foreach SMO Enumerator uses anADO.NET Connection Manager to enumerate objects at a server or database level as well as run queries to return information about certain objects.

Connection lists all the ADO.NETConnection Managers defined in the package.

Enumerate defines the objects to enumerate. This property can be automatically populated by using the Browse dialog box.

Browse opens a dialog box to select the required object from the server. This will automatically generate the necessary expression to populate the Enumerate property.

Foreach Loop Editor—Variable Mappings Page

As the container iterates through the list, it is able to extract information from the enumerator. The elements can be stored in SSIS variables that will be overwritten with new values as the container iterates by configuring the Variable Mappings page, shown in Figure 6-31. Columns need to be defined to accept each of the values, depending on the structure of the enumerator.

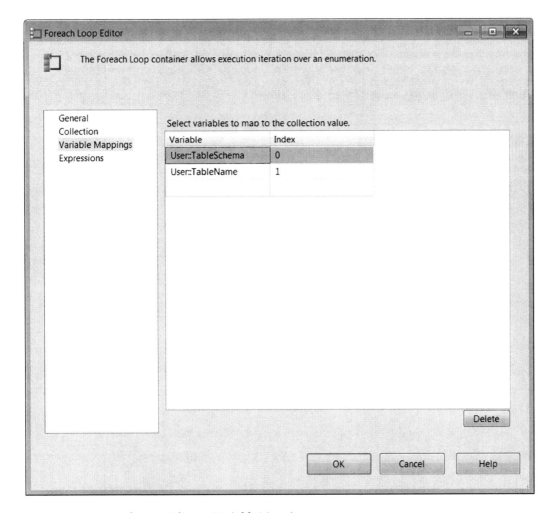

Figure 6-31. Foreach Loop Editor—Variable Mappings page

The Variable Mappings page allows you to configure the following mappings:

Variable lists all the user-defined SSIS variables with appropriate scope for the container.

Index identifies the location of the variable in the enumerator. The index value represents the column number inside the enumerator. The values start with 0 and increase to match the data inside the enumerator.

Task Host Controller

The Task Host container is implicitly configured when an executable is added to the SSIS control flow. The configurations apply exclusively to the executables and their dependents in the case of containers. This container allows for variables and event handlers to be tied directly to the task. This container also limits the scope of variables across the different executables.

Summary

This chapter introduced the advancedcontrol flow items that will allow you to perform many nonfunctional requirements. A majority of the advanced tasks transfer objects between SQL Server instances. We also introduced the advanced containers in the SSIS Toolbox. These containers loop through the execution differently, but they achieve similar goals. The implicit Task Host controller cannot be accessed directly but works behind the scenes to keep the package executables organized.Chapter 7covers the basic components of the Data Flow task.

CHAPTER 7

Source and Destination Adapters

"All rivers flow into the sea, yet the sea is not full."

—King Solomon

In SSIS, the *data flow* is your primary tool for moving data from point A to point B and manipulating it along the way. The data flow is a powerful concept that allows you to encapsulate your data movement and transformation as a self-contained task of the *control flow*. The data flow moves your data from a source to a destination, like King Solomon's river moves water from its source to the sea. This chapter introduces the data flow and discusses data flow source adapters, destination adapters, and the new Source and Destination Assistants.

The Data Flow

The data flow is contained within the confines of the *Data Flow task*, which itself exists in the control flow. The Data Flow task is shown in Figure 7-1.

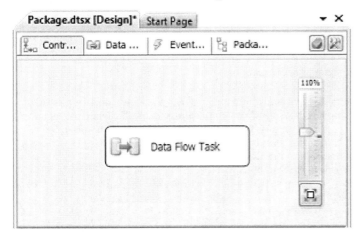

Figure 7-1. The Data Flow task on the BIDS designer surface

You add a Data Flow Task to the control flow by dragging and dropping it from the *SSIS Toolbox* over to the BIDS designer surface. Because the Data Flow Task is a control flow task, the data flow represents a powerful self-contained subset of the control flow. The purpose of having a data flow is to separate data movement and manipulation—the primary purpose of ETL—from work flow management. As you can see in Figure 7-2, any given data flow can be fairly complex. You can also include multiple Data Flow tasks in a single control flow. We cover the sources, destinations, and transformations shown in the sample data flow, and many more, in this chapter and the next.

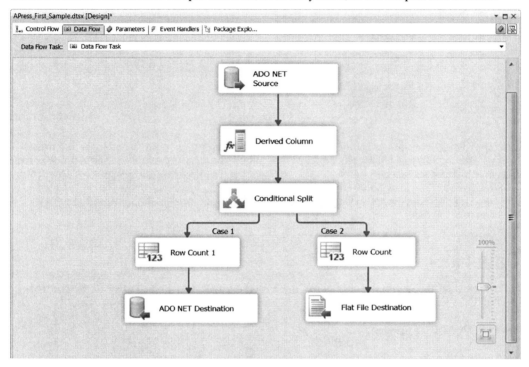

Figure 7-2. *Data flow consisting of several data flow components*

The components that make up the data flow can be divided into three categories: source adapters that pull data into the data flow; transformations that allow you to manipulate, modify, and direct your data; and destination adapters that allow you to push data out of the data flow to persistent storage or into other systems for further processing. In this chapter, we consider the sources and destinations that SSIS provides to pull data into and push data out of your data flows.

Technically speaking, all data flow components derive from a single base class called the PipelineComponent class. This class exposes properties such as BufferManager, which provides access to the two-dimensional storage object (that is to say, a *tabular rowset*) holding your data as it moves through the data flow. The PipelineComponent class also has methods such as AcquireConnection, which establishes connectivity to your data sources via connection managers. In the out-of-the-box stock components we discuss in this chapter, these properties and methods are already fully developed for you, so you don't have to deal with them directly.

> ■ **NOTE:** We discuss the details of the `PipelineComponent` class and developing your own custom components in depth in Chapter 22.

Sources and Destinations

In the SSIS data flow, *source adapters* are components that pull data from well-defined data stores. Source adapters use connection managers to connect to, and pull data from, databases such as SQL Server and Oracle, flat files, XML, or just about any other source you can define. *Destination adapters* are the opposite of source adapters—they push data to data stores. Destination adapters use connection managers to send data to databases, flat files, Excel spreadsheets, or any other destination you can connect to.

Although you can create extremely complex data flows in SSIS, the simplest useful data flow you can create might consist of a single source adapter connected to a single destination adapter. For this example, let's consider a simple data flow that extracts data from a flat file and loads it into a SQL Server database table. This is considered *straight pull*, in that no transformations are applied to the data as it moves from source to destination. For the purposes of this chapter, assume you're editing a brand new SSIS package in BIDS with a single data flow.

Source Assistant

The *Source Assistant* is new to SQL Server 11 SSIS. When you drag this component from the SSIS Toolbox to the designer surface, BIDS opens the Add New Source dialog box. This dialog asks you to choose a type of source and a connection manager to use. As you can see in Figure 7-3, the source assistant window lets you choose from several types of sources. For our simple data flow sample, we've selected a Flat File source type and a <New> connection manager.

> ■ **NOTE:** The Show Installed Only check box limits the types shown to only those that are installed on your local development machine.

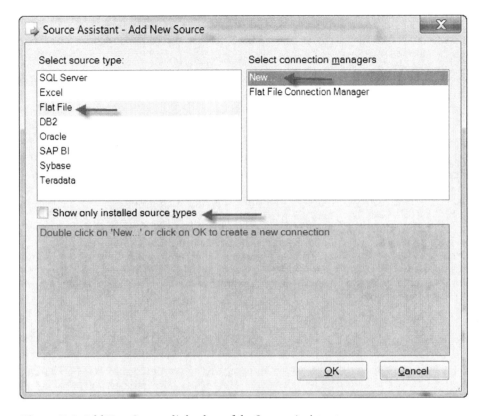

Figure 7-3. Add New Source dialog box of the Source Assistant

When you choose the <New> connection manager, the Connection Manager Editor pops up. The editor is specific to the type of connection manager you want to create—the Flat File Connection Manager Editor has different properties from the SQL Server Connection Manager Editor. The Flat File Connection Manager Editor is shown in Figure 7-4.

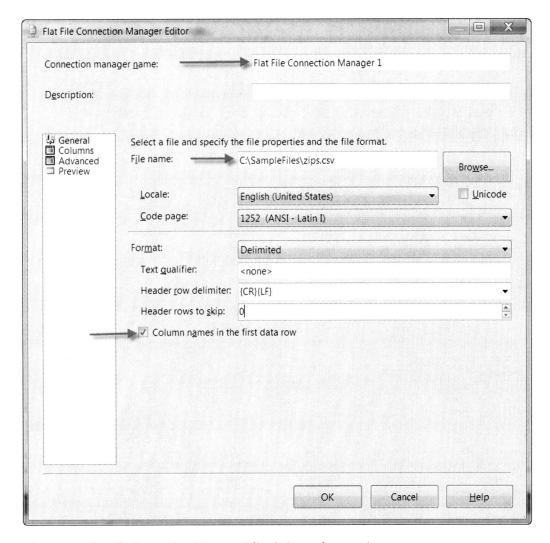

Figure 7-4. *Flat File Connection Manager Editor's General properties*

We'll choose the Flat File source and <New> connection manager from the Add New Source dialog box. Then we use the Flat File Connection Manager Editor to set the properties for the flat file and select a source file. As you can see in Figure 7-4, we chose a comma-delimited file named zips.csv, updated the connection manager name, and selected the Column Names in the First Data Row check box on the General page. We left the Locale, Code Page, and other options at their default values.

On the Columns page of the editor, you have two options for flat files. You can change the *row delimiter*, which is the character or combination of characters that ends each line of the flat file, and you can change the *column delimiter*, which is the character or character combination that separates fields in the file. In this case, we've chosen the default {CR}{LF} (carriage return/line feed) combination for the row delimiter, and the Comma (,) for the column delimiter for .csv files. The Columns page also gives you a preview of the source data. Figure 7-5 highlights these options on the Columns page of the editor.

■ **NOTE:** The {CR}{LF} combination is a common row delimiter for Windows text files. Files generated on some other operating systems, such as Unix, use only the {LF} character as row delimiters. Keep this in mind when dealing with flat files generated by non-Windows systems.

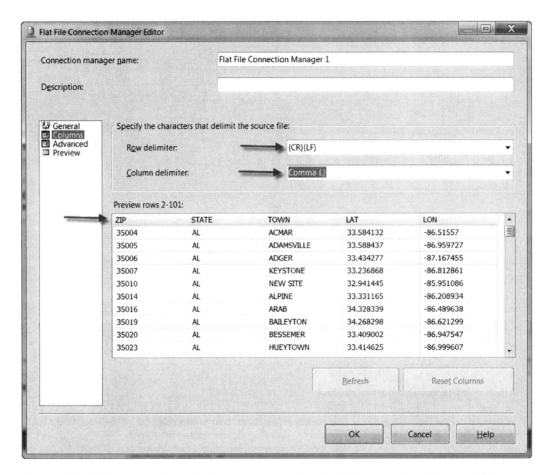

Figure 7-5. *Editing properties in the Columns page of the Flat File Connection Manager Editor*

The Advanced page is the third page of the editor. On this page, you can change column-specific properties for your data source. You can change the ColumnDelimiter property for individual columns, so that one or more columns can have a special delimiter (useful if you have a single input column that needs to be split in two, for instance). You can also change the DataType for the column (default is string, or DT_STR) and the output column width (default is 50 for string). There are additional properties for DataPrecision and DataScale, which determine the number of total digits in a numeric (DT_NUMERIC) column and the number of digits after the decimal point, respectively. Figure 7-6 shows the Advanced page of the Flat File Connection Manager Editor.

For our sample columns, properties were set as shown in Table 7-1.

Table 7-1. Sample Column Settings

Column Name	DataType	OutputColumnWidth	ColumnDelimiter
ZIP	String [DT_STR]	5	Comma (,)
STATE	String [DT_STR]	2	Comma (,)
TOWN	String [DT_STR]	50	Comma (,)
LAT	Double-precision float [DT_R8]	--	Comma (,)
LON	Double-precision float [DT_R8]	--	Comma (,)

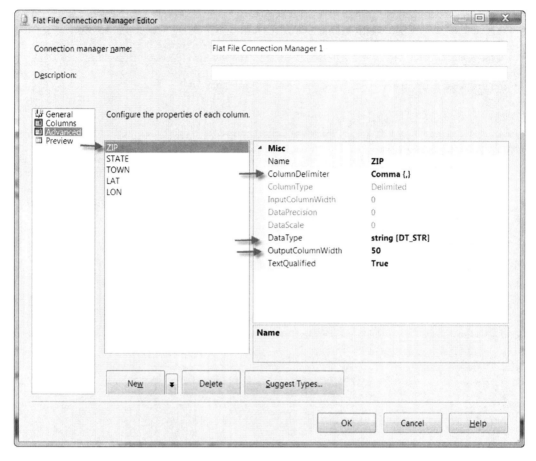

Figure 7-6. *Editing column properties in the Advanced page of the Flat File Connection Manager Editor*

PRECISION AND SCALE

The DataPrecision and DataScale properties in the Flat File Connection Manager Editor's Advanced page apply only to the numeric (DT_NUMERIC) and decimal (DT_DECIMAL) column data types. The precision of one of these columns is the total number of digits that can be held in a number being processed through the column. The precision of the number 123.45 is 5, for instance. The scale of a column is the number of digits allowed after the decimal point, so for 123.45, the scale is 2.

For numeric columns, the precision can be set to a number between 0 and 38, and the scale can also be set to a value between 0 and 38. The precision of the decimal data type is always 29 (can't be changed), and the scale can be set from 0 to 28.

After you configure the connection manager, the Source Assistant adds the appropriate type of source adapter to your data flow, as shown in Figure 7-7. The Flat File Connection Manager you created appears in the Connection Managers tab of the BIDS designer.

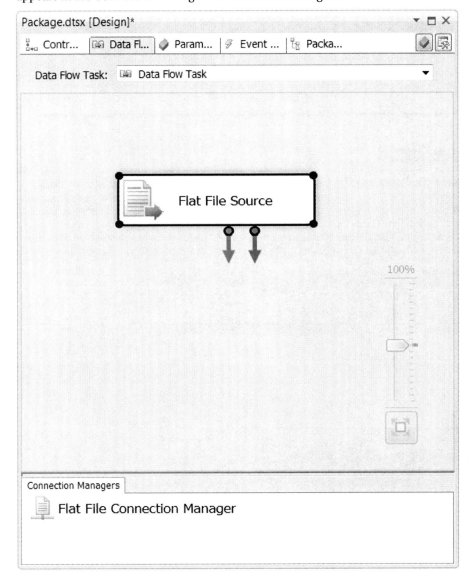

Figure 7-7. Flat File source adapter created by the Source Assistant

EDITING DATA FLOW COMPONENTS

After you add a data flow component to the designer surface, you can edit it at any time by (1) double-clicking it, (2) right-clicking and choosing the Edit option, or (3) right-clicking and choosing the Show Advanced Editor option. The standard editor for most components is generally a simplified user interface that gives access to only the most common modified properties. The Advanced Editor provides access to all available properties of a data flow component, such as direct access to the output column and error output column properties. We cover the capabilities of the Advanced Editor in greater detail later in this chapter.

Destination Assistant

In addition to the new Source Assistant, SQL Server 11 SSIS also includes a new *Destination Assistant*. Whereas the Source Assistant guides you through adding source adapters to data flow, the Destination Assistant walks you through adding destination adapters. Just drag the Destination Assistant to the designer surface, and the Add New Destination dialog box, shown in Figure 7-8, appears. As in the Source Assistant dialog box, you can choose a type and connection manager for your new destination. You can also toggle the Show Installed Only check box to list only currently installed destination types or all supported types.

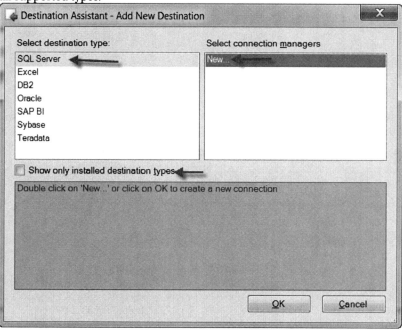

Figure 7-8. Add New Destination dialog box of the Destination Assistant

For this example, we chose the SQL Server destination type and <New> connection manager. The
SQL Server destination type presents us with the OLE DB Connection Manager Editor, with the Native
OLE DB\SQL Server Native Client 11.0 provider selected. This editor allows you to choose the server
name, provide authentication credentials, and choose the database to log into, as shown in Figure 7-9.

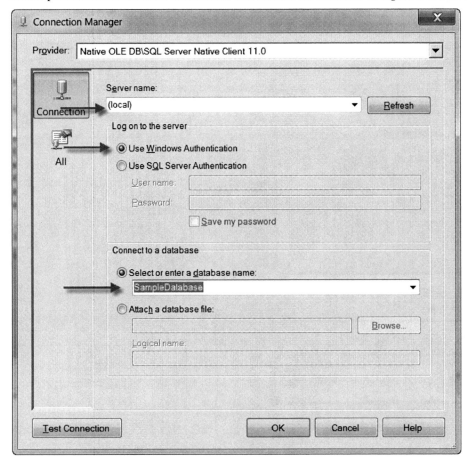

Figure 7-9. *Configuring the OLE DB Connection Manager*

After you edit the connection manager properties, BIDS adds the appropriate destination adapter to
your data flow, in this case an OLE DB destination. If there is a red *x* on the destination adapter, as
shown in Figure 7-10, it means you need to configure additional properties of the destination adapter. In
this case, we need to drag the green Flat File source adapter output path arrow and connect it to the OLE
DB destination adapter and configure the destination adapter's properties to point it at a table in a
database.

■ **NOTE:** The OLE DB Connection Manager created by the Destination Assistant has a default name of the form `server_name.database_name`. You will probably want to change this to a friendlier name. Just right-click the connection manager in the Connection Managers tab and choose Rename from the context menu. In our example, we renamed the database connection manager to `Source_DB`.

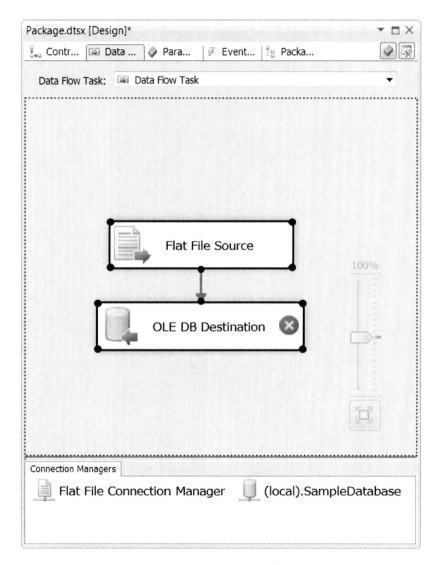

Figure 7-10. *OLE DB destination adapter created by the Destination Assistant*

After connecting the Flat File source adapter to the OLE DB destination adapter, we still need to configure the OLE DB destination adapter. By double-clicking the OLE DB destination adapter, we can pull up the OLE DB Destination Editor. With this editor, we chose the OLE DB Connection Manager, the data access mode, and the name of the target table. We chose Table or View – Fast Load as the data access mode, which lets us also set the Rows per Batch and Maximum Insert Commit Size options. We changed these from the default values. These options are shown in Figure 7-11.

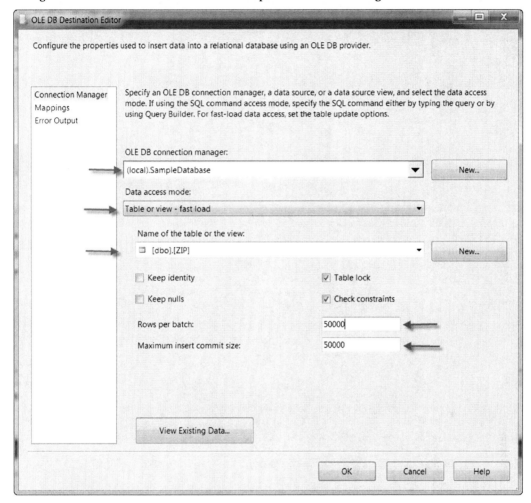

Figure 7-11. Setting properties for OLE DB destination in the editor

The Mappings page of the editor gives you the opportunity to map the destination component's input columns to its output columns. When you connect the destination adapter to the data flow, BIDS tries to automatically map the columns based on name. In our example, all of the columns in the source file have the same names as the columns in the target table, so the mapping is performed for us automatically. If you need to map an input column to a differently named output column, you can change the mappings by connecting them in the upper portion of the mapping window or by changing them in the grid view in the lower portion of the screen, as shown in Figure 7-12.

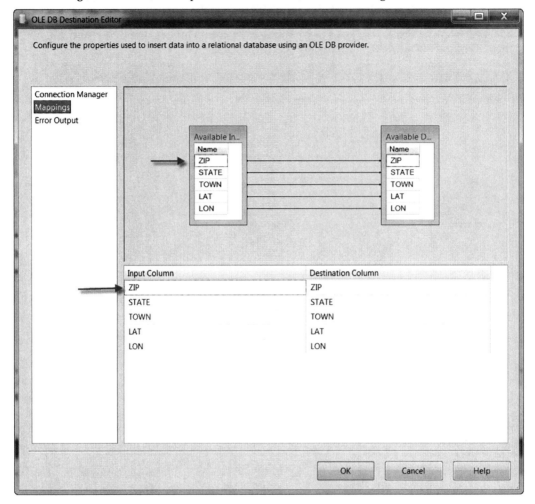

Figure 7-12. Mapping page of the OLE DB destination editor

After you've completed the destination configuration, the red *x* will disappear from the component in the data flow designer in BIDS. Running the package in BIDS shows that 29,470 rows are imported from the flat file to the database table, as you can see in Figure 7-13.

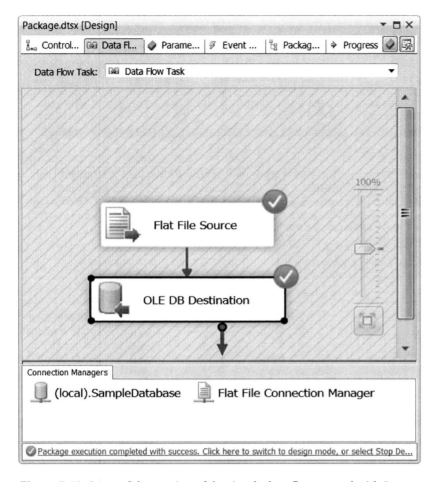

Figure 7-13. Successful execution of the simple data flow created with Source and Destination Assistants

Database Sources and Destinations

In the previous sections, we showed you how to use the Source and Destination Assistants to set up a simple package to pull data out of a flat file and push it into a database. We chose to demonstrate with the Flat File source and OLE DB destination adapters because their use is a very common scenario, especially when using SSIS to pull data from legacy systems for which no direct connection is available and push it into a SQL Server database. This section details database sources and destinations and shows you how to configure their more-advanced features.

OLE DB

OLE DB source and destination adapters allow you to connect to a variety of OLE DB data stores, but they are commonly used for database connectivity because they provide good performance and support a wide variety of relational databases. For this example, we'll configure an OLE DB source adapter and OLE DB destination adapter to both connect to a SQL Server instance and move data from one table to another. This will be a very simple demonstration, but will give you an opportunity to uncover a wide range of OLE DB configuration options.

For our example, we have two tables: one named LastName, containing a list of the most common surnames in the United States (data obtained from US Census Bureau), and one called LastName_Stage that we'll copy the surnames to.

Our first step was to create two connection managers named Source_DB and Dest_DB, respectively. These two connection managers point at the same server and database in the example, but in the real world they would likely point at different servers or different databases on the same server. This is why we created two separate connection managers for them. Table 7-2 shows the variety of options you can choose in the OLE DB Source Editor, which is pictured in Figure 7-14.

Table 7-2. *OLE DB Source Editor Dialog Controls*

Option	Description
OLE DB Connection Manager drop-down	Lets you choose an OLE DB Connection Manager as a source for your data. In the example, we chose the Source_DB connection manager we created earlier.
Data Access Mode drop-down	Determines how the source adapter retrieves data from the OLE DB source. There are four options:
--	Table or View mode lets you choose the name of a table or view in the database as your source. This mode returns all columns from the table, and is similar to a SELECT * query, but with a little more overhead because the source needs to retrieve table metadata itself.
--	Table Name or View Name Variable mode lets you store the name of a table or view in a string variable, to be retrieved at runtime. This mode is also similar to a SELECT * query, returning all columns from a table, including some you may not need.

Option	Description
--	SQL Command mode gives you an opportunity to specify a SQL statement that returns a rowset, such as SELECT or EXECUTE <procedure>. By using SQL Command mode, you can specify only the columns you want returned, and you can limit the rows returned with joins and WHERE clauses.
--	SQL Command from Variable mode gives you the chance to execute a SQL statement that is stored in a string variable. The SQL command stored in the variable is retrieved and executed at runtime.
--	Because you can use them to limit the columns and rows retrieved by the source adapters, the SQL Command and SQL Command from Variable modes are the most efficient methods of retrieving data from a SQL database or other OLE DB source. We chose the SQL Command mode in this example.
SQL Command text box	The SQL Command mode gives you a text box in which you can enter a SELECT or other rowset-producing statement. In our example, we are grabbing the rows from the LastName table. The other access modes give you a drop-down box to choose a table name or variable.
Parameters button	Lets you map variables to parameters if you use them in your query.
Build Query button	Allows you to edit your query in the Query Builder graphical user interface.
Browse button	Lets you load a SQL query script file into the SQL Command text box.
Parse Query button	Parses and validates the syntax of your SQL statement.
Preview button	Gives you a preview of the data produced by your SQL command text.

■ **NOTE:** It's a best practice to use SQL SELECT statements when pulling data from source tables for a couple of reasons. First, your table may have more columns than you actually need to pull. It's a good idea to minimize the amount of data you pull into your data source for efficiency reasons. Second, the Table or View access mode incurs additional overhead that is avoided with the SQL Command or SQL Command from Variable access mode.

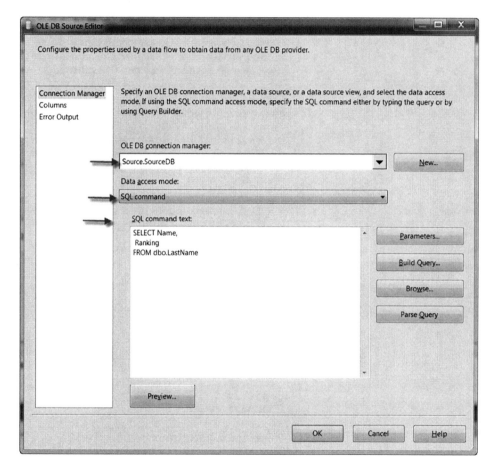

Figure 7-14. Configuring the OLE DB source to pull data from the LastName table

In the OLE DB source, we've used an OLE DB *parameterized query*. In a parameterized query, you define parameters and map variables to those parameters. At query execution time, both the parameterized query and the parameter values are passed on to the server. The server executes the query with the appropriate values in place of the parameters. In our example, we've used the following simple query:

```
SELECT Name,
  Ranking
FROM dbo.LastName
WHERE Name LIKE ?;
```

In OLE DB the ? is used as a parameter placeholder. Parameters in OLE DB are indicated by their *ordinal position* (the order in which they appear in the query). The first parameter is Parameter0, the second is Parameter1, and so on. Clicking the Parameters button on the editor dialog gives you the Set Query Parameters dialog box. In this window, you can map variables to parameters, as shown in Figure 7-15.

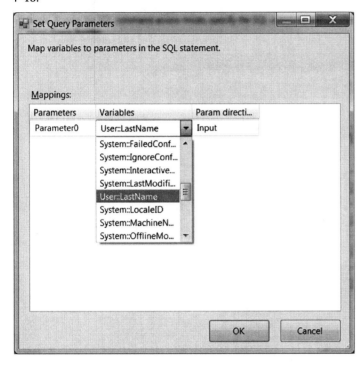

Figure 7-15. *Mapping a variable to an OLE DB parameter in our sample source query*

We created a string variable named User::LastName and populated it with a SQL wildcard LIKE operator pattern (in this case, we chose [A-M]%, which will return all names that start with the letters *A* through *M*). Figure 7-16 shows the Variables portion of the Parameters and Variables window, where we defined the User::LastName variable.

■ **NOTE:** For a detailed discussion of creating and using SSIS variables, see Chapter 9.

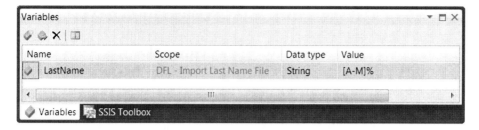

Figure 7-16. *Defining a variable in the Variables portion of the Parameters and Variables window*

The next step in our sample is configuring the OLE DB destination, as shown in Figure 7-17.

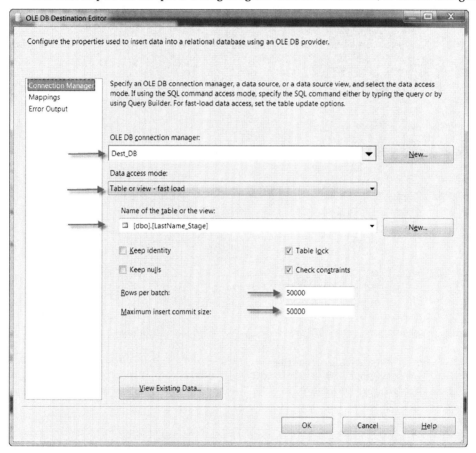

Figure 7-17. *Configuring the OLE DB Destination Editor to output to a table*

With the OLE DB Destination Editor, you can configure exactly where your data is going as well as some of the properties that determine how that data gets there. Table 7-3 is a breakdown of the OLE DB Destination Editor.

***Table 7-3.** OLE DB Destination Editor Dialog Box Controls*

Control	Description
OLE DB Connection Manager drop-down	Lets you choose an OLE DB Connection Manager to use as a destination for your data. Here we chose the Dest_DB connection manager.
Data Access Mode drop-down	Determines how the source adapter sends data to the OLE DB destination. This drop-down has five options:
--	Table or View mode lets you choose the name of a table or view in the database to send data to. This mode incurs a lot of overhead because it generates an INSERT statement for every row sent to the destination.
--	Table or View – Fast Load mode uses the OLE DB fast load option. The fast load option uses the OLE DB IRowsetFastLoad interface to perform an in-memory *bulk copy* of your data. In fast load mode, SSIS queues up rows in memory and sends them to the server in batches. This can be a significant performance boost over the normal access modes.
--	Table Name or View Name Variable mode lets you store the name of a table or view in a string variable, to be used at runtime. Like Table or View mode, this mode generates an INSERT statement per row.
--	Table Name or View Name Variable – Fast Load mode uses the OLE DB fast load option to send data to a table or view whose name is stored in a variable. Like the other fast load option, this access mode batches rows before sending them to the server.

Control	Description
--	SQL Command mode often trips people up when they first see it. You might imagine it providing you a way to give a parameterized INSERT or UPDATE statement; in reality, it gives you a way to define a "virtual view" to insert data into. If you use this option at all, it will probably be with a simple SELECT from a table.
--	In this example, we chose the commonly used Table or View – Fast Load mode. The Table or View mode is also used often. The From Variable and SQL Command modes are usually reserved for special-purpose situations.
Keep Identity check box	In the fast load modes, this option populates an identity column with values from the source.
Keep Nulls check box	Also a fast load option, this determines whether source column nulls are inserted as nulls in the destination column when the destination column has a default constraint applied to it.
Table Lock check box	Another fast load option to lock the destination table during the load. This can improve performance, but prevents other processes from accessing the table during the load.
Check Constraints check box	When on, the check constraints on the target table are checked as the data is loaded.
Rows per Batch	Rows per Batch is used to optimize memory usage during the fast load operation. We find setting this value to 50000–100000 generally works well, although you might play with the value to find an optimal setting for your configuration.
Maximum Insert Commit Size	This value sets the maximum batch size the OLE DB destination queues up before it tries to commit the data to the server. We generally set this value to the same as the Rows per Batch setting.

■ **NOTE:** Generally we set Rows per Batch and Maximum Insert Commit Size to a value between 50000 and 100000. We recommend setting these values to something other than the defaults. Setting these to nondefault values will help the provider optimize its memory usage and avoid some issues reported with older versions of some OLE DB providers.

A successful run of this package results in a screen like the one shown in Figure 7-18.

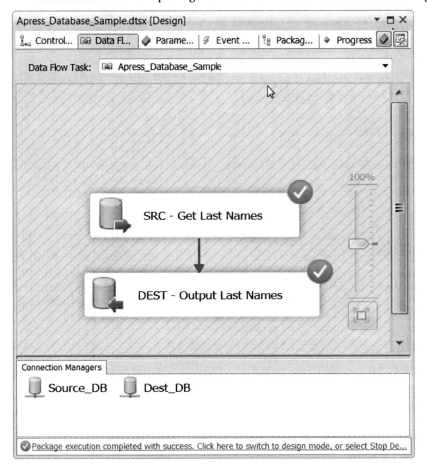

Figure 7-18. *Successful OLE DB source to OLE DB destination package execution*

ADO.NET

The ADO.NET source and destination adapters allow you to create managed .NET SqlClient connections. Because they are managed code, these types of connections tend to provide weaker performance than their native-mode OLE DB counterparts overall. On the other hand, they are easier to access and manage programmatically from within .NET code, such as Script tasks and script components, precisely because they are managed. In many cases, particularly when small numbers of rows are involved, the performance difference between ADO.NET and OLE DB source and destination adapters is negligible.

The ADO.NET source adapter has a simplified interface that allows you to choose an ADO.NET connection manager and one of two access modes: Table or View mode or SQL Command mode. Unlike the OLE DB source adapter, parameters are not supported with the ADO.NET source adapter.

■ **TIP:** Although you can't parameterize an ADO.NET source adapter, you can set the `SqlCommand` property for the component to an expression. You can access this property via the Data Flow task properties. We discuss SSIS expressions in detail in Chapter 9.

The ADO.NET destination adapter also has a simple interface. It allows you to choose an ADO.NET Connection Manager and a table or view to send output to. There is an additional check box to Use Bulk Insert When Possible, which will take advantage of memory-based bulk copy, similar to the OLE DB `IRowsetFastLoad` interface.

SQL Server Destination

The SQL Server destination adapter provides high-speed bulk insert, similar to the Bulk Insert task. The main difference is that, unlike the Bulk Insert task that sits in the control flow, the SQL Server destination sits at the end of a data flow—so you can transform your data prior to bulk loading it. Another difference is that the SQL Server destination doesn't read its source data from a file. Instead it bulk loads from shared memory, which means you can't use it to load data to a remote server.

SQL Server Compact

SSIS has a SQL Server Compact destination adapter that lets you send data to a SQL Server Compact Edition (CE) instance. One thing to keep in mind when connecting to SQL Server CE is that only a 32-bit driver is available.

Files

Flat files and databases are arguably the most common sources and destinations used in SSIS packages, which is why we started this chapter with a detailed discussion of these two classes of adapters. However, there are still more file-based sources and destinations available. We discuss these source and destination adapters, and their properties, in this section.

Flat Files

When you're talking about importing and exporting files, odds are very high you're talking about flat files. Because they're so prevalent, it's no surprise that SSIS provides extensive support and options for importing data from and exporting data to flat files. When we talk about flat files, we're talking about delimited files, fixed-width files, and ragged-right files, which are files with fixed width-columns, except for the very last column, which can be of varying length.

We demonstrated a simple flat-file import in the first sample in this chapter, and now we'll circle back to discuss the advanced options with another example. We started by creating and configuring a Flat File Connection Manager and an ADO.NET Connection Manager in a new package. We configured the Flat File Connection Manager as shown in Figure 7-19.

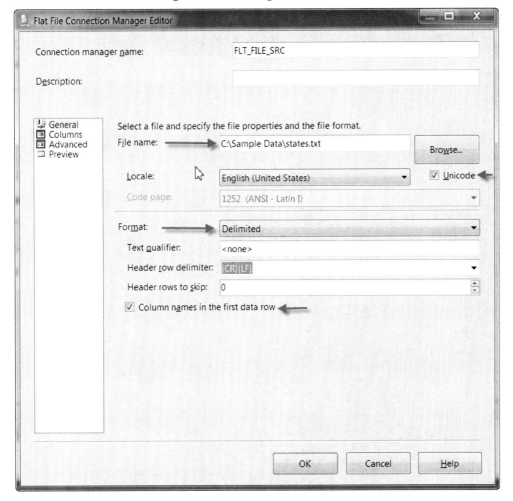

Figure 7-19. Configuring the Flat File Connection Manager

We configured the Flat File Connection Manager to pull data from a delimited file named states.txt. The file holds Unicode data, so we selected the Unicode check box. Because we're using Unicode, the Code Page drop-down is disabled because it is irrelevant. The format is delimited using a pipe delimiter for most columns—more on this later; and finally, the file has the column names in the first row.

We also tweaked some settings on the Advanced page of the Flat File Connection Manager Editor. We set the ColumnDelimiter, which tells SSIS how to divide your file into columns, to the pipe character (|) for *most* of the columns. In the last field of the file, we have the Longitude and Latitude of each state capital, separated by a comma (,), as shown in Figure 7-20. So really we have what's known as a *mixed-delimiter file*.

When you create the flat file connection, all columns default to 50-character strings. In our case, we adjusted the DataType setting on some of the columns: we changed the Long and Lat columns to the double-precision float [DT_R8] data type, for instance.

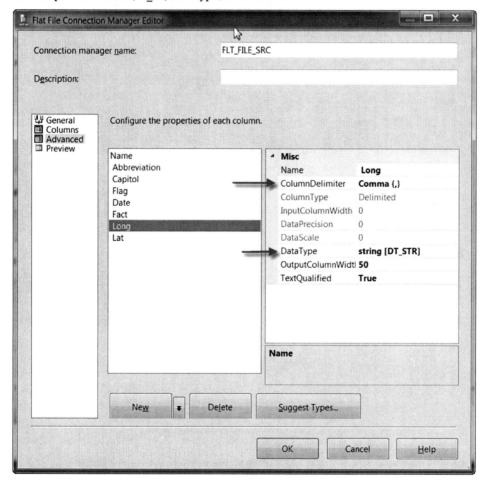

Figure 7-20. *Adjusting column-level settings on the Advanced page of the Flat File Connection Manager Editor*

▪ **NOTE:** We're just giving a brief overview of the Flat File Connection Manager in this section. We discussed the connection managers and their configurations in detail in Chapter 4.

After we configured the Flat File Connection Manager, we configured the Flat File source adapter to use it. Although the Flat File source adapter has a standard, simplified editor, we chose to configure this component by using the Advanced Editor that all components have by default. To access the Advanced Editor, shown in Figure 7-21, simply right-click the Flat File source adapter and choose Show Advanced Editor from the context menu.

The first option we set, on the Connection Managers tab of the Advanced Editor, was to tell the Flat File source adapter to use the Flat File Connection Manager.

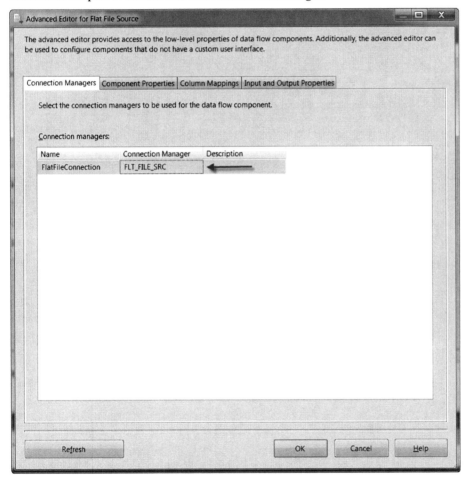

Figure 7-21. Configuring the Flat File source adapter to use the Flat File Connection Manager

The Column Mappings tab maps the *external columns* (which are the columns defined by the connection manager) and the *output columns* (which are the columns that are output by the Flat File source adapter). You can change column mappings in the top portion of the window by dragging and dropping external columns over to the Output Columns box, or you can change them in the lower portion of the window by choosing different columns from the drop-down lists in the grid box. The Column Mappings tab is shown in Figure 7-22.

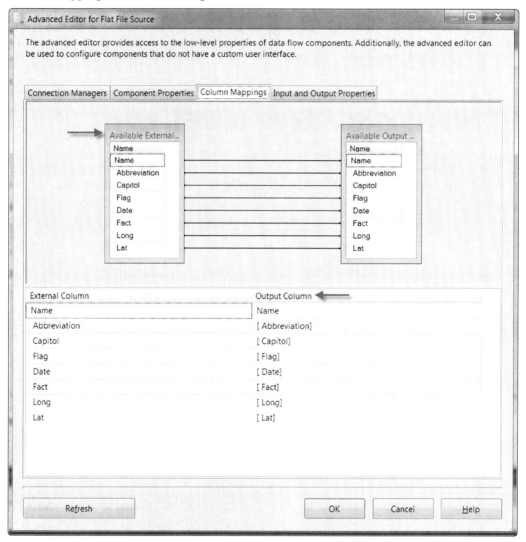

Figure 7-22. *Mapping columns in the Advanced Editor*

The Input and Output Properties tab gives you access to advanced column-level metadata. In this view, you can see the individual external columns, output columns, and their properties, as shown in Figure 7-23.

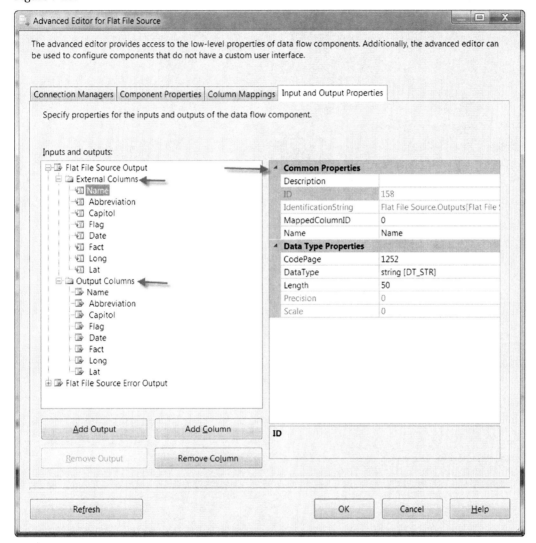

Figure 7-23. *Reviewing column-level metadata in the Input and Output Properties tab*

After configuring the Flat File source adapter, we connected its output to the ADO.NET destination, and configured the ADO.NET destination adapter to use the ADO.NET Connection Manager. The source-to-destination connection and ADO.NET destination adapter are shown in Figure 7-24 and Figure 7-25.

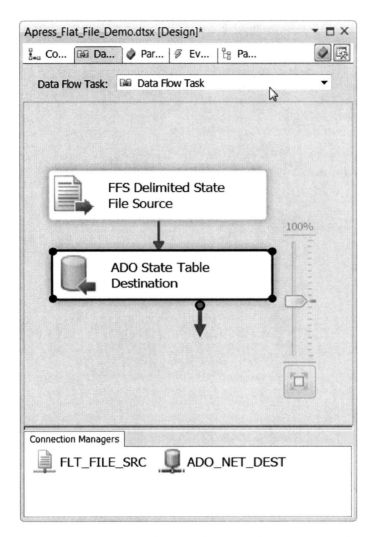

Figure 7-24. Connecting the Flat File source adapter output to the ADO.NET destination adapter input

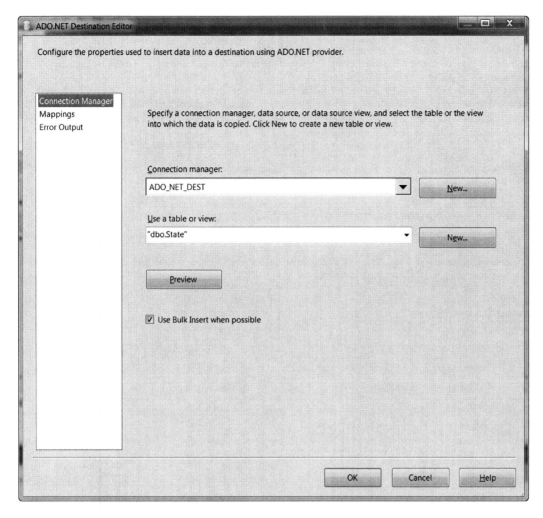

Figure 7-25. *Configuring the ADO.NET destination adapter*

The Flat File destination adapter is the opposite of the Flat File source adapter. Instead of pulling in the contents of a flat file and outputting the data into your data flow, the Flat File destination adapter accepts the input from your data flow and outputs it to a flat file.

Excel Files

Business users often use spreadsheets as ad hoc databases. From a business user's perspective, it makes sense because they, and all their colleagues, are familiar with the spreadsheet paradigm. They all understand the user interface, how to implement simple and even complex calculations, and how to format the interface exactly as they want it. From the IT perspective that developers and DBAs bring to the table, there are few things scarier than the thought of hundreds of gigabytes of business information floating around the aether, possibly unsecured, in ad hoc spreadsheet formats.

The Excel source and destination can help you pull data out of spreadsheets and store it in secure, structured databases, or extract data from well-defined systems and put it in a format your business users can easily manipulate.

For this example, we'll assume a simple package with two data flows in it. One data flow will read the contents of an Excel spreadsheet and store it in a table, and the second will read the contents of that same table and output it to an Excel spreadsheet. Our sample Excel spreadsheet looks like Figure 7-26.

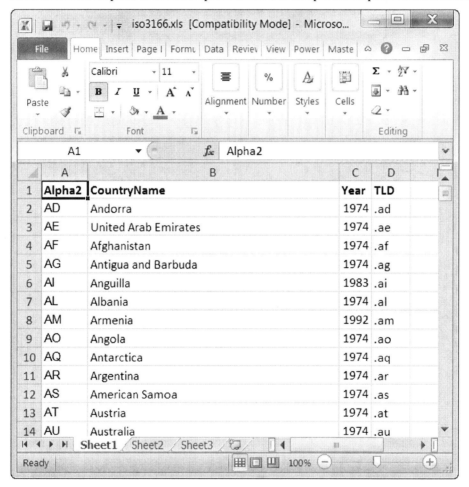

Figure 7-26. *Source Excel spreadsheet containing ISO 3166 country codes and names*

The first step is to create an Excel Connection Manager. Right-click in the Connection Managers tab and choose New Connection. Then choose the EXCEL connection manager type. You'll be presented with the Excel Connection Manager dialog box, shown in Figure 7-27. In this example, we chose an Excel file named iso3166.xls with a list of country names and abbreviations from the ISO 3166 standard, we selected Microsoft Excel 97–2003 format, and we selected the check box indicating that the first row of data on the spreadsheet holds the column names.

■ **NOTE:** ISO 3166 is the international standard for country codes and names. Whenever possible, it's a good idea to use recognized standards instead of reinventing the wheel.

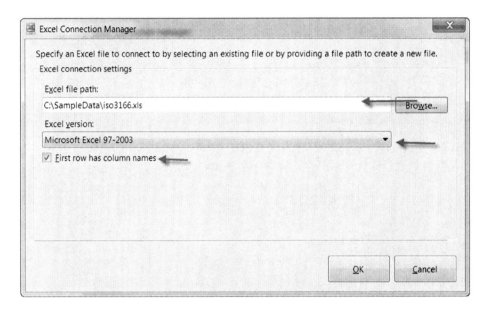

Figure 7-27. Setting Excel Connection Manager properties in the editor dialog box

We also created an OLE DB Connection Manager, as described in the "Destination Assistant" section of this chapter.

The next step is to drag the Excel source adapter and OLE DB destination adapter onto the BIDS designer surface and connect them. We then edited the Excel source by double-clicking it to pull up the Excel Source Editor. In the editor, we chose the Excel Connection Manager we just created, chose a data access mode of Table or View, and selected the first spreadsheet in the Excel workbook, named Sheet1$, as you can see in Figure 7-28.

■ **NOTE:** The Excel Source Editor lets you choose entire worksheets or named ranges of cells from an Excel workbook.

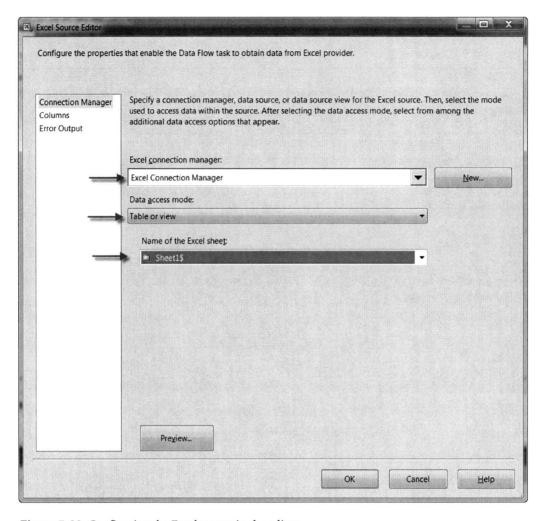

Figure 7-28. *Configuring the Excel source in the editor*

You can look at the source columns by selecting the Columns tab of the Excel Source Editor. The Columns page gives you a list of available *external columns* (the columns in the physical Excel file) with a check box next to each one. You can deselect a given column if you don't want it included in your data flow. Figure 7-29 shows the Columns page of the Excel Source Editor.

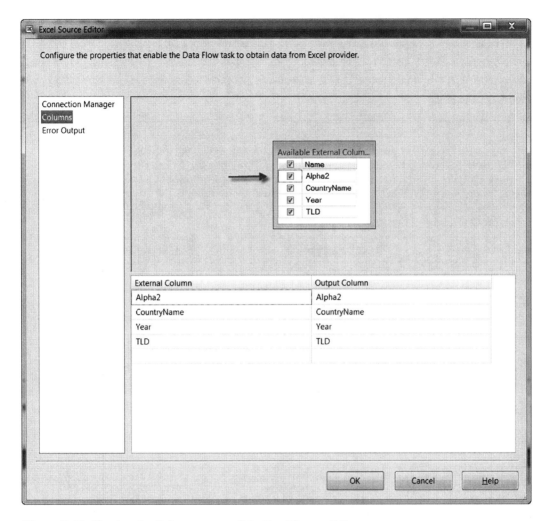

Figure 7-29. Viewing the Columns page of the Excel Source Editor

As an alternative to choosing the Table or View access mode and selecting a worksheet name, you can choose SQL Command mode and enter a SQL-style query to get the same data from your Excel spreadsheet. The following query retrieves the same data from your worksheet that we're grabbing in the current example:

```
SELECT Alpha2,
    CountryName,
    Year,
    TLD
FROM [Sheet1$];
```

■ **NOTE:** The Excel source and Excel destination adapters use the Microsoft OLE DB Provider for Jet 4.0 and the Excel Indexed Sequential Access Method (ISAM) driver to read from and write to Excel spreadsheets. Bear in mind that this driver provides a very limited subset of SQL-style query syntax, and it does not support many T-SQL features you may be used to.

When you set up an Excel source adapter, it tries to automatically determine the data types of the external columns by sampling the data in the spreadsheet. There is currently no way to force or coerce the data type of an Excel column to a more appropriate type, apart from modifying the data in your spreadsheet. Table 7-4 shows all of the data types supported by the Excel ISAM driver.

Table 7-4. Excel to SSIS to SQL Server Data Type Conversions

Excel Data Type	SSIS Data Type	SQL Server Data Type
Boolean	Boolean [DT_BOOL]	bit
Currency	Currency [DT_CY]	money
Date/time	Datetime [DT_DATE]	datetime
Memo	Unicode text stream [DT_NTEXT]	nvarchar(max)
Numeric	Double-precision float [DT_R8]	float
String	Unicode string, length 255 [DT_WSTR]	nvarchar(255)

If SSIS overestimates the size or data type of your Excel columns—for instance, (nvarchar(255) for an nvarchar(2) column—you may need to add a Derived Column transformation (which we cover in the next chapter) to your data flow to convert your columns to the appropriate types. To complete the data flow, we simply configured the OLE DB destination to point at a database table and mapped the columns as we described in the "Destination Assistant" section of this chapter. A successful run of this sample package looks like Figure 7-30.

JET DRIVERS AND 64-BIT

Before you run a package that connects to Microsoft Office files, such as Excel spreadsheets and Access databases, you need to know that the Microsoft Jet 4.0 drivers come in only 32-bit (x86) flavors. If you're developing on a 64-bit machine, you'll need to set your project to run using the 32-bit runtime so that it will use the 32-bit Jet 4.0 drivers to connect to the Excel workbook. You can access this option by right-clicking your project in the BIDS Solution Explorer and choosing Properties. Under the Debugging properties, change the Run64BitRuntime option to False, as shown in Figure 7-30.

This setting makes BIDS use the 32-bit runtime instead of the 64-bit runtime to execute your packages for this project. The setting is good only at design time in BIDS, however. If you execute your package from the command line or by using another tool, you'll have to ensure that the 32-bit runtime is used.

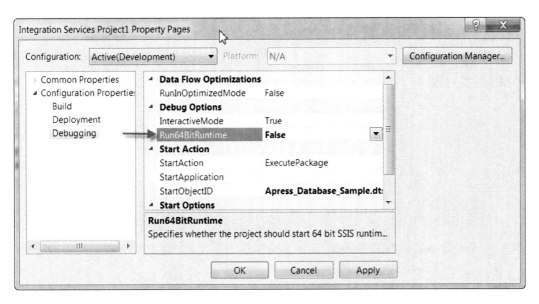

Figure 7-30. Setting the SSIS project to run in 32-bit mode

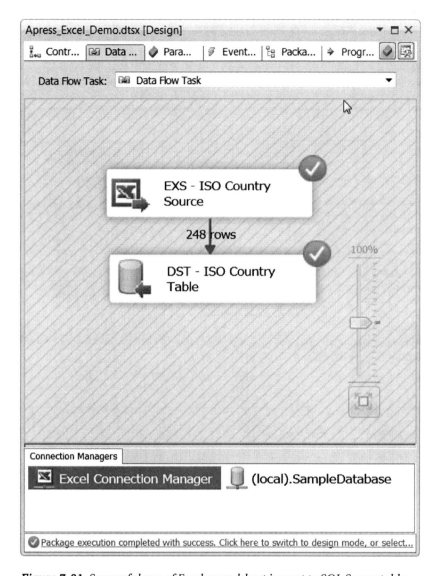

Figure 7-31. *Successful run of Excel spreadsheet import to SQL Server table*

Whereas the Excel source adapter lets you pull data from Excel spreadsheets into your data flow, the Excel destination allows you to output data from a data flow to an Excel spreadsheet. To demonstrate, we'll pull the contents of the Country table we just populated from the database and output it to a new spreadsheet.

We'll add a new Excel Connection Manager to the SSIS package and point it at a new, mostly empty spreadsheet. The new spreadsheet will have only the names of the columns in the first row, as shown in Figure 7-32.

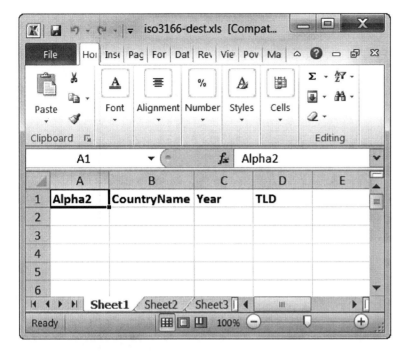

Figure 7-32. New SSIS destination workbook, empty except for column headings

Next we'll add an OLE DB source adapter and an Excel destination adapter to an empty data flow. After we configure the OLE DB source to pull data from the Country table in the database, we link the OLE DB source output to the Excel destination input. The final step is to configure the Excel destination. In the Excel Destination Editor, we selected the newly created Excel Connection Manager, set the data access mode to Table or View, and chose the name of the first worksheet, Sheet1$, as shown in Figure 7-33.

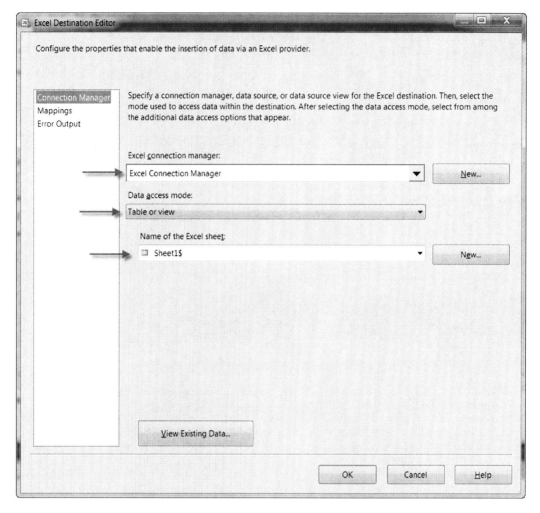

Figure 7-33. Configuring the Excel destination adapter in the Excel Destination Editor

Raw Files

Whenever you read from or write to a flat file, there are thousands of data conversions taking place in the background. Consider an integer number such as 2,147,483,647. This number uses only 4 bytes of memory in your computer. But when you write it out to a flat file, it's converted to a string of numeric digits 10 characters long. That's more than double the storage and a performance hit because of the conversion. When you read the number back in from a flat file, you have to read in 10 characters and you get hit with another conversion penalty. Granted, the size difference and performance impact isn't that much for a single number, but multiply that by 10 columns and 1,000,000 rows (which is not an unreasonable example), and suddenly you're talking about a noticeable change in both performance and storage space.

For day-to-day file transfers and imports/exports from and to other systems, flat files are the way to go. In a lot of cases, flat files aren't all that large, so the size and performance differences aren't significant. But more important, when transferring data between systems, you can't go wrong with plain text. Accounting for some variation between character sets, every system reads text, and every system writes text.

Sometimes, however, you may find a need to temporarily store large volumes of partially processed data during processing. A common example is when a large number of rows have been pushed through an SSIS package, a lot of processing has taken place, and you need to pick up the data in another SSIS package (or a different data flow in the same package) for further processing. To maximize efficiency of your SSIS interpackage processing, raw files are hard to beat.

Raw files are specialized binary format files that eliminate a lot of the conversion overhead associated with normal flat files. Raw files store your data in binary format, so that those 4-byte integers are stored in exactly 4 bytes. Raw files also store metadata about your columns, so the binary data in the raw file can't be accidentally read in as the wrong format. The Raw File destination adapter lets you output data from your data flow to a raw file; the Raw File source adapter lets you read a raw file back into your data flow. The raw file provides an efficient intermediate format for serializing temporary results.

Just as one example of the use of raw files, we recently ran into a situation where we had to dump a large amount of data from a Microsoft Access database using 32-bit Jet 4.0 drivers and import the data into a SQL Server database using 64-bit drivers. You can't mix 32-bit and 64-bit drivers in the same package, so the solution was to create two packages: one to extract the data from Access into a raw file and one to import the data into SQL Server. We ran the Access extract package using the SSIS 32-bit runtime and the SQL Server import package using the SSIS 64-bit runtime. This is just one example, but there are plenty more in which the raw file produces efficient temporary storage of your intermediate results. Anytime you need to temporarily store partially processed data, consider raw files.

XML Files

The XML source adapter lets you use an XML file with an XML Schema document (XSD) as a source for your data flow. The XML Source uses the XSD you provide to extract the data values from your XML file and output it in columns. If you don't have an XSD file, this component will generate a simple one for you. The XML source adapter is useful for relatively simple XML files, or for extracting well-defined subsets of data from more-complex XML files.

▪ **NOTE:** We recommend the book *SSIS Design Patterns* by Matt Masson , Tim Mitchell , Jessica Moss , Michelle Ufford , Andy Leonard (Apress, 2012), which devotes an entire chapter to loading XML files with SSIS.

Special-Purpose Adapters

SSIS has two special-purpose destination adapters, which provide additional functionality, such as writing to in-memory recordsets or to SQL Server Analysis Services (SSAS). These adapters are as follows:

Recordset: The SSIS Recordset destination adapter lets you populate an in-memory recordset. One of the most common uses of the in-memory recordset is to populate it via the data flow and later iterate it with a Foreach Loop Container.

DataReader: The DataReader destination adapter outputs data in a format compatible with the .NET DataReader interface, which can be picked up and consumed by an application that can read a DataReader. SQL Server Reporting Services (SSRS) reports, for instance, can be set to consume the output of an SSIS package using the DataReader interface.

Analysis Services

In addition to all the source and destination adapters we've covered in this chapter, SSIS provides destination adapters for SQL Server Analysis Services (SSAS). This section provides an overview of SSAS capabilities, and Chapter 14 presents detailed information about SSIS's Analysis Services functionality. Table 7-5 lists SSIS's Analysis Services destinations.

Table 7-5. Analysis Services Destinations

Destination Name	Description
Data Mining Model Training	Passes data through data mining model algorithms to train data mining models
Dimension Processing	Loads and processes SQL Server Analysis Services dimensions
Partition Processing	Loads and processes SSAS partitions

Summary

In this chapter, we discussed SSIS's source and destination adapters, the key components required to move data into and out of your SSIS data flows. We began this chapter with a discussion of SSIS's Source and Destination Assistants, two new features designed to make creating source and destination adapters a little more convenient. We then detailed how to create and use different flavors of database-specific source and destination adapters, which are among the most commonly used types of data flow adapters.

Next we discussed the various types of files that SSIS supports reading from and writing to, including flat files, Excel spreadsheets, raw files, and XML. We also talked about the special-purpose destinations: the Recordset and DataReader destination adapters, and we finished up with an introduction to the Analysis Services destinations—a conversation we will pick up again in Chapter 14.

In the next chapter , we introduce the third type of data flow components—transformations.

CHAPTER 8

Data Flow Transformations

The goal is to transform data into information, and information into insight.

—Carly Fiorina

In the previous chapter, you looked at how SSIS pulls data from point A and pushes it out to point B. In this chapter, you'll begin exploring the different types of data manipulations, referred to as *transformations*, which you can perform on your data as it moves from its source to its destination. As Carly Fiorina indicated, our ultimate goal is to start with raw data and use it to reach a state of insight. Data flow transformations are the key to moving your raw data along the first half of that journey, turning it into usable information.

High-Level Data Flow

The SSIS data flow consists of sources, transformations, and destinations. Figure 8-1 shows the high-level view of SSIS's data flow.

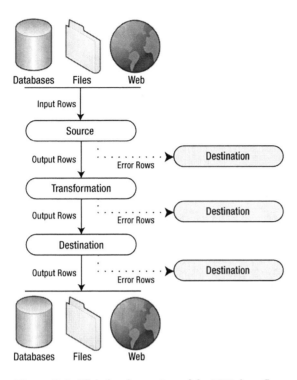

Figure 8-1. *High-level overview of the SSIS data flow*

As you can see from the diagram, SSIS source components pull data from a variety of sources such as databases, files, and the Web. The source component introduces data into the data flow, where it moves from transformation to transformation. After the data has been processed, it moves on to the destination component, which pushes it out to storage, including databases, files, the Web, or any other type of destination you can access. The solid black arrows in the diagram are analogous to the output paths (green arrows) in the SSIS designer. Some components, such as the Multicast transformation we discuss later in this chapter, have more than one output path.

Each type of data flow component (source components, transformations, and destination components) can also have an error output path. These are represented by red arrows in the BIDS designer. When a component runs into a data error while processing a row of data, the erroneous row is redirected to the error output. Generally, you'll want to connect the error output to a destination component to save error rows for later review, modification, and possible reprocessing.

Types of Transformations

SSIS comes with 30 stock transformations out of the box. These standard transformations give you the power to manipulate your data in any number of ways, including modifying, joining, routing, and performing calculations on individual rows or entire rowsets.

Transformations can be grouped along functional lines, which we've done in this chapter. Row transformations and Split and Join transformations are two of the groups we cover, for instance. On a different level, transformations are also classified by how they process data. In particular, data flow transformations can be classified as either synchronous or asynchronous. In addition, they can be further subdivided by their *blocking* behavior.

Synchronous Transformations

Synchronous transformations process each row of input at the time. When sending data through a synchronous transformation, SSIS uses the input buffer (an area of memory set aside for temporary data storage during processing) as the output buffer. This is shown in Figure 8-2.

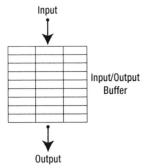

Figure 8-2. *Synchronous transformations use the input buffer as the output buffer.*

Because synchronous transformations reuse the input buffers as the output buffers, they tend to use less memory than asynchronous transformations. Generally speaking, synchronous transformations also share these other properties (though these don't always hold true for every component):

- Synchronous components generally are nonblocking or only partially blocking. This means they tend to process rows and output them immediately after processing, or they process and output rows with minimal delay.

- Synchronous components also tend to output the same number of rows that they receive as input. However, some synchronous components may effectively discard rows, resulting in fewer output rows than input rows.

Asynchronous Transformations

Asynchronous transformations tend to transform data in sets. Asynchronous transformations are used when your method for processing a single row of data is dependent on other rows of data in your input. You may need to sort or aggregate your input data, for instance. In these situations, the transformation needs to see all rows of data at once, and can't transform each row independently.

From a technical perspective, asynchronous transformations maintain separate input and output buffers. Data moves into the input buffers, is transformed, and then moved to the output buffers. The extra data movement between input and output buffers can cost you some performance, and the maintenance of two separate sets of buffers tends to use more memory than synchronous transformations. Figure 8-3 shows data moving between input and output buffers of an asynchronous transformation.

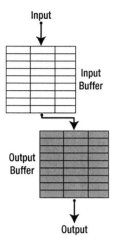

Figure 8-3. *Asynchronous transformations move data from an input buffer to a separate output buffer.*

In general, asynchronous transformations are designed to handle situations such as the following:

- The number of input rows does not equal the number of output rows. This is the case with the Aggregate and Row Sampling transformations.

- Multiple input and output buffers have to be acquired to queue up data for processing, as with the Sort transformation.

- Multiple rows of input have to be combined, such as with the Union All and Merge transformations.

Blocking Transformations

In addition to grouping transformations in synchronous and asynchronous categories, they can also be further subdivided by their *blocking* behavior, as noted earlier. Transformations that are *fully blocking* have to queue up and process entire rowsets before they can allow data to flow through. Consider the Sort transformation, which sorts an entire rowset. Consider pushing 1,000 rows through the Sort transformation. It can't sort just the first 100 rows and start sending rows to output—the Sort transformation must queue up all 1,000 rows in order to sort them. Because it stops data from flowing through the pipeline while it is queuing input, the Sort transformation is fully blocking.

Some transformations hold up the pipeline flow for shorter periods of time while they queue up and process data. These transformations are classified as *partially blocking*. The Merge Join transformation is an example of a partially blocking transformation. The Merge Join accepts two sorted rowsets as inputs; performs a full, left, or inner join of the two inputs; and then outputs the joined rowsets. As data passes through the Merge Join, previously buffered rows can be discarded from the input buffers. Because it has to queue up a limited number of rows from each rowset to perform the join, the Merge Join is a partially blocking component.

Nonblocking transformations don't hold up data flows. They transform and output rows as quickly as they are received. The Derived Column transformation is an example of a nonblocking transformation. Table 8-1 compares the properties of each class of blocking transformations.

Table 8-1. Transformation Blocking Types

Property	Fully Blocking	Semiblocking	Nonblocking
Communication pattern	Asynchronous	Asynchronous	Synchronous
Logical processing (general)	Full rowset	Subsets of rowset	Row level
# rows in must equal # rows out	No	No	Yes
Queues all input rows before processing	Yes	No	No
Can spawn new threads	Yes	Yes	No
Input buffer is output buffer	No	No	Yes
Input sort order preserved	No	No	Yes
Can rename/change data types of input columns	Yes	Yes	No

Row Transformations

Row transformations are generally the simplest and fastest type of transformation. They are synchronous (with the possible exception of some Script Component transformations) and operate on individual rows of data. This section presents the stock row transformations available in SSIS.

■ **NOTE:** We discuss the script component in detail in Chapter 10.

Data Conversion

A common task in ETL is converting data from one type to another. As an example, you may read in Unicode strings that you need to convert to a non-Unicode encoding, or you may need to convert numeric data to strings, and vice versa. This is what the Data Conversion transformation was designed for.

The Data Conversion transformation provides a simple way to convert the data type of your input columns. For our sample, we borrowed some data from the New York City Health Department. We took the data for selected restaurants that had dozens of health violations and saved it in an Excel spreadsheet. As you can see in Figure 8-4, we added a Data Conversion transformation immediately after the Excel source adapter.

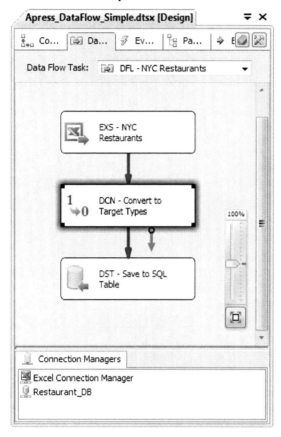

Figure 8-4. *Using the Data Conversion transformation on an Excel spreadsheet*

We're using the Data Conversion transformation in the data flow because the Excel Connection Manager understands only a handful of data types. For instance, it can read character data only as Unicode data with a length of either 255 characters or as a 2.1 GB character large object (LOB). In addition, numbers are recognized only as double-precision floating-point numbers, so you have to explicitly convert them to other data types.

The Data Conversion transformation creates copies of columns that you indicate for conversion to a new data type. The default name for each newly created column takes the form `Copy of <column name>`, but as you can see in Figure 8-5, you can rename the columns in the Output Alias field of the editor. The Data Type field of the editor lets you choose the target data type for the conversion. In this case, we chose to convert the Violation Points column to a signed integer (`DT_I4`) and Unicode string columns to non-Unicode strings of varying lengths.

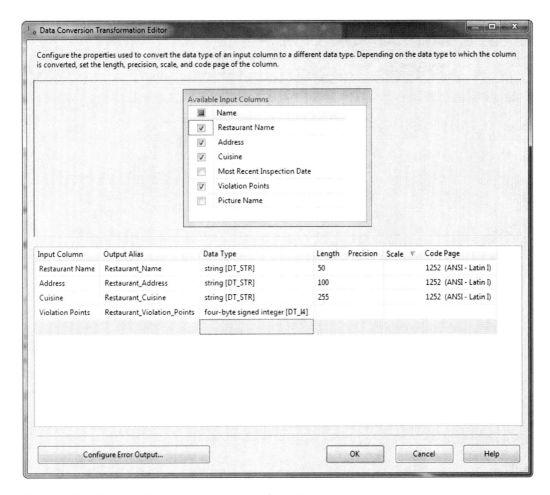

Figure 8-5. *Editing the Data Converstion transformation*

For purposes of data conversion especially, it's important to understand how SSIS data types map to your destination data types. Microsoft Books Online (BOL) documents mappings between SSIS data types and a handful of RDBMSs. We provide an abbreviated list of mappings of SSIS to SQL Server data types and additional conversion options in Table 8-2.

Table 8-2. Mapping SSIS Data Types to SQL Data Types

SSIS Data Type	SQL Type	Length	Precision	Scale	Code Page
Boolean [DT_BOOL]	bit	No	No	No	No
byte stream [DT_BYTES]	varbinary	Yes	No	No	No
currency [DT_CY]	money	No	No	No	No
database date [DT_DBDATE]	date	No	No	No	No
database time [DT_DBTIME]	time	No	No	No	No
database time with precision [DT_DBTIME2]	time	No	No	Yes	No
database timestamp [DT_DBTIMESTAMP]	datetime	No	No	No	No
database timestamp with precision [DT_DBTIMESTAMP2]	datetime2	No	No	Yes	No
database timestamp with timezone [DT_DBTIMESTAMPOFFSET]	datetimeoffset	No	No	Yes	No
date [DT_DATE]	date	No	No	No	No
decimal [DT_DECIMAL]	decimal	No	No	Yes	No
double-precision float [DT_R8]	float	No	No	No	No
eight-byte signed integer [DT_I8]	bigint	No	No	No	No
eight-byte unsigned integer [DT_UI8]	numeric	No	No	No	No
file timestamp [DT_FILETIME]	datetime	No	No	No	No
float [DT_R4]	real	No	No	No	No

SSIS Data Type	SQL Type	Length	Precision	Scale	Code Page
four-byte signed integer [DT_I4]	int	No	No	No	No
four-byte unsigned integer [DT_UI4]	numeric	No	No	No	No
image [DT_IMAGE]	varbinary(max)	No	No	No	No
numeric [DT_NUMERIC]	numeric	No	Yes	Yes	No
single-byte signed integer [DT_I1]	numeric	No	No	No	No
single-byte unsigned integer [DT_UI1]	tinyint	No	No	No	No
string [DT_STR]	varchar	Yes	No	No	Yes
text stream [DT_TEXT]	varchar(max)	Yes	No	No	Yes
two-byte signed integer [DT_I2]	smallint	No	No	No	No
two-byte unsigned integer [DT_UI2]	numeric	No	No	No	No
Unicode string [DT_WSTR]	nvarchar	Yes	No	No	No
Unicode text stream [DT_NTEXT]	nvarchar(max)	No	No	No	No
unique identifier [DT_GUID]	uniqueidentifier	No	No	No	No

Note that SSIS data types can be mapped to additional data types not indicated here, such as the byte stream [DT_BYTES] data type, which can be mapped to varbinary, binary, uniqueidentifier, geography, and geometry data types. Some of the SSIS data types, such as the SSIS-provided unsigned integers, are not natively supported by SQL Server, but we've provided approximations in this table for data types that can be used to store other data types in SQL Server.

■ **TIP:** The Derived Column transformation can perform the same task as the Data Conversion transformation, and more. In fact, you can think of Data Conversion as a convenience transformation that provides a subset of Derived Column functionality. Derived Column is far more flexible than Data Conversion but is a little more complex because you have to write your data type conversion using SSIS Expression Language cast operators. We discuss the Derived Column transformation later in this chapter and dig into the details of the SSIS Expression Language in Chapter 9.

Character Map

The Character Map transformation allows you to perform character operations on string columns. This example expands the previous one by adding a character map to change the case of the string columns, as shown in Figure 8-6.

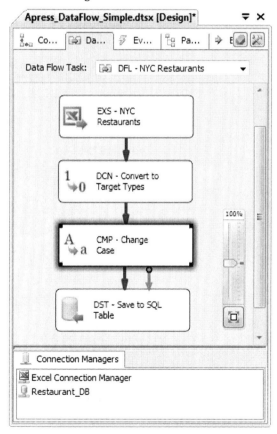

Figure 8-6. *Character Map transformation in the data flow*

■ **NOTE:** Like the Data Conversion transformation, some of the functionality (uppercase and lowercase options) in the Character Map transformation can be performed by using Derived Column instead. We'll look at Derived Column later in this chapter.

The Character Map transformation lets you apply string operations to inbound character data columns. For each selected column, you can choose one or more string operations to perform, such as converting a string to uppercase or lowercase. The Character Map Transformation Editor is relatively simple.

In this editor, you select the columns you wish to update. You then decide whether the result of the operation should be placed in a new column or just replace the value in the same column (*in-place change*). You can change the name of the output column by changing the value in the Output Alias field. Finally, in the Operation field, you can choose the types of transformations to apply to the selected columns. Figure 8-7 shows the transformation editor.

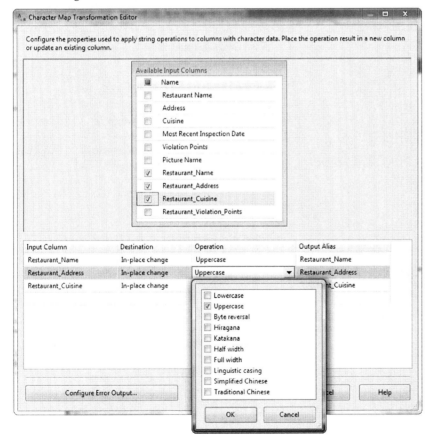

Figure 8-7. *Editing the Character Map transformation*

The Character Map transformation supports 10 string transformations you can perform on inbound data. You can choose more than one from the drop-down list to perform multiple transformations on an input column at once. In this example, we chose to use Uppercase selected string columns. The string operations you can choose from this transformation are listed in Table 8-3.

Table 8-3. *Character Map Transformation Operations*

Operation	Description
Byte Reversal	Reverses byte order of Unicode characters
Full Width	Changes single-byte characters to double-byte characters
Half Width	Changes double-byte characters to upper-byte characters
Hiragana	Maps Katakana characters to Hiragana characters
Katakana	Maps Hiragana characters to Katakana characters
Linguistic Casing	Applies linguistic casing rules; must be used in conjunction with Lowercase or Uppercase
Lowercase	Changes all characters to lowercase
Simplified Chinese	Maps Traditional Chinese characters to Simplified Chinese characters
Traditional Chinese	Maps Simplified Chinese characters to Traditional Chinese characters
Uppercase	Changes all characters to uppercase

Although you can choose more than one operation on a single column, some of these transformations are mutually exclusive, as shown in Table 8-4.

Table 8-4. *Mutually Exclusive Character Map Operations*

If you choose...	You can't also choose...
Full Width	Half Width, Lowercase, Uppercase
Half Width	Full Width, Lowercase, Uppercase
Hiragana	Katakana, Lowercase, Uppercase

If you choose...	You can't also choose...
Katakana	Hiragana, Lowercase, Uppercase
Linguistic Casing	Full Width, Half Width, Hiragana, Katakana, Simplified Chinese, Traditional Chinese, Byte Reversal
Lowercase	Uppercase, Hiragana, Katakana, Half Width, Full Width
Simplified Chinese	Traditional Chinese
Traditional Chinese	Simplified Chinese
Uppercase	Lowercase, Hiragana, Katakana, Half Width, Full Width

Copy Column

The Copy Column transformation creates copies of columns you designate. Figure 8-8 extends the example we've been working on to include a Copy Column transformation.

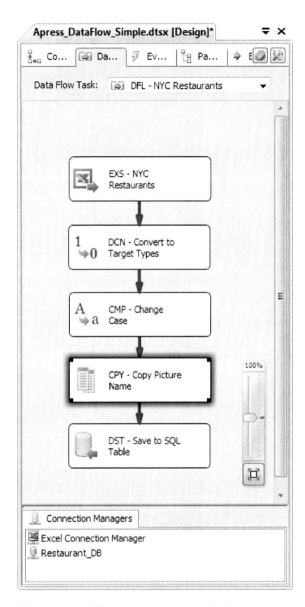

Figure 8-8. Adding Copy Column to the data flow

The editor for this transformation is simple: just check off the columns you want to copy. The duplicated columns are named `Copy of <column name>` by default. You can edit the Output Alias field to change this to a more meaningful name if you choose to. The Copy Column transformation we've added will create a copy of the `Picture Name` column, as you can see in Figure 8-9.

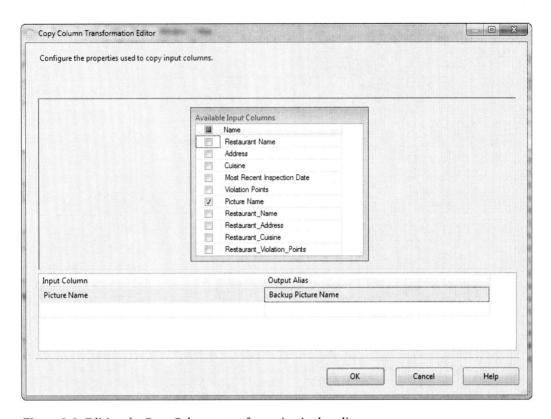

Figure 8-9. Editing the Copy Column transformation in the editor

Derived Column

The Derived Column transformation is one of the most widely used, and flexible, row transformations available in SSIS. This transformation lets you create new columns, or replace existing columns, with values calculated from expressions that you create with the SSIS Expression Language. The *SSIS Expression Language* sports a powerful and flexible syntax supporting mathematical operators and functions, data type conversions, conditional expressions, string manipulation, and null handling.

NOTE: We dive into the details of the SSIS Expression Language in Chapter 9.

To create a Derived Column transformation, we drag it from the toolbar and place it in the data flow between the source and destination. We'll build on the previous example by adding a Derived Column transformation, as shown in Figure 8-10.

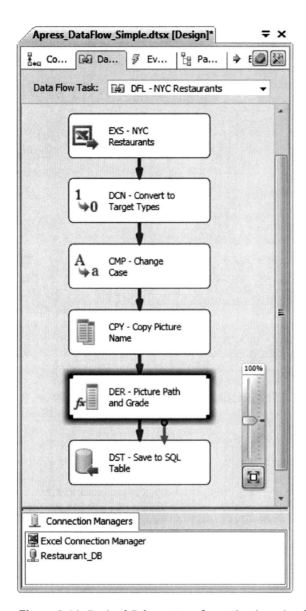

Figure 8-10. Derived Column transformation in a simple data flow

The Derived Column transformation lets us define expressions, the results of which will be added to the output in new columns (or will replace existing columns). Figure 8-11 shows the Derived Column Transformation Editor as it appears in this example.

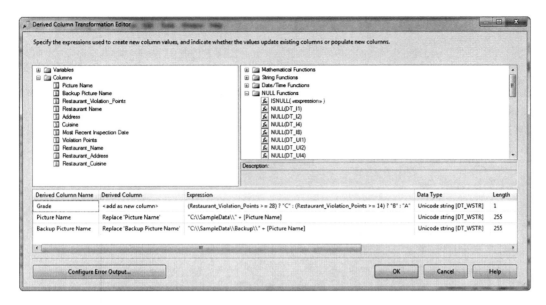

Figure 8-11. *Editing the Derived Column transformation*

As you can see in the transformation editor, two columns have their values replaced with the results of expressions. The new columns are populated with the results of expressions, which are written in the SSIS Expression Language. This powerful language lets you perform mathematical calculations and string manipulation on variables, columns, and constants. The expressions we used for the `Picture Name` and `Copy of Picture Name` columns look like this:

```
Picture Name → "C:\\SampleData\\" + [Picture Name]
```

```
Backup Picture Name → "C:\\SampleData\\Backup\\" + [Picture Name]
```

These expressions use the string concatenation feature of SSIS Expression Language to prepend a file path to the picture name passed into the transformation. SSIS Expression Language uses C#-style syntax, including escape characters, which is why we had to double up the backslashes (\) in the expressions. The result is two full paths to files in the file system. Although these expressions are fairly simple and straightforward, we implemented a more complex derived column that calculates a letter grade based on the NYC Health Department grading scale. The result is stored in a new column that is added to the data flow, called `Grade`:

```
Grade → (Restaurant_Violation_Points >= 28)?"C":(Restaurant_Violation_Points >= 14)?"B":"A"
```

This expression uses the *conditional operator* (`?:`) to assign a grade to each restaurant based on the NYC Health Department grading scale. This scale assigns a grade of A to restaurants with 0 to 13 violation points, B to restaurants with 14 to 27 violation points, and C to restaurants with 28+ points. The conditional operators in this example model those rules exactly.

As you read the expression from left to right, you'll notice the first Boolean expression (`Restaurant_Violation_Points >= 28`), which returns `True` or `False`. If the result is true, the conditional operator returns the value after the question mark (C, in this case). If the result is false, the second

261

Boolean expression, (`Restaurant_Violation_Points >= 14`), is evaluated. If it returns `True`, B is returned; if `False`, A is returned.

■ **NOTE:** The SSIS Expression Language is a powerful feature of SSIS. If you're not familiar with the functions and operators we've used in this example, don't fret. We cover these and more in a detailed discussion of the SSIS Expression Language in Chapter 9.

Import Column

The Import Column transformation provides a way to enrich your rows in the data flow with LOB data from the file system. Import Column allows you to add image, binary, and text files to your data. We added an Import Column transformation to the data flow in Figure 8-12 to import images of restaurants on this list.

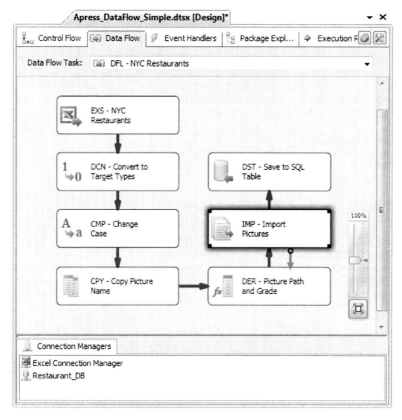

Figure 8-12. Import Column transformation in the data flow

The Import Column transformation is useful when you need to tie LOB data to rows of other data and store both in the database together. One caveat though—this transformation has one of the more arcane editors of any transformation. The first step to configuring Import Column is to select a string column on the Input Columns tab. We selected the `Picture Name` column that we previously populated with a full path to each image coming through the data flow (in the Derived Column transformation). You can see this in Figure 8-13.

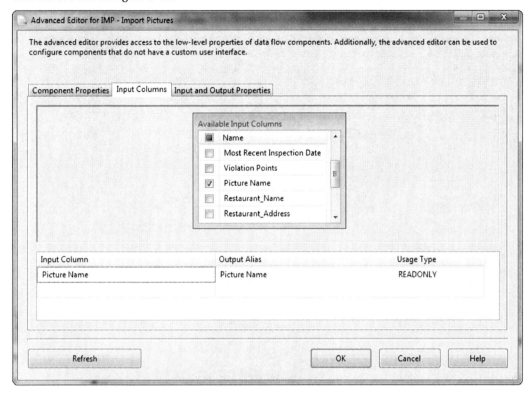

Figure 8-13. *Choosing the input column that points to the file to be imported*

The input column you choose in the first step tells the Import Column transformation which file to import into the data flow. As in our example, the task should contain a full path to the file.

The next step to configure this transformation is to add an output column to the Input and Output Properties. This column will hold the contents of the file after the Import Column reads it in. The following are appropriate data types for this new output column:

- `image [DT_IMAGE]` for binary data such as images, word processing files, or spreadsheets

- `text stream [DT_TEXT]` for text data such as ASCII text files

- `Unicode text stream [DT_NTEXT]` for Unicode text data such as Unicode text files and UTF-16 encoded XML files

One of the more arcane aspects of Import Column is the configuration of the input column on the Input and Output Properties tab. To configure the input column, grab a pen and paper (yes, a pen and paper!) and write down the number you see next to the ID property for your output column. In our example, the number is *201*.

Then edit the input column on the same tab. Scroll to the bottom of the page and type the number you just wrote down into the `FileDataColumnID` property. If you're loading Unicode data, you can set the `ExpectBOM` property to `True` if your data has a byte order mark (BOM), or `False` if it doesn't. This is shown in Figure 8-14.

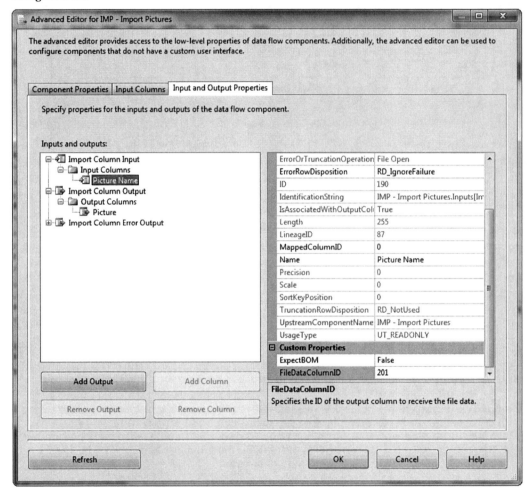

Figure 8-14. *Finishing up configuration of the Import Column transformation*

Finally, if you expect your input column to have nulls in it, you may want to change the `ErrorRowDisposition` property from the default `RD_FailComponent` to `RD_IgnoreFailure` or `RD_RedirectRow`. If `RD_IgnoreFailure` or `RD_RedirectRow` is set, the component will not throw an exception if it hits a null. Unfortunately, there's no way for this component to handle nulls separately from actual file paths that don't exist (you can handle this separately with additional data flow components if you want). The end result of properly configuring Import Column is that the data contained in the image files referenced by the input column are added to the data flow's new output column.

HANDLING ERROR ROWS

Data Flow transformations in SSIS give you considerable flexibility in handling error rows. Many of the components give you granular error handling, allowing you to choose different error handling for different types of exceptions that can occur. In some components, for instance, you can handle truncation differently from other errors.

The Import Column transformation error has less-granular error handling—rows either error out (for any reason) or they don't. Regardless of the error-handling granularity of the transformation you're using, you will have a few options for dealing with error rows:

- RD_FailComponent causes the component to fail when an error is encountered; this is the default error handling for most transformations.

- RD_IgnoreFailure simply ignores errors as they occur.

- RD_RedirectRow redirects error-causing rows to the error output of a component.

In other components with less-arcane interfaces, you'll see these same choices in their editors, but with friendlier names. In these components, you'll see the options listed as *Ignore Failure*, *Redirect Row*, and *Fail Component*. These choices are equivalent to the RD_ options in the preceding list.

OLE DB Command

The OLE DB Command transformation is an interesting row transformation that executes a SQL statement for each and every row that passes through the transformation. Most often, you'll see the OLE DB Command transformation used to issue update statements against individual rows, primarily because SSIS doesn't yet have a Merge Destination that will do the job for you in a bulk update.

▩ **NOTE:** The OLE DB Command transformation uses a processing model known as Row by Agonizing Row, or RBAR (a term popularized by SQL guru and Microsoft MVP Jeff Moden). In terms of SQL, this is not considered a best practice for large sets of data.

To demonstrate, we set up a data flow that reads an Excel spreadsheet containing updates to the restaurant information we loaded earlier and then applies the updates to the database. Figure 8-15 shows OLE DB Command in the data flow.

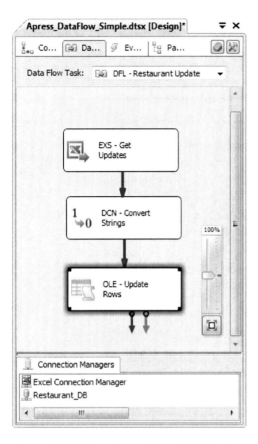

Figure 8-15. *Data flow with an OLE DB Command transformation*

All changes to the OLE DB Command transformation are made in an Advanced Editor window with four tabs. The Connection Managers tab lets you choose the OLE DB Connection Manager the transformation will issue SQL statements against. In Figure 8-16, the `Restaurant_DB` connection manager is selected.

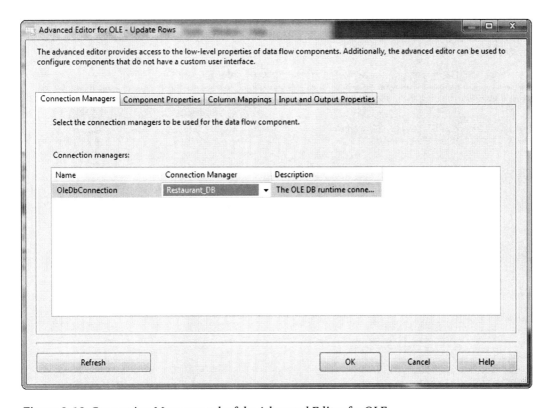

Figure 8-16. *Connection Managers tab of the Advanced Editor for OLE*

The Component Properties tab lets you set the `SqlCommand` property of the OLE DB Command transformation. The `SqlCommand` property holds the SQL statement you want executed against each row passing through the transformation. You can edit the `SqlCommand` property with the String Value Editor dialog box, accessed from the Component Properties tab, as shown in Figure 8-17. In this instance, we've set it to a simple parameterized UPDATE statement.

PARAMETERIZED SQL STATEMENTS

Parameterization allows you to dynamically replace values in your SQL statements. When you parameterize SQL, the statement and parameter values are sent to the server separately. The server dynamically substitutes the parameterized values in the SQL statement at execution time. Parameterized SQL is safer than building SQL statements by concatenating strings, which can leave your code susceptible to SQL injection attacks. Parameterized SQL can also provide performance benefits due to cached query plan reuse.

The OLE DB providers, in particular, use a question mark (?) as a parameter placeholder (some other providers use different parameter placeholders). In our example, we used the following parameterized SQL statement:

```
UPDATE dbo.Restaurant
SET Restaurant_Address = ?
WHERE Restaurant_Name = ?;
```

SQL Server substitutes the parameter markers with actual values at execution time.

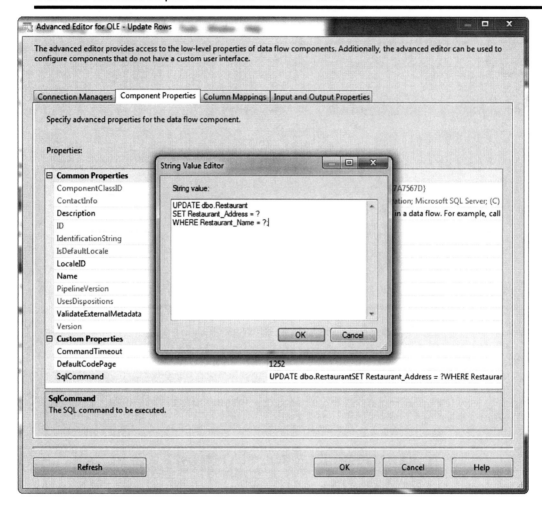

***Figure 8-17.** Component Properties tab of the Advanced Editor for OLE*

The Column Mappings tab of the editor lets you map the OLE DB Command's inbound columns to the parameters in your SQL statement. Because the OLE DB Command uses the question mark as a placeholder for parameters, the parameters are considered *positional*—that is, they can be referenced by their numeric position beginning at zero. Figure 8-18 shows that we mapped the `Address String` column to `Param_0`, and the `Restaurant Name String` column to `Param_1`.

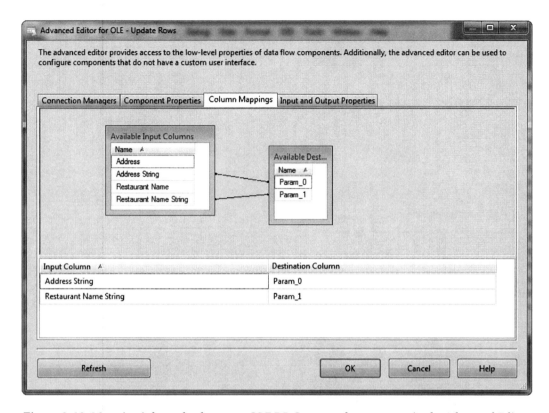

Figure 8-18. Mapping inbound columns to OLE DB Command parameters in the Advanced Editor

The OLE DB Command is useful for some very specific situations you may encounter. However, the performance can be lacking, especially for large datasets (thousands of rows or more). We recommend using set-based solutions instead of the OLE DB Command transformation when possible, and minimizing the number of rows you send through OLE DB Command when you do have to use it.

Export Column

The Export Column transformation performs the opposite function of the Import Column transformation. Export Column allows you to extract LOB data from your data flow and save it to files in the file system. Figure 8-19 shows the Export Column transformation in the data flow.

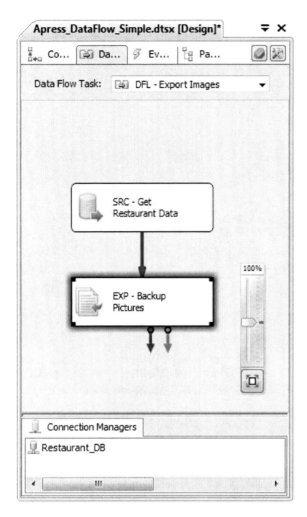

Figure 8-19. *The Export Column transformation in the data flow*

Though the Import Column and Export Column transformations are a matched pair, Export Column is much simpler to configure. The Export Column editor allows you to choose the column containing your LOB data with the `Extract Column` property and the destination file path in the `File Path Column` property. You can also choose from three check box properties: `Allow Append` will append your LOB data to the output file if the target file already exists, `Force Truncate` clears the target file before it starts writing data (if the file already exists), and `Write Byte-Order Mark` outputs a BOM to the output file, which can be important in situations when your LOB data consists of Unicode character data. Figure 8-20 shows the Export Column Transformation Editor.

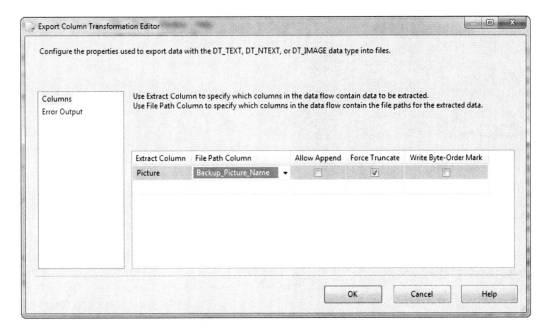

Figure 8-20. Configuring the Export Column transformation

Script Component

The script component lets you use your .NET programming skills to easily create SSIS components to fulfill requirements that are outside the bounds of the stock components. The script component excels at performing the types of transformations that other SSIS stock components do not perform.

With the script component, you can perform simple transformations such as counting rows in the data flow or extremely complex transformations such as calculating cryptographic one-way hashes and performing complex aggregations. The script component supports both synchronous and asynchronous modes, and it can be used as a source, destination, or in-flow transformation.

In this introduction, we'll demonstrate a simple row counting, as illustrated in Figure 8-21.

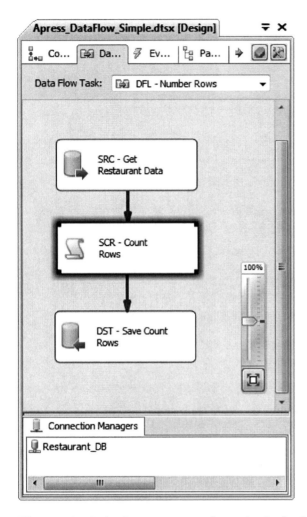

Figure 8-21. *Script Component transformation in the data flow*

In this example, we've used the script component to create a simple synchronous transformation that adds an increasing row number to each of the rows passed through it. To create this transformation, we dragged and dropped the script component from the SSIS Toolbox to the designer surface. It immediately prompted us for the type of component to create, as shown in Figure 8-22.

Figure 8-22. Choosing the type of script component to create

For this sample, we're creating a simple synchronous transformation, so we chose the Transformation script component type. After the script component has been added to the data flow, we configured it through the Script Transformation Editor. We went to the Input Columns page first. On this page, you can choose the input columns, those columns that are accessible from within the script component. You can also indicate whether a column is read-only or read/write, as displayed in Figure 8-23.

▨ **TIP:** Chapter 10 covers how to create sources and destinations, as well as more-complex transformations, with the script component.

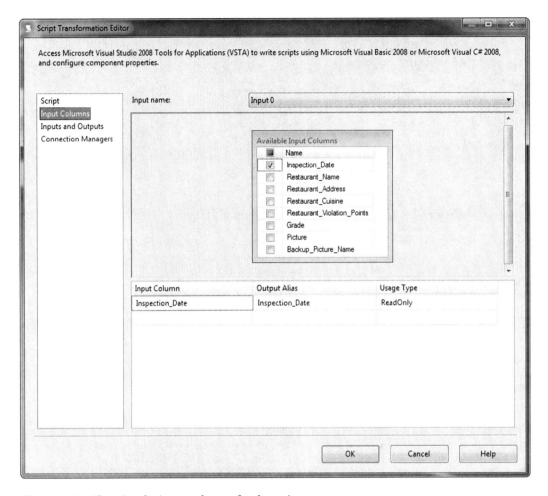

Figure 8-23. *Choosing the input columns for the script component*

Next we added a column to the component's Output Columns collection on the Inputs and Outputs page of the editor. We called the column RowNumber and made it a four-byte signed integer [DT_I4], as shown in Figure 8-24.

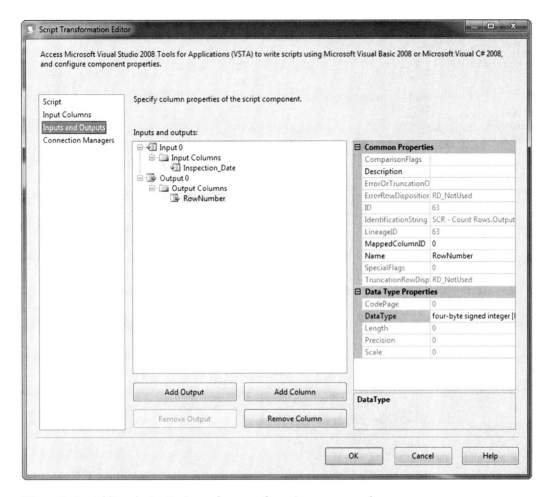

Figure 8-24. *Adding the* `RowNumber` *column to the script component's output*

As we mentioned, this component will be a simple synchronous script component. Script components are synchronous. by default. Whether or not a script component is synchronous is determined by the `SynchronousInputID` property on the output column collection of the Inputs and Outputs page. When this property is set to the name of an input column collection, as shown in Figure 8-25, the component is synchronous. If you set this property to `None`, the component is asynchronous. In this case, we set this property to the name of the input column collection, `SCR - Count Rows.Inputs[Input 0]`.

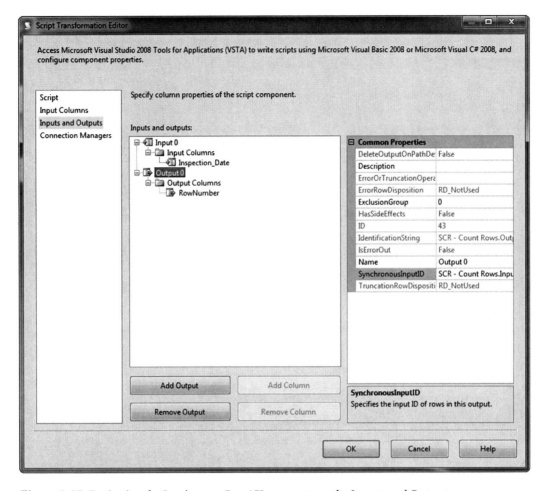

Figure 8-25. *Reviewing the SynchronousInputID property on the Inputs and Outputs page*

Next we went to the Script page to edit the script. On this page, you can set the ScriptLanguage property to Microsoft Visual Basic 2008 or Microsoft Visual C# 2008. As you can see in Figure 8-26, we chose C# as our scripting language of choice. On the Script page, you can also choose any variables you want the script to access through the ReadOnlyVariables and ReadWriteVariables collections. We don't use variables in this example, but we discuss them in detail in Chapter 9.

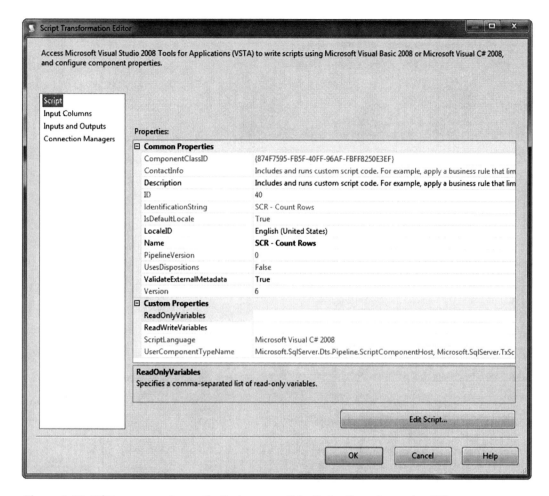

Figure 8-26. *Editing properties on the Script page of the Script Transformation Editor*

After we selected our scripting language, we edited the .NET script by clicking the Edit Scrip button. This pulls up the Visual Studio Tools for Applications (VSTA) Editor with a template for a basic synchronous script component, as shown in Figure 8-27.

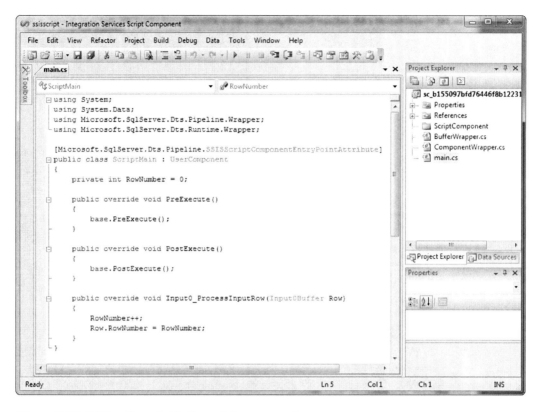

Figure 8-27. Editing the script in the script component

All script components have a default class named ScriptMain, which inherits from the UserComponent class, which in turn inherits from the Microsoft.SqlServer.Dts.Pipeline.ScriptComponent class. The UserComponent class requires you to override three of its methods to implement a synchronous script component:

- The PreExecute() method executes any setup code, such as variable initialization, before the component begins processing rows of data. PreExecute() is called exactly once when the component is first initialized. In this instance, we didn't have any custom pre-execution code to run, so we just called the base.PreExecute() method to perform any standard pre-execution code in the base class.

- The PostExecute() method executes any cleanup code, such as disposing of objects and assigning final values to SSIS variables, after the component has finished processing all rows of data. PostExecute() is called exactly once when the component has finished processing all data rows. Our sample didn't require any custom post-execution code to run, so we called the base.PostExecute() method to perform any standard post-execution code in the base class.

- The `Input0_ProcessInputRow()` method is the workhorse of the script component. This method is called once per input row. It accepts an `InputOBuffer` parameter with the contents of the current row in it. With this `InputOBuffer` parameter, you can read and write values of input fields. In our example, we increment the `RowNumber` variable with each call to the method and assign its value to the `RowNumber` field of the `InputOBuffer`.

The result is a new column added to the data flow called `RowNumber`, which contains an incremental number for each row in the data flow. You can view the data in the data flow by adding a data viewer to the script component output. To do this, right-click the green arrow coming out of the script component and choose the Enable Data Viewer option from the context menu, as shown in Figure 8-28.

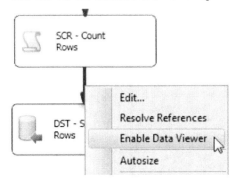

Figure 8-28. Enabling the data viewer on the script component output

After you've added the data viewer to the output path, you'll see a magnifying glass icon appear on the output arrow, as shown in Figure 8-29.

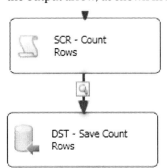

Figure 8-29. Data viewer magnifying glass icon on output path

When you run the package, the data viewer will appear in a pop-up window with a grid containing data from the data flow. The data viewer holds up the data flow, so rows will not move on to the next step until you either click the arrow button or Detach. Clicking the arrow button allows another set of rows to pass through, after which it will pause the data flow again. The Detach button detaches the data viewer from the data flow, causing the data viewer to stop collecting and displaying new rows and allowing all rows to pass through. The results of placing the data viewer in our example package are shown in Figure 8-30.

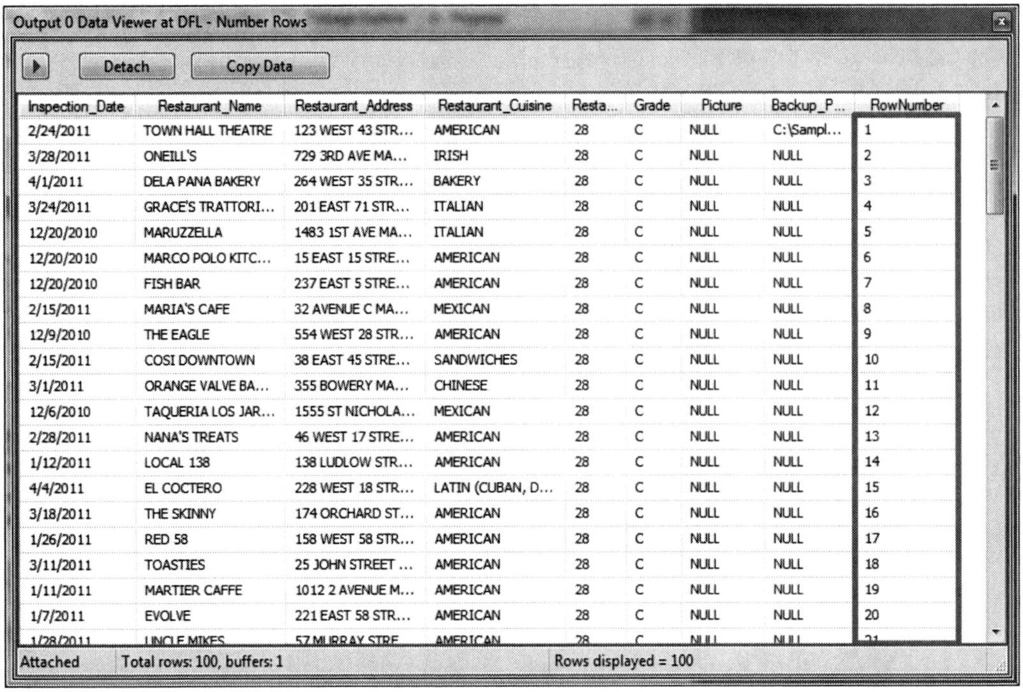

Inspection_Date	Restaurant_Name	Restaurant_Address	Restaurant_Cuisine	Resta...	Grade	Picture	Backup_P...	RowNumber
2/24/2011	TOWN HALL THEATRE	123 WEST 43 STR...	AMERICAN	28	C	NULL	C:\Sampl...	1
3/28/2011	ONEILL'S	729 3RD AVE MA...	IRISH	28	C	NULL	NULL	2
4/1/2011	DELA PANA BAKERY	264 WEST 35 STR...	BAKERY	28	C	NULL	NULL	3
3/24/2011	GRACE'S TRATTORI...	201 EAST 71 STR...	ITALIAN	28	C	NULL	NULL	4
12/20/2010	MARUZZELLA	1483 1ST AVE MA...	ITALIAN	28	C	NULL	NULL	5
12/20/2010	MARCO POLO KITC...	15 EAST 15 STRE...	AMERICAN	28	C	NULL	NULL	6
12/20/2010	FISH BAR	237 EAST 5 STRE...	AMERICAN	28	C	NULL	NULL	7
2/15/2011	MARIA'S CAFE	32 AVENUE C MA...	MEXICAN	28	C	NULL	NULL	8
12/9/2010	THE EAGLE	554 WEST 28 STR...	AMERICAN	28	C	NULL	NULL	9
2/15/2011	COSI DOWNTOWN	38 EAST 45 STRE...	SANDWICHES	28	C	NULL	NULL	10
3/1/2011	ORANGE VALVE BA...	355 BOWERY MA...	CHINESE	28	C	NULL	NULL	11
12/6/2010	TAQUERIA LOS JAR...	1555 ST NICHOLA...	MEXICAN	28	C	NULL	NULL	12
2/28/2011	NANA'S TREATS	46 WEST 17 STRE...	AMERICAN	28	C	NULL	NULL	13
1/12/2011	LOCAL 138	138 LUDLOW STR...	AMERICAN	28	C	NULL	NULL	14
4/4/2011	EL COCTERO	228 WEST 18 STR...	LATIN (CUBAN, D...	28	C	NULL	NULL	15
3/18/2011	THE SKINNY	174 ORCHARD ST...	AMERICAN	28	C	NULL	NULL	16
1/26/2011	RED 58	158 WEST 58 STR...	AMERICAN	28	C	NULL	NULL	17
3/11/2011	TOASTIES	25 JOHN STREET ...	AMERICAN	28	C	NULL	NULL	18
1/11/2011	MARTIER CAFFE	1012 2 AVENUE M...	AMERICAN	28	C	NULL	NULL	19
1/7/2011	EVOLVE	221 EAST 58 STR...	AMERICAN	28	C	NULL	NULL	20
1/28/2011	UNCLE MIKES	57 MURRAY STRE...	AMERICAN	28	C	NULL	NULL	21

Attached   Total rows: 100, buffers: 1   Rows displayed = 100

Figure 8-30. Looking at data in the data viewer

The data viewer is a very handy data-debugging tool, and one you'll probably want to become familiar with—you'll undoubtedly find yourself using it often to troubleshoot data flow issues and data errors.

■ **NOTE:** Previous versions of SSIS included four types of data viewer—the Grid, Histogram, Scatterplot, and Column Chart data viewers. Because the Grid data viewer is the most commonly used, the SSIS team removed the other types of data viewers from SSIS 11.

Rowset Transformations

Rowset transformations generate new rowsets from their input. The Rowset transformations are asynchronous, and the number of rows in the input is often not the same as the number of rows in the output. Also the "shape" of the output rowsets might not be the same as the shape of the input rowsets.

The Pivot transformation—which we discuss later in this section—turns the input rowset on its side, for instance.

Aggregate

The Aggregate transformation performs two main tasks: (1) it can apply aggregate functions to your input data and (2) it allows you to group your data based on values in your input columns. Basically, it performs a function similar to the T-SQL aggregate functions (for example, MIN, MAX, COUNT) and the GROUP BY clause.

In the sample package shown in Figure 8-31, we are importing sample aviation incident data from the National Transportation Safety Board and perform two aggregations on the inbound data, each represented in the data flow by a different output from the Aggregate transformation.

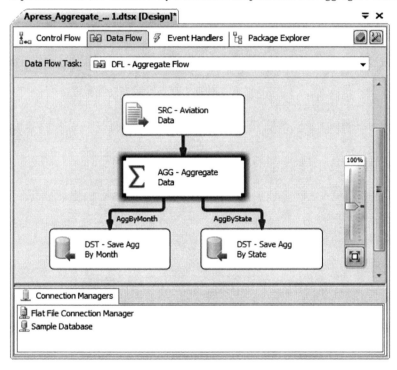

Figure 8-31. *Sample package with Aggregate transformation*

The Aggregate transformation can be configured in Basic mode or Advanced mode. In Basic mode, the transformation has one output; in Advanced mode, it can have more than one output, each containing the result of a different aggregation. In this example, we have configured two aggregations:

- The first aggregation is called AggByMonth. This aggregation sums the injury count fields in the input, and groups by EventYear and EventMonth.

- The second aggregation is called AggByState. This aggregation sums the injury count fields, grouping by State, EventYear, and EventMonth.

Figure 8-32 shows the Aggregate Transformation Editor.

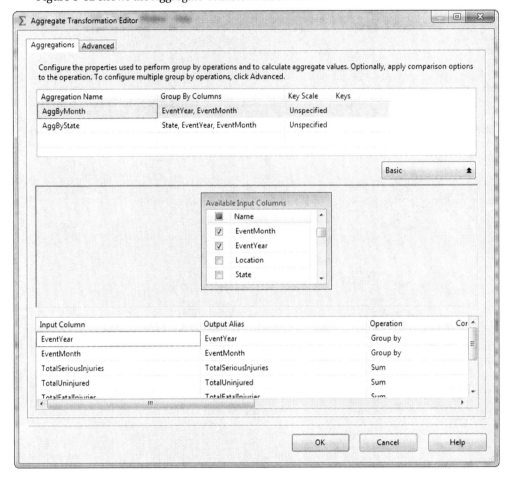

Figure 8-32. *Editing the Aggregate transformation in Advanced mode*

The Advanced/Basic button reveals or hides the multiple aggregation configuration box at the top of the editor. You can choose columns from the input column list and select the operations to perform on those columns in the lower portion of the editor. The operations you can choose include the following:

Group By groups results based on this column, just like the GROUP BY clause in SQL SELECT queries.

Count returns the count of values in this column. Nlls are included in the count if you select (*) as the input column. Otherwise, nulls are ignored. This operation is equivalent to the SQL COUNT aggregate function.

Count Distinct returns the count of distinct values in this column. Equivalent to the SQL COUNT(DISTINCT ...) aggregate function.

Sum returns the sum of the values in this column. Equivalent to the SQL SUM aggregate function.

Average returns the average of the values in the selected column. Equivalent to the SQL AVG aggregate function.

Minimum returns the minimum of values from the column. Equivalent to the SQL MIN aggregate function.

Maximum returns the maximum of values from the column. Equivalent to the SQL MAX aggregate function.

The Group By, Count, and Count Distinct operations can be performed on numeric or string data. The Sum, Average, Minimum, and Maximum operations can be performed on only numeric data.

■ **TIP:** The Aggregate transformation does not require inbound data to be sorted.

Sort

The Sort transformation sorts inbound rows based on the values from columns that you select in the designer. There are several reasons you may need to sort your input data in the data flow, including the following:

- Some transformations, such as Merge Join presented later in this chapter, require input data to be sorted.

- Under some circumstances, you can achieve better performance when saving data to a relational database when the data is presorted.

- In some instances, data needs to be processed in a specific order, or sorted before being handed off to another data flow or ETL process.

In any of these instances, you'll need to sort your data prior to passing it on, as shown in Figure 8-33.

■ **TIP:** Because Sort is a fully blocking asynchronous transformation, it will hold up the data flow until it has completed the sort operation. It's a good idea to sort data at the source when possible. If you're pulling data from a relational database, consider putting an ORDER BY clause on your query to guarantee order, for instance. If the order of your input is not guaranteed—for instance, when you pull data from a flat file or perform transformations on your data that could change the order of your data in the data flow, the Sort transformation may be the best option. If your data is not indexed on the sort columns in SQL Server, an ORDER BY clause might use a lot of server-side resources. If, however, your data is indexed, the SSIS Sort transformation will not be able to take advantage of the index.

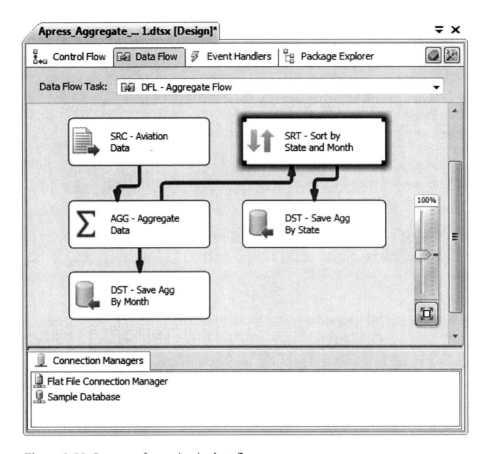

Figure 8-33. Sort transformation in data flow

The Sort transformation offers several options applicable to sorting. In the Sort editor, you can choose the columns that you want to sort by, and choose the Sort Type (ascending or descending options) and Sort Order for each column. The Sort Order indicates the order of the columns in the sort operation. In our example, we're sorting by the `State` column, and then by `EventYear` and `EventMonth`.

The Comparison Flags option provides several sort-related options for character data, such as ignoring case and symbols during the sort process. In our example, we chose to ignore case on the `State` column when sorting the inbound data. You can also choose to remove rows with duplicate sort values. Figure 8-34 shows the Sort Transformation Editor.

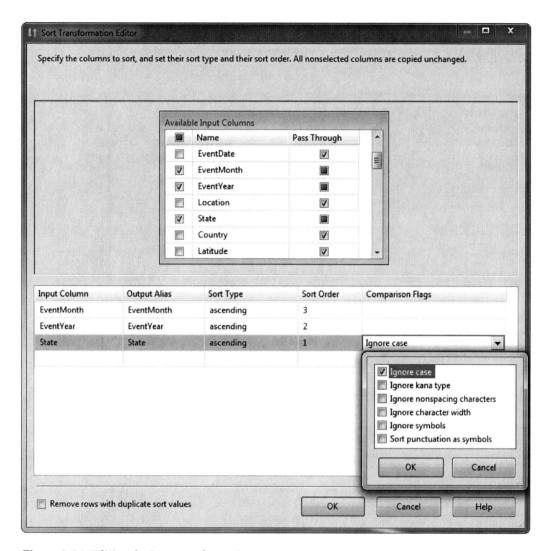

Figure 8-34. *Editing the Sort transformation*

THE ISSORTED PROPERTY

One of the features of note in the Sort transformation is exposed in the Advanced Editor, via the Input and Output Properties. The `IsSorted` property is automatically set by the Sort transformation, as you can see in Figure 8-35.

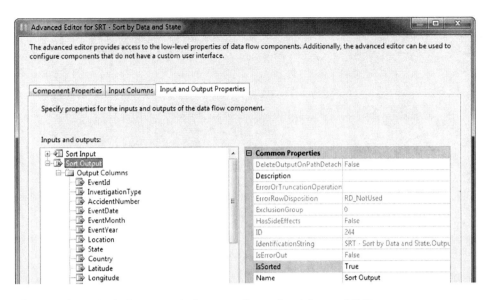

Figure 8-35. IsSorted property in Sort transformation Advanced Editor

This property is checked by transformations that require sorted input, such as Merge Join covered later in this chapter. If it's not set to True on an output further up the data flow, the transformation requiring sorted input will complain about it.

Closely related to the IsSorted output property is the column-level SortKeyPosition property, which is shown in Figure 8-36.

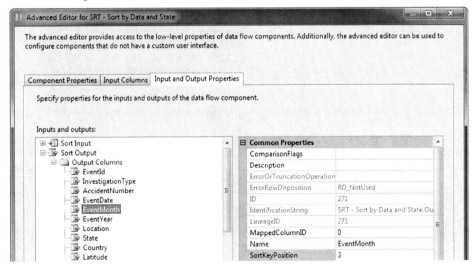

Figure 8-36. SortKeyPosition property in the Advanced Editor

For the Sort transformation, the `SortKeyPosition` can be set through the Basic Editor. If you presort your inbound data, as with an `ORDER BY` clause in a source query, you'll have to set these properties on the source adapter manually.

Pivot

The Pivot transformation allows you to perform a pivot operation on your input data. A pivot operation means you take your data and "turn it sideways," essentially turning values from a column into columns in the result set. As shown in Figure 8-37, we added a Pivot transformation to the data flow to denormalize our aggregated aviation data, creating columns with month names.

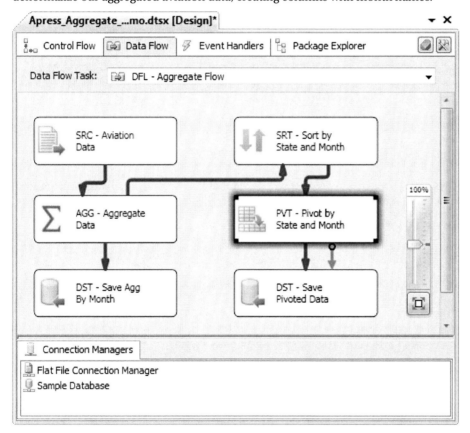

Figure 8-37. *Adding a Pivot transformation to pivot aggregated aviation data*

This Pivot transformation takes the individual rows of input and pivots them based on the `EventMonth`. The pivot operation turns the months into columns, as shown in Figure 8-38.

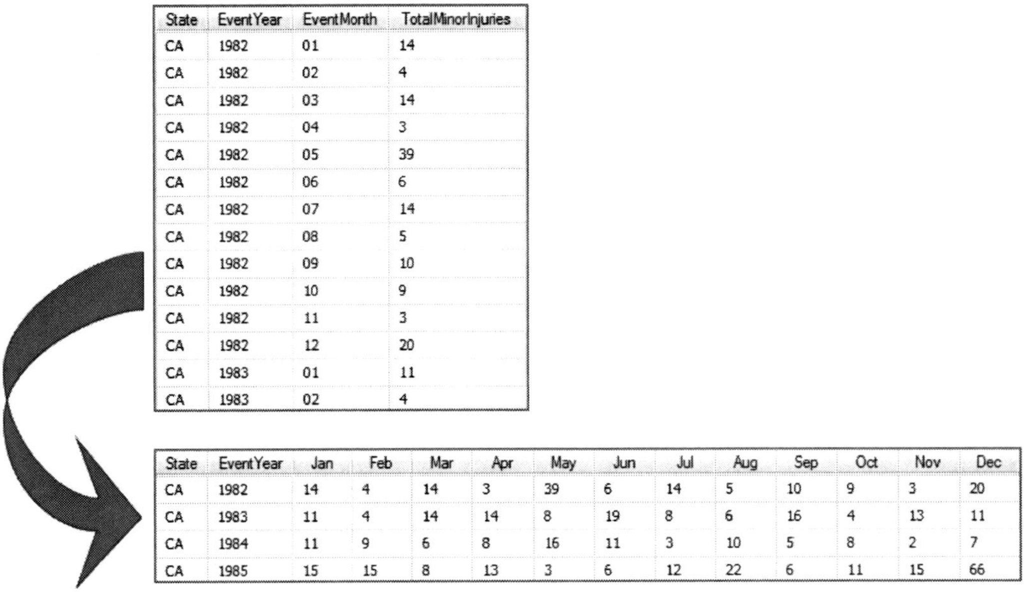

State	EventYear	EventMonth	TotalMinorInjuries
CA	1982	01	14
CA	1982	02	4
CA	1982	03	14
CA	1982	04	3
CA	1982	05	39
CA	1982	06	6
CA	1982	07	14
CA	1982	08	5
CA	1982	09	10
CA	1982	10	9
CA	1982	11	3
CA	1982	12	20
CA	1983	01	11
CA	1983	02	4

State	EventYear	Jan	Feb	Mar	Apr	May	Jun	Jul	Aug	Sep	Oct	Nov	Dec
CA	1982	14	4	14	3	39	6	14	5	10	9	3	20
CA	1983	11	4	14	14	8	19	8	6	16	4	13	11
CA	1984	11	9	6	8	16	11	3	10	5	8	2	7
CA	1985	15	15	8	13	3	6	12	22	6	11	15	66

Figure 8-38. Result of Pivot transformation

In previous releases of SSIS, the Pivot Transformation Editor was difficult to work with—a situation that has been corrected in this new release. The newly redesigned Pivot Transformation Editor is shown in Figure 8-39.

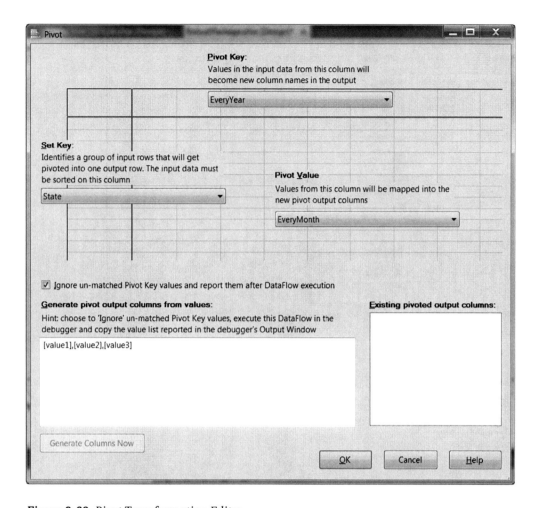

Figure 8-39. *Pivot Transformation Editor*

■ **NOTE:** The Pivot transformation requires input data to be sorted, or incorrect results may be produced. Unlike other transformations that require sorted input data, Pivot doesn't enforce this requirement. Make sure your input to Pivot is sorted.

Percentage Sampling

The Percentage Sampling transformation selects a given percentage of sampled rows from the input to generate a sample dataset. This transformation actually splits your input data into two separate datasets—one representing the selected sampling of rows and another containing the rows from your dataset that were not selected for sampling. Figure 8-40 demonstrates a simple data flow that samples rows from the aviation flat file we've used in the examples in this section.

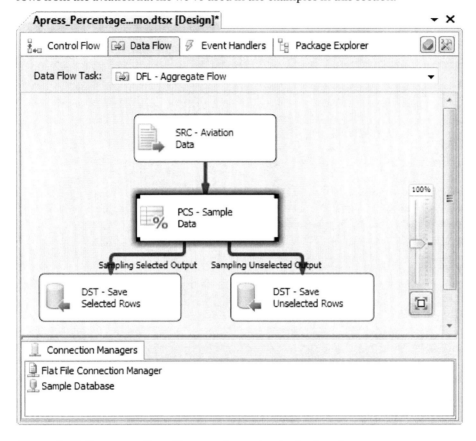

Figure 8-40. *Percentage Sampling transformation in the data flow*

As you can see in the data flow, the Percentage Sampling transformation splits your inbound dataset into two separate outputs:

> **Sampling Selected Output** contains all the rows selected by the component for the sample set
>
> **Sampling Unselected Output** contains the remaining rows that were not selected by the component for the sample set

The Percentage Sampling Transformation Editor makes it very easy to edit this transformation. Simply select the Percentage of Rows you wish to sample (the default is 10%), and change the names of the outputs if you want to. You can also set the random seed for the transformation. If you do not set the random seed, the component uses the operating system tick counter to randomly seed a selection of sample rows from your input data, so the sample dataset will change during each run. If you do set a random seed, the same sample dataset is generated each time (assuming the source data does not change between runs, of course). Figure 8-41 shows the Percentage Sampling Transformation Editor.

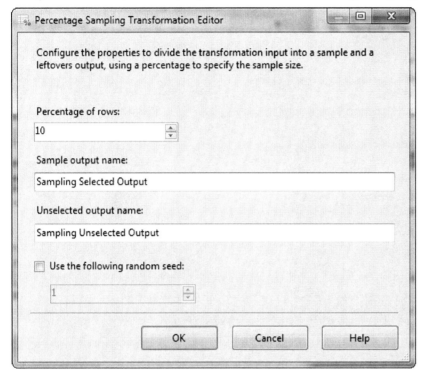

Figure 8-41. *Editing the Percentage Sampling transformation*

Percentage Sampling is useful when you want to train and test data-mining models, or if you want to efficiently test your ETL processes with a representative sample of input data.

▪ **TIP:** The Percentage Sampling Transformation Editor allows you to choose the percentage of rows to include in your sample, but keep in mind that because of the sampling algorithm used by SSIS, your sample dataset may be slightly larger or smaller than this percentage. This transformation is similar to the T-SQL TABLESAMPLE with PERCENT option.

Row Sampling

The Row Sampling transformation is similar to the Percentage Sampling transformation, except that you choose the number of rows to sample instead of the percentage of rows to sample. Figure 8-42 shows the Row Sampling transformation in the data flow.

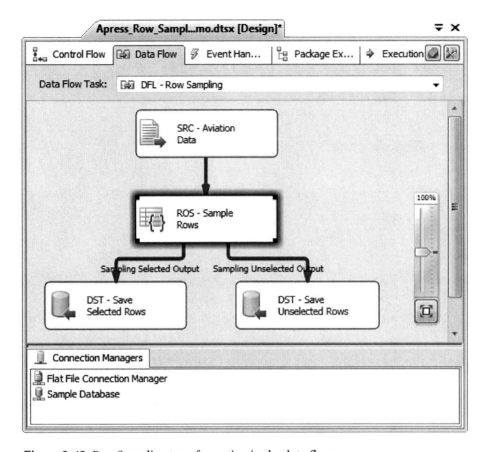

Figure 8-42. Row Sampling transformation in the data flow

The Row Sampling Transformation Editor, shown in Figure 8-43, is very similar to the Percentage Sampling editor. The only real difference is that with Row Sampling, you choose a number of rows instead of a percentage of rows to sample.

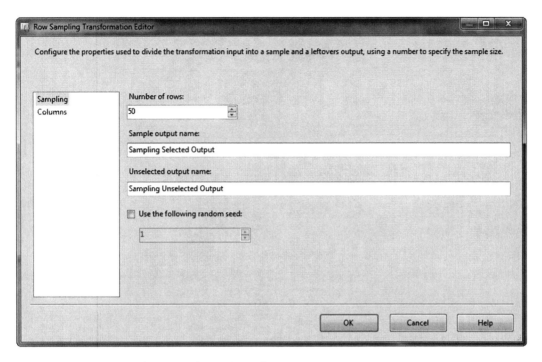

Figure 8-43. *Row Sampling Transformation Editor*

There is a slight behavior difference between the Percentage Sampling and Row Sampling transformations. With Percentage Sampling, you may end up with a sample set that is slightly larger or smaller than the percentage sample size you've requested. With Row Sampling, however, you'll get exactly the number of rows you request, assuming you request a sample size that is less than the number of rows in the input dataset. If your sample size is equal to (or greater than) the number of rows in your input dataset, all rows are selected in the sample. The Row Sampling transformation is similar in functionality to the T-SQL `TABLESAMPLE` clause with `ROWS` option.

Unpivot

The Unpivot transformation normalizes denormalized datasets. This transformation takes selected columns from an input dataset and unpivots them into more-normalized rows. Taking the example of denormalized aviation data we used in the Pivot transformation example, we can Unpivot it back into a more normalized version, as shown in Figure 8-44.

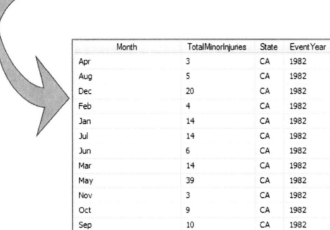

State	EventYear	Jan	Feb	Mar	Apr	May	Jun	Jul	Aug	Sep	Oct	Nov	Dec
CA	1982	14	4	14	3	39	6	14	5	10	9	3	20
CA	1983	11	4	14	14	8	19	8	6	16	4	13	11
CA	1984	11	9	6	8	16	11	3	10	5	8	2	7
CA	1985	15	15	8	13	3	6	12	22	6	11	15	66
CA	1986	6	0	8	5	11	8	6	25	3	7	7	7
CA	1987	11	19	4	15	19	9	5	7	8	6	9	1

Month	TotalMinorInjuries	State	EventYear
Apr	3	CA	1982
Aug	5	CA	1982
Dec	20	CA	1982
Feb	4	CA	1982
Jan	14	CA	1982
Jul	14	CA	1982
Jun	6	CA	1982
Mar	14	CA	1982
May	39	CA	1982
Nov	3	CA	1982
Oct	9	CA	1982
Sep	10	CA	1982
Apr	14	CA	1983

Figure 8-44. *Unpivoting a denormalized dataset*

The Unpivot transformation is shown in the sample data flow in Figure 8-45.

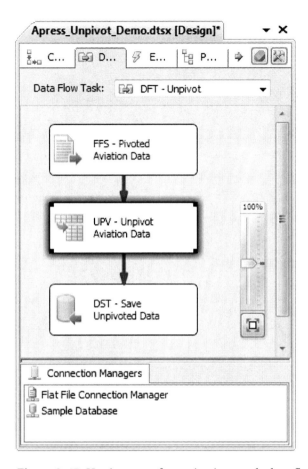

Figure 8-45. *Unpivot transformation in sample data flow*

Configuring the Unpivot transformation requires choosing the columns to unpivot and giving the newly unpivoted destination column and the pivot key value column names. Figure 8-46 shows the Unpivot Transformation Editor.

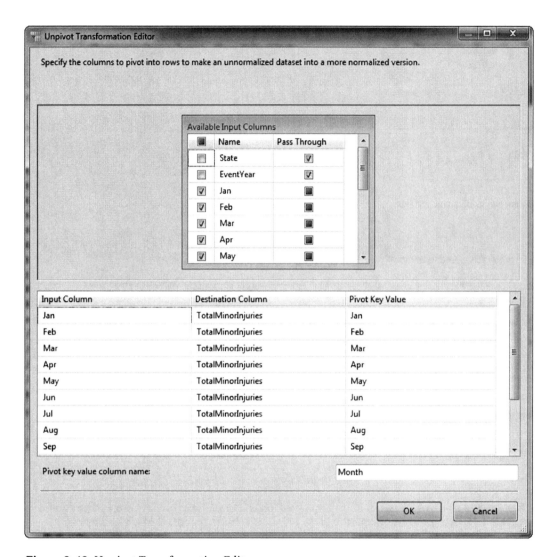

Figure 8-46. *Unpivot Transformation Editor*

In the editor, you select the columns you want to pivot from the Available Input Columns section. Any columns you don't want to be pivoted are checked off as Pass Through columns. In the bottom-right corner, you choose a pivot key value column name—this is the name of the column you wish to place your pivot key values into. In this example, we chose the column name Month, and the pivot key values are the month names for each column.

If you choose to, you can change the pivot key values to something else, although they must all be unique. In our example, we went with the default, which is the same value as the Input Column name. We could, for instance, use the full month names (January, February, and so forth) as pivot key values.

The Destination Column is the name of the column you wish to place the unpivoted values into. In this case, the name is `TotalMinorInjuries`. The values for each unpivoted column are added in this newly created column.

▪ **TIP:** The Destination Column name must be the same for all your input columns.

Splits and Joins

SSIS includes several transformations that allow you to split, merge, and join datasets in the data flow. These transformations are useful for combining multiple datasets, duplicating datasets, performing lookups, and creating copies of datasets.

Lookup

The Lookup transformation lets you enrich your data by retrieving related data from a reference dataset. Lookup is similar in functionality to a join operation in SQL Server. In the Lookup Transformation Editor, you choose the source data columns and the related columns from the reference dataset. You also choose the columns you wish to add to your data flow from the reference dataset. Figure 8-47 is a sample data flow that pulls in National Football League game data from a flat file and performs lookups against team data stored in a SQL Server database table.

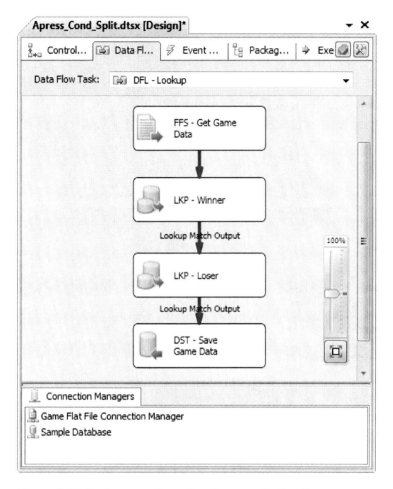

Figure 8-47. *Lookup transformations in a sample data flow*

There are two lookups in this data flow: one looks up the winning team's name, and the other looks up the losing team's name. The LKP - Winner lookup was configured with the Lookup Transformation Editor, shown in Figure 8-48.

■ **TIP:** If your reference data has multiple rows with the same values in the join key columns, duplicates are removed. SSIS will generate warning messages when duplicates are encountered. The reference data rows are considered in the order in which they are retrieved by the lookup component.

LOOKUPS AND CASE SENSITIVITY

One thing to keep in mind with the Lookup transformation is that it is case-sensitive, accent-sensitive, Kana-sensitive, and so forth. This is true regardless of the collation and sensitivity settings of the source of your input or reference data. That is to say, if you are pulling your reference data from a database with a case-insensitive collation and pulling your input data from a database with a case-insensitive collation, it doesn't matter to the Lookup transformation—the string comparisons performed by the Lookup transformation are still case-sensitive. If you want to simulate case sensitivity, convert your input string data and related reference data to all uppercase or all lowercase prior to the comparison.

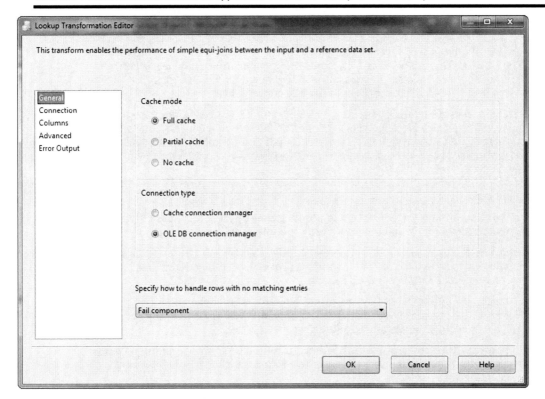

Figure 8-48. *General page of the Lookup Transformation Editor*

The General page of the editor lets you choose the connection manager that will be the source of the reference data. Your options are an OLE DB Connection Manager or a Cache Connection Manager. For this sample, we went with the default OLE DB Connection Manager.

You can also choose the cache mode on this page. You have three options for cache mode:

Full Cache mode preloads and caches the entire reference dataset into memory. This is the most commonly used mode, and it works well for small reference datasets or datasets for which you expect a large number of reference rows to match.

Partial Cache mode doesn't preload any reference data into memory. With this cache mode, reference data rows are retrieved from the database as they are needed and then cached for future lookups. Individual SELECT statements are issued to retrieve each data row. This mode is useful when you have a small reference dataset, or when you expect very few reference rows to match many records in the input dataset.

No Cache mode doesn't preload any reference data. In No Cache mode, reference data rows are retrieved as needed, one at a time using individual SELECT statements. Technically speaking, the No Cache mode does in fact cache the last reference row it retrieved, but discards it as soon as a new reference row is needed. This mode is normally not recommended unless you have a very small reference dataset and expect very few rows to match. The overhead incurred by this cache mode can hurt your performance.

The Lookup transformation is generally closely tied to the OLE DB Connection Manager. By default, the lookup wants to pull its reference data from an OLE DB source, such as a SQL Server or other relational database. When you want to pull reference data from another source, such as a flat file or Excel spreadsheet, you need to store it in a Cache transformation first. We cover the Cache transformation in the next section.

The final option on this first page lets you specify how to handle rows with no matching entries. You have four options:

Fail Component (default): If an input row passes through that does not have a matching row in the reference dataset, the component fails.

Ignore Failure: If an input row passes through that does not have a matching reference row, the component continues processing, setting the value of reference data output columns to null.

Redirect Rows to No Match Output: When this option is set, the transformation creates a "no match" output and directs any rows that don't have matching reference rows to the new output.

Redirect Rows to Error Output: When this option is set, the component directs any rows with no matching reference rows to the transformation's standard error output.

The Connection page of the editor lets you select an OLE DB Connection Manager that points to the database where your reference data is stored. On this tab, you also choose the source table or a SQL query, as shown in Figure 8-49.

▪ **TIP:** Specifying a SQL query instead of a table as your source is a best practice. There is less overhead involved when you specify a SQL query, because SSIS doesn't have to retrieve table metadata. You can also minimize the amount of data retrieved with a SQL query (both columns and rows), and you can't do that if you specify a table.

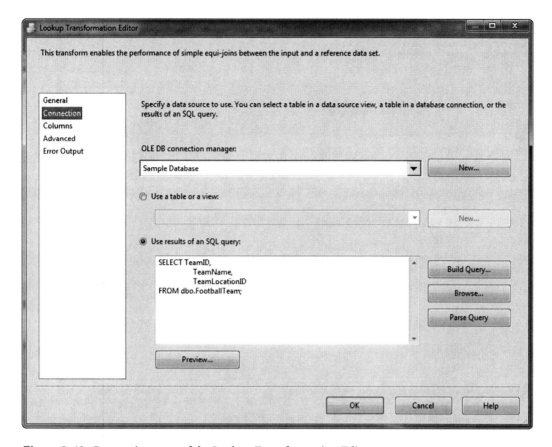

Figure 8-49. Connection page of the Lookup Transformation Editor

The third page of the editor—the Columns page—is where you define the join between your input dataset and your reference dataset. Simply click on a column in the Available Input Columns box and drag it to the corresponding column in the Available Lookup Columns box. Select the check boxes next to the reference data columns you wish to add to your data flow. Figure 8-50 shows the Columns page.

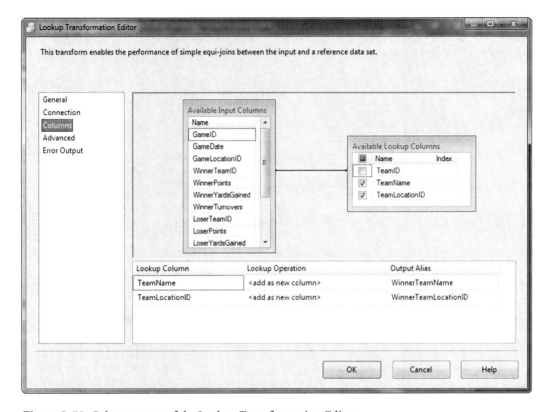

Figure 8-50. *Columns page of the Lookup Transformation Editor*

In this example, we joined the `WinnerTeamID` column of the input dataset to the `TeamID` column of the reference data, and chose to add `TeamName` and `TeamLocationID` to the destination. The columns you select from the Available Lookup Columns box are added to the grid in the lower portion of the editor. Each Lookup Column has a Lookup Operation assigned to it that can be set to *<add as new column>* or *Replace 'Column*, indicating whether the column values should be added to the data flow as new columns or if they should replace existing columns. Finally, the Output Alias column allows you to change the name of the output column in the data flow.

The Advanced page lets you set Lookup caching properties. The Cache Size property indicates how much memory should be used for caching reference data. The maximum 32-bit cache size is 3,072 MB, and the maximum 64-bit cache size is 17,592,186,044,416 MB.

In Partial Cache mode, you can also set the Enable Cache for Rows with No Matching Entries option and set a percentage of allocation from the cache (default is 20%) on this tab. This option caches data values that don't have matching reference rows, minimizing round-trip queries to the database server.

The Custom Query option lets you change the SQL query used to perform database lookups in Partial Cache or No Cache mode, as referenced in the figure below.

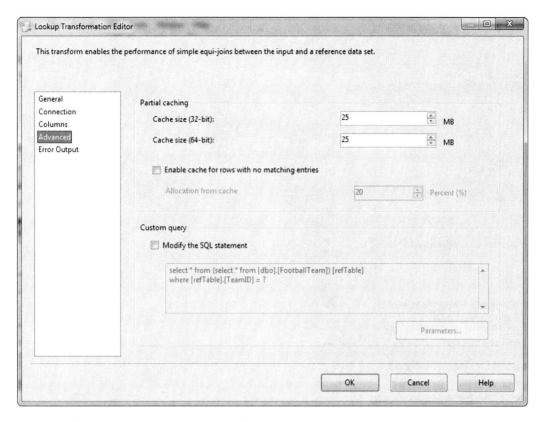

Figure 8-51. *Advanced page of the Lookup Transformation Editor*

Cache Transformation

As we mentioned in the previous section, the Lookup transformation, by default, looks for an OLE DB Connection Manager as its source for reference data. Other sources can be used, but they must be used indirectly via a Cache transformation. The Cache transformation can read data from a wide variety of sources, including flat files and ADO.NET data sources that aren't supported directly by the Lookup transformation as illustrated in Figure 8-52.

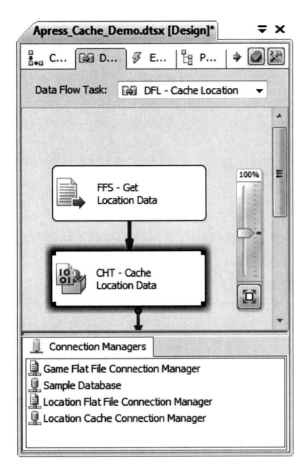

Figure 8-52. *Populating the Cache transformation*

As you can see in the figure, the Cache transformation accepts the output of a source component in the data flow as its input. It uses a Cache Connection Manager to cache the reference data in memory for use by the lookup component. Because the Cache transformation has to be populated before your lookup executes, you generally want to populate it in a separate data flow that precedes the data flow containing your lookups. In our sample, we populated the Cache transformation in one data flow, performed the lookup in a second data flow, and linked them with a precedence constraint, as shown in Figure 8-53.

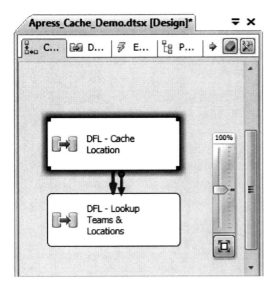

Figure 8-53. *Populating the Cache transformation in a separate data flow*

The Cache transformation is configured through the Cache Transformation Editor. The Connection Manager page lets you choose the Cache Connection Manager that will be populated with your cached reference data, as shown in Figure 8-54.

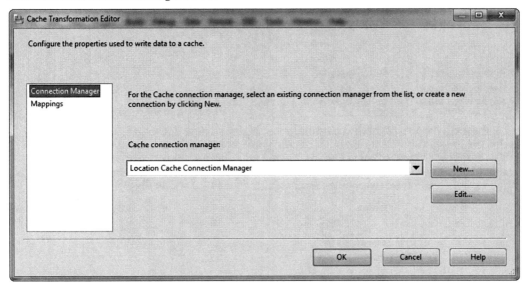

Figure 8-54. *Connection Manager page of the Cache Transformation Editor*

You can edit the Cache Connection Manager by clicking the Edit button to pull up the Connection Manager Editor. On the General tab of the editor, shown in Figure 8-55, you can change the name of the connection manager and choose to use a file cache. If you choose to use a file cache, the connection manager will write cached data to a file. You can also use an existing cache file as a source instead of pulling data from an upstream source in the data flow.

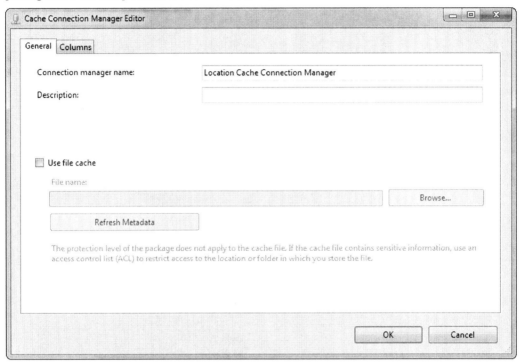

Figure 8-55. *General tab of the Cache Connection Manager Editor*

The Columns tab shows a list of the columns in the cache and their data types and related information. The Index Position column must be configured to reflect the columns you want to join in the lookup component. Columns that are not part of the index have an Index Position of 0; index columns should be numbered sequentially, beginning with 1. In our example, the `LocationID` column is the only index column, and is set to an Index Position of 1. Figure 8-56 shows the Columns tab.

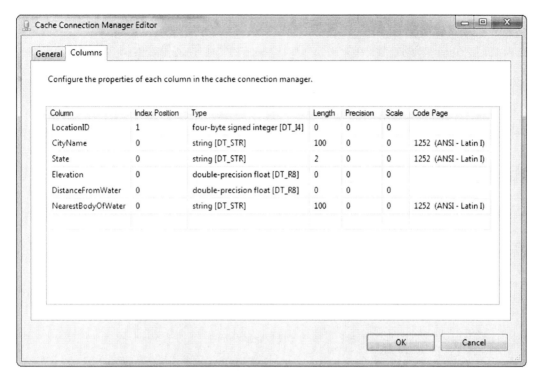

Figure 8-56. Columns tab of the Cache Connection Manager Editor

Our sample package demonstrating the Cache transformation expands on the previous example by performing a lookup against the Cache transformation, as shown in Figure 8-57.

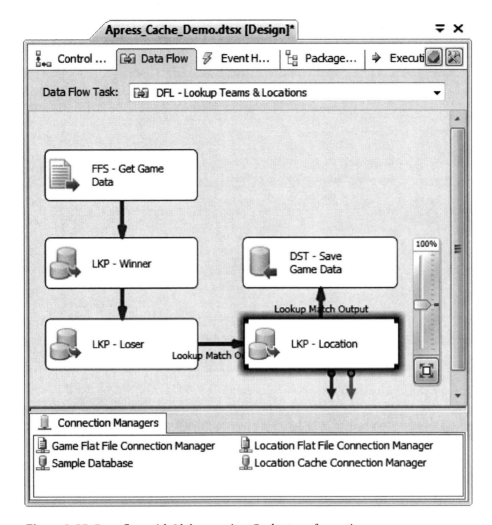

Figure 8-57. *Data flow with Llokup against Cache transformation*

The Lookup transformation against a cache is configured similarly to the lookup against an OLE DB source. The main differences are as follows:

- You must choose Full Cache mode. Partial Cache and No Cache are not valid options for lookups against a cache.

- The Connection type must be set to Cache Connection Manager.

- On the Connection tab of the Lookup transformation, you must choose a Cache Connection Manager instead of an OLE DB Connection Manager.

On the Columns tab, you'll also notice a magnifying glass icon in the Index column of the Available Lookup Columns box, as shown in Figure 8-58. These columns are the columns you will map to your input data. Other than these minor differences, the operation of the lookup against a Cache Connection Manager is exactly the same as against an OLE DB source.

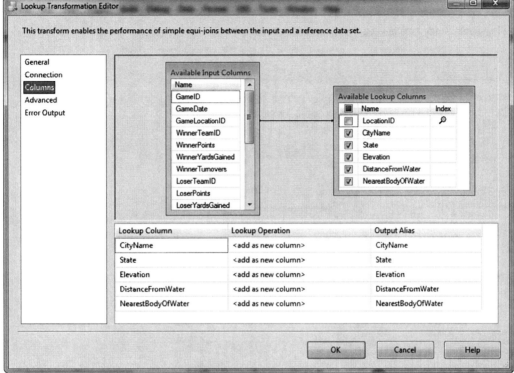

Figure 8-58. *Columns tab of the Lookup transformation against a Cache Connection Manager*

Conditional Split

The Conditional Split transformation lets you redirect rows of data that meet specific conditions to different outputs. You can use this functionality as a tool to direct data down different processing paths, much like an if...then...else construct in procedural programming languages (such as C# or VB), or as a filter to eliminate data from your dataset, as with the SQL WHERE clause. We've expanded the previous example to filter out any games that did not occur during the regular season, as shown in Figure 8-59.

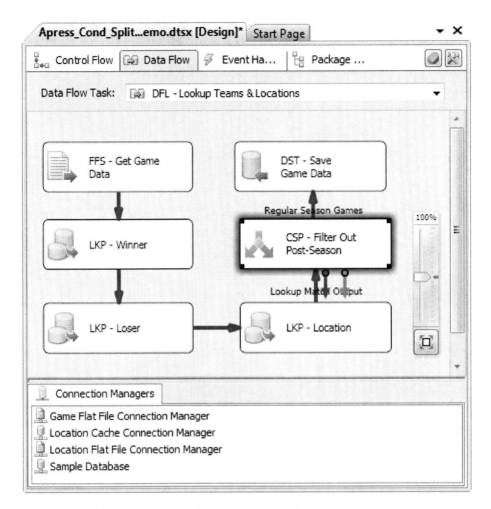

Figure 8-59. Adding a Conditional Split transformation to the data flow

The Conditional Split Transformation Editor gives you control to add as many outputs as you like to the transformation. Each output has rows redirected to it based on the condition you provide for it. The condition is written in the form of an SSIS Expression Language expression. Often you'll use variables or columns in your conditions, to make your data self-directing. In this example, we've added one output to the transformation called Regular Season Games. The condition we applied to this output is [GameWeek] == "Regular Season", refer to Figure 8-60 below. We discuss the SSIS Expression Language in Chapter 9.

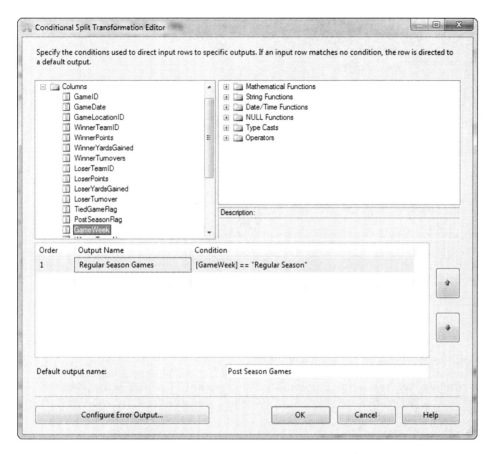

Figure 8-60. *Editing the Conditional Split transformation*

When the GameWeek column contains the value Regular Season, data is redirected to the Regular Season Games output. Note that string comparisons in SSIS Expression Language are case-sensitive. Any rows that do not match this condition are directed to the default output, which we've named Post Season Games in this example.

TIP: When you define multiple outputs with conditions, they are evaluated in the order indicated by the Order field. As soon as a row matches a given condition, it is immediately redirected to the appropriate output, and no comparisons are made against subsequent conditions.

When you connect the output of the Conditional Split transformation to the input of another data flow component, you'll be presented with an Input Output Selection box. Choose which output you want to send to the next component, as shown in Figure 8-61.

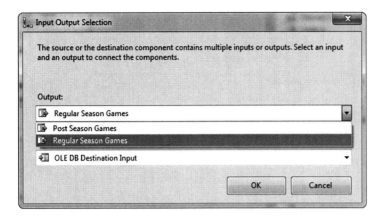

Figure 8-61. *Input Output Selection when connecting the Conditional Split transformation*

We didn't connect the Post Season Games output to any downstream components in this case, which means the rows directed to it won't be sent down the data flow. This is effectively a filter on the input data.

Multicast

The Multicast transformation duplicates your data in the data flow, which comes in very handy in many situations where you want to apply different transformations to the same source data in parallel, or when you want to send your data to multiple destinations simultaneously. To build on the previous sample, we've added a Multicast transformation just before the OLE DB destination in our data flow. We'll use the Multicast transformation to send the transformed data to two destinations: the OLE DB destination and a flat file destination, as shown in Figure 8-62.

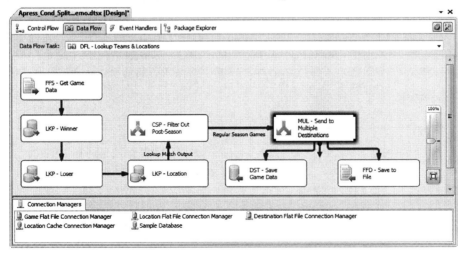

Figure 8-62. *Multicast transformation sending data to multiple destinations*

You can use the Multicast transformation to duplicate your data as many times as necessary, although it's most often used to create one copy of its input data.

Union All

The Union All transformation combines the rows of two or more datasets into a single dataset, like the UNION ALL operator in SQL. For this sample, we've taken two flat files with daily weather data in them and combined them into a single dataset in the data flow, as shown in Figure 8-63.

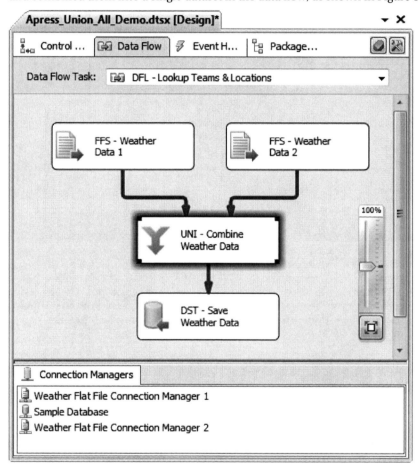

Figure 8-63. *Combining data from two source files with the Union All transformation*

When you add the first input to the Union All transformation, it defines the structure of the output dataset. When you connect the second and subsequent inputs to the Union All transformation, they are lined up, column by column, based on matching column names. You can view the columns from all the inputs by double-clicking the Union All transformation to reveal the editor, as shown in Figure 8-64.

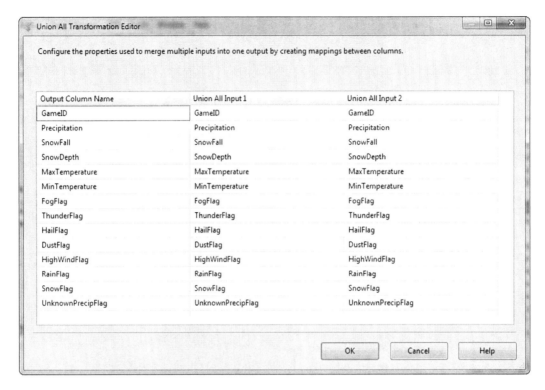

Figure 8-64. *Union All Transformation Editor*

The Output Column Name entries list the names of each column added to the output. The names are editable, so you can change them to your liking. If you have different names for columns that should be matched in the outputs, you can choose them from drop-down lists in the Union All Input lists. Choosing *<ignore>* will put a null in the column for that input.

■ **TIP:** The output from the Union All transformation is not guaranteed to be in order when more than one input is involved. To guarantee order, you'll need to perform a Sort after the Union All.

Merge

The Merge transformation is similar to the Union All, except that it guarantees ordered output. To provide this guarantee, the Merge transformation requires all inputs to be sorted. This is particularly useful when you have to merge inputs from two separate sources and then perform a Merge Join with the resulting dataset. Figure 8-65 shows the Merge transformation with two sorted inputs.

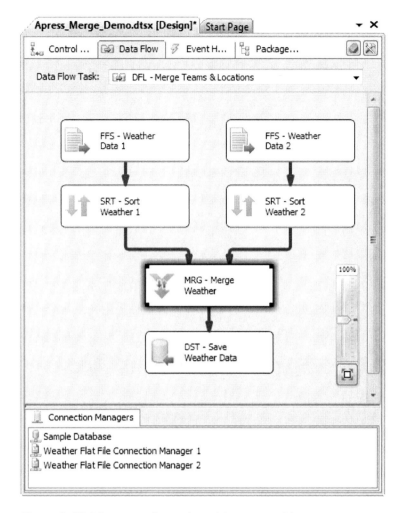

Figure 8-65. *Merge transformation with two sorted inputs*

In our example, we sorted the weather data from both sources by the GameID field and then performed a merge on them. The Merge Transformation Editor can be viewed by double-clicking the transformation. The editor is very similar to the Union All Transformation Editor, with one minor difference: the Sort key fields are all labeled in the Merge Input and Output Column lists, as shown in Figure 8-66.

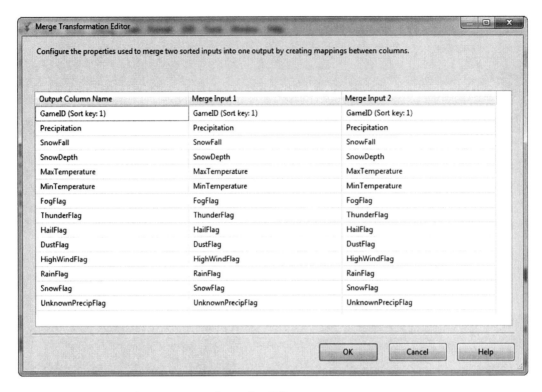

Figure 8-66. *Viewing the Merge Transformation Editor*

When properly configured, the Merge transformation guarantees that the output will be sorted based on the sort keys.

Merge Join

The Merge Join transformation lets you perform joins on two input datasets, much like SQL joins. The major difference is that unlike SQL Server, which handles data sorting/ordering for you when performing joins, the Merge Join transformation required you to presort your inputs on the join key columns. Figure 8-67 expands the previous Merge transformation example and adds a Merge Join to the input Football Game data.

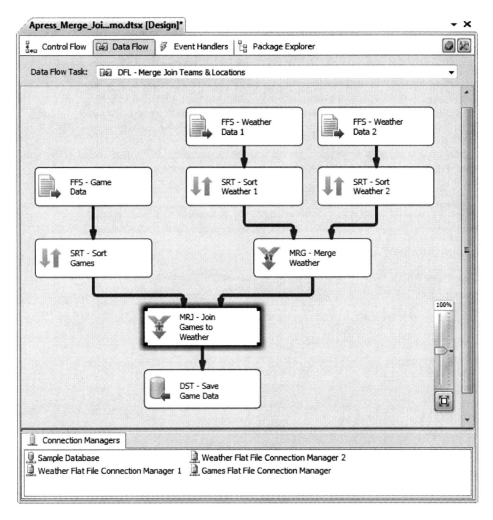

Figure 8-67. Merge Join added to the data flow

The Merge Join Transformation Editor, shown in Figure 8-68, lets you choose the join type. You can select an inner join, left outer join, or full outer join. All of these joins work as you'd expect from working with SQL:

Inner Join returns only rows where the left input key and right input keys match. If there are rows from either input with join key values that don't match the other input, the rows are not returned.

Left Outer Join returns all the rows from the left input and rows from the right input where the join keys match. If there are rows in the left input that don't have matching rows in the right input, nulls are returned in the right-hand columns.

317

Full Outer Join performs all rows from the left and right inputs. Where the join keys don't match on either the right or left side, nulls are returned in the columns on the other side.

One thing you might notice is that the Merge Join doesn't support the SQL equivalent of the cross-join or the right outer join. You can simulate the right join by selecting Left Outer Join as the join type and then clicking the Swap Inputs button. This moves your left input to the right, and vice versa. The cross-join could be simulated by adding a derived column to both sides with a constant value in it and then joining on those two columns. The cross-join functionality isn't as useful, though, except for generating large datasets (for testing purposes, for instance).

In the editor, you can link the join key columns and choose the columns from both sides to return. You can also rename the output columns in the Output Alias list at the bottom of the editor, shown in Figure 8-68.

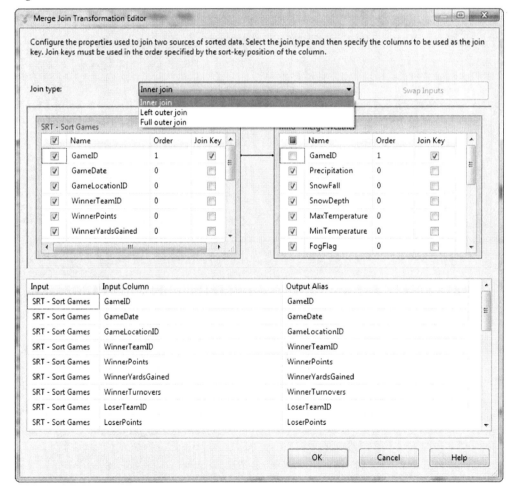

Figure 8-68. *Setting attributes in the Merge Join editor*

Auditing

SSIS includes a handful of transformations that perform "auditing" functions. Essentially, these tasks allow you to capture metadata about your package or the data flow itself. You can use this metadata to analyze various aspects of your ETL process at a granular level.

Row Count

The Row Count transformation does just what its name says—it counts the rows that pass through it. Row Count sets a variable that you specify to the result of its count. Figure 8-69 shows the Row Count transformation in the data flow.

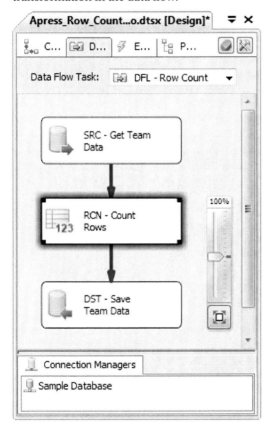

Figure 8-69. *Row Count transformation in the data flow*

After you've added the Row Count transformation to the data flow, you need to create a variable on the Parameters and Variables tab and add an integer variable to the package, as shown in Figure 8-70. In this case, we've chosen to add a variable named RowCount.

> ▪ **NOTE:** If you're not familiar with SSIS variables, don't fret. We cover them in detail in Chapter 9. For now, it's just important to know that SSIS variables are named temporary storage locations in memory, as in other programming languages. You can access variables in expressions, which we also discuss in Chapter 9.

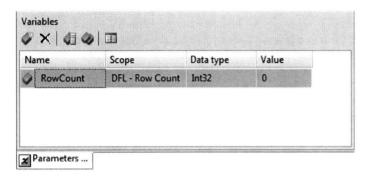

Figure 8-70. Adding a variable to the Parameters and Variables tab

The final step in configuring the Row Count transformation is to choose the variable it will transform. You associate the variable with the Row Count transformation by using the `VariableName` property of the Row Count editor, shown in Figure 8-71.

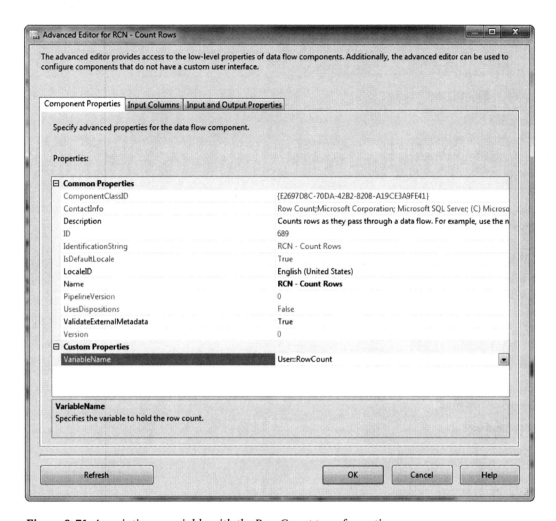

Figure 8-71. *Associating a variable with the Row Count transformation*

■ **TIP:** Don't try to access the value of the variable set by your Row Count transformation until the data flow is finished. The value is not updated until after the last row has passed through the data flow.

Audit

The Audit transformation gives you a shortcut to add various system variables as columns in your data flow. Figure 8-72 shows the Audit transformation in the data flow.

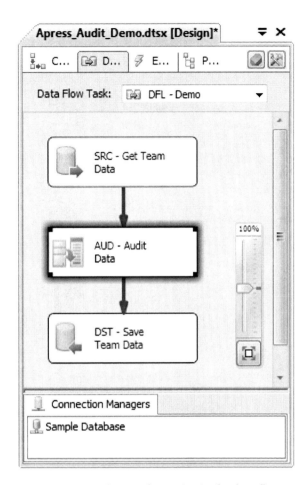

Figure 8-72. *Audit transformation in the data flow*

After you add the Audit transformation to your data flow, double-click it to edit the properties in the editor. In the editor, you can choose the audit columns to add to your data flow. You can also rename the default output column names. Figure 8-73 shows the audit column selection.

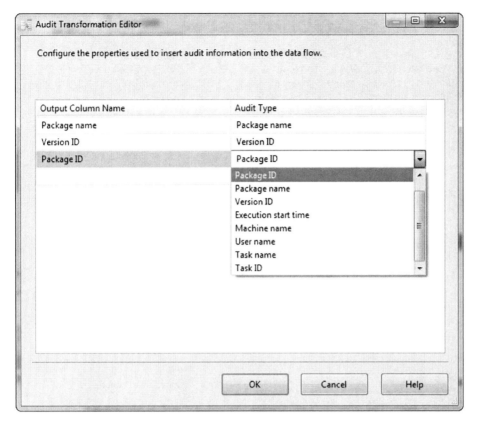

Figure 8-73. Choosing audit columns in the Audit Transformation Editor

■ **TIP:** The Audit transformation is a convenience transformation. As an alternative, you can access all of the same system variables and add them to columns in your data flow with the Derived Column transformation.

Business Intelligence Transformations

In addition to the transformations covered so far, SSIS provides a handful of Business Intelligence transformations. One of these transformation, the Slowly Changing Dimension transformation, is specific to Dimensional Data ETL. We present this component and efficient alternatives to it in Chapter 17. The remaining components are designed for data scrubbing and validation. We cover these transformations in detail in Chapter 12.

Summary

This chapter presented SSIS data flow transformation components. We talked about the differences between synchronous and asynchronous transformations, as well as blocking, nonblocking, and partially blocking transformations. You looked at the individual transformations you can apply in your data flow, including the wide variety of settings available to each, with examples. The next chapter introduces SSIS variables and the SSIS Expression Language.

CHAPTER 9

Variables, Parameters, and Expressions

Old expressions are the best, and short ones even better.

—Prime Minister Winston Churchill

In order to create modular and robust solutions, developers will often create variables and routines to access those variables. Integration Services is no different in this regard. The variables available to SSIS have their own data types that often correlate to SQL Server data types. Parameters are used to pass values between parent and child packages to extend the modularity of an ETL project. And an expression language is provided to allow the ETL process to read or modify the values of both during runtime. The expression language can certainly get convoluted, so it is recommended that you take Churchill's words to heart and keep the logic minimal, readable, and easily modifiable.

Variables allow flexibility when running packages by allowing you to evaluate conditions, modify data in the stream, parameterize SQL, and many other options. These variables can be used to store scalar values or tabular values, depending on their data types. Scalar values are useful for parameterizing SQL, whereas tabular values can control loop containers. This chapter covers the data types that SSIS variables can have and shows how they interact with the package during runtime.

What Are Variables and Expressions?

Variables are used to store values that SSIS executables can access at runtime. Defaults can be provided at design time for variables of certain data types, but it is during runtime that they truly shine. There are two kinds of variables: system variables and user-defined variables.

The *system variables* capture the status of the package during runtime. They are defined by SSIS and in some cases will automatically update. You can neither modify the values of system variables nor define any system variables. You can, however, access the values of the system variables such as System::StartTime in order to store the execution information for tracing the process. System:: denotes the namespace that the variable belongs to; we introduce namespaces later in this chapter. Variable names are case sensitive in SSIS.

User-defined variables are extremely useful because they can extend the functionality of SSIS by making processes modular. Scalar variables defined as String and Date data types, among others, can be used to parameterize Execute SQL tasks and source queries. Tabular variables defined as Object data types can be used to control loop containers as well as allow script components access to the data. You can create user-defined variables and can define the level of access, read-only or read/write, that individual components may have to the variables. In order to add variables to a package, you can use the Variables window. The window can be opened by right-clicking on the control flow of the package and selecting the Variables option, as shown in Figure 9-1. The other option is to use the View menu to choose Other Windows ➤ Variables.

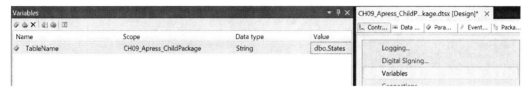

Figure 9-1. *Variables window in Visual Studio*

Expressions are used in SSIS to return a value based on the evaluation of criteria. The expression language itself consists of identifiers, literals, functions, and operators. Some expressions can be written to assign values to variables, return the value of a calculation, or be used as conditional statements. The expressions, just like most programming languages, adhere to a strict grammar. The grammar determines the proper usage of the identifiers, literals, functions, and operators. In order to assist you with writing expressions, SSIS provides an expression evaluator and builder. Figure 9-2 shows the Expression Builder with the expression evaluator. The evaluator will parse and validate the expression's adherence to the grammar. The Expression Builder provides quick access to all the available variables, functions, type casts, and operators. You can click and drag the item you need from its respective position into the expression text box to add it to the expression.

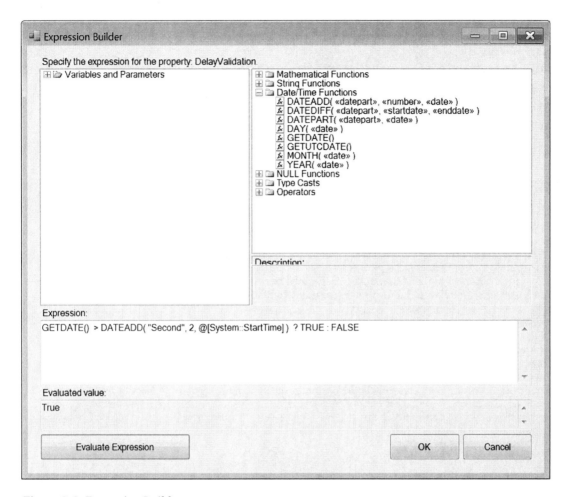

Figure 9-2. Expression Builder

The expression GETDATE() > DATEADD("Second", 2, @[System::StartTime]) ? TRUE : FALSE evaluates to a Boolean value. It performs a simple check to determine whether 2 seconds have passed since the package's execution began. This particular expression uses the ? : syntax to handle an IF THEN statement. The DATEADD function allows us to adjust the time interval for our check. We use this expression to modify the values of control flow task properties such as DelayValidation. This expression can be set only to properties that have Boolean definitions.

■ **NOTE:** The system variables will store the values once the package is opened for design time evaluation. For example, the System::StartTime variable will maintain the timestamp from when the package was initially opened. This value will not update even if the package is run using Debug mode. It will update only if you close and reopen the package.

What Are Parameters?

In order to support the new deployment model for SSIS, parameters have been introduced in this version. *Parameters* basically replace the need for configurations to specify values. Parameters can be used at the package level or at the project level.

Package-level parameters are extremely useful for the parent-child package design. They allow you to pass specific values between the parent packages in order to configure the child packages. Prior to passing the parameters to the child package, you need to create the package parameters. Certain objects within a package can be bound to properties so that when a value is inherited from the parent, it will directly impact the child package's property. Bindings can also be created to map to the objects' properties that exist within the child package.

Figure 9-3 demonstrates how to bind the parameter to a package property. You can either create a new parameter by using the wizard or you can use a project parameter whose value is available to all the packages in the project. Parameter names are case sensitive. We discuss parameterizing packages later in this chapter. All the executables, containers, and event handlers can be parameterized as well. The package parameters that are created can be bound to the specific properties of each of these objects in the package. Connection managers cannot be parameterized directly but properties such as ConnectionString can be modified by using Script tasks and variables that inherited values from parent packages.

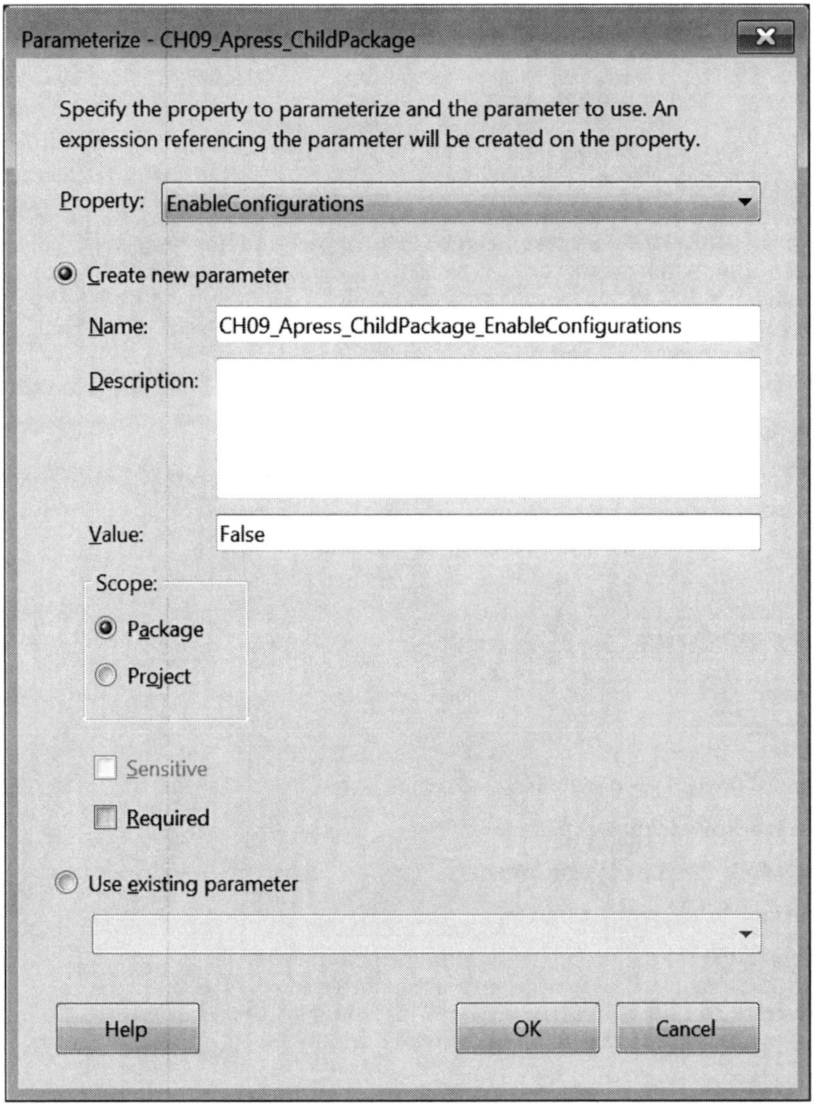

Figure 9-3. Parameterizing a package

The Parameterize dialog box appears when you right-click the control flow background or when you right-click an object and select Parameterize. Using the dialog box will create any new parameters you require. All package parameters can be seen in the new Parameters designer window that has been added to the BIDS. The designer window is shown in Figure 9-4.

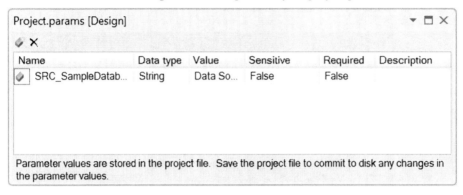

	Control Flow		Data Flow		Parameters		Event Handlers		Package Explorer	

◇ ✕

	Name	Data type	Value	Sensitive	Required	Description
◇	ParentTableName	String		False	False	Derives value from parent package binding.

Figure 9-4. *Parameters designer window*

Project parameters are available to all the packages included in the project. Adding project parameters creates a file in the solution that allows you to view all the parameters that exist at the project level. Visual Studio has a designer window specifically for project parameters, shown in Figure 9-5.

Project.params [Design]   ▼ ☐ ✕

◇ ✕

	Name	Data type	Value	Sensitive	Required	Description
◇	SRC_SampleDatab...	String	Data So...	False	False	

Parameter values are stored in the project file. Save the project file to commit to disk any changes in the parameter values.

Figure 9-5. *Project-level parameters*

Following are descriptions of the various parameters:

Name specifies the name of the project parameter.

Data Type specifies the data type of the parameter.

Value provides a default value for the parameter.

Sensitive specifies whether the data contained within the parameter is sensitive. This is so that sensitive data may be encrypted, not saved or left as is depending of the level of security behind the project. This field may come in handy if username and password information is contained within the parameter.

Required specifies that this parameter must be provided during the execution of the package, after it has been deployed to a server.

Description provides a short synopsis of the parameter.

The parameters are not limited to just modifying package properties. They can be accessed in the Expression Builder just like the rest of the variables. This allows you to access strings or integer values set at the project level without having to worry about keeping multiple package variables in sync, as was the case in older versions. With this ability, configuration files will no longer be required to maintain variable values across multiple packages.

SSIS Data Types

As with most programming languages, SSIS variables also require data types. For the most part, these data types match up with SQL Server data types. When extracting data from SQL Server, each column is recognized as one of these data types. The Data Conversion task will use these data types to convert data types from other sources so that the data can seamlessly map into a SQL Server database.

Table 9-1 shows the data types that SSIS uses. We included a column that shows the Type Cast function that can be used in expressions to convert a value. You can use the functions in expressions in the following manner: (<<type cast function>> [, <<param1>>, <<param2>>, …]) (<<expression>>). The parentheses around the expression are not required, but will make it easier to determine what is being type casted.

Table 9-1. *SSIS Data Types*

Data Type	Description	Domain/Size	Type Cast Function
DT_BOOL	Boolean value.	True/False.	(DT_BOOL)
DT_BYTES	Binary data value.	Binary data with a maximum size of 8,000 bytes.	(DT_BYTES, «length»)
DT_CY	Currency value.	8-byte signed integer with precision and scale of (19,4)	(DT_CY)
DT_DATE	Date data type that supports YYYY/MM/DD HH:MM:SS. Provided by floating-point number whose whole-number portion represents the date and whose fractional portion represents the timestamp.	0001/01/01 00:00:00– 9999/12/31 23:59:59.	(DT_DBDATE)
DT_DBDATE	Date data type that supports YYYY/MM/DD.	0001/01/01– 9999/12/31.	(DT_DBDATE)
DT_DBTIME	Time data type that supports hh:mm:ss.	00:00:00–23:59:59.	(DT_DBTIME)
DT_DBTIME2	Time data type that supports hh:mm:ss[.fffffff].	00:00:00.0000000– 23:59:59.9999999.	(DT_DBTIME2, «scale»)

Data Type	Description	Domain/Size	Type Cast Function
DT_DBTIMESTAMP	Date data type that supports YYYY/MM/DD hh:mm:ss[.fff].	1753/01/01 00:00:00.000– 9999/12/31 23:59:59.997.	(DT_DBTIMESTAMP)
DT_DBTIMESTAMP 2	Date data type that supports YYYY/MM/DD hh:mm:ss[.fffffff]	0001/01/01 00:00:00.0000000– 9999/12/31 23:59:59.9999999.	(DT_DBTIMESTAMP2 , «scale»)
DT_DBTIMESTAMP OFFSET	Date data type that supports YYYY/MM/DD hh:mm:ss[.fffffff] +/- 14hh, +/- .59mm. This timestamp consists of an offset to support the Coordinated Universal Time (UTC). The hour and minute offsets must match in sign. If they don't match, the minute offset or the hour offset must be 0.	0001/01/01 00:00:00.0000000 +/– 14hh, +/– .59mm– 9999/12/31 23:59:59.9999999 +/– 14hh, +/– .59mm.	(DT_DBTIMESTAMP OFFSET, «scale»)
DT_DECIMAL	A precise numeric value with defined precision and scale. 12-byte unsigned value.	Scale can vary from 0– 28 while the maximum precision is 29.	(DT_DECIMAL, «scale»)
DT_FILETIME	64-bit value that returns 100-nanosecond intervals that have occurred since 1601/01/01.	1601/01/01 00:00:00.000– 9999/12/31 23:59:59.997.	(DT_FILETIME)
DT_GUID	Globally unique identifier that is stored as binary data.	16-byte binary string.	(DT_GUID)
DT_I1	Signed integer.	1 byte. 0 to 255.	(DT_I1)
DT_I2	Signed integer.	2 bytes. –32,768 to 32,767 (-2^{15} to (2^{15}) - 1).	(DT_I2)
DT_I4	Signed integer.	4 bytes. –2,147,483,648 to 2,147,483,647 (-2^{31} to (2^{31}) -1).	(DT_I4)

Data Type	Description	Domain/Size	Type Cast Function
DT_I8	Signed integer.	8 bytes. –9,223,372,036,854,775,808 to 9,223,372,036,854,775,807 (−2^63 to (2^63)-1).	(DT_I8)
DT_NUMERIC	Precise numeric value with defined precision and scale.	Scale can vary from 0–38, with a maximum precision of 38.	(DT_NUMERIC, «precision», «scale»)
DT_R4	Floating-point value.	4 bytes.	(DT_R4)
DT_R8	Floating-point value.	8 bytes.	(DT_R8)
DT_STR	American National Standards Institute, ANSI/Member British Computer Society, MBCS character string that is null terminated. If a string is entered with multiple nulls, the string will terminate at the first null value.	Maximum length of 8,000 bytes. Accepts ANSI/MBCS characters.	(DT_STR, «length», «code_page»)
DT_UI1	Unsigned integer.	1 byte.	(DT_UI1)
DT_UI2	Unsigned integer.	2 bytes.	(DT_UI2)
DT_UI4	Unsigned integer.	4 bytes.	(DT_UI4)
DT_UI8	Unsigned integer.	8 bytes.	(DT_UI8)
DT_WSTR	Unicode character string that is null terminated.	Maximum length of 4,000 bytes. Accepts Unicode characters.	(DT_WSTR, «length»)
DT_IMAGE	Binary data.	Maximum size of 2,147,483,647 ((2^31)-1) bytes.	(DT_IMAGE)
DT_NTEXT	Unicode character string.	Maximum length of 1,073,741,823 characters.	(DT_NTEXT)

Data Type	Description	Domain/Size	Type Cast Function
DT_TEXT	ANSI/MBCS character string.	Maximum length of 2,147,483,647 characters.	(DT_TEXT, «code_page»)

Variable Scope, Default Values, and Namespaces

SSIS provides several ways to group variables so that you do not end up with a confusing mass. Your naming conventions will assist you greatly in keeping the variables in order. If you do not have these standards, the methods that come by default in SSIS should assist in providing some semblance.. The variable's scope physically limits your variable from being accessed by all methods. Namespaces assist you in grouping variables that serve a particular purpose. Assigning a default value insures that a user defined variable will have a value other than NULL. The default values will be used during Debug mode and runtime unless they are modified by using expressions or Script tasks.

Scope

Most programming languages provide scope for their variables. *Scope* is defined as the context of the variables with relation to the values and expressions. For SSIS, this translates to which executables, containers, and event handlers have access to the variables. To define a variable at the package implies that all the objects within the package will have access to the variable. In order to limit the variable's scope to a particular executable, you should select the object in the control flow designer window when you add the variable. If you do not select any object, the default is the package scope. The variable window has several icons at the top that allow you to modify the variables, as shown in Figure 9-6.

Figure 9-6. Variable options

The following list describes the functions of each of the buttons on the Variables toolbar:

Add Variable adds a variable to the collection by using selected objects as the defined scope of the variable.

Move Variable moves the variable to a different scope.

Delete Variable deletes the highlighted variables.

Show System Variables displays all the system variables.

Show Variables of All Scopes displays all the user-defined variables defined in the package. By default, only the variables of the selected object are shown. This helps to quickly identify only the available variables.

Choose Variable Columns opens a dialog box that allows you to quickly look at all the available columns.

The Choose Variable Columns icon is important because it allows you to gain control over all the aspects of a variable. By default, the only columns provided are Name, Scope, Data Type, and Value, as shown earlier in Figure 9-1. Figure 9-7 shows all the available columns that you can modify for the user-defined variables. The Namespace and Description columns are left out, but with the dialog box, you can add them back. The Raise Event When Variable Value Changes check box shows whether the specific variable is tied to an event that will fire when the value changes.

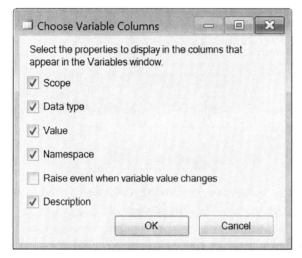

Figure 9-7. Choose Variable Columns dialog box

⬚ **NOTE:** You have to add the Namespace and Description column back every time you restart Visual Studio. The columns reset to the default after the Visual Studio window is closed.

Figure 9-8 shows the Variables window after we add all the variables we will need for this package. The objective of the CH09_Apress_ChildPackage is to extract the states that were accepted after 1900, convert the Date column into a DateTime column, and load only the states whose capitals lie north of 35.493259. The purpose of using two variables for row filtering is to demonstrate that a SQL query in a source component can be parameterized and to show that a conditional split can be used to filter out based on a variable value after the data has entered the data stream.

Name	Scope	Data type	Value	Namespace	Description
Long	CH09_Apress_ChildPackage	Double	0	Audit	Iterates through all the Longitude values in the State table.
Lat	CH09_Apress_ChildPackage	Double	0	Audit	Iterates through all the Latitude values in the State table.
RunTime	CH09_Apress_ChildPackage	Int32	0	Audit	Tracks the number of seconds for the package execution.
StateName	CH09_Apress_ChildPackage	String		Audit	Used to store state name as container loops through.
StateAcceptanceTime1	CH09_Apress_ChildPackage	DateTime	8/30/2011 1:55 AM	Audit	Iterates through all the acceptance times values derived.
Abbreviation	CH09_Apress_ChildPackage	String		Audit	Iterates through all the Abbreviation values in the State table.
Capital	CH09_Apress_ChildPackage	String		Audit	Iterates through all the Capital values in the State table.
Date	CH09_Apress_ChildPackage	DateTime	8/30/2011 1:55 AM	Audit	Iterates through all the Date values in the State table.
Flag	CH09_Apress_ChildPackage	String		Audit	Iterates through all the Flag values in the State table.
Fact	CH09_Apress_ChildPackage	String		Audit	Iterates through all the Fact values in the State table.
StateYearFilter	CH09_Apress_ChildPackage	Int32	1900	Extract	Used to limit the states extracted based on year of acceptance.
StateCapitalFilter	CH09_Apress_ChildPackage	Decimal	35.493259	Load	Limits the data loaded base on the state capital's latitude.
States	CH09_Apress_ChildPackage	Object	System.Object	Load	Stores all the states that pass through in a tabular object.
StateColumnName	CH09_Apress_ChildPackage	String		Load	Iterates through all the column names in the State table.
StateColumns	CH09_Apress_ChildPackage	Object	System.Object	Load	Stores all the columns in the State table.
StateAcceptanceTime	CH09_Apress_ChildPackage	DateTime	8/28/2011 3:43 PM	Transform	Adds a time stamp to the acceptance date.
StateQuery	CH09_Apress_ChildPackage	String		Transform	Stores SQL Query to execute against State table.

Figure 9-8. *Variables defined in* `CH09_Apress_ChildPackage.dtsx`

■ **NOTE:** The variable SSIS data types map to the SSIS data types that are used in the ETL. For example, the Int32 data type refers to a 32-bit signed integer, the String data type maps to a Unicode character string, and Decimal refers to the DT_NUMERIC data type. The data type names shown in Figure 9-8 are more reader friendly than the names that appear in a metadata viewer inside a data flow.

After the variables have been added, their scope can be changed by using the Select New Scope dialog box shown in Figure 9-9. This process works by copying all the properties of the selected variables to the new scope. After these new variables have been created, the names will have a 1 appended, and the original variables will be deleted. The dialog box will display all the available objects and the containers that they may be nested in so that you can move the variable scope to that object. The dialog box will also display all the event handlers that you may have created.

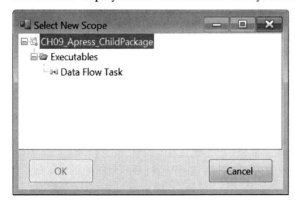

Figure 9-9. *Select New Scope dialog box*

Default Values

For most programming languages, you need to initialize a variable or at the least assign it a value before you can use it in a statement. The Value column allows you to specify the *default values* for the variables in SSIS. Certain data types automatically provide a default such as the DateTime and Int32, while others such as the Object data type will not accept any default values. The DateTime variables will use the time and date that they were created as their default value, while the default value for Int32 variables is 0. If you do not provide a valid value when setting defaults, you will receive an error dialog box similar to the one shown in Figure 9-10. The most common places for the values of variables to change are Execute SQL task and Script tasks.

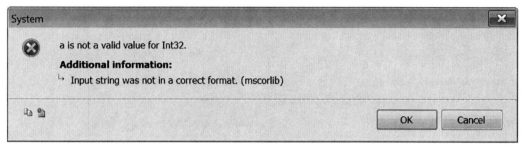

Figure 9-10. *Invalid Variable Default Value error message*

Namespaces

Namespaces are one of the best ways to organize your variables. They allow you to group your variables in any way you see fit. The convention we showed in Figure 9-8 groups the variables by the function they serve in the ETL process. We use the Extract namespace when we need variables that will be used during the extract phase, the Transformation namespace when we need a variable to use in the transformation of the data, and the Load namespace if we need to modify the data before we load it. The default namespace for a user-defined variable is User, and because we always create variables with a very specific purpose in mind, we should use this feature to our advantage.

One slight drawback to using namespaces is that the lists of variables are sorted by the name rather than the extended name (`Namespace::Name`) in the Expression Builder or any editor that exposes the list in a drop-down. In Expression Builder, the `RunTime` variable will be referred to as `@[Audit::RunTime]`. In the drop-down lists that show variables, it will appear as `Audit::RunTime`. The namespaces are case sensitive, because they are part of the variable identifier.

System Variables

SSIS provides variables that allow you to view minute details about a package and its objects. These variables are known as *system variables*, and they belong to the System namespace. These variables are accessible in most of the scopes, but depending on the scope in which they are area accessed the values might be different In order to access these variables, you must use `@[System::<<variable_name>>]`.

Package System Variables

System variables that belong to the package show important information about the package itself. All the objects defined within the package have access to these variables. Table 9-2 lists all the package system variables and their data types.

Table 9-2. Package System Variables

Name	Data Type	Description
CancelEvent	Int32	Identifier for a Windows Event object that signals the task to stop execution.
CreationDate	DateTime	The date on which the package was created.
CreatorComputerName	String	The computer on which the package was created.
CreatorName	String	The username of the package creator.
ExecutionInstanceGUID	String	Unique identifier of the package's execution. The string represents hexadecimal values.
InteractiveMode	Boolean	Indicates whether the package is being executed in interactive mode. Interactive mode indicates whether the SSIS designer (True) is used to execute or DTExec command line utility is used (False).
LocaleID	Int32	Identifies the locale that the package is using. By default it is English (US).
MachineName	String	The name of the computer on which the package is currently being executed.
OfflineMode	Boolean	Indicates whether the package is in offline mode and not acquiring connections to the data sources.
PackageID	String	Unique identifier of the package. The string represents hexadecimal values.
PackageName	String	The name of the package without the file extension.
StartTime	DateTime	The timestamp indicating when the package began execution.

Name	Data Type	Description
UserName	String	The username of the account that is currently executing the package.
VersionBuild	Int32	The package's version.
VersionComment	String	Displays the comments about the package's version.
VersionGUID	String	Uniquely identifies the package's version. The string represents hexadecimal values.
VersionMajor	Int32	Identifies the major version of the package.
VersionMinor	Int32	Identifies the minor version of the package.

Container System Variable

The *containers* have only one system variable that is specific to them, LocaleID. This 32-bit integer identifies the locale that the container uses. This variable can be used within Sequence, For Loop, and Foreach Loop containers. Accessing the LocaleID variable within a container will default to this value rather than the package's LocaleID.

Task System Variables

The control flow tasks get their own set of system variables after they are created. These variables are usually not directly accessible for most of the tasks other than the Data Flow task. The Data Flow task allows you to access its variables by using Script transformation tasks, Derived Column transformations, and Conditional Split transformations. Using these transformations, you can access these variables and use their values as part of your data stream. Table 9-3 shows all the system variables that are available with tasks.

Table 9-3. Task System Variables

Name	Data Type	Description
CreationName	String	The name of the task as recognized by SSIS.
LocaleID	Int32	Identifies the locale the task uses. By default it is English (US).

Name	Data Type	Description
TaskID	String	Unique identifier of the task. The string represents hexadecimal values.
TaskName	String	The unique name given to the task at design time.
TaskTransactionOption	Int32	Identifies the transaction option the task is utilizing.

Event Handler System Variables

The last type of executables in SSIS, event handlers, also has its own set of system variables. These variables often do not apply to all the event handlers. The general rule that applied to the tasks also applies to the event handler system variables. Table 9-4 describes all the event handler system variables.

Table 9-4. *Event Handler System Variables*

Name	Data Type	Description
Cancel	Boolean	Identifies whether the event handler stops execution after error, warning, or query cancellation. Available to only OnError, OnWarning, and OnQueryCancel.
ErrorCode	Int32	Identifies the error code that occurred. Available to only OnError, OnInformation, and OnWarning.
ErrorDescription	String	String that describes the error event. Available to only OnError, OnInformation, and OnWarning.
ExecutionStatus	Boolean	Identifies whether the event is currently executing. Available to only OnExecStatusChanged.
ExecutionValue	DBNull	Returns the execution value. Available to only OnTaskFailed.
LocaleID	Int32	Identifies the locale that the event handler uses. Available to all event handlers.
PercentComplete	Int32	Returns the progress on the completion of the event handler. Available to only OnProgress.

Name	Data Type	Description
ProgressCountHigh	Int32	Works in conjunction with `ProgressCountLow` to show the total number of operations completed by the `OnProgress` event. Represents the high values of a 64-bit composite. Available to only `OnProgress`.
ProgressCountLow	Int32	Works in conjunction with the `ProgressCountHigh` to show the total number of operations completed by the `OnProgress` event. Represents the low values of a 64-bit composite. Available to only `OnProgress`.
ProgressDescription	String	Describes the progress of the event handler. Available to only `OnProgress`.
Propagate	Boolean	Identifies whether the event handler propagates to higher-level event handlers. Available to all event handlers.
SourceDescription	String	Description of the source that triggered the event handler to fire. Available to all event handlers.
SourceID	String	The unique identifier of the source that triggered the event handler to fire. Available to all event handlers.
SourceName	String	The name of the source that triggered the event handler to fire. Available to all event handlers.
VariableDescription	String	Description of the variable that triggered the event handler to fire. Available to only `OnVariableValueChanged`.
VariableID	String	The unique identifier of the variable that triggered the event handler to fire. Available to only `OnVariableValueChanged`.

Accessing Variables

After you create all the variables you need for your ETL process, you will most probably want to access them. SSIS provides multiple ways to access the variables. Only the user-defined variables are modifiable. The values stored within the variables can be used to either construct a new value based on the variable value or to divert rows in the data flow.

To illustrate the different methods for accessing variables and parameters, we created two packages, CH09_Apress_ParentPackage.dtsx and CH09_Apress_ChildPackage.dtsx. The parent package's sole task is to execute the child package by using the Execute Package task. Figure 9-11 demonstrates the contents of the parent package's Package Explorer. The variable is in place to show the passing of variables to child packages by using parameters.

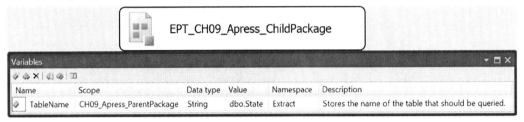

Figure 9-11. CH09_Apress_ParentPackage.dtsx Package Explorer

The child package is a little bit more complicated, as you can see in Figure 9-12. It serves to show two examples. The first example to execute is the SEQC_States sequence container. Its goal is to demonstrate how variables can be accessed by using transformations in a Data Flow task, a Foreach Loop container, and a Script task. The end result of this example is showing a message box displaying a string repeatedly until all the records have been iterated by the Foreach Loop container. The second example's main purpose is to show the implementation of generating and executing dynamic SQL. This is done by using an Execute SQL task to retrieve a set of strings that will help create the different SQL statements, a Script task to concatenate the strings into executable SQL, and a final Execute SQL Task to execute the query stored within that string.

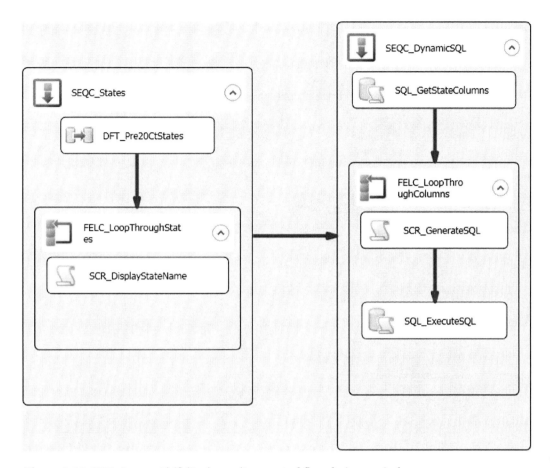

Figure 9-12. `CH09_Apress_ChildPackage.dtsx` *control flow designer window*

Parameterized Queries

Another excellent way that SSIS allows us to use variables is to parameterize source queries in Data Flow tasks. In order to parameterize queries, you need to use the SQL Command option as the data access mode. Listing 9-1 demonstrates the query we used inside the source component, `SRC_GetPre20CtStates`.

Listing 9-1. *Parameterized Source Query*

```
SELECT DISTINCT Name
      ,Abbreviation
      ,Capital
      ,Flag
      ,Date
      ,Fact
      ,Long
```

```
    ,Lat
FROM dbo.State s
WHERE YEAR(s.Date) < ?;
```

The question mark is the qualifier used to mark the placement of the parameter. We recommend placing all the required parameters in the same area so that reading and maintaining the SQL does not become a nightmare. In order to map the proper variable value to this qualifier, we must use the Parameters button on the source editor. Figure 9-13 shows our configuration for the parameter mapping. We used the Extract::StateYearFilter variable in order to limit the data that is coming through. The Parameter0 name is predetermined because we are using the OLE DB source component. Refer to Chapter 7 for more information about the parameter-naming conventions required with the different providers.

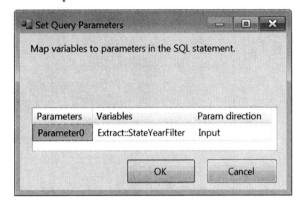

Figure 9-13. Set Query Parameters dialog box for SRC_GetPre20CtStates

---

■ **NOTE:** We provided a default value for the Extract::StateYearFilter variable. This value can be modified by using the Script task and using an assignment statement after listing the variable in the ReadWriteVariables field.

Derived Column Transformations

After the data starts flowing through the pipeline, SSIS allows you to use Derived Column transformations to access the value stored in the variables. The same functionality can be used through a Script task transformation using similar code as shown earlier. For this particular part of the data flow, we want to be able to replace null values with a default value and add this transformation as a new column to the pipeline. In order to achieve this requirement, we use the expression ISNULL([Date]) ? @[Transform::StateAcceptanceTime] : (DT_DATE)   [Date]. Figure 9-14 demonstrates how the Derived Column transformation automatically reads in the data type information from the type casts. We discuss type casts in more depth later in this chapter.

The ISNULL() function returns a Boolean value similar to the SQL Server function. If the conditional evaluates to True, we provide the value of the Transform::StateAcceptanceTime. Otherwise, we maintain the original date. The only difference is that this column contains timestamp information.

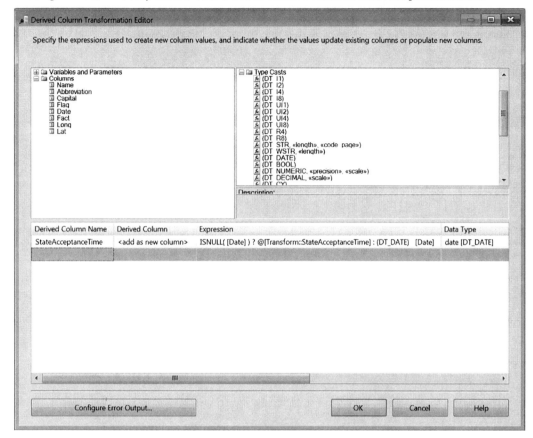

Figure 9-14. Derived column to replace missing data

■ **NOTE:** Because we used a WHERE clause with the equal operator in the source SQL query, the ISNULL([Date]) condition will always return False. Without that condition in the initial query, it is possible for ISNULL([Date]) to return True.

Conditional Splits

SSIS provides a Conditional Split transformation that can redirect data to multiple streams. In the simplest case, it can act as a WHERE clause, and in the more complicated cases, it can act as a CASE statement. For our example, we have a very simple criterion: we want to load only states whose capitals are north of Oklahoma City. We set the latitude value of Oklahoma City as the default value of `Transform::StateCapitalFilter`. With this value in place, we use the expression `Lat > @[Load::StateCapitalFilter]` in the conditional split shown in Figure 9-15 to pass through only the desired records. Because the latitude values increase as we approach the North Pole, the Greater Than comparison operator was used to determine whether the record should pass through.

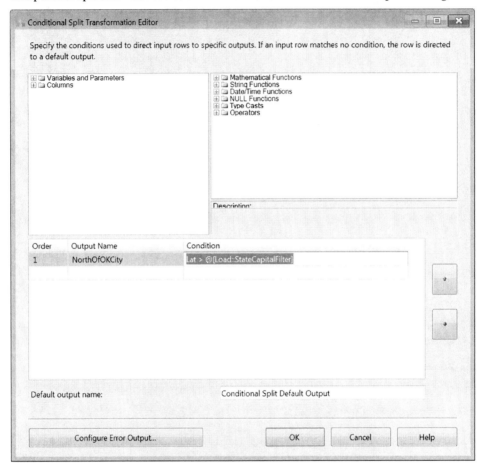

Figure 9-15. *Conditional split to exclude values based on the variable value*

Recordset Destinations

After we perform all the transformations that are required, we need to store the data somewhere. The recordset destination allows us to load the data into an Object data type variable. This functionality works similarly to the Execute SQL task storing a Full result set output in a variable. Figure 9-16 shows the recordset destination configuration that is required to load the data into a variable. The essential part is to determine which variable to use.

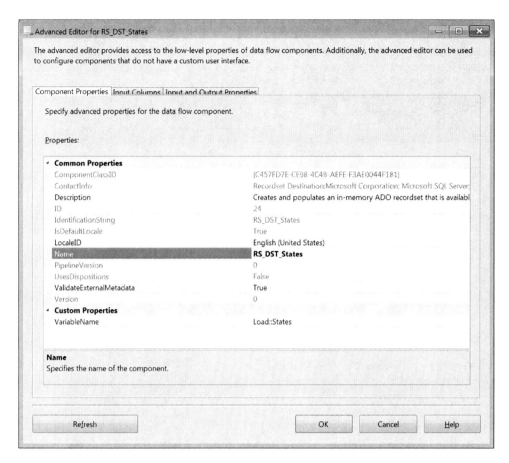

Figure 9-16. Configuration of the recordset destination

■ **NOTE:** Reusing object variables for storing data will cause them to be cleared before they are loaded with the new data. Object variables do not append data after they are loaded. This can allow you to reuse the same variable for various datasets, but we do not recommend this approach because you will start to lose track of the tabular structure of the variable. Each load can add or remove columns, making the reuse of the variable a development pitfall. It is pretty easy to lose track of the column mappings in the objects, especially with entities that have numerous columns. Changing the structure several times will create an even greater complexity. This becomes especially noticeable if you use the object as the iterator in multiple Foreach Loop containers. You need to go back and forth to make sure that you are mapping the results in the proper order based on how the latest dataset was loaded.

After the variable is chosen as the destination, we need to specify the columns we will need to access. Figure 9-17 shows the column mapping that we can pass to a Foreach Loop container as we iterate through the object. After we have the dataset in the variable, the Foreach Loop container can read the values and assign them to other variables whose purpose is to hold the value during that iteration. This is very similar to the functionality provided by a cursor in SQL Server.

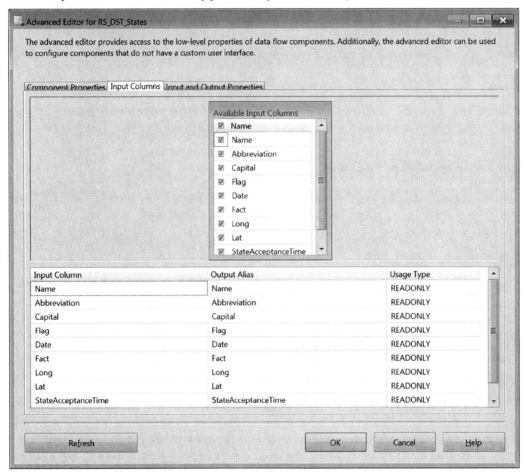

Figure 9-17. *Recordset destination—column mapping*

Foreach Loop Containers

Foreach Loop containers within SSIS can utilize Object data type variables as their iterators. In order to load the data, we need to first load data into the variable we intend to use. We demonstrated loading the data by using the recordset destination. As Figure 9-18 demonstrates, the Foreach Loop container utilizes the Foreach ADO enumerator as its iterator. We specified the Load::States variable as the enumerator because we populated it with the States dataset.

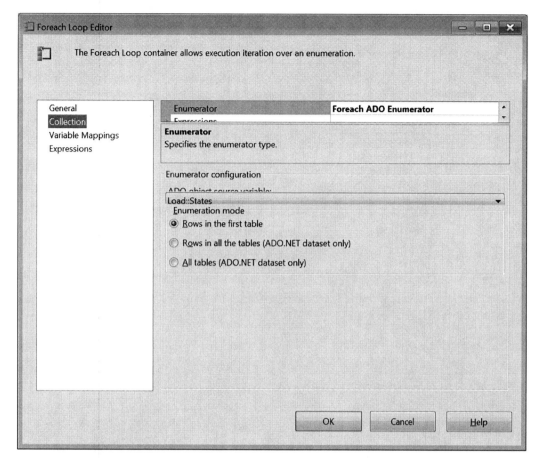

Figure 9-18. Foreach Loop container—Collections page

After the enumerator has been defined, we need to ensure that every column that is populated in the object is mapped to a variable. As the container loops through the object, the Foreach Loop container will assign the data value in each column to a variable. Skipping mappings will result in SSIS throwing unfriendly error messages. The container will automatically assign the index value shown in Figure 9-19, so we recommend mapping the variables in the same order as the columns are mapped to the enumerator variable.

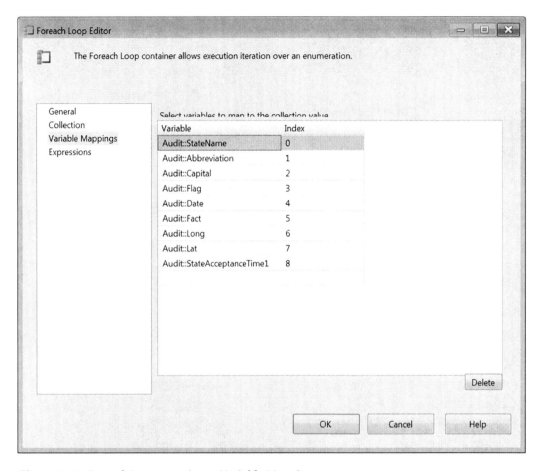

Figure 9-19. Foreach Loop container—Variable Mappings page

Script Tasks

One of the easiest ways to access variables is by using the SSIS Script tasks in either the control flow or the data flow. In our sample package, CH09_Apress_ChildPackage.dstx, we will use the Script task at the control-flow level to display a string in a message box. Figure 9-20 demonstrates the ability to specify the access mode of the variables in a Script task. In our case, we only want to be able to read the value of the System::PackageName variable. Because we will not be modifying any existing variable values, we leave the ReadWriteVariables field empty.

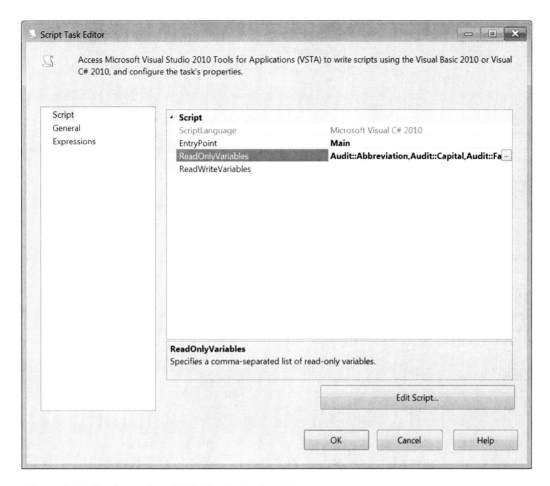

Figure 9-20. Configuration of SCR_DisplayPackageName

Using Visual C#, we can access only the variables listed in the configuration shown in Figure 9-20. The code goes directly into the main method of the script. Listing 9-2 demonstrates the C# that we used to access the value of the variable and display it in a message box at runtime. The section highlighted in bold allows the Script task to access the variables collection in Dts. After we extract the value, we can manipulate it in any manner we need. The quotes around the fully qualified variable name are necessary to properly identify the variable. The variable is case sensitive, so the code needs to be very precise.

Listing 9-2. Variable Accessor Script

```
MessageBox.Show("The name current state's name is: " +
    Dts.Variables["Audit::StateName"].Value.ToString()+"\n"+
    "Its abbreviation is: " + Dts.Variables["Audit::Abbreviation"].Value.ToString() + "\n"
+
    "A fact about this state: " + Dts.Variables["Audit::Fact"].Value.ToString() + "\n" +
```

```
"The state capital is: " + Dts.Variables["Audit::Capital"].Value.ToString() + "\n" +
"The capital is located at: (" + Dts.Variables["Audit::Lat"].Value.ToString() + ", " +
Dts.Variables["Audit::Long"].Value.ToString() + ")." + "\n" +
"The state was accepted at: "+Dts.Variables["Audit::StateAcceptanceTime1"].
Value.ToString());
```

With Listing 9-2 code, when we execute the package, we receive a small message box. The code concatenates the values extracted from the object variable into one string that is used to populate the message box. Figure 9-21 shows the value that is concatenated by the code. The package will not proceed until you close the message box. After the message box is closed, the Foreach Loop will proceed to the next record in the enumerator and expose its values in a similar message box.

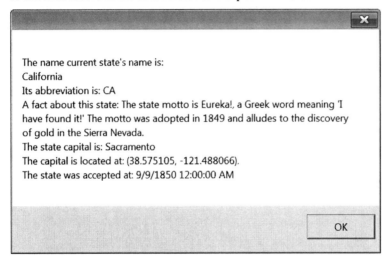

Figure 9-21. Message box displaying the package name derived from the system variable

Execute SQL Task Result Sets

The Execute SQL task allows you to store result sets directly from the executed query. The query can return a scalar value, a one-column value with one row, a full result set, or an XML value. These result sets can be stored in variables with the proper data types. In our example, we will store a full result set based on the query shown in Listing 9-3. This query retrieves all the columns in the dbo.State table. With this result set, we will show a quick data-profiling process contained in CH09_Apress_ChildPackage.dtsx. Figure 9-22 shows the configuration of the SQL_GetStateColumns task that stores the result of the query.

Listing 9-3. SQL_GetStateColumns—column names query

```
SELECT c.COLUMN_NAME
FROM INFORMATION_SCHEMA.COLUMNS c
WHERE c.TABLE_NAME = 'State';
```

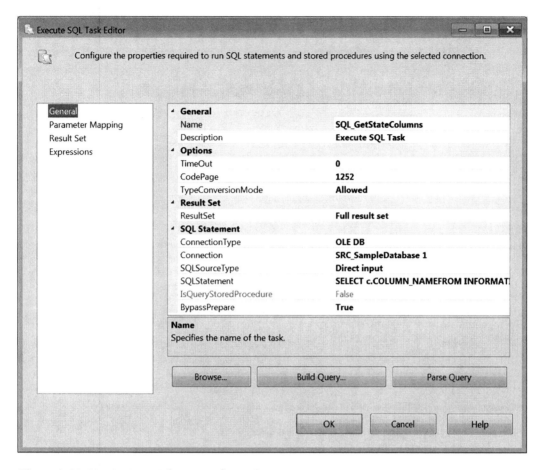

Figure 9-22. SQL_GetStateColumns configuration

▨ **NOTE:** If the variable contains values prior to the execution of this task, those values will be overwritten by its results.

Source Types

The final way to access variables is not exactly a single task or transformation but rather a property that appears in several tasks. This is the source type property that usually allows you to specify Direct input, Variable, or File. In our example for the profiling process, we use an Execute SQL task, SQL_ExecuteSQL, to execute a query stored within the variable, Transform::StateQuery. The process we use to modify this variable is covered in the following "Dynamic SQL" section. Figure 9-23 shows the configuration of the SQL_ExecuteSQL task that accesses the dynamically generated query.

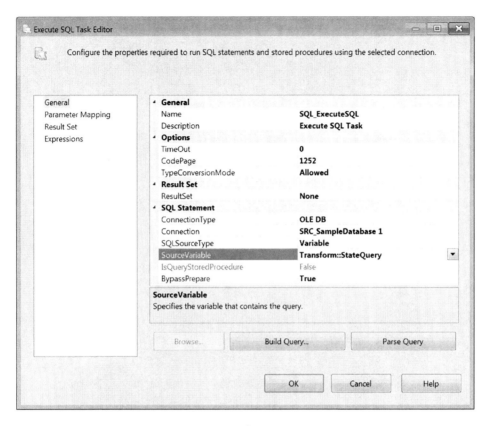

Figure 9-23. SQL_ExecuteSQL sourcing Transform::StateQuery

Dynamic SQL

In most of our examples, we have demonstrated only reading the variable values without actually modifying any values. One of the most frequent areas that require variable modification is in generating dynamic SQL queries. In SSIS, this process usually replaces cursors and runs a set of queries that can vary in number, but have some very important components that are similar in structure. As mentioned in the preceding section, we want to demonstrate a very basic data-profiling process. We already showed you how we retrieved our controller set by using the Execute SQL task to store the column names in the Load::StateColumns variable. We also showed you how we executed the resulting query by using the SQLSourceType option on a separate Execute SQL task. This section shows you how the variable's value is set so that it becomes an executable query.

The first step we need to take is to extract the name of each column as we iterate through all the columns. We implemented this by using a Foreach Loop container, FELC_LoopThroughColumns. Because Load::StateColumns has only one column, Name, the variable mappings are very simple, as we demonstrate in Figure 9-24. This configuration overwrites the value of Load::StateColumnName with every row in the object, one iteration at a time.

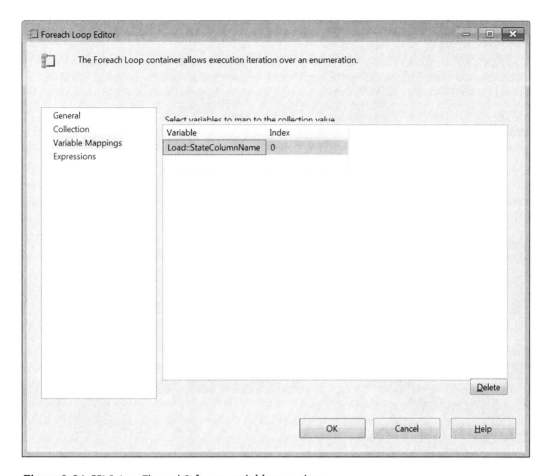

Figure 9-24. FELC_LoopThroughColumns variable mappings

With the variable value changing with every row in the object, we can run some queries that can give some meaningful insight into the data. For our query, we chose to perform a distinct count on the values stored in each column in the dbo.State table. Options include loading the data into a table by using INSERT INTO. We included a sample value in the commented-out C# on the last line of the code sample. The Execute SQL task, SQL_ExecuteSQL, will run a query for every column name that is stored in the object. With this particular query, you can see how the values in each of your columns vary.

Listing 9-4. StateQuery Assignment

```
Dts.Variables["Transform::StateQuery"].Value =
        "SELECT COUNT(DISTINCT " + Dts.Variables["Load::StateColumnName"].Value.ToString()
            + ") FROM dbo.State WITH (NOLOCK);";

// SELECT COUNT(DISTINCT Name) FROM dbo.State WITH (NOLOCK);
```

Passing Variables

One of the main difficulties with parent-child design patterns in prior versions of SSIS was the dependency of the child packages on the parent packages. At first glance this may not seem like an obstacle, but in some cases the dependency would make it very difficult to unit-test the child package on its own. With the introduction of parameters in this version of SSIS, this obstacle disappears. You essentially have the ability to define a default value for a parameter that under normal execution would be overwritten.

We begin by adding a parameter to the child package, as shown earlier in Figure 9-4. This will provide us with a parameter that can be accessed just like a variable in SSIS expressions and script components. We can provide a default if we are anticipating that the package may be executed on its own. With the parameter added, the parent package's Execute Package task should automatically detect it. You can create a mapping that allows the parent value to overwrite the child value while configuring the other properties of the Execute Package task. The mapping in CH09_Apress_ParentPackage.dtsx is shown in Figure 9-25.

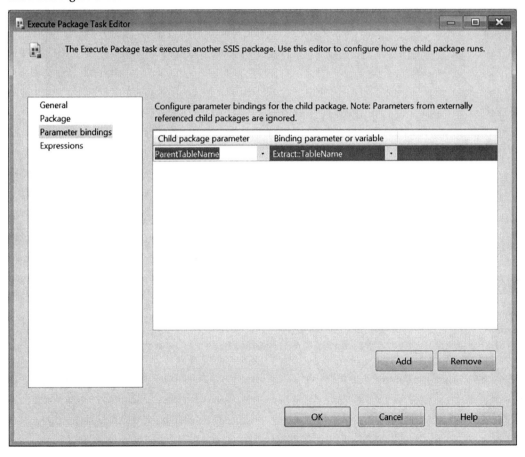

Figure 9-25. Execute Package task parameter bindings

SSIS Expression Language

The SSIS Expression Language allows you to extend the functionality of your process to incorporate variables. The language contains a whole set of functions and operators that can be used to evaluate columns, variables, or expressions. The functions return different data type values. They are usually grouped by their input types in the Expression Builder. We already covered the casting functions in the "SSIS Data Types" section of this chapter. The function names are not case-sensitive, unlike most of the other identifiers in the expression language. We recommend that you use a distinct case when using functions in order to make the code a little easier to read.

Functions

Mathematical functions accept numeric values as their inputs to return numeric values after performing operations on them. The following are the mathematical functions available within SSIS:

ABS(«numeric_expression») returns the absolute value of the input.

CEILING(«numeric_expression») returns the smallest integer greater than or equal to the input.

EXP(«numeric_expression») returns the exponent to base e of the input.

FLOOR(«numeric_expression») returns the largest integer less than or equal to the input.

LN(«numeric_expression») returns the natural logarithm of the input.

LOG(«numeric_expression») returns the base-10 logarithm of the input.

POWER(«numeric_expression», «power») returns the value of raising the first parameter to the power specified in the second parameter.

ROUND(«numeric_expression», «length») returns the first input round to the length specified in the second parameter.

SIGN(«numeric_expression») returns the positive, negative, or zero sign of the input.

SQUARE(«numeric_expression») returns the value of the input raised to the second power.

SQRT(«numeric_expression») returns the square root of the input.

String functions evaluate character expressions. These are the string functions available in the Expression Builder:

CODEPOINT(«character_expression») returns the Unicode value of the first character in the input.

FINDSTRING(«character_expression», «string», «occurrence») returns the index of the occurrence of the specified string in the input. The index values start at 1.

HEX(«integer_expression») returns a string hexadecimal value of the input.

LEFT(«character_expression», «number») returns a string that consists of the specified number of characters at the beginning of the first parameter.

LEN(«character_expression») returns the length of the input.

LOWER(«character_expression») returns a string that consists of the lowercase characters of the input.

LTRIM(«character_expression») returns a string stripped of the leading whitespaces from the input.

REPLACE(«character_expression», «search_expression», «replace_expression») returns the character expression value after a string that has been replaced with another string or empty string within the original character expression.

REPLICATE(«character_expression», «times») returns a string with the character expression repeated a specified number of times.

REVERSE(«character_expression») returns a string whose characters are in the reverse order of the input.

RIGHT(«character_expression», «number») returns a string consisting of the specified number of the rightmost characters in the character expression.

RTRIM(«character_expression») returns a string stripped of the trailing whitespaces in the input.

SUBSTRING(«character_expression», «start», «length») returns a string consisting of the characters from the specified starting index to the specified length of the character expression.

TOKEN(«character_expression», «delimiter_expression», «occurrence») returns a string consisting of all the characters between the specified occurrence and the first delimiter expression that is encountered in the character expression.

TOKENCOUNT(«character_expression», «delimiter_expression») returns the number of tokens that are present in the character expression based on the delimiter expression as the token terminator.

TRIM(«character_expression») returns a string stripped of the leading and trailing whitespaces in the input.

UPPER(«character_expression») returns a string that consists of the uppercase of the characters of the input.

The date functions perform operations on date and timestamp values. The following are the available date functions in the Expression Builder:

DATEADD(«datepart», «number», «date») returns a date value after adding the specified number of time units to the specified part of the date input.

DATEDIFF(«datepart», «startdate», «enddate») returns the value of the length of time units between the starting date and the ending date supplied.

DATEPART(«datepart», «date») returns an integer value representing part of the specified date. A date in the month of January would return 1 if the datepart was specified as the month.

DAY(«date») returns an integer value that represents the day of month of the input date.

GETDATE() returns the current date and time set on the host machine.

GETUTCDATE() returns the current date and time set on the host machine in Universal Time Coordinate.

MONTH(«date») returns an integer representing the number of the month of the input date.

YEAR(«date») returns an integer representing the number of the year of the input date.

The last category of functions that exists in SSIS is composed of the NULL functions. All but one of the functions in this category returns a NULL value type casted for a certain data type. In order to return a NULL of a certain data type, you pass the function as your expression NULL(«data type») and fill in the required data type name. The ISNULL(«expression») function will evaluate the input expression and return a Boolean indicating whether it evaluates to NULL.

Operators

The operators in the expression language work similarly to the operators in C#. There are unary operators and binary operators. The operators do have a hierarchy when the expression is being evaluated. To maintain clarity, we recommend using parentheses whenever possible, or ambiguity may appear when reading the code quickly. The following are the operators available in SSIS:

+ **(Add/Concatenate)** adds two expressions together. It can also be used to concatenate strings.

- **(Subtract/Negate)** subtracts two expressions. It can also be used to return the negative value of a numeric expression.

* **(Multiply)** multiplies two numeric expressions.

/ **(Divide)** divides two numeric expressions.

% **(Modulo)** returns the integer remainder of the division of two numeric expressions.

() **(Parentheses)** are used to prioritize the evaluation of expressions.

== **(Equal)** logically evaluates two expressions for equality.

!= **(Unequal)** logically evaluates two expressions for inequality.

> (Greater Than) logically evaluates whether the expression on the left side of the operator is greater than the expression on the right side.

< (Less Than) logically evaluates whether the expression on the left side of the operator is less than the expression on the right side.

>= **(Greater Than or Equal To)** logically evaluates whether the expression on the left side of the operator is greater than or equal to the expression on the right side.

<= **(Less Than or Equal To)** logically evaluates whether the expression on the left side of the operator is less than or equal to the expression on the right side.

&& **(Logical AND)** performs a logical AND operation on the expressions on the left and right side of the operator.

|| **(Logical OR)** performs a logical OR operation on the expression on the left and right side of the operator.

? : **(Conditional)** performs a conditional check on the expression preceding the question mark. If the expression evaluates to True, the expression between the question mark and the colon is returned. If the expression evaluates to False, the expression following the colon is returned.

& **(Bitwise AND)** performs a bitwise AND operation on two integer values on either side of the operator.

| **(Bitwise Inclusive OR)** performs a bitwise inclusive OR operation on two integer values on either side of the operator.

^ **(Bitwise Exclusive OR)** performs a bitwise exclusive OR operation on two integer values on either side of the operator.

~ **(Bitwise Not)** performs a bitwise negation of an integer value.

! **(Logical Not)** negates the value of a Boolean expression.

Summary

SQL Server 11 offers many ways to make your ETL processes dynamic and modular. This chapter introduced the SSIS variables, parameters, and expression language. The code we provided allowed you to see in depth the different roles that variables and parameters can play in an ETL process. We also introduced how to pass variable values between packages. We concluded by describing all functions and operators that make up the expression language. Chapter 10 will walk you through scripting in SSIS.

Scripting

You're darn right more power!

—Tim Allen, *Home Improvement*

SSIS provides several stock control flow tasks and data flow components out of the box, all described in the previous chapters. Despite all these great tools, you'll inevitably encounter a situation when you need to do something that's not covered by the stock toolkit. The Script task and script component are two tools that give you an extra power boost. With the Script task and script component, you can use .NET code to enhance your SSIS packages and to manipulate and transform your data in ways the stock components can't.

Script Task

SSIS comes with more than 20 stock control flow tasks that perform a variety of functions. Whether you need to put or get files via File Transfer Protocol, FTP, execute another package or process, or perform common DBA database maintenance tasks, SSIS control flow tasks have you covered. Sometimes, though, you need a little more flexibility. At times like these, you can whip out the Script task and embed .NET code directly in your control flow.

One of the simplest tasks for which SSIS developers use the Script task is SSIS variable initialization in the control flow. For this example, we'll set a string variable to the postal abbreviation for a state to limit results returned by a query in a data flow. To start our example, we dragged a Script task and a Data Flow task onto the designer surface, as shown in Figure 10-1.

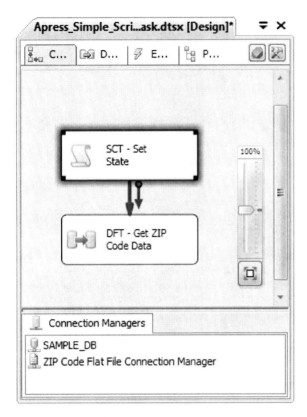

Figure 10-1. *Control flow with Script task*

We then declared a string variable named State with package scope, as shown in Figure 10-2.

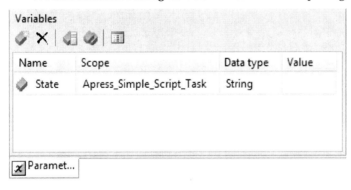

Figure 10-2. *Declaring a variable*

At this point, we're ready to use the Script task to initialize our variables. When you double-click the Script task, you'll see the editor shown in Figure 10-3.

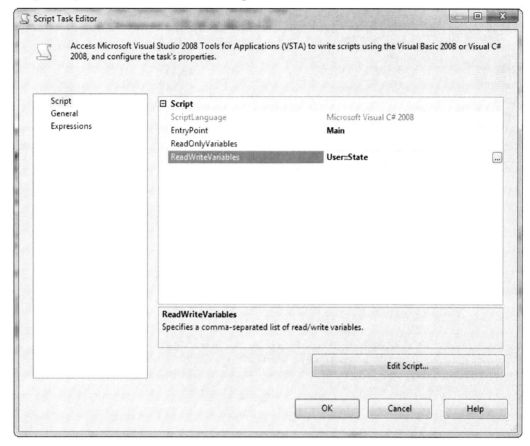

Figure 10-3. *Script page of the Script Task Editor*

On the Script page of the editor, you can choose your preferred scripting language with the ScriptLanguage parameter. The current options are Microsoft Visual C# 2008 and Microsoft Visual Basic 2008. Our preference is for C#, so our script code samples will be presented in this .NET language. You can also choose the EntryPoint for the Script task, which is the name of the function in the script that the task will execute when it runs. The default EntryPoint function name is Main.

You can also choose to expose variables to your script as read-only variables or read/write variables from pop-up dialog boxes, shown in Figure 10-4. The ReadOnlyVariables property lets you choose a list of SSIS variables to expose as read-only. Your script can't change the values of read-only variables. The ReadWriteVariables property exposes a list of variables to your script for reading and writing. You can change the values of read/write variables in your script. Because we're changing the value of the User::State variable in the script, we've exposed it as a read/write variable.

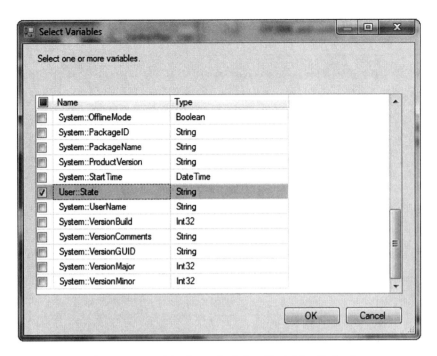

Figure 10-4. Choosing variables from the Select Variables dialog box

To write your script, click the Edit Script button to open the Visual Studio Tools for Applications (VSTA) Editor. By default, the Script task generates a class called ScriptMain, which inherits from the VSTARTScriptObjectModelBase class. There are also some autogenerated comments in the script that provide tips on how to access particular functionalities. Comments aside, the generated script code looks like this:

```
using System;
using System.Data;
using Microsoft.SqlServer.Dts.Runtime;
using System.Windows.Forms;

namespace ST_ab23c7f2534d47459000c7bfe5e99f2e.csproj
{
  [System.AddIn.AddIn("ScriptMain", Version = "1.0", Publisher = "", Description = "")]
  public partial class ScriptMain :
    Microsoft.SqlServer.Dts.Tasks.ScriptTask.VSTARTScriptObjectModelBase
  {

    #region VSTA generated code
    enum ScriptResults
    {
      Success = Microsoft.SqlServer.Dts.Runtime.DTSExecResult.Success,
      Failure = Microsoft.SqlServer.Dts.Runtime.DTSExecResult.Failure
    };
```

```
    #endregion

    public void Main()
    {
        Dts.TaskResult = (int)ScriptResults.Success;
    }
  }
}
```

The `Main` function, shown in bold in the preceding script, is where the magic happens. This function is called every time the Script task runs—it's where your code begins. Our task here is simple: we just want to set a variable. To do this, we'll change the `Main` function to set our variable as shown here:

```
public void Main()
{
    Dts.TaskResult = (int)ScriptResults.Success;
    Dts.Variables["User::States"].Value = "LA";
}
```

After editing the script, click the Save (disk icon) button. To finish off this sample, we created a simple data flow with an OLE DB source and a flat file destination, as shown in Figure 10-5.

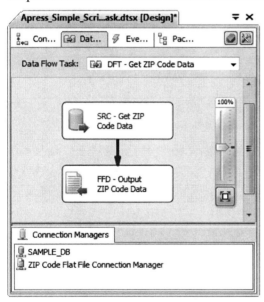

Figure 10-5. *Moving ZIP Code data from a database table to a flat file*

We used the following query in the OLE DB source component:

```
SELECT ZIP,
    State,
    Town,
    Lat,
    Lon
```

```
FROM dbo.ZIP
WHERE State = ?;
```

And we set the source's `Parameter0` value to the `User::State` variable. The end result is a flat file with the ZIP codes from the database, but only those for the state of Louisiana (LA).

Advanced Functionality

Our first Script task example was admittedly simplistic, but its goal was just to introduce the concept of adding .NET scripting to the control flow. The Script task lets you perform processing tasks that range from very simple to extremely complex, and they allow you to do things that are not always directly supported by the other stock control flow tasks. This section gives you a sample with a little more meat on it to demonstrate.

For this example, we want to reference back to the Foreach loop container, discussed in Chapter 5. The Foreach loop container has a Foreach File Enumerator mode, which iterates files in a directory for you, populating a string variable with the file names and/or fully qualified file paths in turn. Figure 10-6 shows the editor for the Foreach loop container in Foreach File Enumerator mode.

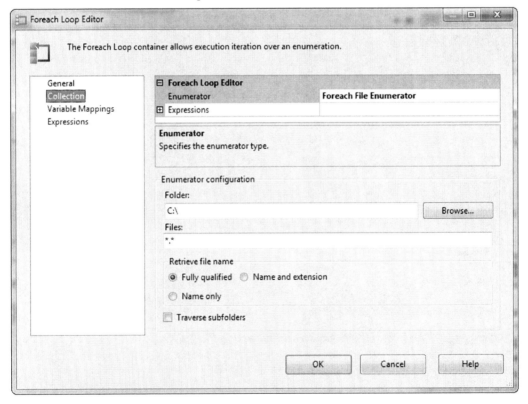

Figure 10-6. Foreach loop container in File Enumerator mode

The Foreach loop container's File Enumerator mode is very useful, but it is limited—it returns only file names and/or file paths. Files in the file system have a lot more metadata attached to them that can be useful for processing. Every file has a creation date and read-only flag attached to it, for instance. This information comes in handy if you want to process or archive files older than a specified date, or if you need to check whether a file is read-only before trying to delete it. We can get at this extra information by using a Script task.

To create our sample package, we dragged a Script task onto the designer surface, followed by a Foreach loop container with another Script task inside it, as shown in Figure 10-7.

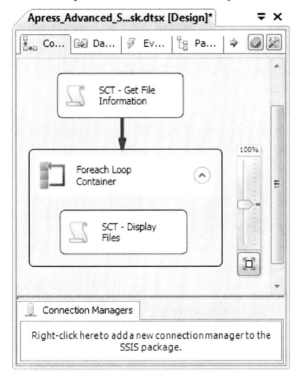

Figure 10-7. *Script tasks with Foreach loop container package*

We also created some variables scoped at the package level and some scoped at the Foreach loop container level. The two variables at the package level are as follows:

> User::Path: A string containing the full path of the directory in which we wish to enumerate files.

> User::Files: An object that will hold the results of the file enumeration, which will be stored as an ADO.NET DataTable object.

The variables at the Foreach loop container level are populated with file names, dates, and other related information on each iteration of the loop. Figure 10-8 shows the variables we declared at both levels.

■ **NOTE:** We discuss variables and variable scope in detail in Chapter 9.

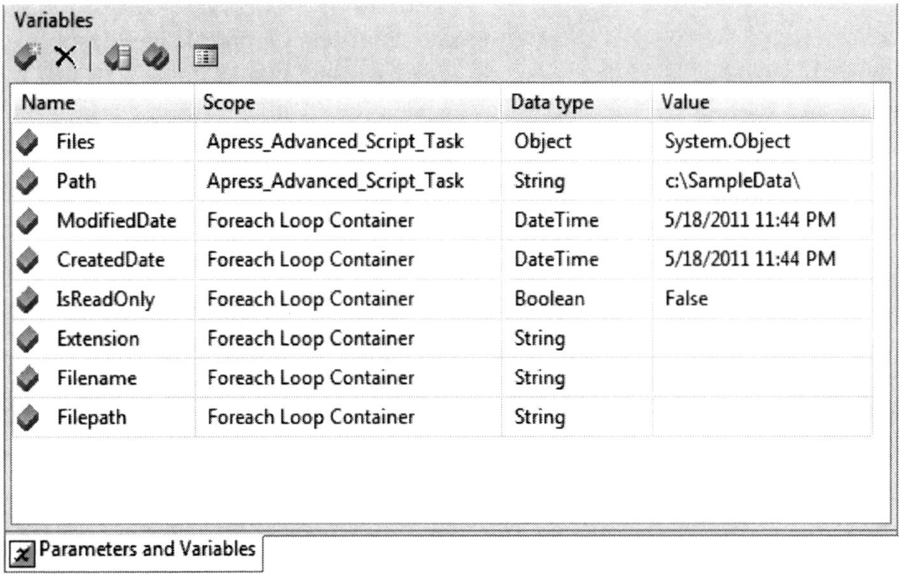

Variables			
Name	Scope	Data type	Value
Files	Apress_Advanced_Script_Task	Object	System.Object
Path	Apress_Advanced_Script_Task	String	c:\SampleData\
ModifiedDate	Foreach Loop Container	DateTime	5/18/2011 11:44 PM
CreatedDate	Foreach Loop Container	DateTime	5/18/2011 11:44 PM
IsReadOnly	Foreach Loop Container	Boolean	False
Extension	Foreach Loop Container	String	
Filename	Foreach Loop Container	String	
Filepath	Foreach Loop Container	String	

Parameters and Variables

Figure 10-8. *Variables, scoped at two levels in the sample package*

After the Script tasks, Foreach loop container, and variables were added to the package, we edited them. The first Script task (outside of the Foreach loop container) requires access to two of the variables we created: User::Path and User::Files. We're also passing in a system variable named System::TaskName, which holds the name of the current Script task so we don't have to hard-wire the name into any of our messages. The Script task needs only read-only access to the User::Path and System::TaskName variables, but needs read/write access to the User::Files variable because the task will place its results in this variable. Figure 10-9 shows the Script Task Editor with the variables.

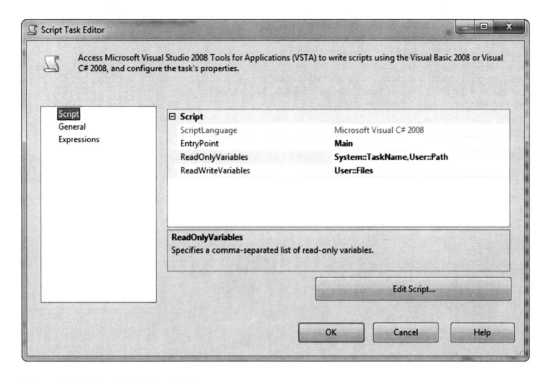

Figure 10-9. *First Script Task Editor*

The script we created in this Script task creates a .NET DataTable object with columns to hold the file name, path, and other file attributes. Each row in the DataTable represents a different file. The following code creates the DataTable, populates it with file information, and returns the DataTable in an SSIS object variable named User::Files:

```
public void Main()
{
  Dts.TaskResult = (int)ScriptResults.Success;

  // Get the name of the current task
  string TaskName = Dts.Variables["System::TaskName"].Value.ToString();
  bool b = true;

  try
  {
    // Fire an OnInformation event that we're starting
    Dts.Events.FireInformation(-1, TaskName, "Starting", "", 0, ref b);

    // Define our output data table
    DataTable dt = new DataTable();
    dt.Columns.Add("Filename", typeof(string));
    dt.Columns.Add("Extension", typeof(string));
    dt.Columns.Add("Filepath", typeof(string));
```

```
dt.Columns.Add("CreatedDate", typeof(DateTime));
dt.Columns.Add("ModifiedDate", typeof(DateTime));
dt.Columns.Add("IsReadOnly", typeof(Boolean));

// Get the file info and add it to the data table
string path = Dts.Variables["User::Path"].Value.ToString();
DirectoryInfo di = new DirectoryInfo(path);
FileInfo[] fi = di.GetFiles("*.*", SearchOption.AllDirectories);
foreach (FileInfo f in fi)
{
  dt.Rows.Add(new object[] { f.Name, f.Extension, f.DirectoryName, f.CreationTime,
    f.LastWriteTime, f.IsReadOnly });
}

// Output the data table
Dts.Variables["User::Files"].Value = dt;
}
catch (Exception ex)
{
  // If an error occurs fire an OnError event
  Dts.Events.FireError(-1, TaskName, ex.ToString(), "", 0);
}
finally
{
  // Fire a final OnInformation event that we're finished
  Dts.Events.FireInformation(-1, TaskName, "Finished", "", 0, ref b);
}
}
```

■ **TIP:** It's a good idea to use `try-catch` blocks in any .NET code that accesses external resources (such as the file system in this case). If the external resource is not accessible, you may need to set the `TaskResult` to the `Failure` value or perform other cleanup tasks before returning from the script.

SCRIPT TASK EVENTS

The Script task supports several event and logging options via the `Dts` object. Astute .NET developers might have noticed we used the `Dts.Events.FireError()` method in the `catch` part of the `try-catch` block instead of the usual `throw` statement to rethrow the exception. The call looks like the following:

```
Dts.Events.FireError(-1, "SCT - Get File Information", ex.ToString(), "", 0);
```

The parameters are as follows:

- The first parameter is an `int` named `errorCode`. This is a user-defined identifier for the error.

- Next is a `string` named `subComponent`. This is normally set to the name of the Script task for reference when the `OnError` event is logged.

- Then we have a `string` named `description` that contains the error description. If you use the `ToString()` method of the exception, you'll capture the exception information and inner exception stack in the `description`.

- The fourth and fifth parameters are a `string` named `helpFile` and an `int` named `helpContext`. These represent the path to a help file and the identifier for a topic within that file, if you have one. In our case, we set these to an empty string and 0, respectively, because we don't have a supporting help file.

We also don't assign a `Failure` value to the `Dts.TaskResult` property of the component. There are a couple of reasons for this. First, when you use the `FireError()` method, SSIS respects the `MaximumErrorCount` properties of the Script task and the package. Setting `Dts.TaskResult` or using a `throw` statement does not respect the `MaximumErrorCount` and causes the Script task to stop immediately. `FireError()` actually fires the `OnError` event, which means SSIS will handle logging for you, if you have logging turned on for your package and are capturing the `OnError` event.

In addition to `FireError()`, SSIS exposes methods to fire other events as well:

- `FireWarning()` fires an `OnWarning` event to log warning messages. Warning messages generally indicate a potential issue, but are not as severe as error messages.

- `FireInformation()` fires an `OnInformation` event that logs informational messages. Informational messages are generally softer than warning messages, in that they don't imply a problem or potential issue.

- `FireProgress()` fires an `OnProgress` event that logs progress messages. `OnProgress` events are fired when "measurable progress" is made within a component. In a nutshell, this means `OnProgress` events are fired for completion percentages.

- `FireQueryCancel()` fires an `OnQueryCancel` event, which checks whether the task should stop running. The method returns a `bool` result: `true` means the task should stop running, and `false` means to keep going.

- `FireCustomEvent()` fires a custom event.

The Script task `Dts.Log()` method lets you write messages directly to the SSIS log without the overhead of invoking an event. Normally you'll want to use the preceding event-driven methods to log information as they respect the package and task settings such as `MaximumErrorCount`.

After we populate the SSIS object variable with the list of files in DataTable format, we need to use those results. For this task, we pass the User::Files variable in to a Foreach loop container in Foreach ADO Enumerator mode. This mode lets you iterate the rows in an ADO.NET DataTable or DataSet or an ADO Recordset. We configured the Collection tab of the Foreach Loop Editor to iterate the rows in the first table and set the ADO object source variable to User::Files, as shown in Figure 10-10.

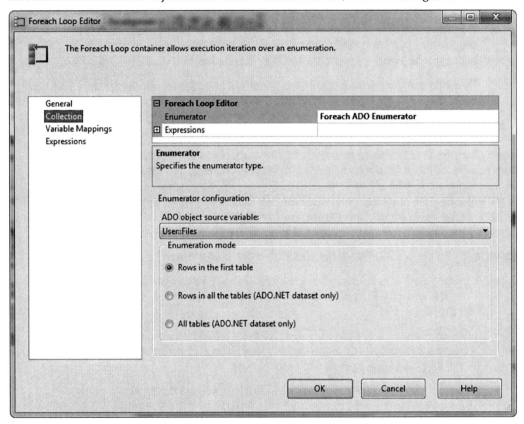

Figure 10-10. *Configuring the Foreach loop container to iterate rows in a .NET DataTable*

We finished configuring the Foreach loop container by setting the options on the Variable Mappings page of the editor, as shown in Figure 10-11. This page has two columns named Variable and Index. The Index column holds the zero-based indexes of the columns in your DataTable; the Variable column holds the variables these columns are mapped to. On each iteration of the loop, the variables listed will be populated with the values from the columns they are mapped to for each row in the DataTable.

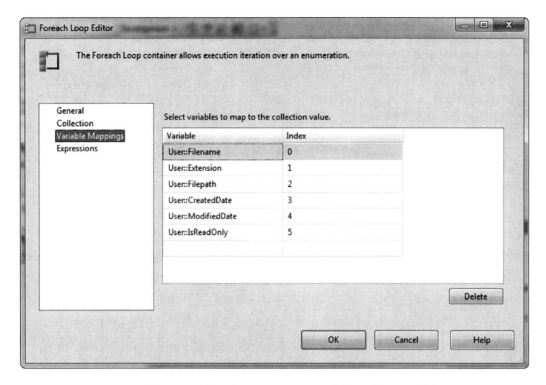

Figure 10-11. *Mapping the* DataTable *columns to SSIS variables in the Foreach loop container*

We put a second Script task inside the Foreach loop container and passed it the variables we populate on each loop, as shown in Figure 10-12. All we need to do is read the values of these variables, so we passed them in as read-only variables.

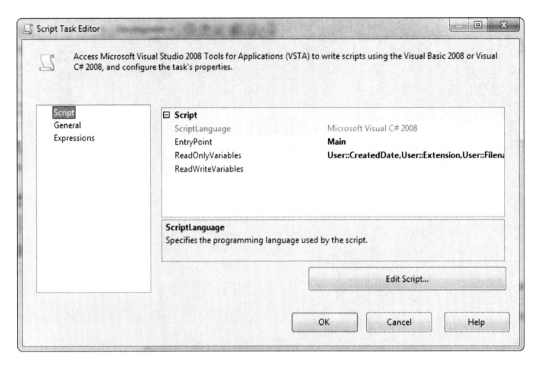

Figure 10-12. *Configuring the read-only variables in the inside Script task*

The script for this Script task is simple, as you can see here:

```
public void Main()
{
  Dts.TaskResult = (int)ScriptResults.Success;
  MessageBox.Show(String.Format("{0}, {1}, {2}, {3}, {4}, {5}",
    Dts.Variables["User::Filename"].Value.ToString(),
    Dts.Variables["User::Extension"].Value.ToString(),
    Dts.Variables["User::Filepath"].Value.ToString(),
    Dts.Variables["User::CreatedDate"].Value.ToString(),
    Dts.Variables["User::ModifiedDate"].Value.ToString(),
    Dts.Variables["User::IsReadOnly"].Value.ToString()));
}
```

This script simply takes the values of the read-only variables passed in and displays them in a Windows message box. The result, as you can see in Figure 10-13, is a pop-up message box displaying the metadata for each file on each iteration.

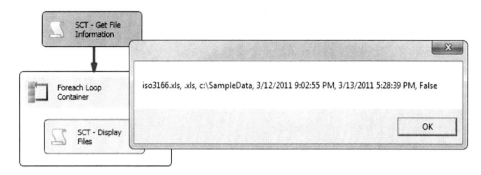

Figure 10-13. *Displaying file metadata on each loop iteration*

For this example, we simplified the result, simply displaying the file metadata in pop-up message boxes, but in a real application, you might use this metadata to back up, delete, or choose files to process based on some specific criteria. The important point here is that the first Script task retrieves the data and makes it accessible to the second Script task via variables set by the Foreach loop container.

■ **CAUTION:** In our example, we used a Windows message box to display variable values in the Script task. This is a very useful feature for SSIS script development and troubleshooting. Make sure you don't use message boxes in packages that you deploy to production, however, because this will cause a scheduled job to hang or fail.

Script Component Source

SSIS allows you to add .NET to your control flow with the Script task. You can also use .NET to manipulate your data in ways the other SSIS stock components don't natively support with the SSIS Script Component transformation. The Script Component transformation has three modes of operation: you can use it to create .NET script-based source, destination, and transformation components. As with the stock data flow components, a Script Component source retrieves data and pushes it into the data flow, a Script Component destination accepts data from the data flow and pushes it out to storage, and a Script Component transformation manipulates your data within the data flow.

When you drag a script component into your data flow, BIDS presents you with a pop-up menu to select the component type, as shown in Figure 10-14. To create a Script Component source, choose Source from the pop-up menu. The Script Component source has no inputs, but at least one output, and is always synchronous by design.

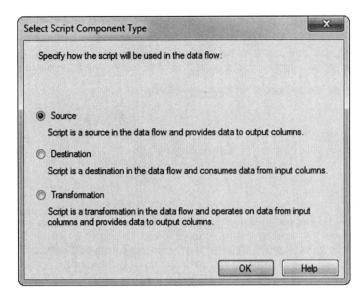

Figure 10-14. *Selecting the script component type from the pop-up menu*

Instead of pushing the data from our Script Component source to an output, we just pushed it into a Row Count component and enabled the data viewer on the source's output. This is a common method of testing SSIS data flows, because it allows you to review your data "in flight" during the ETL process without the hassle of persisting it to output. The data flow for our example looks like Figure 10-15.

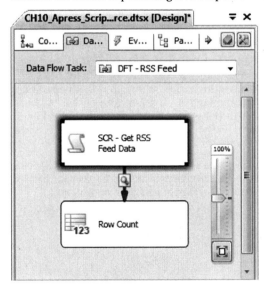

Figure 10-15. *Data flow with Script Component source*

After we dragged the script component onto the data flow and selected the source type, we had to configure it. The first step was adding columns to the script component output. To do this, we opened the Script Component Editor and went to the Inputs and Outputs page. Once there, we clicked on the Output Columns of Output 0 and clicked the Add Column button seven times. The columns are added with default names such as Column 1, Column 2, and so on, all with a default data type of four-byte signed integer [DT_I4].

We renamed each column to make the names more descriptive and changed the data type for each to string [DT_STR] with a length of 200. The one exception is the Description column, which we changed to string [DT_STR] with a length of 2000. Figure 10-16 shows the Inputs and Outputs page of the editor.

■ **TIP:** In addition to changing the name of the columns in the output, you can also change the name of the output itself. In this example, we kept the default name of Output 0.

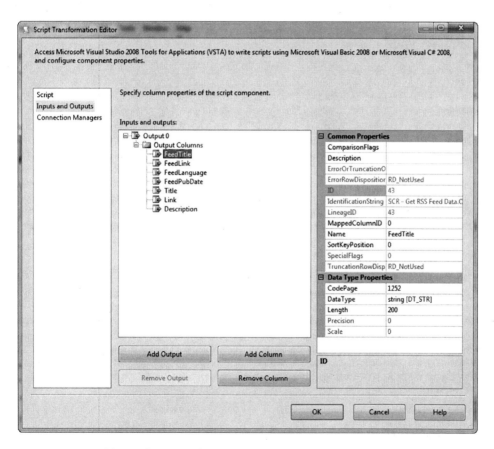

Figure 10-16. *Adding columns to the script component output*

The Script Component source inherits from the UserComponent class and implements three of its methods. The methods are called in the following order when the script component executes:

1. The PreExecute() method fires exactly once when the script component starts, before any rows are added to the output.

2. The CreateNewOutputRows() method is also called once for the script component. It is in this method that you can add new rows to the output, most often with a loop of some sort.

3. The PostExecute() method fires once when the script component ends, after you have finished adding rows to the output. This method is useful for performing any cleanup tasks after your script component has completed.

In our example, we grabbed the CNN Top Stories RSS feed. *Really Simple Syndication (RSS)* is an XML format used for syndicating web content, such as blog posts and news stories. In the script component, we used .NET to grab the latest RSS feed document and shred the XML to rows and columns, which we then placed into the component's output buffer. To begin, we declared a .NET XmlDocument object at the ScriptMain class level to hold our RSS feed page first, as shown here:

```
[Microsoft.SqlServer.Dts.Pipeline.SSISScriptComponentEntryPointAttribute]
public class ScriptMain : UserComponent
{
  // XML Document to hold RSS feed page
  XmlDocument RssXML = null;
  bool b = true;
  string ComponentName = "";

  // Method overrides will go here...

  ...

}
```

The PreExecute() method starts by grabbing the name of the script component for use in logging messages later. It then calls the base.PreExecute() method. Although it may not always be necessary to call base methods, it's a good idea to call them to ensure that any functionality they provide is not missed. Next we used .NET's built-in HttpWebRequest and HttpWebResponse classes to retrieve the CNN RSS feed and place it in the RssXML variable.

We also used the ComponentMetaData.FireInformation() method here, which fires OnInformation events that are useful for logging debugging information. Because our code is dependent on an external resource out of our control (namely a web site), we wrapped the web request in a try-catch block. If an exception is caught, we fire an OnError event with the FireError() method. The FireError() method in a data flow component doesn't stop the data flow. The error is propagated up to the Data Flow task, at which point SSIS decides whether to stop processing or not (based on package settings). In the case of the pre-execute phase of this component, a failure means we don't have good XML data to process for some reason, so there's no point in continuing. Therefore, we force a hard stop by rethrowing the exception with a throw statement.

```
public override void PreExecute()
{
  // Get Name of Component
  ComponentName = this.ComponentMetaData.Name;
```

```
// Fire OnInformation event for starting
this.ComponentMetaData.FireInformation(-1, ComponentName, "Beginning Pre-execute", "",
  0, ref b);

// Perform base PreExecute() method
base.PreExecute();

try
{
  // Fire OnInformation event for getting RSS feed data
  this.ComponentMetaData.FireInformation(-1, ComponentName,
    "Start - Getting RSS Feed data (Pre-execute)", "", 0, ref b);

  // Retrieve RSS feed
  HttpWebRequest req = (HttpWebRequest)HttpWebRequest.Create
    (
      "http://rss.cnn.com/rss/cnn_topstories.rss"
    );
  HttpWebResponse res = (HttpWebResponse)req.GetResponse();
  Stream str = res.GetResponseStream();

  // Put RSS feed document into XML Document
  RssXML = new XmlDocument();
  RssXML.Load(str);

  // Fire OnInformation event for getting RSS feed data
  this.ComponentMetaData.FireInformation(-1, ComponentName,
    "Complete - Getting RSS Feed data (Pre-execute)", "", 0, ref b);
}
catch (Exception ex)
{
  // Fire OnError event if an error occurs
  this.ComponentMetaData.FireInformation(-1, ComponentName, ex.ToString(), "", 0, ref b);

  // Rethrow exception to stop processing
  throw (ex);
}
finally
{
  // Fire OnInformation event for finished
  this.ComponentMetaData.FireInformation(-1, ComponentName, "Finished Pre-execute", "",
    0, ref b);
}
}
```

We don't have any special post-execution processing to perform, but we still have to override the PostExecute() method. In this case, all we did in PostExecute() was call the base.PostExecute() method:

```
public override void PostExecute()
{
  // Perform base PostExecute() method
```

```
    base.PostExecute();
}
```

The CreateNewOutputRow() method is where the real processing takes place. First we grabbed the RSS feed header information including feed title, link, and publication date and placed it in string variables. Then we looped over the <item> tags in the RSS feed, each one representing a syndicated article, and put the article title, link, and description in string variables. In the loop, we called the AddRow() method of the output buffer and assigned our string values pulled from the XML document to the output buffer columns. After the loop completed, and all rows were added to the output, we called the SetEndOfRowset() method on the buffer to signal SSIS that no more rows were coming.

▓ **TIP:** Even if you don't think you need any special error handling right now, putting try-catch blocks around your .NET code will make it easier to add special handling for errors in the future.

SCRIPT COMPONENT EVENTS

Like the Script task, the Script component allows you to fire events that SSIS may log based on your settings. In the Script task, event-firing methods are accessed through the Dts.Events object. In the Script component, they are accessed via the ComponentMetaData object. The methods that ComponentMetaData exposes include the following:

- FireError() fires an OnError event, which indicates a serious condition that affects processing and could stop a package from running. Note that FireError() by itself does not stop a data flow from running, but when the error propagates back up to the Data Flow task, SSIS will decide whether the control flow will fail based on its properties. To force a hard stop in the data flow, you should throw an exception as we do in our sample.

- FireWarning() fires an OnWarning event, which indicates an issue that is not as serious as an error but could affect processing nonetheless.

- FireInformation() fires an OnInformation event that contains informational messages. These messages are generally useful for debugging and troubleshooting issues.

- FireProgress() fires the OnProgress event, which in itself indicates component progress. We use the FireProgress() event in our sample.

- FireCustomEvent() fires a custom event of your creation within the package.

The event-firing methods exposed by the ComponentMetaData object are extremely useful when debugging, and we highly recommend using them liberally in your script components.

Along the way, we keep a count of processed rows, and report our progress by firing OnProgress events with the FireProgress() method. Like OnInformation, these events are useful for troubleshooting and debugging code. If we encounter an exception in this code, it's with a single row, so we call FireError() to log the error and let SSIS decide whether to stop processing at the task level. The code listing is as follows:

```
public override void CreateNewOutputRows()
{
  // Fire OnInformation event for starting
  this.ComponentMetaData.FireInformation(-1, ComponentName,
    "Start - Create new output rows", "", 0, ref b);

  try
  {
    // Get feed properties
    string feed_title = RssXML.SelectSingleNode("(/rss/channel/title)[1]").InnerText;
    string feed_link = RssXML.SelectSingleNode("(/rss/channel/link)[1]").InnerText;
    string feed_language = RssXML.SelectSingleNode("(/rss/channel/language)[1]").InnerText;
    string feed_pubDate = RssXML.SelectSingleNode("(/rss/channel/pubDate)[1]").InnerText;

    // Initialize counters and shred articles
    int CurrentRowCount = 0;
    int CurrentPercent = 0;
    int LastPercent = 0;
    XmlNodeList xl = RssXML.SelectNodes("/rss/channel/item");
    int TotalRows = xl.Count;

    // Iterate articles
    foreach (XmlNode xn in xl)
    {
      // Get article properties
      string title = xn.SelectSingleNode("(title)[1]").InnerText;
      string link = xn.SelectSingleNode("(link)[1]").InnerText;
      string description = xn.SelectSingleNode("(description)[1]").InnerText;

      // Create new output row
      OutputOBuffer.AddRow();

      // Assign values to the output buffer columns
      OutputOBuffer.FeedTitle = feed_title;
      OutputOBuffer.FeedLink = feed_link;
      OutputOBuffer.FeedLanguage = feed_language;
      OutputOBuffer.FeedPubDate = feed_pubDate;
      OutputOBuffer.Title = title;
      OutputOBuffer.Link = link;
      OutputOBuffer.Description = description;

      // Increment row counter, log progress
      CurrentRowCount++;
      CurrentPercent = CurrentRowCount * 100 / TotalRows;

      // Log progress every time % changes
```

```
      if (LastPercent != CurrentPercent)
      {
        // Fire OnProgress event
        this.ComponentMetaData.FireProgress(string.Format("{0} of {1} rows processed.",
          CurrentRowCount, TotalRows), CurrentPercent, CurrentRowCount, 0,
          ComponentName, ref b);

        // Update % complete
        LastPercent = CurrentPercent;
      }
    }
  }
  catch (Exception ex)
  {
    // Fire OnError event if an error occurs
    this.ComponentMetaData.FireInformation(-1, ComponentName, ex.ToString(), "", 0, ref b);
  }
  finally
  {
    // Perform base CreateNewOutputRows() method
    base.CreateNewOutputRows();

    // End of rows
    OutputOBuffer.SetEndOfRowset();

    // Fire OnInformation event for starting
    this.ComponentMetaData.FireInformation(-1, ComponentName,
      "Complete - Create new output rows", "", 0, ref b);
  }
}
```

■ **NOTE:** The .NET `SelectNodes()` and `SelectSingleNode()` methods we used in this example accept an XPath expression and return XML nodes. *XPath* is a language that allows you to locate and retrieve individual nodes, or sets of nodes, from XML documents. A discussion of the details of XPath is beyond the scope of this book. However, if you want more details on this technology, check out the .NET XPath Reference at `http://msdn.microsoft.com/en-us/library/ms256115.aspx`.

When this package is executed, the data viewer displays the results—the contents of the CNN Top Stories RSS feed, shown in Figure 10-17. Note that because CNN is constantly updating its news feeds, the content of your results is likely to differ from those shown in the figure.

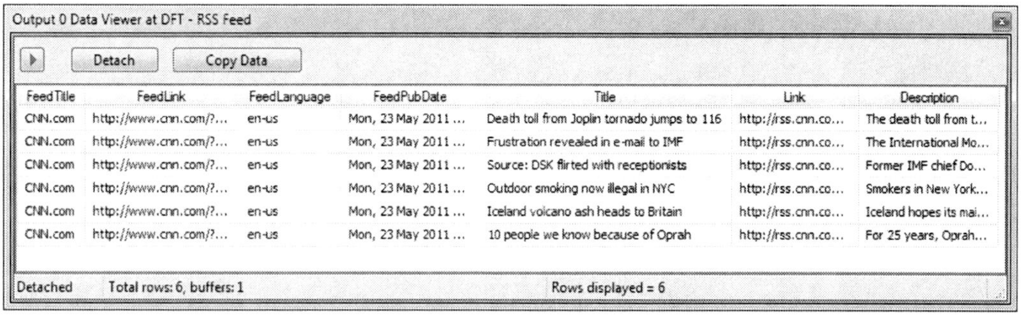

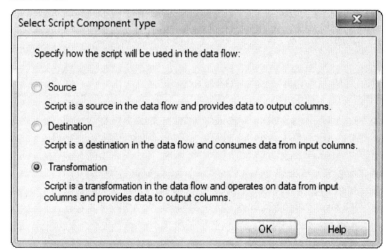

Figure 10-17. RSS feed contents in the data viewer

Synchronous Script Component Transformation

The Script Component synchronous transformation is extremely flexible. It differs from the Script Component source in that it has an input and an output. This section demonstrates a simple synchronous transformation with the script component. For this example, we expanded the previous package by adding another script component to the designer and selecting the transformation type, as shown in Figure 10-18. This new script component will perform a commonly needed—yet simple—function that is not included in the stock components. It will simply number the columns of the data flow for us.

Figure 10-18. Selecting the transformation script component type

After we added the new script component to the designer, we routed the data flow through it, as shown in Figure 10-19.

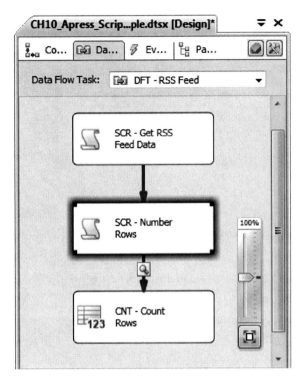

Figure 10-19. Adding the Script Component synchronous transformation to the data flow

SYNCHRONOUS OR ASYNCHRONOUS?

We discussed the differences between synchronous and asynchronous transformations in Chapter 8. The script component allows you to create both types of transformations. By default, the Script Component synchronous transformations are synchronous, and our sample is synchronous.

The setting that determines whether a script component is synchronous or asynchronous is the SynchronousInputID, which can be found on the Inputs and Outputs page of the editor. When this property of the component is set to the name of the input (Input o by default), the component is synchronous. When it's set to None, the component is asynchronous. The below figure shows how to set the SynchronousInputID property of the component.

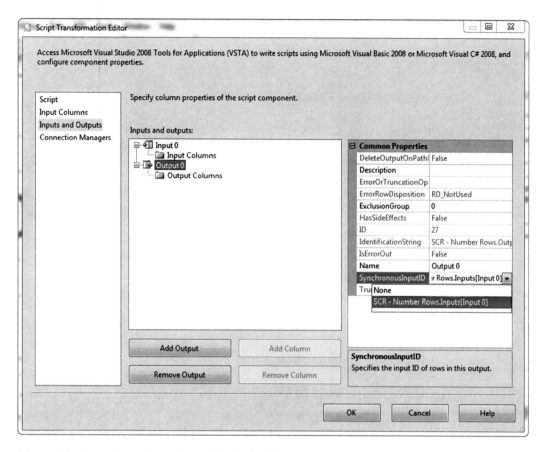

Figure 10-20. *Setting the SynchronousInputID of the script component*

On the Input Columns page of the editor, you can choose Input Columns and Output Columns. The Input Columns you choose are accessible from within the script; all other columns are "passed through" the component to the next component in the data flow. You can add Output Columns to the data flow on this tab as well. In our simple example, we've added a four-byte signed integer [DT_I4] type column named RowNumber to the output, as shown in Figure 10-21. This new column will hold the number assigned to each row, beginning with 1.

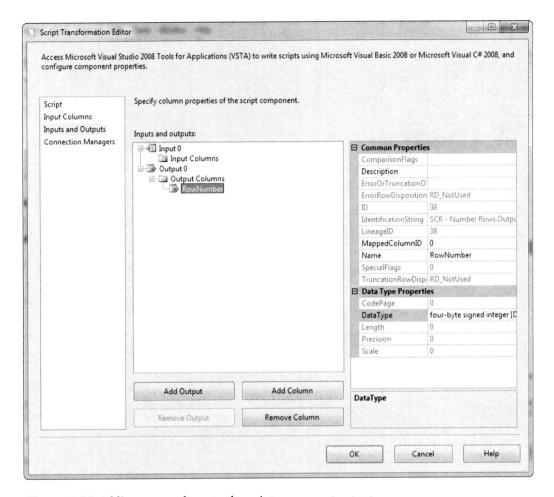

Figure 10-21. Adding a new column to the script component output

The Script Component synchronous transformation overrides three methods:

- Like the Script Component source, the asynchronous transformation type overrides the PreExecute() method. This method is executed exactly once at the start of the script component, before any data is processed. This method is useful for performing initialization tasks in your transformation.

- The Script Component synchronous transformation also supports the PostExecute() method. This method is executed exactly once, when all data has been processed by the component. This method allows you to perform any cleanup steps after the transformation is complete.

- Finally, the transformation provides the ProcessInputRow() method, which has the name of your input prepended to it. In our example, where the input is named Input 0, the ProcessInputRow() method is named Input0_ProcessInputRow(). In a synchronous transformation, this method is called once for every single row of data that passes through it. This method is "where the magic happens" in your transformation.

The script we used in this script component starts by declaring a class-level integer variable named row_number to keep track of our row count, as shown here:

```
[Microsoft.SqlServer.Dts.Pipeline.SSISScriptComponentEntryPointAttribute]
public class ScriptMain : UserComponent
{

  int row_number;

  ...
}
```

The PreExecute() method calls the base.PreExecute() method and initializes the row_number variable to 1:

```
public override void PreExecute()
{
  // Execute base PreExecute() method
  base.PreExecute();

  // Initialize row number
  row_number = 1;
}
```

The PostExecute() method simply calls the base.PostExecute() method:

```
public override void PostExecute()
{
  base.PostExecute();
}
```

The Input0_ProcessRow() method is called once for each row of the input. For each row passed in, we assign the value of the row_number variable to the RowNumber column of the data flow and then increment the row_number by 1.

```
public override void Input0_ProcessInputRow(Input0Buffer Row)
{
  // Assign row_number to RowNumber column
  Row.RowNumber = row_number;

  // Increment row_number
  row_number++;
}
```

The results of our simple row-numbering script component are shown in Figure 10-22.

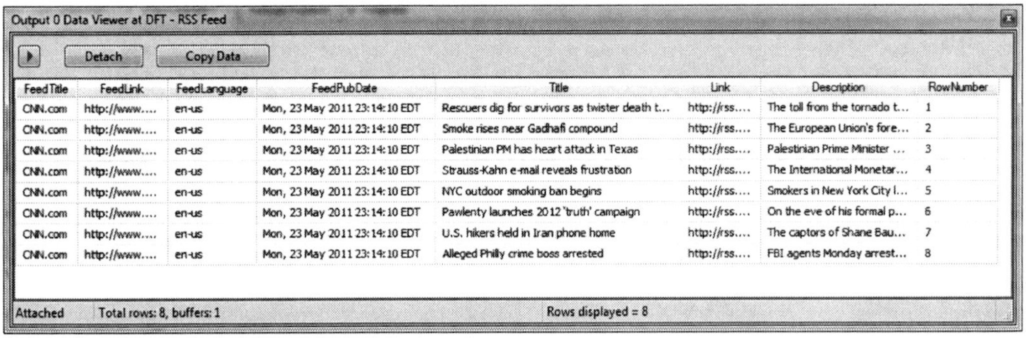

Figure 10-22. Results of row-numbering script component

Asynchronous Script Component Transformation

In addition to synchronous transformations, the script component allows you to create powerful asynchronous transformations. As we discussed in Chapter 8, asynchronous transformations are useful when you want to change the "shape" of your dataset by pivoting it, aggregating it, or by adding and removing rows. This example extends the previous package to incorporate a new asynchronous script component into the data flow. We will parse the article Title and Description columns into individual words and output them in a single column, along with an occurrence count for each word. In the real world, this type of transformation can be useful for performing text data mining and analysis.

We begin this sample by adding another script component to the task, as we did when adding a syncronous Script Component transformation. As before, we chose the Transformation option from the dialog box. We directed the data flow from the synchronous row-numbering script component to the new script component. We also added a new Row Count transformation to catch the input of the second output and enabled the data viewer on the output. The result looks like Figure 10-23.

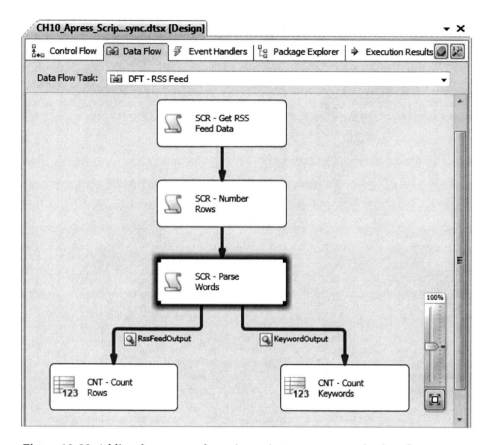

Figure 10-23. Adding the new word-parsing script component to the data flow

In this example, we're going to introduce two features of script transformations: (1) processing input data by using asynchronous transformations and (2) multiple outputs. For one of the outputs, which we've renamed RssFeedOutput, we'll output the RSS feed articles in the same form that we retrieved them in. The transformation will also extract the keywords out of the RSS feed Description column and count the number of occurrences of that word in each article. The results are sent to the second output, which we renamed KeywordOutput.

After dragging the new script component onto the designer surface, we went into the Input Columns page of the editor. We selected all inbound columns from the data flow, making them available to the script component, as you can see in Figure 10-24.

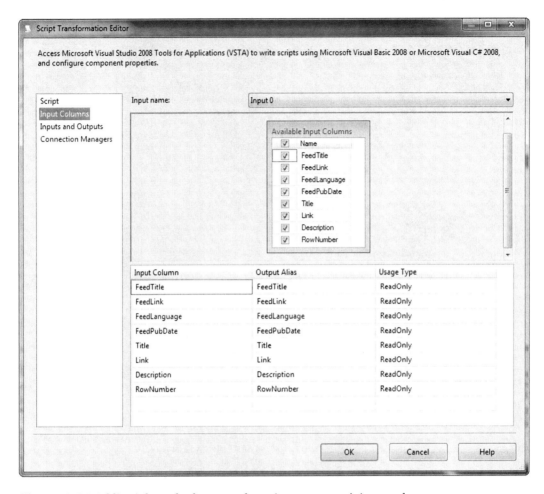

Figure 10-24. *Adding inbound columns to the script component's input columns*

After we added the inbound columns to the script component's input columns, we went to the Inputs and Outputs page. Once there, we added a second output to the Inputs and Outputs page. We then changed the SynchronousOutputID to None on both outputs. This disconnects them from the input and makes them asynchronous.

■ **TIP:** Although you can add multiple outputs to a Script Component transformation, you can have only one input. If you need multiple inputs (one example is the stock Union All component), you'll need to create a custom component, which we discuss in Chapter 22.

By default, the outputs are named Output 0 and Output 1—for this sample, we renamed them to RssFeedOutput and KeywordOutput to better reflect the data we'll push into it. We then created the output columns under each output. RssFeedOutput will contain the RSS feed contents exactly as they come into the component, while KeywordOutput will hold all the parsed keywords. You can see the Inputs and Outputs page with two asynchronous outputs in Figure 10-25.

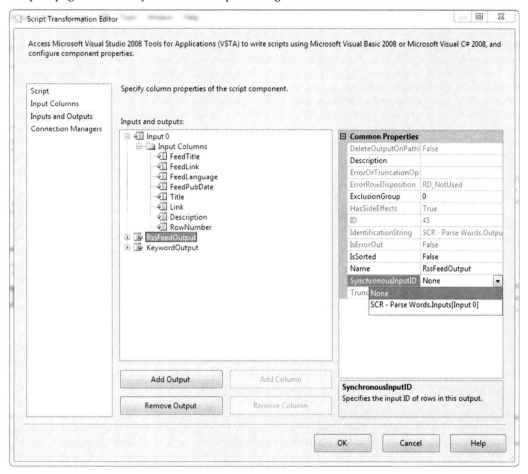

Figure 10-25. *Adding two asynchronous outputs to the script component*

When building a Script Component synchronous transformation, as we saw previously, the inbound columns flow through to the output by default. This is because in synchronous transformations, the input and output buffer are one and the same. You need to explicitly name only those columns that your transformation adds to the output. In an asynchronous transformation, the input and outputs are disconnected, so you need to explicitly create every single column you want in every output. In our example, the RssFeedOutput columns mirror the input columns, while the KeywordOutput contains only four columns, as shown in Figure 10-26. Table 10-1 lists the details of the KeywordOutput columns.

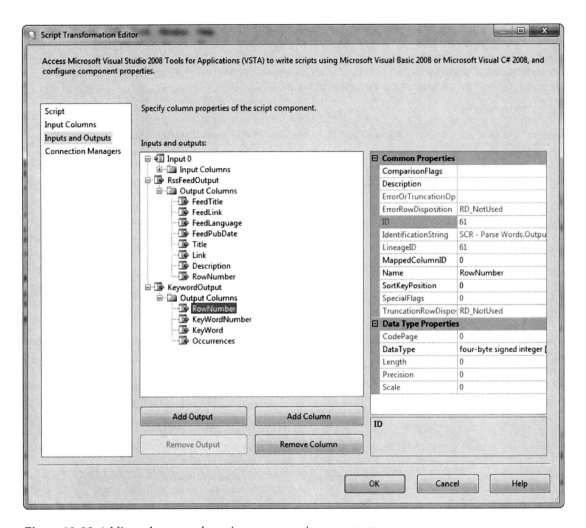

Figure 10-26. Adding columns to the script component's two outputs

Table 10-1. KeywordOutput Column Listing

Column Name	Data Type	Content
RowNumber	four-byte signed integer [DT_I4]	A copy of the RowNumber value assigned to each row of the input
KeyWordNumber	four-byte signed integer [DT_I4]	A unique number assigned to each keyword found within the RSS data Description column

Column Name	Data Type	Content
KeyWord	string [DT_STR], length 100	The keyword found within the Description column
Occurrences	four-byte signed integer [DT_I4]	The number of occurrences of the keyword within the Description column for each article

In the Script Component asynchronous transformation, we have four main methods that need to be overridden:

- The PreExecute() method fires once for the component before any rows are processed.

- The PostExecute() method fires once for the component after all rows have been processed.

- The ProcessInput() method fires once during execution of the component. This method iterates the rows of the buffer, calling another method—ProcessInputRow()—to process them. The ProcessInput() method is prefixed with the name of the input; in our example, it is Input0_ProcessInput().

- The ProcessInputRow() method fires once for every row passed to it. Normally, this will be once for every row in the input buffer, although this depends on the ProcessInput() method. The ProcessInputRow() method is also prefixed with the name of the input. In our example, it is named Input0_ProcessInputRow().

The PreExecute() and PostExecute() methods in our sample simply call the base methods shown here:

```
public override void PreExecute()
{
  // Call base method
  base.PreExecute();
}

public override void PostExecute()
{
  // Call base method
  base.PostExecute();
}
```

The Input0_ProcessInput() method uses a while loop and the input buffer's NextRow() method to iterate the inbound rows. It calls the Input0_ProcessInputRow() method for each row along the way. After the input buffer has been completely processed, the base ProcessInput() method is called, and then the SetEndOfRowset() method for both output buffers is called to signal to the SSIS runtime that all rows have been processed through the script component.

```
public override void Input0_ProcessInput(Input0Buffer Buffer)
{
  // Get Component Name
```

```
ComponentName = this.ComponentMetaData.Name;
// Iterate rows and process them one at a time
while (Buffer.NextRow())
{
   Input0_ProcessInputRow(Buffer);
}

// Call base method
base.Input0_ProcessInput(Buffer);

// At end of input buffer set end of rowset market on both outputs
if (Buffer.EndOfRowset())
{
   KeywordOutputBuffer.SetEndOfRowset();
   RssFeedOutputBuffer.SetEndOfRowset();
}
}
```

Finally, the Input0_ProcessInputRow() method processes each inbound row from the buffer. In our sample, we add a new row to the RssFeedOutputBuffer for each row and then assign the inbound values to the corresponding columns of the output buffer. For the KeywordOutputBuffer, we do a bit more work. First we clean up the incoming Description column, eliminating all punctuation except for spaces. Then we use the .NET Regex (regular expression) class to split up the text into individual words. Next, we iterate those words and count them, storing the words and their occurrence counts in a .NET Hashtable. The last step is to iterate the entries in the hash table and add them to the output.

■ **NOTE:** A detailed discussion of the .NET Regex and Hashtable classes is beyond the scope of this book. Detailed information can be found on MSDN, at http://msdn.microsoft.com, with a search for either.

```
public override void Input0_ProcessInputRow(Input0Buffer Row)
{
   bool b = true;
   try
   {
      // Add a new row to RssFeedOutputBuffer
      RssFeedOutputBuffer.AddRow();

      // Set columns of new rows on output
      RssFeedOutputBuffer.Description = Row.Description;
      RssFeedOutputBuffer.FeedLanguage = Row.FeedLanguage;
      RssFeedOutputBuffer.FeedLink = Row.FeedLink;
      RssFeedOutputBuffer.FeedPubDate = Row.FeedPubDate;
      RssFeedOutputBuffer.FeedTitle = Row.FeedTitle;
      RssFeedOutputBuffer.Link = Row.Link;
      RssFeedOutputBuffer.RowNumber = Row.RowNumber;
      RssFeedOutputBuffer.Title = Row.Title;
```

```
      // Eliminate all punctuation from description, except spaces
      StringBuilder sb = new StringBuilder(2200);
      foreach (char c in Row.Description)
      {
        if (Char.IsLetterOrDigit(c) || c == ' ')
          sb.Append(c);
        else
          sb.Append(' ');
      }

      // Split the clean string
      string[] words = Regex.Split(sb.ToString(), " ");
      int i = 1;

      // Loop iterate keywords and count occurrences; store in hash table
      Hashtable occurrence = new Hashtable(100);
      foreach (string keyword in words)
      {
        if (occurrence.ContainsKey(keyword))
          occurrence[keyword] = ((int)occurrence[keyword]) + 1;
        else
          occurrence.Add(keyword, 1);
      }

      // Send results stored in hash table out to second output
      foreach (DictionaryEntry d in occurrence)
      {
        if (d.Key != "")
        {
          KeywordOutputBuffer.AddRow();
          KeywordOutputBuffer.RowNumber = Row.RowNumber;
          KeywordOutputBuffer.KeyWordNumber = i;
          KeywordOutputBuffer.KeyWord = (string)d.Key;
          KeywordOutputBuffer.Occurrences = (int)d.Value;
          i++;
        }
      }
    }
    catch (Exception ex)
    {
      this.ComponentMetaData.FireError(-1, ComponentName, ex.ToString(), "", 0, out b);
    }
}
```

Figure 10-27 shows a sample result from both outputs of the asynchronous script component.

RssFeedOutput Result

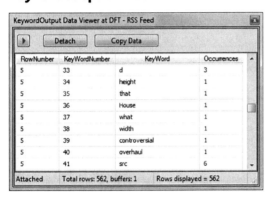

KeywordOutput Result

Figure 10-27. Sample results of both outputs of the asynchronous script component

Script Component Destination

The final type of script component you can create is the destination. In our example, we'll create Script Component destinations that output the results of the previous samples in HTML table format in output files. To start, we replaced the Row Count components in the previous sample with script components. When we added the script components to the data flow, we selected the Destination option from the pop-up menu, as shown in Figure 10-28.

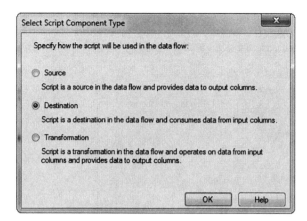

Figure 10-28. *Choosing the Destination script component type*

Next we opened the editor on each and chose all columns on the Input Columns page. The input columns for the first script component are shown in Figure 10-29.

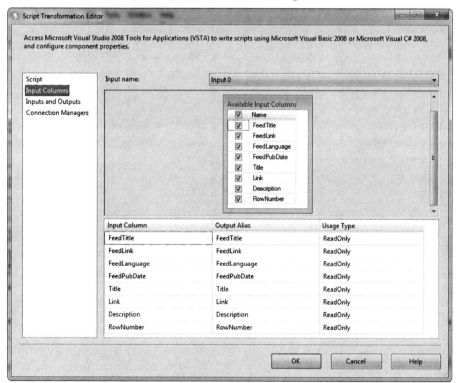

Figure 10-29. *Choosing input columns on the destination script component*

Now, as we explained previously, this destination script component will accept columns as input and then output them, formatted as HTML files. To make this work, we need to define an output file. We defined a File Connection Manager on the Connection Managers page of the editor. We gave it the name FileConnection, and created a new connection from the Connection Manager drop-down menu. This option displays the Add SSIS Connection Manager dialog box, shown in Figure 10-30.

Figure 10-30. *Choosing a* FILE *connection manager from the Add SSIS Connection Manager menu*

After we chose to create a FILE connection manager, we configured it by choosing Create File from the drop-down menu and entering a full path for the file, as shown in Figure 10-31.

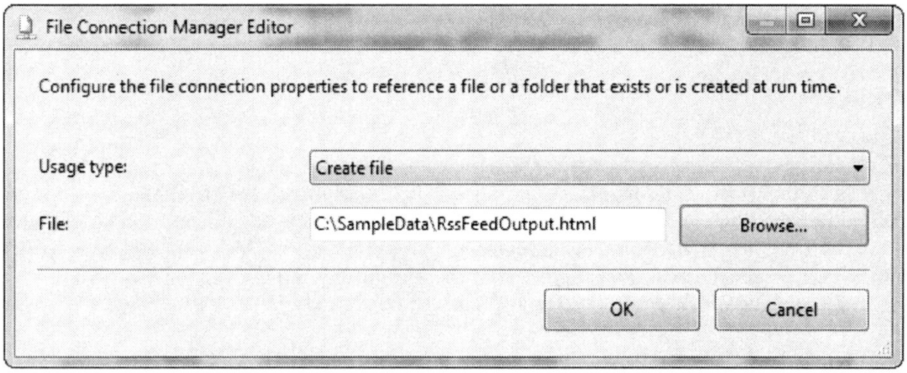

Figure 10-31. Choosing the name of the target file

After we finish the connection manager configuration, the editor looks like Figure 10-32.

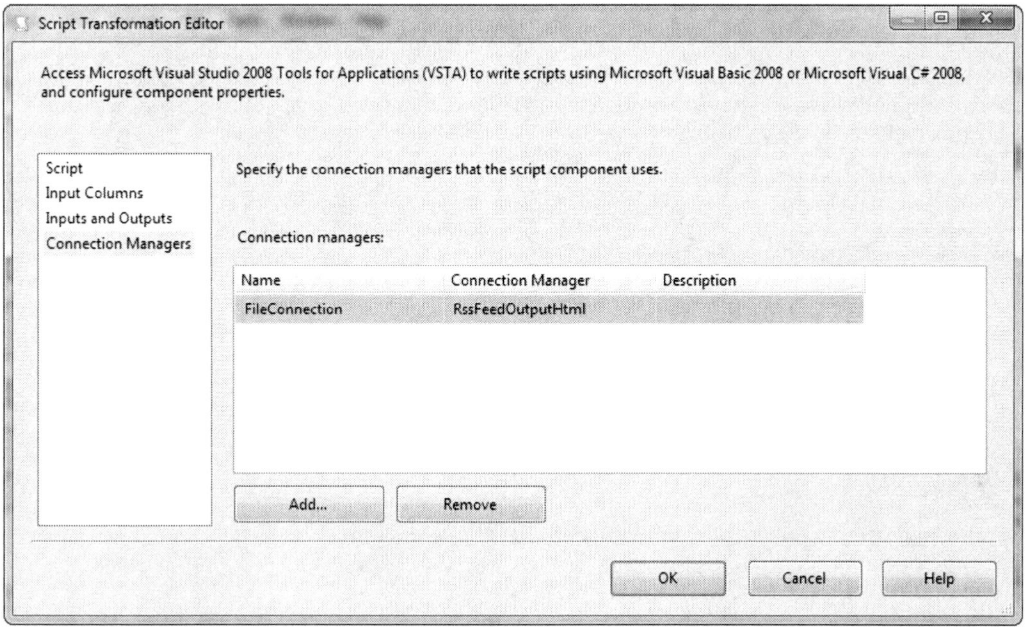

Figure 10-32. Assigning the connection manager to the script component

After we configured the script component, we edited the script. The body of the ScriptMain class, the default entry point for the script, is as follows:

```
[Microsoft.SqlServer.Dts.Pipeline.SSISScriptComponentEntryPointAttribute]
public class ScriptMain : UserComponent
{
  string filename;
```

```
TextWriter outputfile;
bool headerout = false;

// Method overrides go here ...
...
}
```

We declared a few variables at the class level to hold the name of the output HTML file, a TextWriter to write out to the target file and a bool variable that tells us whether we've already written a header out to the HTML file. We talk more about this later in this section.

The first method, which is called during package design in BIDS and when the package is run, is AcquireConnections(). We use this method to grab the full path to the target file from the FileConnection connection manager.

```
public override void AcquireConnections(object Transaction)
{
    base.AcquireConnections(Transaction);
    IDTSConnectionManager100 connmanager = this.Connections.FileConnection;
    filename = (string)connmanager.AcquireConnection(null);
}
```

Our next methods are PreExecute() and PostExecute(). These methods are called at the beginning and end of package execution. In the PreExecute() method, we open the output file for writing. In the PostExecute() method, we write the closing tags for our HTML table and page out to the file, and then flush and dispose of the TextWriter object.

```
public override void PreExecute()
{
    base.PreExecute();
    outputfile = new StreamWriter(filename, false);
}
```

```
public override void PostExecute()
{
    base.PostExecute();
    outputfile.Write("</table></body></html>");
    outputfile.Flush();
    outputfile.Dispose();
}
```

As we showed with the previous components, the script component exposes inbound columns by name, by using the buffer object in the ProcessInputRow() method. For instance, we could access the FeedTitle columns by using syntax such as the following:

```
string title = Row.FeedTitle;
```

In this instance, however, we want to be a little cleverer in our solution. Partly because we have to create this same destination script component twice (once for each output of our asynchronous transformation script component), we don't want to hard-code the column names into the component. We'd rather just copy and paste the code. This means we need to output every input column regardless of the inbound column metadata. To do this, we need to introduce a new method of the script component, the ProcessInput() method:

```
public override void ProcessInput(int InputID, string InputName, PipelineBuffer Buffer,
    OutputNameMap OutputMap)
{
    if (!headerout)
    {
        outputfile.Write("<html>\n<body>\n<table border=\"1\">\n<tr>");
        foreach (IDTSInputColumn100 column in
            this.ComponentMetaData.InputCollection[0].InputColumnCollection)
        {
            outputfile.Write("<th>{0}</th>", column.Name);
        }
        outputfile.Write("</tr>");
        headerout = true;
    }
    while (Buffer.NextRow())
    {
        outputfile.Write("<tr>");
        for (int i = 0; i < Buffer.ColumnCount; i++)
        {
            outputfile.Write(string.Format("<td>{0}</td>", Buffer[i].ToString()));
        }
        outputfile.Write("</tr>");
    }
}
```

The ProcessInput() method (notice the lack of an input name prefix on this method) gives us direct access to the ComponentMetadata and the PipelineBuffer. This means we can get the column names for writing out our table header row and the contents of every column of every row, all accessible by indexer (essentially array subscripts).

The first step in our implementation was to check whether we'd written out the HTML table header. If not, we iterate the input columns (IDTSInputColumn) in the InputColumnCollection. We grab the names from these and write them out to the HTML table header. We also set the flag indicating the header has been written, so we don't write it out again. This is important because the ProcessInput() method may be called multiple times by the SSIS runtime. Finally we iterate the buffer rows with the Buffer.NextRow() method. In this loop, we iterate the input buffer columns and output the values as HTML table data elements.

We copied and pasted the destination script component and put the copy at the end of the KeywordOutput to generate a second HTML file. The result looks like Figure 10-33.

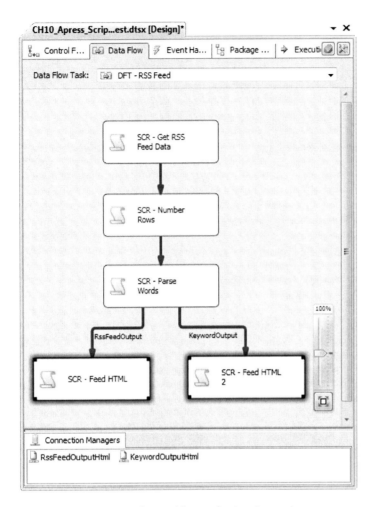

Figure 10-33. SSIS package with two destination script components

The end result of our destination script components are a couple of HTML files with the data flow column data saved in HTML files, as shown in Figure 10-34.

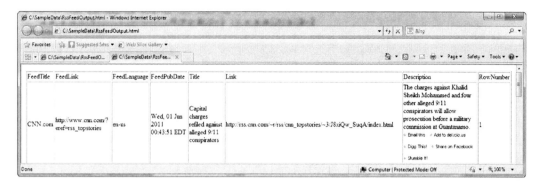

Figure 10-34. HTML file generated by destination script component

---

■ **NOTE:** You'll notice we had to copy and paste the script component in this example to duplicate its functionality. This makes these script components in particular prime candidates for conversion to SSIS custom components. We explore custom components in Chapter 22.

Summary

This concludes our discussion of scripting in SSIS. In this chapter, we discussed the Script task, which lives in the control flow, and the flexible script component, which can serve multiple purposes within a data flow. The script component can act as a data flow source, a transformation, or a destination, allowing you to take full advantage of .NET scripting in either VB or C# to add powerful processing capabilities to your package, above and beyond what the stock components offer. The next chapter covers SSIS errors and event handling.

CHAPTER 11

Events and Error Handling

We are ready for any unforeseen event that may or may not happen.

—Dan Quayle, former vice president of the United States

One of your tasks in building enterprise ETL solutions is making it ready to deal with unforeseen events—the kind that may or may not happen, as Dan Quayle so eloquently points out. Some of this planning comes in the form of infrastructure planning (such as hardware sizing and network and storage capacity planning), but a robust ETL system requires that you also focus attention on building in error handling. Although much of your attention will be focused on issues you can anticipate, unforeseen events can cause the biggest heartburn. This chapter covers SSIS events and event handling, as well as error handling and recovery.

SSIS Events

If you've written .NET Windows Forms programs or JavaScript functions for dynamic web pages, you are probably already familiar with the concept of *events*. Events are fired in response to specified activities. In a GUI-driven .NET application, you might capture events such as mouse clicks and keystrokes. In an application such as SSIS, which is not GUI driven, the events don't depend on external user interface interactions but are instead driven by data processing activities.

Events in SSIS come in two flavors: events with event handlers, and *logging events*, which simply log information but have no event handlers. Events with event handlers give you an opportunity to run your own customized subroutines in response to events. In SSIS, event handlers are simply containers that hold a control flow which fires in response to an event. You can add any tasks to this control flow, although the most commonly used tasks tend to be Script tasks, Execute SQL tasks, and Data Flow tasks.

SSIS incorporates events into every ETL package you design. By default, SSIS raises several types of standard events at the task, container, and package levels. The built-in SSIS events are listed in Table 11-1 with the level at which they are fired.

Table 11-1. Common SSIS Events

Event	Event Is Fired...
Diagnostic	...to log diagnostic information at the package level
OnError	...when an error occurs
OnExecStatusChanged	...when execution status changes
OnInformation	...when an information event occurs
OnPipelinePostEndOfRowset	...after the end-of-rowset signal is sent in the data flow
OnPipelinePostPrimeOutput	...after the call to the PrimeOutput() method
OnPipelinePreEndOfRowset	...immediately before the end-of-rowset signal is sent
OnPipelinePrePrimeOutput	...before the call to the PreOutput() method
OnPipelineRowsSent	...when rows are provided to a data flow component as input
OnPostExecute	...after execution completes
OnPreExecute	...before execution begins
OnPreValidate	...before validation
OnProgress	...at specified progress intervals
OnQueryCancel	...when the QueryCancel() event is called to determine whether to cancel package execution
OnTaskFailed	...when a task fails
OnVariableValueChanged	...when the value of a variable changes (when its RaiseChangedEvent property is set to True)
OnWarning	...when a warning occurs

The events listed in Table 11-1 are available at the task, container, and package level—with the exception of the Diagnostic event, which is available at only the package level. These events *bubble* (aside from the Diagnostic logging event), or propagate upwards, from the lowest-level task, up through the containers that hold them, and ultimately to the package level.

Figure 11-1 shows an OnError event fired at the Data Flow task level. This event propagates up through a Foreach loop container, which in turn fires it up to the package level. The package fires the event again. Each level has its own event handler for the OnError event, although you don't have to implement code for all (or any) event handlers.

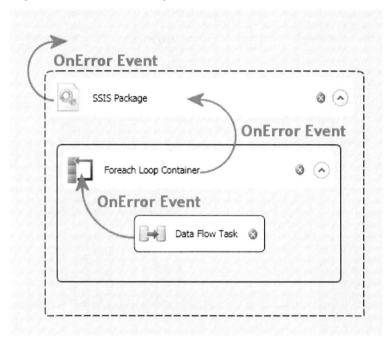

Figure 11-1. OnError event propagation in an SSIS package

Logging Events

SSIS supports several task-specific logging events. These logging events, with the exception of two we'll talk about in a moment, are designated for logging additional information at the task level. These logging events do not have event handlers and cannot be propagated up to the container and package levels.

The Data Flow task is arguably the most important task in SSIS. As we discussed in previous chapters, the data flow provides the functionality for retrieving, transforming, and outputting your data. Because of its prominence and the complexity of the data flows you can create, it comes as no surprise that the Data Flow task exposes several task-specific logging events to help you troubleshoot and optimize your data movement and manipulation. These logging events are listed in Table 11-2.

Table 11-2. Data Flow Task Logging Events

Event	Task Name	Fired...
BufferSizeTuning	Data Flow task	...when data flow changes the size of a buffer during execution
PipelineComponentTime	Data Flow task	...to return information about validation and execution of each data flow component
PipelineExecutionPlan	Data Flow task	...to return the data flow execution plan
PipelineExecutionTrees	Data Flow task	...to return the input the scheduler had when creating the data plan
PipelineInitialization	Data Flow task	...to return data flow initialization information
PiplineBufferLeak	Data Flow task	...when buffers are left outstanding after data flow execution

Data Preparation tasks include the File System task, FTP task, Web Service task, and Data Profiling task. These tasks support the task-specific logging events listed in Table 11-3.

Table 11-3. Data Preparation Tasks Logging Events

Event	Task Name	Fired...
DataProfilingTaskTrace	Data Profiling task	...to provide descriptive information about the task status, such as request and query start and end
FileSystemOperation	File System task	...to log the start of the file system operation; includes source and destination information
FTPConnectingToServer	FTP task	...to report the start of a connection to FTP server
FTPOperation	FTP task	...to log start and type of FTP operation performed

Event	Task Name	Fired...
WSTaskBegin	Web Service task	...to log start of Web service access
WSTaskEnd	Web Service task	...to log completion of Web service method
WSTaskInfo	Web Service task	...to log additional information about the task
XMLOperation	XML task	...to log information about the XML operation performed

The Workflow tasks group includes the Execute Package task, Execute Process task, Message Queue task, Send Mail task, WMI Data Reader task, and WMI Event Watcher task. These tasks support the logging events listed in Table 11-4.

The WMIEventWatcherEventOccurred and WMIEventWatcherEventTimedout events are the exceptions in this group. Unlike the other task-specific logging events in this category, you can create event handlers for these two events, and they will bubble up to the container and package levels.

Table 11-4. Workflow Tasks Logging Events

Event	Task Name	Fired...
ExecuteProcessExecutingProcess	Execute Process task	...to log the name and location of the executable task running and the exit from the executable
ExecuteProcessVariableRouting	Execute Process task	...to log standard input, standard output, and standard error output entries
MSMQAfterOpen	Message Queue task	...after a message queue is opened
MSMQBeforeOpen	Message Queue task	...before a message queue is opened
MSMQBeginReceive	Message Queue task	...before a message is received
MSMQBeginSend	Message Queue task	...before a message is sent
MSMQEndReceive	Message Queue task	...after a message is received
MSMQEndSend	Message Queue task	...after a message is sent

Event	Task Name	Fired...
MSMQTaskInfo	Message Queue task	...to log information about the task
MSMQTaskTimeOut	Message Queue task	...if a task times out
SendMailTaskBegin	Send Mail task	...when an e-mail message send is initiated
SendMailTaskEnd	Send Mail task	...when an e-mail message send is completed
SendMailTaskInfo	Send Mail task	...to log additional information about the task
WMIDataReaderGettingWMIData	WMI Data Reader task	...to indicate the WMI data read has begun
WMIDataReaderOperation	WMI Data Reader task	...to log the WMI query that was run
WMIEventWatcherEventOccurred	WMI Event Watcher task	...when a monitored event occurs
WMIEventWatcherEventTimedout	WMI Event Watcher task	...if the task times out
WMIEventWatcherWatchingForWMIEvents	WMI Event Watcher task	...to indicate the start of a WMI Query Language (WQL) query, including actual query text

■ **TIP:** The Execute Package task does not have any task-specific logging events. However, the child package forwards log details to the parent package, which may log those details.

The group of SQL Server tasks includes the Bulk Insert task, Execute SQL task, Transfer Database task, Transfer Error Messages task, Transfer Jobs task, Transfer Logins task, Transfer Master Stored Procedures task, and Transfer SQL Server Objects task. The task-specific logging events supported by these tasks are listed in Table 11-5.

Table 11-5. *SQL Server Tasks Logging Events*

Event	Task Name	Fired...
BulkInsertBegin	Bulk Insert task	...to signal the start of a bulk insert operation
BulkInsertEnd	Bulk Insert task	...to signal the end of a bulk insert operation
BulkInsertTaskInfo	Bulk Insert task	...to give additional information about the bulk insert operation
DestSQLServer	Transfer Database task	...to log the name of the destination SQL Server
ExecuteSQLExecutingQuery	Execute SQL task	...to provide information about an executing SQL query
SourceDB	Transfer Database task	...to log the name of the source database
SourceSQLServer	Transfer Database task	...to log the name of the source SQL server
TransferErrorMessagesTaskFinishedTransferringObjects	Transfer Error Messages task	...to log the end of a transfer task
TransferErrorMessagesTaskStartTransferringObjects	Transfer Error Messages task	...to log the start of a transfer task
TransferJobsTaskFinishedTransferringObjects	Transfer Jobs task	...to log the end of a job transfer
TransferJobsTaskStartTransferringObjects	Transfer Jobs task	...to log the start of a job transfer

411

Event	Task Name	Fired...
TransferLoginsTaskFinishedTransferringObjects	Transfer Logins task	...to log the end of a login transfer
TransferLoginsTaskStartTransferringObjects	Transfer Logins task	...to log the start of a login transfer
TransferSqlServerTaskFinishedTransferringObjects	Transfer SQL Server Objects task	...to log the end of an object transfer
TransferSqlServerTaskStartTransferringObjects	Transfer SQL Server Objects task	...to log the start of an object transfer
TransferStoredProceduresTaskFinishedTransferringObjects	Transfer Master Stored Procedures task	...to log the end of a stored procedure transfer
TransferStoredProceduresTaskStartTransferringObjects	Transfer Master Stored Procedures task	...to log the start of a stored procedure transfer

The Scripting task group includes just one task, the Script task. This group provides the task-specific logging event shown in Table 11-6.

Table 11-6. *Scripting Tasks Logging Events*

Event	Task Name	Fired...
ScriptTaskLogEntry	Script task	...in response to Dts.Log() method calls

Log Providers

In SSIS terminology, a *log provider* is a component that persists details about your package execution. SSIS logs the events you choose to log providers that you select in your package. SSIS provides several stock log providers to cover the most commonly used types of logging. These log providers are selected by right-clicking on an empty area of the control flow within BIDS and selecting Logging to access the logging options shown in Figure 11-2.

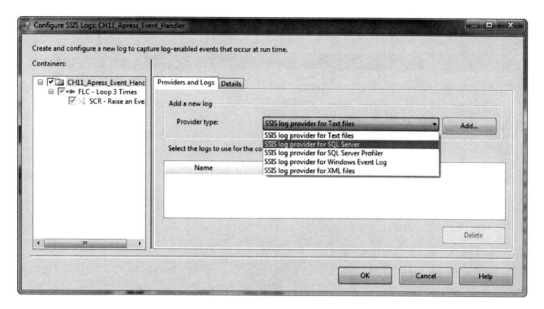

Figure 11-2. *Choosing a log provider in an SSIS package*

The containers and tasks are listed in the tree view on the left side of the editor. The Providers and Logs tab lets you configure the appropriate log providers. The stock log providers supplied by SSIS are listed in Table 11-7. Of these, the SQL Server provider, Text File provider, and Windows Event Log provider are the most commonly used log providers.

Table 11-7. *SSIS Stock Log Providers*

Log Provider	Description
SSIS Log Provider for Text Files	Logs to comma-separated values (CSV) log files
SSIS Log Provider for SQL Server	Logs to the `dbo.sysssislog` table in a SQL Server database
SSIS Log Provider for SQL Server Profiler	Logs to SQL Server Profiler trace files (only available in 32-bit mode)
SSIS Log Provider for Windows Event Log	Logs to the Windows Event log Application log
SSIS Log Provider for XML Files	Logs to XML files

After choosing a log provider, many of them require you to choose a connection in the Configuration column. For the SQL Server provider, you need to choose an OLE DB Connection Manager. The text file, XML file, and SQL Server Profiler providers require a file connection. The

Windows Event Log provider doesn't require a connection. In Figure 11-3, we've selected the SQL Server log provider with an OLE DB Connection Manager named LOG.

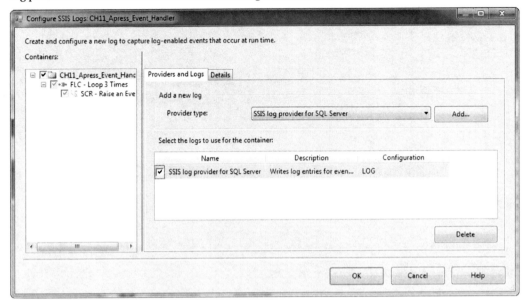

Figure 11-3. *Configuring an SSIS log provider for SQL Server*

In the Details tab of the editor, you can choose the events that you want to log, as shown in Figure 11-4. You can choose different events to log for the package and for individual containers and tasks, or you can choose to log the same events for everything in the package.

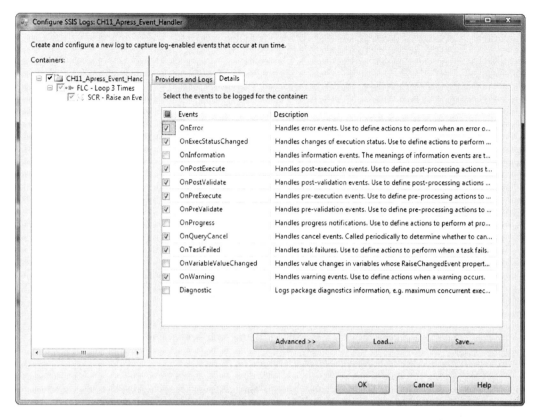

Figure 11-4. *Selecting events to log in the Details tab*

You can even choose which elements of each event are logged by clicking the Advanced button. Generally speaking, you probably won't need to change the default (log all elements) unless you have an event that logs very large MessageText or DataBytes entries, for instance. Figure 11-5 shows the Advanced options of the Details tab.

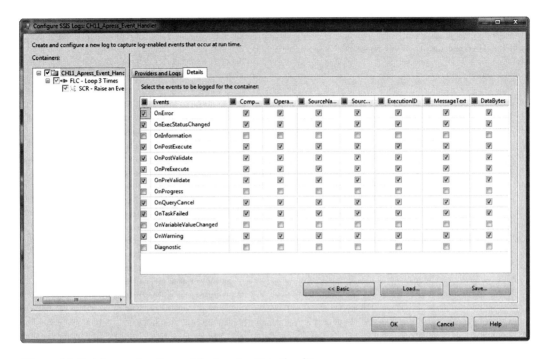

Figure 11-5. *Advanced options of the logging Details editor*

Figure 11-6 shows a sample of the log entries saved in the dbo.sysssislog table by the SQL Server log provider. The information logged includes the name of the event being logged; the name of the package, container, or task that fired the event; the start and end times; and a descriptive message of the event.

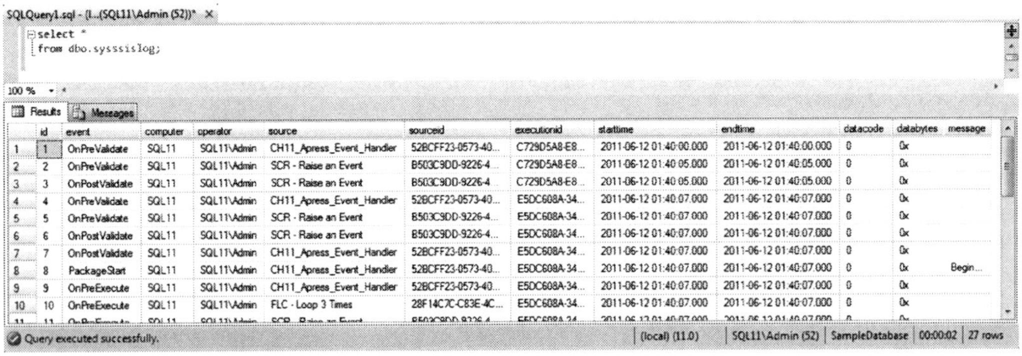

Figure 11-6. *Sample SSIS log entries*

When you run SSIS packages in BIDS, the events fired by the package can be viewed on the Progress tab, shown in Figure 11-7. The Progress tab is updated in real-time as the package runs, which is useful for package testing and debugging purposes.

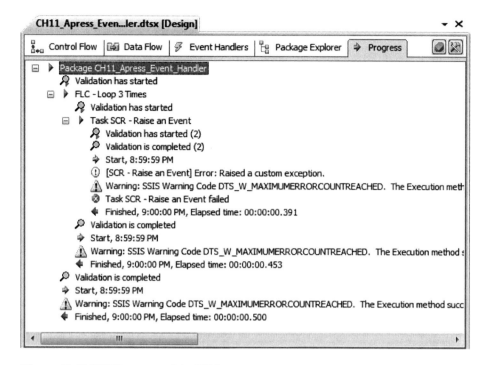

Figure 11-7. SSIS Progress tab in BIDS

CHOOSING EVENTS TO LOG

You can log dozens of events in your SSIS packages, but logging everything is not necessarily the best idea. Logging takes time and uses server resources. Logging too many events can slow down your SSIS packages and result in bloated logs that make it difficult to find specific events. Which events you choose to log depends on your environment: often you'll need to log more-detailed events in a development or testing environment than in a production setting.

Take the OnInformation and OnProgress events, for instance. These events occur frequently—OnProgress can fire up to 100 times per task. Wrap that task in a loop container and you can get thousands of instances of this event logged per package execution. While OnInformation and OnProgress are useful in a debugging scenario, they're usually overkill for production environments.

Some events, such as OnPreExecute and OnPostExecute, don't add a lot of value to the logged information, but they do not generate the extensive logging activity of some other events. The primary events that we log in every environment include OnError, OnWarning, OnTaskFailed, and OnQueryCancel. These events give you the bare-minimum information you need to begin troubleshooting SSIS packages.

Script Events

SSIS lets you fire events from Script tasks and script components. Both options give you the opportunity to add context, task-specific error messaging, and additional debugging and performance information to your packages. We discuss firing events from script in this section.

In your .NET script code, you can (and generally should) use try-catch exception handling within your code. If you need to raise an SSIS error within your component, you'll want to use the events covered in the following sections.

Script Task Events

You can fire logging events with the Dts.Log() method in Script tasks. These logging events are like the built-in logging events in that they are sent to your log provider but do not have associated event handlers. They're captured in your logging details with the ScriptTaskLogEntry event and are useful for sending user-defined informational messages to your log.

The Dts.Events object also provides several Fire methods to fire associated events, which can in fact have event handlers associated with them. These methods are listed in Table 11-8.

Table 11-8. Dts.Events *Event-Firing Methods*

Method	Fires...
Dts.Events.FireCustomEvent()	...a user-defined custom event
Dts.Events.FireError()	...the OnError event, which indicates an error condition in your package
Dts.Events.FireInformation()	...the OnInformation event, which sends informational messages
Dts.Events.FireProgress()	...the OnProgress event, which indicates task progress and is useful in long-running tasks
Dts.Events.FireQueryCancel()	...the OnQueryCancel event, which checks for a Query Cancel state to determine whether a query should be stopped
Dts.Events.FireWarning()	...the OnWarning event, which indicates a warning (which is less severe than an error condition)

Most of these methods fire predefined standard events such as OnError and OnProgress. The FireCustomEvent() method, on the other hand, fires a custom event. The downside is that the Script task doesn't provide a mechanism to register custom events in the task itself, so you can't create an event handler for it. You also can't choose it from the list of events to log in your package's logging details. The best you can do is turn on logging for all events for the Script task, which will cause your custom events to be logged also. If you decide to not log even one event, SSIS won't log your custom events either.

The Script task also exposes a `Dts.Events.FireBreakpointHit()` method, but this event is for internal use by the SSIS and BIDS infrastructure and is not designed to be used directly from your code. To demonstrate Script task event firing, we put together the sample package shown in Figure 11-8.

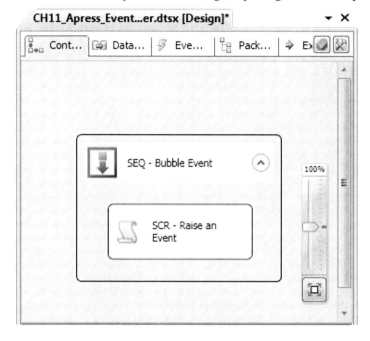

Figure 11-8. *Sample package to demonstrate Script task events*

In this package, we have a Sequence container that contains a Script task. In the Script task, we use `Dts.Log()` to generate a logging event and `Dts.Events.FireError()` to fire an `OnError` event. The sample script is as follows:

```
public void Main()
{
  Dts.TaskResult = (int)ScriptResults.Success;
  Dts.Log("We're about to throw an error.", -1, new byte[0]);
  Dts.Events.FireError(-1, "SCR - Raise an Event", "Raised a custom exception.", "", 0);
}
```

The `Dts.Log()` method takes three parameters: a string message to log, an integer data code value, and a byte array representing the binary data bytes to log. The `Dts.Events.FireError()` method takes five parameters: an integer error code, a string subcomponent name, a string error description, a help file name, and an integer help context value. When there is no help file or help context, just use an empty string for the help file name and 0 for the help context. When run, this package fails with an error, as shown in Figure 11-9.

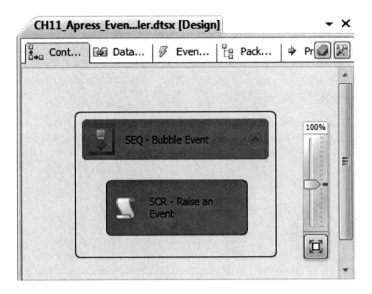

Figure 11-9. Sample package errors out

The events raised by the sample package can be viewed in the log, as shown in Figure 11-10. Notice that User:ScriptTaskLogEntry contains the data logged by the call to Dts.Log(). Also notice that the OnError event was logged three separate times: once by the Script task, then by the Sequence container, and again by the package. This is due to the event bubbling we discussed previously in this chapter.

SQLQuery1.sql - (I...(SQL11\Admin (52))* ×

```sql
select id,
    event,
    computer,
    source,
    datacode,
    databytes,
    message
from dbo.sysssislog
order by id desc;
```

100 % ▾ ◂

▦ Results | ▤ Messages

	id	event	computer	source	datacode	databytes	message
11	155	OnWarning	SQL11	SCR - Raise an Event	-2147381246	0x	SSIS Warning Code DTS_W_...
12	154	OnError	SQL11	CH11_Apress_Event_Handler	-1	0x	Raised a custom exception.
13	153	OnError	SQL11	SEQ - Bubble Event	-1	0x	Raised a custom exception.
14	152	OnError	SQL11	SCR - Raise an Event	-1	0x	Raised a custom exception.
15	151	User:ScriptTaskLogEntry	SQL11	SCR - Raise an Event	-1	0x	We're about to throw an error.
16	150	OnPostValidate	SQL11	SCR - Raise an Event	0	0x	
17	149	OnPreValidate	SQL11	SCR - Raise an Event	0	0x	
18	148	OnPreExecute	SQL11	SCR - Raise an Event	0	0x	

◯ Query executed successfully. | | (local) (11.0) | | SQL11\Admin (52) | SampleDatabase | 00:00:00 | 165 rows

Figure 11-10. Reviewing the log after package failure

Script Component Events

Script components in the data flow also allow you to fire events. Within script components, you can log entries by using the Log() method. This is the script component equivalent of the Script task's Dts.Log() method. Like the Dts.Event object, the ComponentMetaData object exposes a handful of Fire methods to fire events. These methods are listed in Table 11-9.

Table 11-9. Script Component Event-Firing Methods

Method	Fires...
ComponentMetaData.FireCustomEvent()	... a custom event
ComponentMetaData.FireError()	... an OnError event
ComponentMetaData.FireInformation()	... an OnInformation event
ComponentMetaData.FireProgress()	... an OnProgress event
ComponentMetaData.FireWarning()	... an OnWarning event

FIREERROR() AND MAXIMUMERRORCOUNT

Script component event methods are similar to Script task event methods in most respects. The events raised in a component are passed along to the containing Data Flow task. There's one big difference, though. When you invoke the FireError() method on a Script task, the method immediately counts against the MaximumErrorCount property for the task, any containers holding the task, and the package itself. If you reach the MaximumErrorCount value, the package halts immediately.

In a script component, the FireError() method immediately fires an OnError event that bubbles up to the higher levels. When fired at the component level, however, the FireError() method does not immediately count against your MaximumErrorCount. Instead, the data flow keeps moving data despite the error event. The OnError events you raise in the script component are accumulated and counted against the MaximumErrorCount properties after the data flow has completed processing.

If you encounter an error within the data flow that you want to stop processing immediately, use the .NET throw method. As an example, a script component source that can't establish a connection to an external data store might halt processing immediately.

In the example shown in Figure 11-11, we created a simple package with a Data Flow task in a Sequence container. We then added a script component source and script component destination to the data flow. The script component source logs two messages, one each in the PreExecute() and PostExecute() methods, and fires an OnError event in the CreateNewOutputRows() method, as shown here:

```
public override void PreExecute()
{
  base.PreExecute();
  this.Log("Logging the first sample message.", -1, new byte[0]);
}

public override void PostExecute()
{
  base.PostExecute();
  this.Log("Logging the second sample message.", -1, new byte[0]);
}

public override void CreateNewOutputRows()
{
  bool b = false;
  this.ComponentMetaData.FireError
  (
    -1,
    this.ComponentMetaData.Name,
    "Firing an OnError event.",
    "",
    0,
    out b
  );
}
```

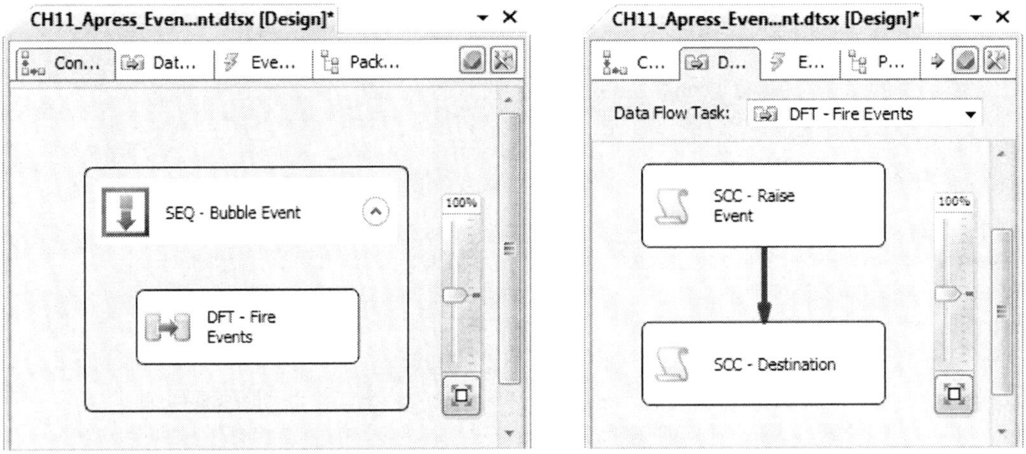

Figure 11-11. Raising events in script components

A quick query of the SSIS log shows that the two log entries and the OnError event were all logged in the correct order. Figure 11-12 shows the results as logged to the dbo.sysssislog table.

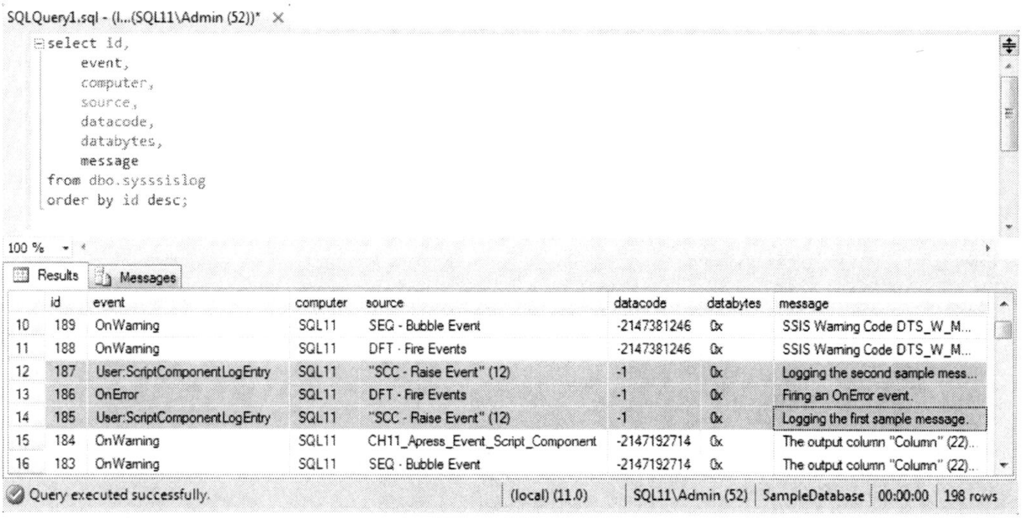

Figure 11-12. Results of script component log entries

Event Handlers

Event handlers are containers for control flows that are executed in response to SSIS events. Generally speaking, the SSIS stock events whose names begin with On, such as OnError and OnWarning, can have event handlers associated with them. For our example, we extended the previous sample to include OnError event handlers.

We created an event handler for the Data Flow task by highlighting it on the design surface and selecting the Event Handlers tab in BIDS. Then we selected the OnError event from the Event Handler drop-down list. We were presented with the window shown in Figure 11-13.

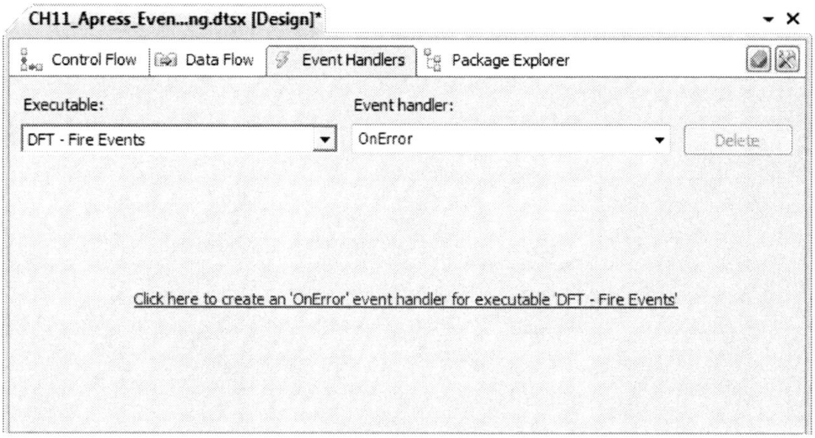

Figure 11-13. Adding an event handler to a task

At this screen, we clicked the blue link. BIDS created a container for us to hold a control flow associated with the event. In our example, the control flow was created on the OnError event. We added a Script task to the event handler that simply displays the message *Task Error Raised*. The completed OnError event handler is shown in Figure 11-14.

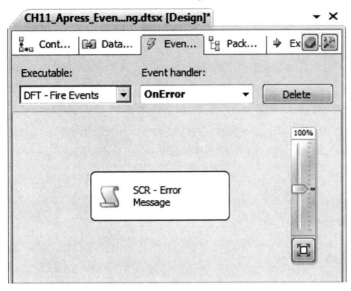

Figure 11-14. *Completed* OnError *event handler*

We then repeated the process to create OnError event handlers for our Sequence container and the package itself. When the sample package was run, it raised an OnError event at the Data Flow task level, which then bubbled up to the Sequence container and the package level. As the event bubbled upward, the event handler at each level displayed a message box, in the order shown in Figure 11-15.

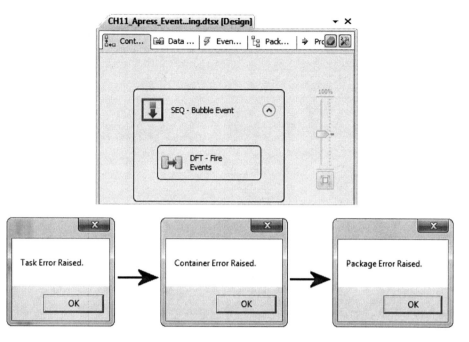

Figure 11-15. Demonstrating OnError *event bubbling in a package*

In this example, we used the .NET MessageBox.Show() method to demonstrate event handlers and event bubbling in SSIS. Your event handlers can be much more complex and might include considerable logic. It's common, for instance, to use event handlers to implement customized auditing and logging processes or to send e-mails to alert administrators of error conditions.

■ **CAUTION:** he .NET MessageBox.Show() method is very handy when debugging and troubleshooting SSIS packages. Be careful to remove these method calls when you deploy a package to production, however. If your package tries to display a message box in an automated job, no one can click the OK button, and your package may stop responding.

Summary

This chapter presented SSIS events and error handling, including event bubbling and Script tasks and script component methods for firing events. You looked at the different types of events you can fire and the purpose behind each. In the next chapter, you will consider how to incorporate data profiling and data scrubbing into your ETL processes.

CHAPTER 12

Data Profiling and Scrubbing

Code, load, and explode.

—Steve Hitchman

Projects that require bringing together data from multiple sources—for example, data warehouse, data mart, or operational data store (ODS) projects— are extremely common. You could spend months gathering business requirements, putting together technical specifications, designing target databases, and coding and testing your ETL process. You could spend an eternity in "ad hoc maintenance mode" rewriting large sections of code that don't handle unanticipated bad or nonconforming data. This scenario is the result of a failure to properly plan and execute data integration projects—a phenomenon known as *code, load, and explode.*

Anytime you need to bring together data from two or more systems, you have a *data integration* project on your hands. Proper data integration requires a lot of grunt work. Unfortunately, it's one of the least exciting and glamorous parts of any project—thorough planning and process formalization, investigation of source systems, interrogation of source data, generation of large amounts of documentation . By accident or by choice, the scope of data integration requirements and the cost of not doing it right are often underestimated in enterprise projects. Data integration requires a lot of generally low-profile analysis, but failure to do it properly can result in high-profile project failures. This chapter shows how SSIS can help you properly profile and cleanse your data.

Data Profiling

Data profiling, at its core, is the process of gathering statistical information about your data. The purpose is to ensure that your source data meets your expectations by answering questions such as the following:

> **Does my source data contain nulls?** You may expect certain source data columns to contain no nulls, or to contain a certain number of nulls (fewer than 10 percent, for instance). Profiling your source data will reveal whether the number of nulls meets your expectations.

> **Does my source data contain all valid values?** This involves defining *domains*, or sets of valid values, for your source data. As examples, you might expect a Gender column to contain only Male or Female values, or you might expect a Price column to contain only positive numeric values between 0.01 and 500.00. Profiling will tell you whether your source data falls within its expected domains.

427

Does the distribution of my data fit my expectations? Answering this question requires industry- and business-specific domain knowledge. For instance, you might expect most of the prices for items in your inventory to fall between $20 and $50. An analysis of your data might show that the majority of items in inventory are actually priced lower than $20, which could point to either (1) a bad initial assumption about the business, or (2) a data quality problem.

How does my source data align with data from other systems? Consider reference data such as US state codes. Several types of codes could be used by any given source system: two-character Postal Service codes such as AL, DE, and NY; two-digit FIPS (Federal Information Processing Standard) numeric codes such as 01, 02, 03; or even integer surrogate keys. Answering this question will let you recognize differences in key attributes and align the values in key attributes.

What are my business keys? Successful data integration projects, such as BI projects, require identification of business keys in your source data. Data warehouse updates and data mart slowly changing dimension (SCD) processing depend on knowledge of your source data business keys.

Answering these questions might require profiling single columns or sets of columns. As an example, most industrialized countries implement postal code systems to facilitate mail delivery. The format and valid characters in postal codes vary from country to country. Postal codes in the United States (also known as Zone Improvement Plan, or ZIP, codes) consist of either five or nine numeric digits, such as 90071 or 10104-0899. In Canada, postal codes consist of six alphanumeric characters—for example, K1P 1J9. You may need to profile country names and postal codes from your source data in combination with one another to validate proper postal code formats.

In addition to answering questions about the quality and consistency of your source data, you may also isolate information about the relationships in your source databases. One thing that many legacy source databases seem to have in common is a lack of referential integrity and check constraints. Throw in an utter lack of documentation, and these source systems present themselves as complex puzzles, often requiring you to establish relationships between tables yourself.

Data Profiling Task

The *Data Profiling task* is a useful way to grab statistical information about your source data. Much of the major functionality is comparable in many respects to other data-profiling software packages available on the market. The Data Profiling task grabs the specified source data, analyzes it based on the criteria you specify, and outputs the results to an XML file. The Data Profiling task is shown in Figure 12-1.

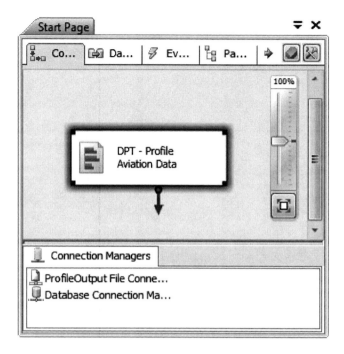

Figure 12-1. Data Profiling task in a package control flow

The Data Profiling task requires a File Connection Manager pointing to the XML file you want it to create or overwrite. We configured our File Connection Manager to point at a file named C:\SampleData\ProfileOutput.xml, as shown in Figure 12-2.

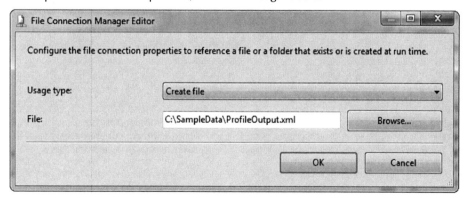

Figure 12-2. Configuring the File Connection Manager to point at an XML output file

One drawback of the Data Profiling task is that it is limited to data that can be retrieved via an ADO.NET Connection Manager. The Data Profiling task requires a connection to SQL Server and uses the *SqlClient Data Provider*, shown by the ADO.NET Connection Manager Editor in Figure 12-3.

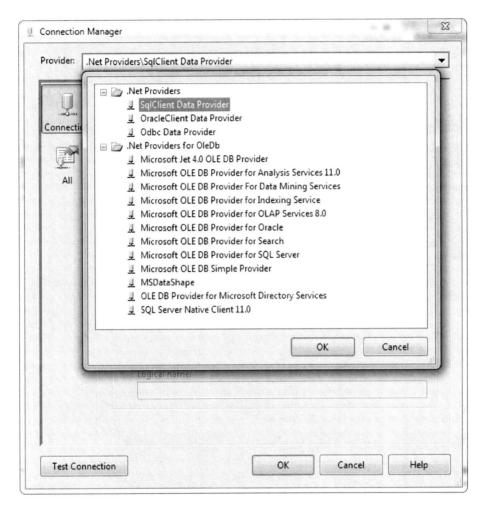

Figure 12-3. Connection Manager editor providers

The General page of the Data Profiling Task Editor lets you choose destination options including the destination type, the destination connection manager, whether the destination should be overwritten if it exists already, and the source time-out (in seconds). Figure 12-4 shows the editor's General page.

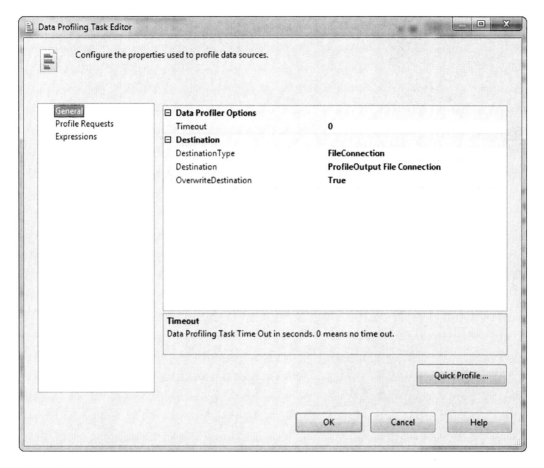

Figure 12-4. *General page of the Data Profiling Task Editor*

On the Profile Requests page, you can choose and configure profile requests, each representing a specific type of analysis to perform and a set of statistics to collect about your source data. Figure 12-5 shows many of the types of profile requests that can be selected. Table 12-1 describes the profile requests you can choose. You'll look at configuring individual data profile requests in the following sections.

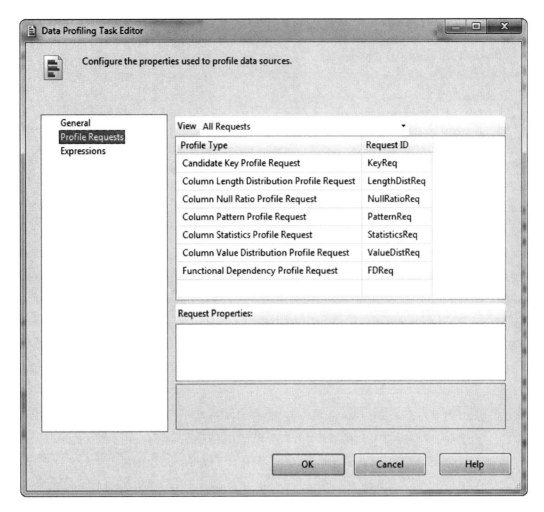

Figure 12-5. *Profile Requests page of the Data Profiling Task Editor*

Table 12-1. *Data Profile Request Types*

Profile Request	Description
Column Length Distribution Profile	Returns distinct lengths of string values in selected columns. This can help to quickly identify string data that is too long or too short for the columns containing it.

Profile Request	Description
Column Null Ratio Profile	Returns percentage of nulls in selected columns. This helps identify issues such as large numbers of unexpected missing data values.
Column Pattern Profile	Returns a set of regular expressions that match a percentage of values in selected columns. This profile helps identify problems with string data formatting.
Column Statistics Profile	Returns statistics such as minimum, maximum, mean, and standard deviation for selected columns.
Column Value Distribution Profile	Returns all distinct values in selected columns and the percentage of times those values occur.
Candidate Key Profile	Attempts to determine whether a column, or set of columns, is a candidate key for the selected table.
Functional Dependency Profile	Attempts to determine the dependency relationship between the values in one column and those in another column (or set of columns). As an example, a given airport code should always be associated with a given state; the airport code is functionally dependent on the state.
Value Inclusion Profile	Computes the union, or overlap, between the values of two columns or two sets of columns. This is useful for determining whether a foreign-key relationship can be established between the columns of two tables.

Data Profile Viewer

After the Data Profiling task generates an XML output file, you can view the results by using a tool called the *Data Profile Viewer*, which is found in the SQL Server Integration Services folder on the Windows Start menu. Figure 12-6 shows the Data Profile Viewer on the Start menu.

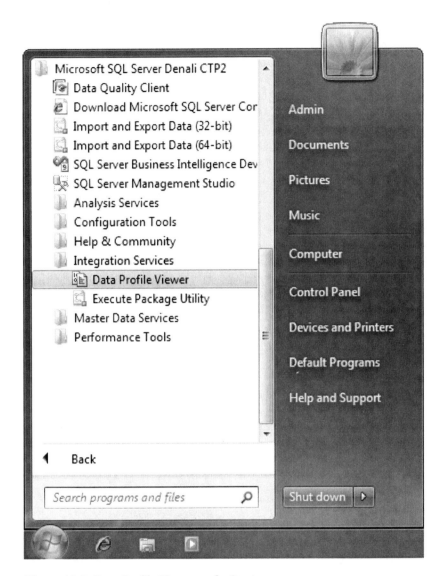

Figure 12-6. *Data Profile Viewer on the Start menu*

After you launch the Data Profile Viewer, you can open the XML file generated by the Data Profiling task by clicking the Open button and selecting the file, as shown in Figure 12-7.

Figure 12-7. Opening the Data Profiling task output in the Data Profile Viewer

After you open the Data Profiling task output file in the Data Profile Viewer, you'll see a list of all the profile requests you selected on the left side of the window. Clicking one of the profile requests displays the details on the right side of the window. You can click the detail rows on the right side to show even more detail. In Figure 12-8, we've selected the Candidate Key profile request and drilled into the details of the EventId column.

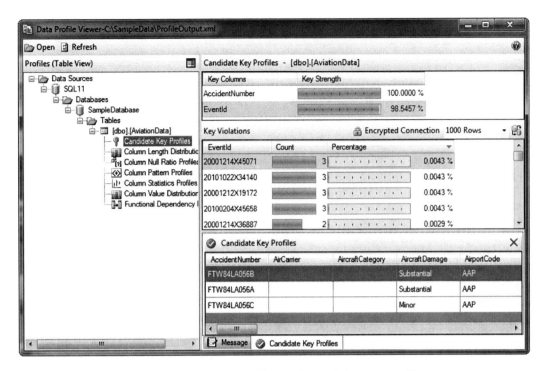

Figure 12-8. *Viewing the results of a Data Profiling task Candidate Key profile request*

■ **TIP:** You'll look at the results of the profile requests in the following sections.

Column Length Distribution Profile

The *Column Length Distribution profile* reports the distinct lengths of string values in the columns you select, and the percent of rows in the table that each length represents. As an example, US ZIP codes must be five to ten characters in length (ZIP+4, including the hyphen); any other string length for these data values may be considered invalid. When analyzing your data, you may find that some of your ZIP codes are the wrong length. After choosing the Column Length Distribution profile request, you can configure it as shown in Figure 12-9.

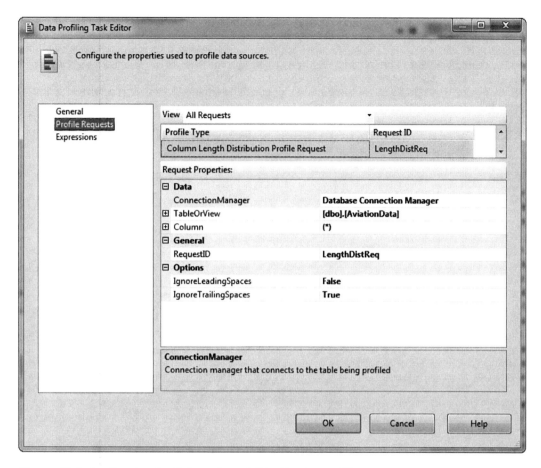

Figure 12-9. *Configuring the Column Length Distribution profile request*

For the Column Length Distribution profile request, you need to configure the source connection manager and choose the table and columns you wish to profile. Choosing wildcard (*) as the column indicates that you want to use all the columns in the table (nonstring columns are ignored). You can also choose to ignore leading or trailing spaces in your data.

▪ **NOTE:** Every profile request is assigned a unique `RequestID`. You can rename the `RequestID` to suit your needs.

After you run the Data Profiling task, the Column Length Distribution profile request generates a list of string-value columns. Selecting one of these columns shows you the distribution of string data lengths in that column. Clicking one of the lengths in the Length Distribution list shows the details, listing the values that match that length.

In Figure 12-10, we've selected the AccidentNumber column, which has data in three lengths: 9 characters, 10 characters, and 11 characters. We then drilled into the 9-character values to see the rows containing these values. After viewing the column-length distributions, we can see that the AccidentNumber column generally holds 10-character lengths. The small percentage of 9-character and 11-character values may represent a data quality issue with the source data.

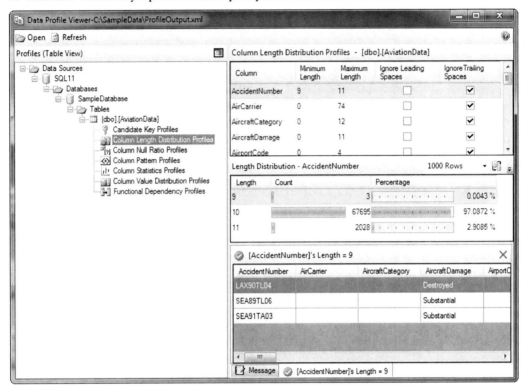

Figure 12-10. *Reviewing details of the Column Length Distribution profile*

Column Null Ratio Profile

The *Column Null Ratio profile* helps you identify columns that contain more (or fewer) nulls than expected. If you have a column for which you expect very few nulls, but discover a very large number of nulls, it could indicate a data quality issue (or it may mean that the assumptions about your data need to be changed). The Column Null Ratio profile is simple to configure. Like the Column Length Distribution profile request, you must choose an ADO.NET Connection Manager, a table or view, and the column you want to profile. Like the Column Null Ratio profile request, the Column Null Ratio request lets you choose (*) to profile all columns. In Figure 12-11, we've chosen to profile all columns in the AviationData table.

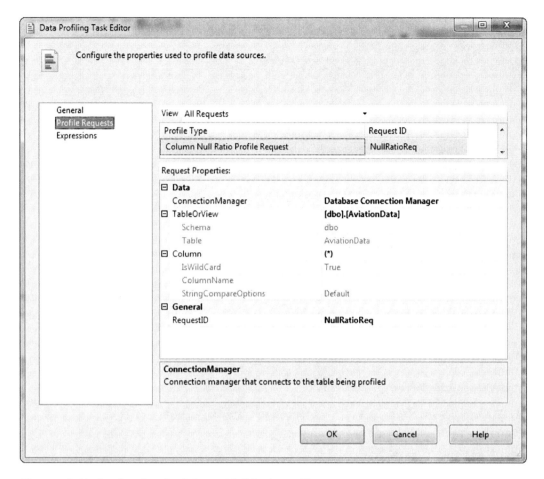

Figure 12-11. Configuring the Column Null Ratio profile request

The results can be viewed in the Data Profile Viewer. In our example, we've focused on the AircraftDamage column, which contains no nulls, as shown in Figure 12-12.

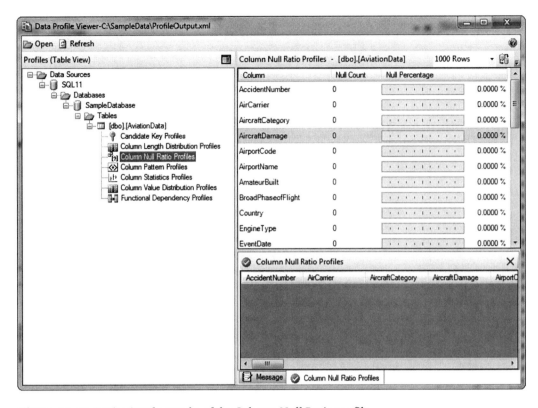

Figure 12-12. *Reviewing the results of the Column Null Ratio profile*

Column Pattern Profile

The *Column Pattern profile* is useful for identifying patterns in string data, such as postal codes that aren't formatted according to the standards for a given country. This profile returns regular expression patterns that match your string data, which can make it easy to identify string data that does not fit expected patterns. As an example, a US five-digit ZIP code should fit the regular expression pattern \d{5}", which represents a string of exactly five numeric digits. Any five-digit US ZIP codes that do not match this pattern are invalid.

■ **NOTE:** A detailed discussion of regular expressions and regular expression syntax is beyond the scope of this book. However, MSDN covers .NET Framework regular expressions in great detail at http://bit.ly/dotnetregex.

Like the other profile requests, the Column Pattern profile request requires an ADO.NET Connection Manager, a table or view, and a source column. In addition, the Column Pattern profile request has many more options available than the other profile requests we've covered so far. The following options allow you to refine your Column Pattern profile request:

MaxNumberOfPatterns: The maximum number of patterns that you want the Data Profiling task to compute. The default is 10, and the maximum value is 99.

PercentageDataCoverageDesired: The percentage of rows to sample when computing patterns. The default is 95.

CaseSensitive: A flag indicating whether the generated patterns should be case-sensitive. The default is False.

During the process of computing patterns to fit your string data, the Data Profiling task tokenizes your strings (breaks them into individual "words" or substrings). Two options are included for controlling this tokenization behavior:

Delimiters: This is a list of characters that are treated as spaces when tokenizing strings. By default, the delimiters are the space, the tab (\t), carriage return ("\r"), and newline ("\n").

Symbols: The list of symbols to keep when tokenizing data. By default, this list includes the following characters: ,.;:-"'`~=&/\@!?()<>[]{}|#*^%.

The Column Pattern profile request also allows you to tag, or group, tokens. Tags are stored in a database table with two-character data columns named Tag and Term. The Tag column holds the name of the token group, and the Term column holds the individual tokens that belong to the group. For performance reasons, it's recommended that if you use this option, use 10 tags or fewer and no more than 100 terms per tag. The following options control the tagging behavior:

TagTableConnectionManager: An ADO.NET Connection Manager using the SqlClient provider to connect to a SQL Server database.

TagTableName: The name of the table holding the tags and terms. Must have two columns named Tag and Term.

Figure 12-13 shows how we configured the Column Pattern profile request for our sample.

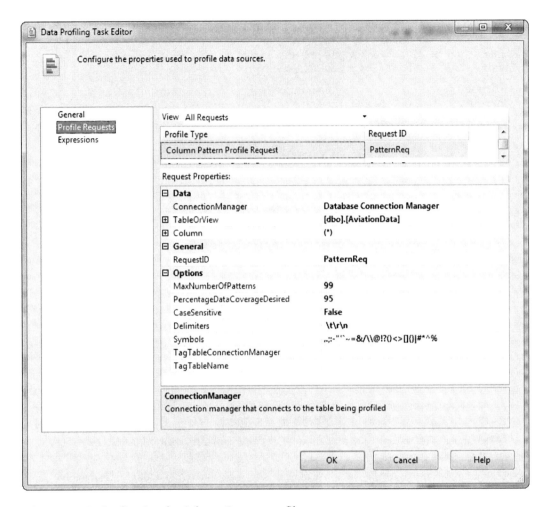

Figure 12-13. Configuring the Column Pattern profile request

The results of the Column Pattern profile are shown in Figure 12-14. We focused on the EventYear column and found that all data matched the pattern \d\d\d\d, which is the expected pattern of four numeric characters in a row. Because all of the string values in this column match the valid pattern, we are a little closer to confirming that the values are valid.

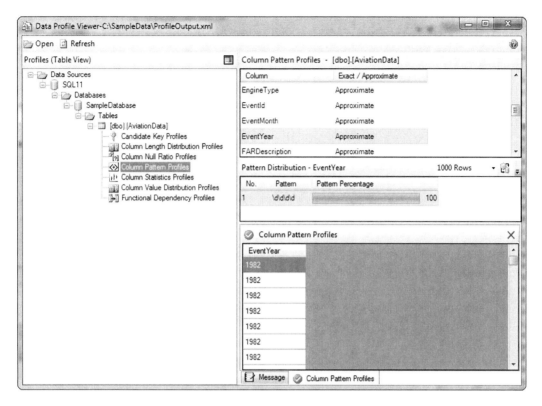

Figure 12-14. Reviewing the Column Pattern profile results

Column Statistics Profile

The *Column Statistics profile* helps to quickly assess data that is outside of the normal range, or *tolerances*, for a given column. You might find that your column contains dates of birth that are in the future, for example. You can also use the basic statistical information provided to determine whether your data fits the statistical normal distribution.

Configuring the Column Statistics profile request is similar to the previously described profile requests. You need to choose a connection manager, table or view, and a source column. As before, you can you can use (*) to profile all columns. We configured our Column Statistics profile request to use the AviationData table, as shown in Figure 12-15.

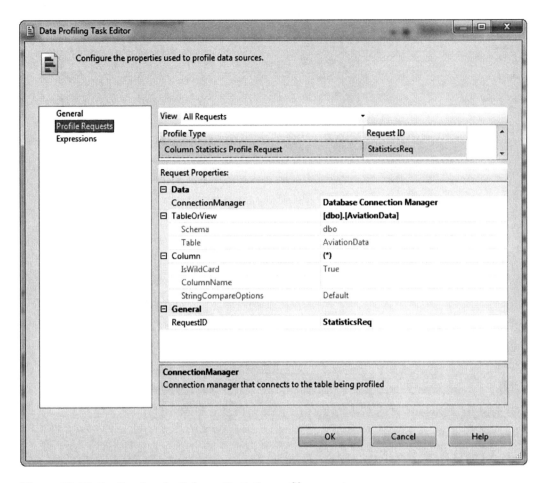

Figure 12-15. *Configuring the Column Statistics profile request*

The Column Statistics profile will profile columns that hold date/time and numeric data, such as DATETIME, INT, FLOAT, and DECIMAL columns, for example. For date/time data, the profile calculates the minimum and maximum; for numeric data, it calculates the minimum, maximum, mean (average), and standard deviation. Results of our sample Column Statistics profile are shown in Figure 12-16.

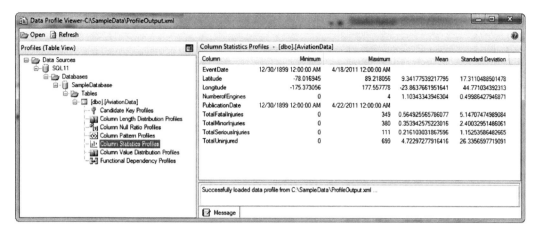

Figure 12-16. Reviewing the results of the Column Statistics profile request

Column Value Distribution Profile

The *Column Value Distribution profile* reports all the distinct values in a column and the percentage of rows in the table that each value represents. You can use this information to determine whether different values occur with the expected frequency. You may find, for instance, that a column's default value occurs far more often than you anticipated.

The Column Value Distribution profile request has several options to configure. The usual suspects are here: you need to configure an ADO.NET Connection Manager, choose the source table or view, and select the column to profile. You also need to choose a ValueDistributionOption: FrequentValues (the default) limits the results reported to those that meet or exceed a given threshold, and AllValues reports all the results regardless of how many times they occur. The FrequentValueThreshold option is a numeric value—the minimum threshold used to limit the results returned when the FrequentValues option is selected. Figure 12-17 shows how we configured the Column Value Distribution profile request by using the AllValues options.

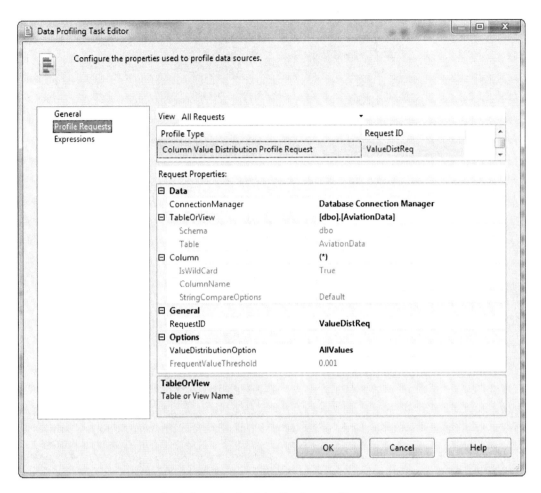

Figure 12-17. Configuring the Column Value Distribution profile request

The results of profiling the columns of the AviationData table are shown in Figure 12-18. The column displayed is the State column, with occurrence counts and occurrence percentages shown.

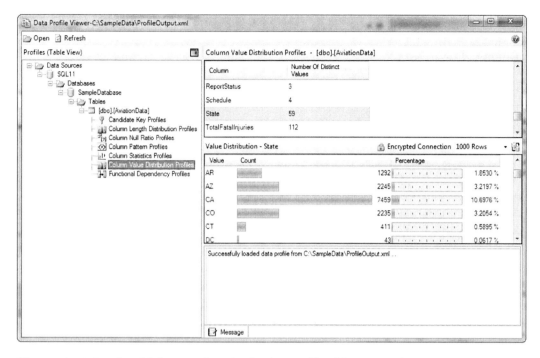

Figure 12-18. Results of Column Value Distribution profile of the State column

Candidate Key Profile

The *Candidate Key profile* profiles one or more columns to determine the likelihood that a column (or set of columns) would be a good key, or approximate key, for your table. The Candidate Key profile is a useful tool when you are trying to identify your *business keys* (attributes that uniquely identify business transactions or objects).

■ **NOTE:** A *candidate key* is a column, or set of columns, that can be used to uniquely identify rows in a table. Although a table can have many candidate keys, you'll usually identify one of them as the *primary key*.

As with the other profile requests, you must configure the Candidate Key profile with an ADO.NET Connection Manager, a source table or view, and columns. Unlike the other profile requests, in which you choose only a single column or all columns by using the wildcard (*), this profile request allows you to choose many columns. This makes sense because a given candidate key can consist of multiple columns, and you may want to test several permutations of column sets for viability as candidate keys. The drop-down menu for choosing KeyColumns is shown in Figure 12-19. You can choose one or more columns in several combinations, such as the following:

Single named column: If you choose a single column, it will be tested for usefulness as a candidate key.

Multiple named columns: If you choose multiple named columns, they are all tested together for usability as a composite candidate key. For instance, if you choose the `AirCarrier`, `AircraftCategory`, `EventDate`, and `State` columns, the Data Profiling task will test all of the columns together for usability as a single candidate key.

Single wildcard: If you choose the wildcard (*) as your column, the Data Profiling task profiles every column in your table, testing each individually for usability as a candidate key.

Single wildcard and named columns: If you choose the wildcard (*) and one or more named columns, the Data Profiling task will test combinations of the named columns and the other columns in the table for candidate key viability. As an example, you might choose `AirportCode` and (*) in your profile request, in which case the Data Profiling task will test the `AirportCode` column in combination with every other column in the table.

Multiple wildcards: If you choose multiple wildcard (*) columns, the Data Profiling task tests the permutations of the specified number of column combinations for usability as candidate keys. For instance, if you choose two wildcards, the task profiles all combinations of two columns in your table for uniqueness.

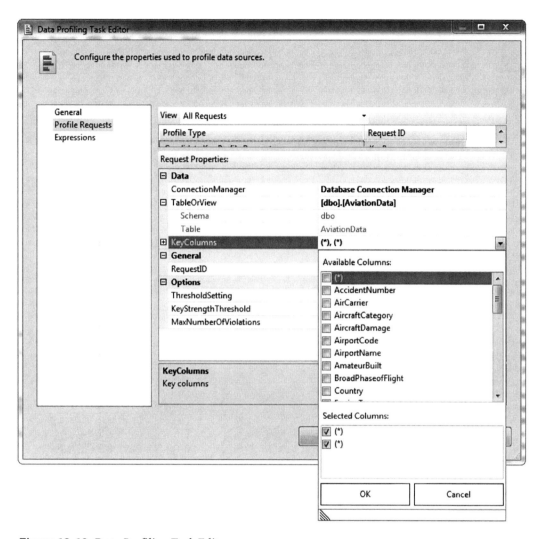

Figure 12-19. Data Profiling Task Editor

Figure 12-20 demonstrates the Candidate Key profile output. The strength of the proposed key columns AirCarrier, AircraftCategory, EventDate, and State are approximately 87 percent unique. The output goes even further and shows the duplicate rows for each of the key violations as well as the count of the infractions.

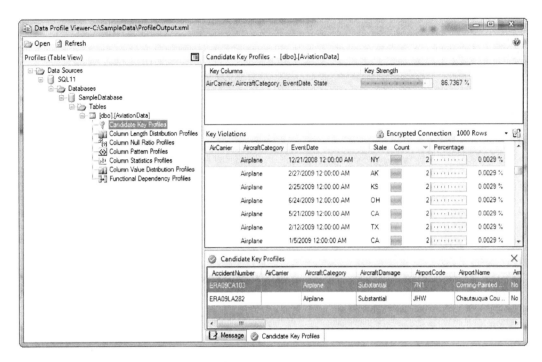

Figure 12-20. *Tolerances for candidate keys*

Functional Dependency Profile

The *Functional Dependency profile* allows you to use the profiling task to find dependencies on the table. The dependencies test to see how the values in the specified columns determine the values of the dependent columns. Using the (*) as the DeterminantColumns property allows us to test every column as the determinant of all the combinations allowed by the DependentColumns. The (*) value in the DependentColumn property allows us to test every combination of the columns in the table to be dependent on the specified determinant. Using the (*) notation for both properties will pit each column against every combination of all the columns for a dependency report. The 0.95 threshold indicates that only 95 percent or better will define a useful data dependency, as displayed in Figure 12-21.

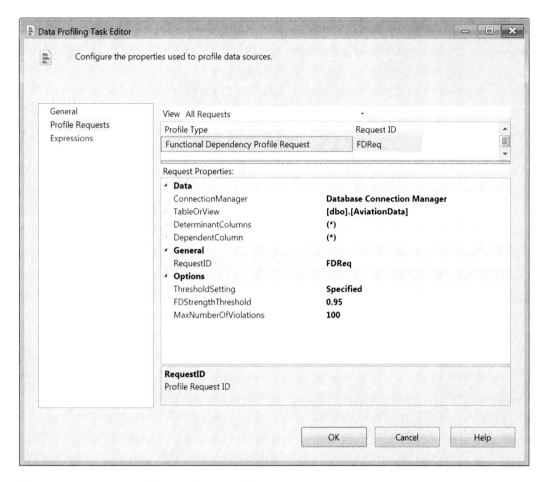

Figure 12-21. *Functional Dependency profile request*

Figure 12-22 demonstrates the results of the Functional Dependency profile request. The report shows you the overall strength of each of the tests as well as the different violations. The tab below the report shows the individual data elements that were used for profiling the dependency and their strengths.

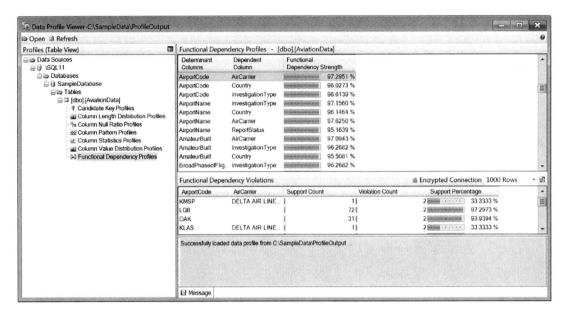

Figure 12-22. *Functional Dependency profile output*

Fuzzy Searching

One of the risks of adding new data to any set is the possibility of unclean, or nonconforming, data entering the system. This usually comes in the form of violating the rules of a character column's domain—for example, alphabet characters for a US ZIP code column being entered. SSIS provides two data flow transformations to clean up the data inconsistencies: the Fuzzy Lookup and the Fuzzy Grouping. They both utilize a token-based approach to determine matches between incoming data and the reference data. After the matches are successfully completed, you can replace the old data with the new conforming data.

Fuzzy Lookup

The *Fuzzy Lookup* returns close matches of reference data for the incoming data stream. This is in contrast to the Lookup transformation, which returns exact matches. One of the advantages to using the Fuzzy Lookup is its ability to return data that contains the strings stored in the lookup table. The lookup table in this instance would be representative of clean data. The Fuzzy Lookup task can be used to allow only data with acceptable matches to be passed through.

For this example, we are using our dbo.State table as the source of data. We set a list of lookups to isolate the states that match any members of the list. The code in Listing 12-1 demonstrates the table structures and the lookup list.

Listing 12-1. *Table Structures and Fuzzy Lookup Elements*

```
CREATE TABLE dbo.StateFuzzyMatch
(
  FuzzyMatchData NVARCHAR(50) NOT NULL
);
GO

INSERT INTO dbo.StateFuzzyMatch
  (FuzzyMatchData)
  SELECT N'Headquarters'
  UNION ALL
  SELECT N'pINEAPPLES'
  UNION ALL
  SELECT N'russia'
  UNION ALL
  SELECT N'FIRST';
GO

CREATE TABLE dbo.StateFuzzyLookup
(
  Name nvarchar(50) NULL,
  Capital nvarchar(50) NULL,
  Flag nvarchar(10) NULL,
  Date date NULL,
  Fact nvarchar(500) NULL,
  Long float NULL,
  Lat float NULL,
  FuzzyMatchData nvarchar(50) NULL,
  _Similarity real NULL,
  _Confidence real NULL
);
GO
```

The dbo.StateFuzzyMatch table contains all the key words that we will be searching for in the State data. We inserted some keywords that we need to find in the Fact attribute of the dbo.State data. We will store the successful matches of the Fuzzy Lookup operation in dbo.StateFuzzyLookup. This table includes additional columns that include the fuzzy match details, including the following:

> FuzzyMatchData is the element in the lookup table that matched the incoming data.

> _Similarity represents the level of similarity between the incoming data and the lookup element. This value can be used to adjust the similarity threshold on the Fuzzy Lookup component to eliminate unwanted matches. This alias can be modified for each of the separate columns handled in the fuzzy matching.

> _Confidence represents the confidence of the match. Previous versions of SSIS have taken into account the best similarity and the number of positive matches for a given data row to calculate this value.

Performing a Fuzzy Lookup and limiting the data to only rows that successfully match will result in the data shown in Figure 12-23. Listing 12-2 shows the query that will retrieve the positive matches and the statistics of the operation. As the results of the query demonstrate, a direct correlation between similarity and confidence does not necessarily exist for the matches in this dataset.

Listing 12-2. SELECT *Query for the Fuzzy Lookup Data*

```
SELECT Name,
  Capital,
  Flag,
  Date,
  Fact,
  Long,
  Lat,
  FuzzyMatchData,
  _Similarity,
  _Confidence
FROM dbo.StateFuzzyLookup
ORDER BY _Similarity DESC,
  _Confidence;
```

Name	Capital	Flag	Date	Fact	Long	Lat	FuzzyMatchData	_Similarity	_Confidence
Ohio	Columbus	OH.gif	1803-03-01	The Cincinnati Reds were the first professional baseball team.	-83.000311	39.961124	FIRST	0.1111111	0.7974399
South Carolina	Columbia	SC.gif	1788-05-23	The first battle of the Civil War took place at Fort Sumter.	-81.031514	34.000454	FIRST	0.08333334	0.557237
Wyoming	Cheyenne	WY.gif	1890-07-10	Wyoming was the first state to give women the right to vote.	-104.819379	41.138741	FIRST	0.08333334	0.9334746
Delaware	Dover	DE.gif	1787-12-07	Delaware was the first state to ratify the U.S. Constitution on Dec. 7, 1787.	-75.520208	39.156598	FIRST	0.07142961	0.9149016
Wisconsin	Madison	WI.gif	1848-05-29	In 1882 the first hydroelectric plant in the United States was built at Fox River.	-89.38308	43.073887	FIRST	0.0666667	0.9826713
Maryland	Annapolis	MD.gif	1788-04-28	In 1830 the Baltimore & Ohio (B&O) Railroad Company built the first railroad station.	-76.49149	38.978635	FIRST	0.06250003	0.9875
Virginia	Richmond	VA.gif	1788-06-25	Jamestown was the first English settlement in the U.S. It was also the first capital o	-77.434505	37.539746	FIRST	0.05882356	0.8228378
Montana	Helena	MT.gif	1889-11-08	Yellowstone National Park in southern Montana and northern Wyoming was the firs	-112.0202	46.586832	FIRST	0.05882356	0.9875
North Carolina	Raleigh	NC.gif	1789-11-21	The Wright Brothers made the first successful powered flight at Kill Devil Hill, near Ki	-78.638982	35.781207	FIRST	0.05555558	0.674367
New Mexico	Sante Fe	NM.gif	1912-01-06	The world's first Atomic Bomb was detonated on July 16, 1945 on the White Sands	-105.937976	35.68153	FIRST	0.0526316	0.9496188
Alaska	Juneau	AK.gif	1959-01-03	In 1867 United States Secretary of State William H. Seward offered Russia $7,200,...	-134.410699	58.301072	russia	0.05000002	0.8228378
Illinois	Springfield	IL.gif	1918-12-03	The world's first Skyscraper was built in Chicago, 1885. The Sears Tower, also in C	-89.653399	39.79825	FIRST	0.04545456	0.8228378
Kansas	Topeka	KS.gif	1861-01-29	Fort Riley was the headquarters of the United States Cavalry for 8 decades. Georg	-95.678724	39.046754	Headquarters	0.04347828	0.5000005
Hawaii	Honolulu	HI.gif	1959-08-21	More than a third of the world's commercial supply of pineapples comes from Hawai	-157.859171	21.310671	pINEAPPLES	0.04347828	0.7217442
New Hampshire	Concord	NH.gif	1788-06-21	New Hampshire was the first of the original thirteen colonies to declare independen	-71.537993	43.208542	FIRST	0.04166668	0.9149016
Kentucky	Frankfort	KY.gif	1792-06-01	Held on the first Saturday in May, the Kentucky Derby at Churchill Downs racetrack	-84.875103	38.189638	FIRST	0.04000001	0.7217441
Georgia	Atlanta	GA.gif	1788-01-02	Coca-Cola was invented in May 1886 by Dr. John S. Pemberton in Atlanta, Georgia,	-84.387887	33.750597	FIRST	0.03703705	0.8228378

Figure 12-23. Fuzzy Lookup matches

Having seen the output and the SQL Server table set up, let us tie back to the SSIS package development that is required for implementing the Fuzzy Lookup. The Fuzzy Lookup is a Data Flow task component and requires a data stream for the matching. The OLE DB source we utilize contains the query in Listing 12-3 to extract all the data that we have on the states that make up the United States of America.

Listing 12-3. State Data

```
SELECT DISTINCT s.Name,
  s.Capital,
  s.Flag,
  s.Date,
  s.Fact,
  s.Long,
```

```
    s.Lat
FROM dbo.State s;
```

At the onset of development, our requirement was to isolate states whose fact contained some very specific tokens. We loaded these tokens in dbo.StateFuzzyMatch. Unlike the Lookup component, which can use a query to create the lookup list, the Fuzzy Lookup must point to the table in order to perform its matches. The component creates indexes on the table in order to expedite the match operations. Figure 12-24 demonstrates the options we used for the Fuzzy Lookup. We did not choose to save the index but instead allow the component to regenerate a new index at each execution. The index used for that execution is not saved. For static tables, it is recommended that the index is saved.

Figure 12-24. FZL_MatchFact—*Reference table configuration*

NOTE: In case you choose to save the index and need to remove it later on, the sp_FuzzyLookupTableMaintenanceUnInstall stored procedure allows you to remove the index. It will take the index name specified in the Fuzzy Lookup as its parameter.

After the table is specified for the component, you can select the column mapping for the lookup matching, as shown in Figure 12-25. If you are required to do matches on multiple columns, you can perform the matches here. The editor draws lines to easily identify the mappings between the input columns and the lookup columns. In our sample, the match is performed on one column, but just like the Lookup component, the Fuzzy Lookup component can utilize multiple columns for its matching criteria.

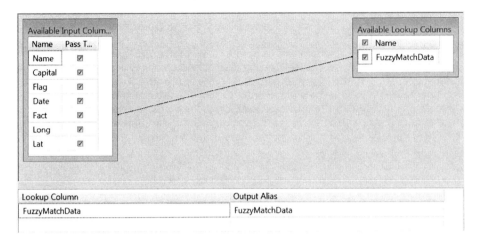

Figure 12-25. `FZL_MatchFact`—*Columns*

The Create Relationships Editor, shown in Figure 12-26, allows you to specify the criteria for each of the mappings involved in the lookup. To open this editor, you have to right-click on the background of the Columns mapping area and select Edit Mappings. The key fields in this editor are Mapping Type, Comparison Flags, and Minimum Similarity. The options for Mapping Type are Fuzzy and Exact. Selecting Exact is the same as forcing Lookup component restrictions on the Fuzzy Lookup. It will forcibly change the Minimum Similarity to be 1, a 100 percent match. The Comparison Flags allow flexibility in terms of how the matches are performed. In our example, we were concerned with ignoring only the case of the characters of the data. The Minimum Similarity sets the threshold for the match to be successful for each of the relationships. The Similarity Output Alias allows you to store the similarity information for each relationship. In our example, we are storing only the overall similarity of the lookup. Because it is a one-column match, the similarity matches the relationship similarity. Just like the Lookup component, the lookup column can be added to the pipeline and sent to the destination. The editor allows you to alias the lookup column if you need to add it to the pipeline.

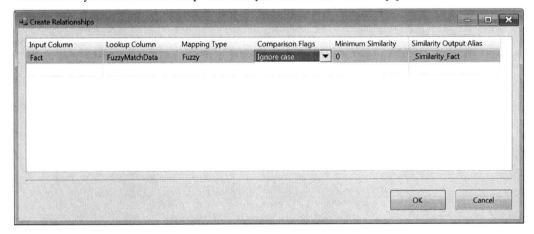

Figure 12-26. `FZL_MatchFact` *Create Relationships*

The Advanced tab of the Fuzzy Lookup Editor, shown in Figure 12-27, allows you to define the delimiters and the overall similarity threshold for each of the matches. The option that allows you to define the maximum number of matches will duplicate data rows for each successful match. For this example, we are using only whitespaces as delimiters for the tokens. By default, a few punctuation characters are defined as delimiters.

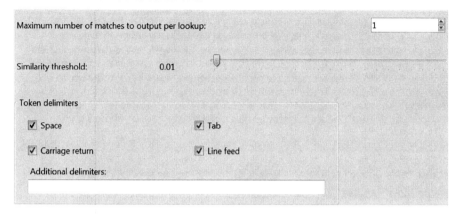

Figure 12-27. FZL_MatchFact—*Advanced*

The entire Data Flow task is shown in Figure 12-28. The Fuzzy Lookup component has a warning message because the sizes of the Fact column and the FuzzyMatchData column do not match. We added the Conditional Split component so that only rows with matching data pass through to the table. The FuzzyMatch output uses !ISNULL(FuzzyMatchData) as the splitting condition.

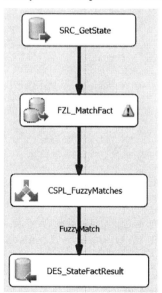

Figure 12-28. DFT_FuzzyLookupSample

Fuzzy Grouping

The *Fuzzy Grouping* component attempts to reduce the number of duplicates within a dataset based on the match criteria. The component will accept only the string data types, Unicode and Code page, to perform the matching operations. The transformation itself will create temporary tables and indexes on the server in order to perform the matching operations efficiently. For this example, we will use the same source component that we used for the Fuzzy Lookup example. The configuration of the Fuzzy Grouping transformation is very similar to Fuzzy Lookup in that it allows you to choose the Match Type, the Minimum Similarity, Comparison Flags, and other options as well. In addition, Fuzzy Grouping allows you to specify whether data may contain numeric characters by providing the Numerals option. The Numerals option enables you to perform better matches on alphanumeric information for which the numeric data poses significant implications at the beginning or end of the string. This option becomes useful for street address information or alphanumeric postal codes. For our example of Fuzzy Grouping, we will utilize the table shown in Listing 12-4 as the destination table for the results of the match.

■ **TIP:** For some performance gains, let the host machine executing the package be the OLE DB connection for the Fuzzy Grouping transformation, if possible. The factors that directly impact the performance of the Fuzzy matching transformations are the dataset size (number of rows and columns) and the average token appearance in the matched column.

Listing 12-4. Fuzzy Grouping Destination

```
CREATE TABLE dbo.StateFactGrouping
(
    _key_in int,
    _key_out int,
    _score real,
    Name nvarchar(50),
    Capital nvarchar(50),
    Flag nvarchar(10),
    Date date,
    Fact nvarchar(500),
    Long float,
    Lat float,
    Fact_clean nvarchar(500),
    _Similarity_Fact real
);
GO
```

The Fuzzy Grouping transformation adds a few columns to the pipeline in order to track the grouping. Some of the columns track the statistics behind the grouping, while others trace the records as they come through the pipeline:

> _key_in traces the original record as it comes through the Data Flow task. This column is for all intents and purposes an identity column. Every row in the dataset receives its own unique value.

_key_out connects a grouped row to the _key_in value of the matching row that it most closely resembles.

_score displays the similarity between the row and the matching row.

Fact_clean represents the matching row's value for the Fact column.

_Similarity_Fact shows the similarity between the Fact column of the row and the matching row's Fact value.

Listing 12-5 shows how the grouping matched the states based on the facts recorded about them. The join conditions in the first query show how the columns added by the Fuzzy Grouping allow you to trace back the data to their original form. The second query allows you to replace the state's original fact with the fact that the Fuzzy Grouping transformation calculated to be the closest.

Listing 12-5. *Fuzzy Grouping Results*

```
SELECT sfg1.Name AS GroupedState,
       sfg1.Fact AS GroupedFact,
       sfg1._score AS GroupedScore,
       sfg2.Name AS MatchingState,
       sfg2.Fact AS MatchingFact
FROM dbo.StateFactGrouping sfg1
INNER JOIN dbo.StateFactGrouping sfg2
       ON sfg1._key_out = sfg2._key_in
       AND sfg1._key_in <> sfg2._key_in
;
GO

SELECT sfg.Name,
       sfg.Capital,
       sfg.Fact_clean
FROM dbo.StateFactGrouping sfg
;
GO
```

Figures 12-29 and 12-30 demonstrate the results of the queries shown in Listing 12-5. You may even be able to determine the tokens used to determine the matches just by looking at Figure 12-28. For example, for Colorado and Louisiana, the tokens used for the matching were most likely the `only state`. As for Arizona and Montana, `National Park` was the most likely candidate. The scores for these matches are relatively low because we set the similarity threshold to 0.08. The facts that match are usually shorter strings matching to longer strings that contain a significant number of the tokens.

GroupedState	GroupedFact	GroupedScore	MatchingState	MatchingFact
Wyoming	Wyoming was the first state to give women the right to vote.	0.1099583	Alabama	Rosa Parks refused to give up her seat on a Montgomery bus in 1955. The Montgomery Bus ...
Colorado	Colorado became the only state to turn down the Olympics when vot...	0.1099872	Louisiana	Louisiana is the only state that does not have counties. Its political subdivisions are called paris...
Mississippi	Mississippi suffered more casualties than any other Confederate St...	0.1005985	South Carolina	The first battle of the Civil War took place at Fort Sumter
Arizona	Arizona is home of the Grand Canyon National Park	0.1747695	Montana	Yellowstone National Park in southern Montana and northern Wyoming was the first national p...
West Virginia	West Virginia broke away from Virginia to form a separate state in 1...	0.1557799	Texas	Texas was an independent nation from 1836 to 1845. It is the only state to enter the United St...
Pennsylvania	The Declaration of Independence was signed in Philadelphia in 1776.	0.1802283	New Hampshire	New Hampshire was the first of the original thirteen colonies to declare independence England...

Figure 12-29. *Fuzzy Grouping results*

The result set shown here simply demonstrates how the matched data is used rather than the original values. This transformation can provide some useful insight when attempting to initiate a data cleansing project. Business names, addresses, and other contact information can be easily consolidated with the proper use of this component. The value of the Fuzzy Grouping transformation begins to show itself when the data starts following a standardized set.

Name	Capital	Fact_clean
Alabama	Montgomery	Rosa Parks refused to give up her seat on a Montgomery bus in 1955. The Montgomery Bus Boycott kicked off the Civil Rights era a few days later.
Wyoming	Cheyenne	Rosa Parks refused to give up her seat on a Montgomery bus in 1955. The Montgomery Bus Boycott kicked off the Civil Rights era a few days later.
Alaska	Juneau	In 1867 United States Secretary of State William H. Seward offered Russia $7,200,000, or two cents per acre, for Alaska.
Arkansas	Little Rock	The state has 6 national parks, 2.5 million acres of national forests, 7 national scenic byways, 3 state scenic byways, and 50 state parks.
California	Sacramento	The state motto is Eureka!, a Greek word meaning 'I have found it!' The motto was adopted in 1849 and alludes to the discovery of gold in the Sierra ...
Connecticut	Hartford	The oldest U.S. newspaper still being published is The Hartford Courant, established in 1764.
Delaware	Dover	Delaware was the first state to ratify the U.S. Constitution on Dec. 7, 1787.
Florida	Tallahassee	Prior to becoming a territory (and later a state), Florida had two capitals: St. Augustine and Pensacola.
Georgia	Atlanta	Coca-Cola was invented in May 1886 by Dr. John S. Pemberton in Atlanta, Georgia; it was first sold at a soda fountain in Jacob's Pharmacy in Atlanta.
Hawaii	Honolulu	More than a third of the world's commercial supply of pineapples comes from Hawaii; Hawaii is also the only state that grows coffee.
Idaho	Boise	The Seven Devils' Peaks mountain ranges in Idaho includes Heaven's Gate Lookout, where sightseers can look into four states.
Illinois	Springfield	The world's first Skyscraper was built in Chicago, 1885. The Sears Tower, also in Chicago, is the tallest building in North America.
Indiana	Indianapolis	Explorers Lewis and Clark set out from Fort Vincennes in Indiana to explore the Northwest Territory.
Iowa	Des Moines	Iowa State University is the oldest land grant college in the U.S.A.
Kansas	Topeka	Fort Riley was the headquarters of the United States Cavalry for 8 decades. George Custer's famous 7th Cavalry was formed there in 1866.

Figure 12-30. Fuzzy Grouping data replaced

Data Previews

One of the most useful features of SSIS is the ability to see the data as it flows through the Data Flow task. There are a few options that allow you to sample the data. Data Viewers allow you to see the data in various forms between two different components of the Data Flow task. The Row Sampling and Percentage Sampling transformations allow you to extract sample data directly from the dataset.

Data Viewer

The *Data Viewer* option allows you to get a quick snapshot of your data stream as it moves through your Data Flow task. The viewers can be enabled between any two components within your Data Flow task. Figure 12-31 demonstrates how the Data Viewer is defined on a Data Flow task. In order to enable a Data Viewer, you have to right-click a connector between two components and select Enable Data Viewer.

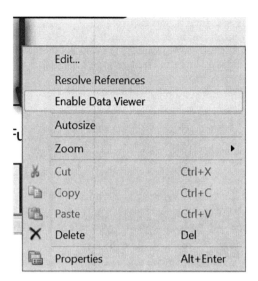

Figure 12-31. Enabling the Data Viewer

After the Data Viewer has been enabled, a small icon will appear on the connector you chose. The icon is a small magnifying glass indicating an in-depth look at the pipeline at a singular point in time. Figure 12-32 demonstrates a connector with a Data Viewer enabled. The Data Viewer can greatly assist you during development because it can allow you to look at data without having to commit it to a table or an object variable. One of the areas this object helps in data profiling is during data conversions. Suppose your Data Conversion transformation is failing without very specific error messages. The Data Viewer can help you identify the rows that are causing the error, allowing you to initiate actions to either fix the bad data or to ignore it. The Data Viewer can also be utilized to gauge the success of Lookup components or Merge Join transformations.

Figure 12-32. Enabled Data Viewer

The Data Viewer shows the data during runtime. The data is shown buffer by buffer as it passes through the connector between two components. There are options on how to display the data, the most popular being the grid. The grid displays the data in a tabular format with the ability to copy the data to the clipboard for later use. The grid appears in a separate window during the Debug mode of Visual Studio. Figure 12-33 shows the Data Viewer after a Fuzzy Lookup component.

Name	Capital	Flag	Date	Fact	Long	Lat	FuzzyMatchData	_Similarity	_Confidence	_Similarity_Fact
Alabama	Montgomery	AL.gif	12/14/1819	Rosa Parks refused to give u...	-86.301963	32.377189	NULL	0	0	0
Alaska	Juneau	AK.gif	1/3/1959	In 1867 United States Secret...	-134.410699	58.301072	russia	0.05000002	0.8228378	0.05000002
Arizona	Phoenix	AZ.gif	2/14/1912	Arizona is home of the Grand...	-112.095704	33.448543	NULL	0	0	0
Arkansas	Little Rock	AR.gif	6/15/1836	The state has 6 national park...	-92.28785	34.746292	NULL	0	0	0
California	Sacramento	CA.gif	9/9/1850	The state motto is Eureka!, a ...	-121.488066	38.575105	NULL	0	0	0
Colorado	Denver	CO.gif	8/1/1876	Colorado became the only st...	-104.986236	39.740086	NULL	0	0	0
Connecticut	Hartford	CT.gif	1/9/1788	The oldest U.S. newspaper st...	-72.68227	41.762664	NULL	0	0	0
Delaware	Dover	DE.gif	12/7/1787	Delaware was the first state t...	-75.520208	39.156598	FIRST	0.07142861	0.9149016	0.07142861
Florida	Tallahassee	FL.gif	3/3/1845	Prior to becoming a territory ...	-84.280499	30.439	NULL	0	0	0
Georgia	Atlanta	GA.gif	1/2/1788	Coca-Cola was invented in M...	-84.387887	33.750597	FIRST	0.03703705	0.8228378	0.03703705
Hawaii	Honolulu	HI.gif	8/21/1959	More than a third of the worl...	-157.859171	21.310671	pINEAPPLES	0.04347828	0.7217442	0.04347828
Idaho	Boise	ID.gif	7/3/1890	The Seven Devils' Peaks mou...	-116.200362	43.617246	NULL	0	0	0
Illinois	Springfield	IL.gif	12/3/1918	The world's first Skyscraper ...	-89.653399	39.79825	FIRST	0.04545456	0.8228378	0.04545456
Indiana	Indianapolis	IN.gif	12/11/1816	Explorers Lewis and Clark set...	-86.1617640...	39.7671542724714	NULL	0	0	0
Iowa	Des Moines	IA.gif	12/28/1846	Iowa State University is the o...	-93.604559	41.591974	NULL	0	0	0
Kansas	Topeka	KS.gif	1/29/1861	Fort Riley was the headquart...	-95.678724	39.046754	Headquarters	0.04347828	0.5000005	0.04347828
Kentucky	Frankfort	KY.gif	6/1/1792	Held on the first Saturday in ...	-84.875103	38.189638	FIRST	0.04000001	0.7217441	0.04000001
Louisiana	Baton Rouge	LA.gif	4/30/1812	Louisiana is the only state tha...	-91.188407	30.45639	NULL	0	0	0
Maine	Augusta	ME.gif	3/15/1820	Main supplies 90% of the lob...	-69.751913	44.414056	NULL	0	0	0
Maryland	Annapolis	MD.gif	4/28/1788	In 1830 the Baltimore & Ohi...	-76.49149	38.978635	FIRST	0.06250003	0.9875	0.06250003
Massachu...	Boston	MA.gif	2/6/1788	Norfolk County is the birthpla...	-71.127607	42.352507	NULL	0	0	0

Attached Total rows: 0. buffers: 0   Rows displayed = 50

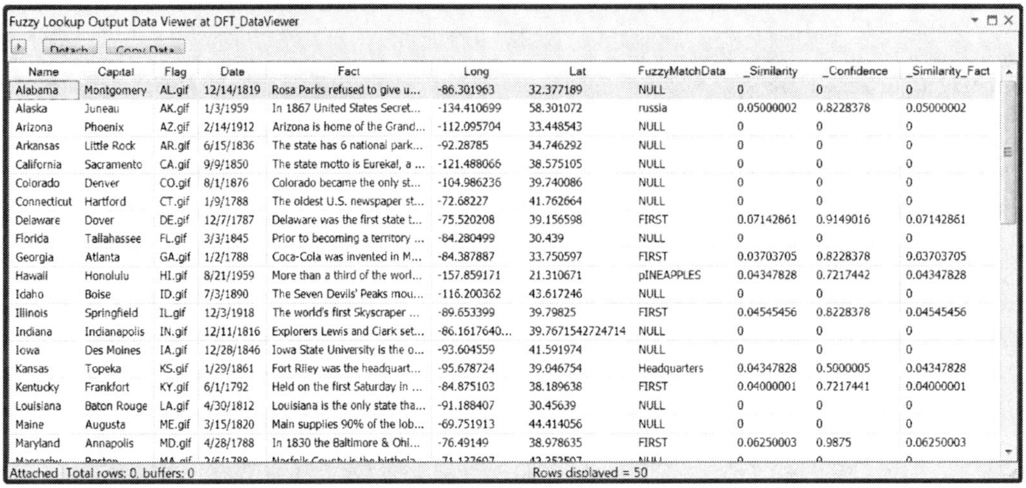

Figure 12-33. *Data Viewer of Fuzzy Lookup output*

The name of the window helps identify its placement in the package. In this case, the Data Viewer is enabled after a Fuzzy Lookup component, and therefore the window's derived name is Fuzzy Lookup Output Data Viewer at DFT_DataViewer. The window also contains a green arrow button that informs Visual Studio to proceed with the execution of the package and allow the data rows to pass through the connector. The Detach button will preserve the window and allow the package to proceed with its execution. The Copy Data button will copy highlighted rows and the column headers of the dataset to the clipboard. Clicking a particular column header will automatically sort the data according to the values in that particular buffer. Closing the Data Viewer window will also force the Visual Studio debugger to continue the execution of the package.

Data Sampling

The SSIS Data Flow task has some useful components that assist in viewing random data samples during runtime. These components are the Row Sampling and Percentage Sampling transformations. These transformations will extract the defined sampling of rows from the data stream as it passes through. Without a Sort transformation or ORDER BY clause, the data should be in random order as it passes through. The sampling transformations will reflect this by selecting a random sample set from the data. The alternative to the sampling transformations is the TOP N recordset from SQL Server. The main difference is that SSIS will attempt a truly random set, whereas TOP N will return that number or percentage of records as they are read from disk.

Row Sampling

The *Row Sampling transformation* allows you to define the number of rows that you would like to extract from the data stream as your sample set. This sample set is completely removed from the pipeline. The data is randomly selected unless you select a seed. If you specify a seed, you will use it in the random-number generation when selecting the rows for your row sample. Figure 12-34 demonstrates a Data Flow task utilizing a Row Sampling component.

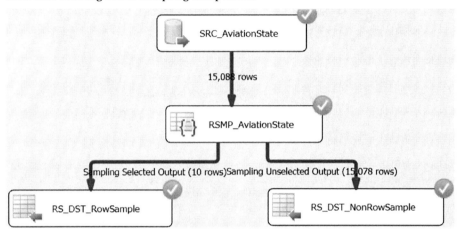

Figure 12-34. *Row Sampling example*

The destinations for the datasets are recordet destinations. We used object data type variables to store each of the outputs. The Row Sampling transformation was configured to use only 10 rows from the dataset as the sample set. The rest of the rows were to be ignored for the sampling exercise. In execution results, you can see that the Sampling Selected Output completely removed the rows from the original pipeline and created as a separate stream, Sampling Unselected Output. In this functionality, the Row Sampling transformation works similarly to the Conditional Split transformation. The Conditional Split transformation may also be used to extract a sample from your dataset by using a condition that will randomly change between True and False for certain rows. The main challenge would be defining the size of the sample set.

Percentage Sampling

The *Percentage Sampling transformation* works similarly to the Row Sampling transformation. Instead of relying on a predefined number of rows, the Percentage Sampling transformation relies on a required percentage of the dataset to be used as the sample set. Figure 12-35 demonstrates a Data Flow task utilizing a Percentage Sampling transformation to extract a sample dataset.

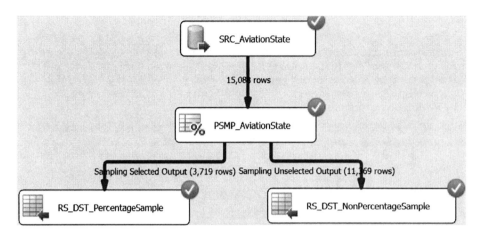

Figure 12-35. *Percentage Sampling example*

For this example, we configured the Percentage Sampling transformation to select 25 percent of the rows from the dataset as the sample set. The initial row count from the source is 15,088. The 3,719 rows are approximately 24.64 percent of 15,088 rows; 25 percent would have been 3,722 rows. The Percentage Sampling transformation does not provide exact percentage breaks when it comes to sampling the rows, but it comes very close. After executing the Data Flow task several times, you will realize that the number of records is not always consistent. The number will be around the percentage specified but will not necessarily be exact.

Summary

Data integration projects require a lot of overheard to synchronize the data from various systems. SSIS provides various tools to analyze this data so that a well-informed plan can be formalized. These tools include the Data Profiling task, Fuzzy search transformations, data sampling transformations, and viewers to analyze data that traverses your data flow. Using these built-in tools enables you to get a snapshot of the data's state very quickly. The next chapter covers the logging and auditing options available to you as you extract, transform, and load your data from various systems into potentially different systems.

Logging and Auditing

Uncontrolled access to data, with no audit trail of
activity and no oversight would be going too far.

—US Naval Officer John Poindexter

A couple of key advantages provided by enterprise systems, which are often overlooked until the auditors start poking around, are process logging,auditing, and data lineage. The conceptsare simple: when you move data from system to system and manipulate it along the way,you might need to keep track of where it came from, maintain summary information about data processing, and know which processes touched that data along the way. There are a few reasons for keeping track of this additional information:

- You may need to keep it for troubleshooting purposes, to trace data issues backward through your processes to their source.

- The legal department may have mandated a new legal requirement to document every step of processing in real-time in the event of issues.

- Your business may fall under a regulation such asSarbanes-Oxley Act, SOX, or Health Insurance Portability and Accountability Act ,HIPAA, that requires high levels of security and controls around confidential medical or consumer data.

SSIS provides extensive standard logging functionality that captures runtime information about the status of ETL processing. In addition, it is relatively simple to add auditing capabilities to your enterprise ETL applications with SSIS. In this chapter, you'll look at ways to take advantage of standard logging and ways to add auditing to your SSIS packages.

Logging

SSIS provides built-in *logging* capabilities that are easy to enable. In previous chapters, we've enabled this feature in some code samples to demonstrate SSIS's logging capabilities. In this section, we'll review how to enable and configure logging in your SSIS packages. We'll also talk about SSIS logging best practices.

Enabling Logging

Logging options in SSIS are accessed at the package level by right-clicking on the control flow and choosing the Logging option from the pop-up context menu, as shown in Figure 13-1.

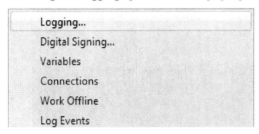

Figure 13-1. *Selecting the Logging option from the pop-up menu*

The logging configuration screen allows you to configure SSIS logging options, as shown in Figure 13-2. In this screen, you can set the following logging options:

- The SSIS log provider to use. The most common options are the SSIS log provider for SQL Server, which logs to a SQL Server table, and the SSIS log provider for text files, which outputs logging information to text files. You can, however, choose to log information to the Windows event log, XML files, or SQL Server profiler trace files. The latter options are generally used for specialized troubleshooting tasks.

- The containers for which events should be logged. You can configure logging of specific events at the package, container, and Data Flow task levels. In our example, we're going to configure at both the package and Data Flow task levels.

- The details you would like logged at the event level. You choose these details from the Details tab.

■ **NOTE:** As a general rule, we tend to prefer the SSIS log provider for SQL Server over other logging methods. Becausethis log provider logs to a SQL Server database table, the logged information is easy to query, simplifying troubleshooting exercises. When you designate the SSIS log provider for SQL Server, it will automatically generate the dbo.sysssislog table and dbo.sp_ssis_addlogentry procedure in your database (if they don't exist), both of which it marks as system objects.

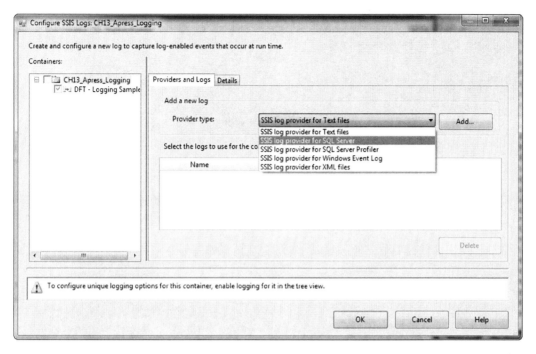

Figure 13-2. SSIS logging configuration screen

To configure logging, choose the package, or the containers or tasks in the package, for which you want logging turned on. Then choose a log provider and click the Add button. In Figure 13-3, we've added the SSIS log provider for SQL Server to a package and turned on logging at the package level. For many log providers, you must choose a connection from the Configuration drop-down. In the figure, we've selected an OLE DB connection named LOG, which is pointed at a SQL Server database we wish to log to.

■ **NOTE:** When we configure the SSIS log provider for SQL Server, we prefer to create an OLE DB Connection Manager specifically for the log provider connection. This keeps the logging information and data connections separate. One of the main reasons to do this is to avoid the occasional "Connection is busy with results for another command" error, which can be difficult to troubleshoot in some cases.

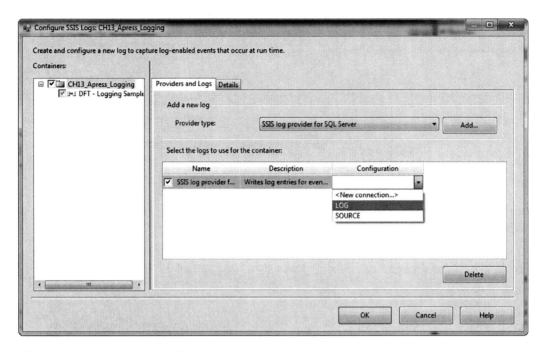

Figure 13-3. Configuring the SSIS log provider for SQL Server

In our example, we've enabled logging at the package level, but we did not change settings for the Data Flow task contained in the package. In this case, all containers and tasks in the package inherit their logging settings from the package as indicated by the grayed-out checkboxes. To configure the events that are logged, choose the Details tab of the logging configuration page. All the events you can log are listed, as shown in Figure 13-4.

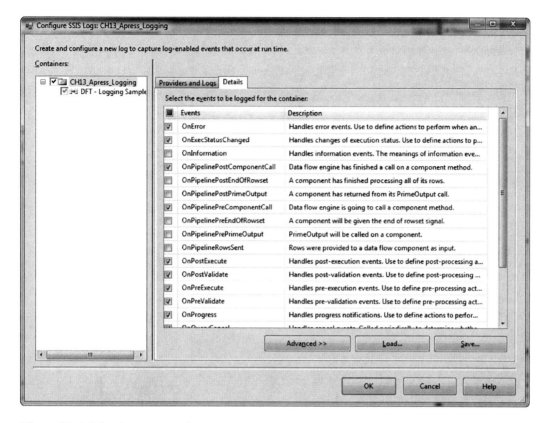

Figure 13-4. *Selecting events to log*

You can also choose the detailed information to log for each event by clicking the Advanced button, as shown in Figure 13-5. The default logs all relevant information for every event. Unless you have a specific reason to eliminate some data from the logs, the default is normally adequate.

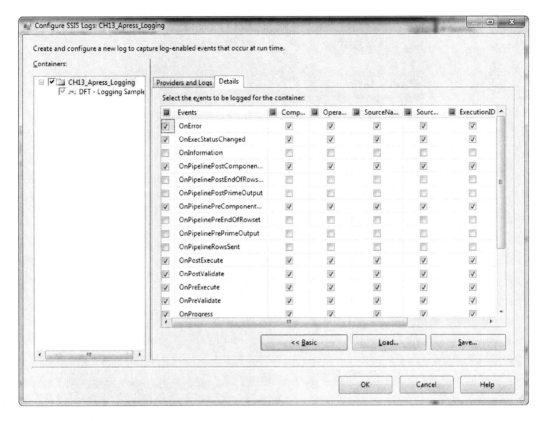

Figure 13-5. Selecting data to log for each event

Choosing Log Events

When configuring logging, one of the things to keep in mind is that each logged event consumes some resources. In the case of the SSIS log provider for SQL Server, each event requires a call to a SQL Server stored procedure, which then writes to a table in the database. Logging large quantities of events can slow down packages and require large amounts of storage.

Although all of the SSIS events provide some level of insight into your package executions, some are better saved for specialized debugging situations. Therefore, we recommend limiting the events you log in production settings. There is a performance and storage hit associated with logging too much information, and when troubleshooting, you can encounter "information overload" if you choose to log too much information. The following list indicates the core events we recommend capturing in a production environment. Note that this list is just a starting point, and you may encounter a need to capture other events in your production environments:

- OnError

- OnExecStatusChanged

- OnPipelinePostComponentCall

- OnPipelinePreComponentCall

- OnPostExecute

- OnPostValidate

- OnPreExecute

- OnPreValidate

- OnQueryCancel

- OnTaskFailed

- OnWarning

Events we recommend avoiding include OnInformation, OnProgress, and Diagnostic, among others. Although often useful in debugging and test scenarios, these events in particular log a very high ratio of "noise" to useful information. They tend to clutter up the log and complicate troubleshooting while adversely affecting performance to varying degrees.

On SQL Logging

As mentioned previously in this chapter, we tend to handle our SSIS logging needs with the SSIS log provider for SQL Server. This log provider relies on two database objects to log information: a stored procedure named dbo.sp_ssis_addlogentry and a table named dbo.sysssislog, both marked as system objects. SSIS calls the stored procedure every time an event occurs. The procedure, in turn, writes an entry to the dbo.sysssislog table. The SSIS log table can be queried to retrieve relevant information with a query similar to the one shown in Figure 13-6.

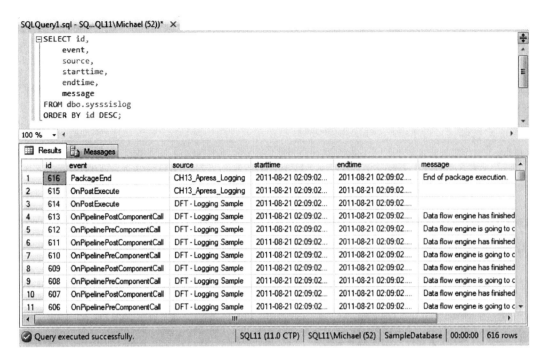

Figure 13-6. Querying the SSIS log table

Summary Auditing

Summary auditing encompasses grabbing and storing abridged processing information for the SSIS packages. As part of auditing, we generally store package auditing information that can be grabbed from system variables in the SSIS package, start and end times, and other summary execution information.

The easiest way to enable auditing is to create and call stored procedures that start and end your auditing processes.In the model the authors normally employ, we like to divide the process into batch-level and package-level auditing. Figure 13-7 is a logical representation of this two-part batch/package auditing process. Note that a *batch* can encompass one or more packages.

■ **NOTE:** Multiple packages can be wrapped in a single batch by using the Execute Package task to implement the parent-child SSIS design pattern.

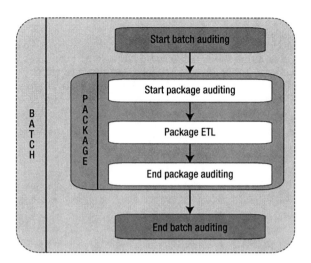

Figure 13-7. *Logical view of batch/package auditing*

Batch-Level Auditing

Batch-level auditing encompasses all of the packages executed during a given run. At the batch level, we record the start time and end time of the entire batch, as well as summary information about the tables in the database. For security purposes, and for simplified management, the implementation of our auditing processes puts its database objects in a new schema. In this instance, we named it Audit:

```
IF SCHEMA_ID(N'Audit') IS NULL
EXEC(N'CREATE SCHEMA Audit;')
GO
```

We first create a table named AuditBatch, which contains batch-level auditing information including the start and end times for a given batch. You can use the information stored in the AuditBatch table to determine the performance of an entire batch of packages, and to wrap up log entries that belong to a single batch execution. Here is the code we are executing:

```
IF OBJECT_ID(N'Audit.AuditBatch') IS NOT NULL
  DROP TABLE Audit.AuditBatch;
GO

CREATE TABLE Audit.AuditBatch
(
  BatchID BIGINT NOT NULL IDENTITY(1, 1),
  BatchStartTime DATETIMEOFFSET,
  BatchEndTime DATETIMEOFFSET,
  BatchElapsedTimeMS AS (DATEDIFF(MILLISECOND, BatchStartTime, BatchEndTime)),
  BatchStatus NVARCHAR(20),
  CONSTRAINT PK_AUDIT_AUDITBATCH PRIMARY KEY CLUSTERED
  (
    BatchID
  )
```

```
);
GO
```

We also create, in this next example, a batch-level auditing table called AuditTable, which captures state information for tables in the database including the number of rows in each table and how much space each table consumes. The information stored in this table can be used to determine resource usage for a given batch process. You can use this raw data to estimate long-term storage requirements, for instance.

```
IF OBJECT_ID(N'Audit.AuditTable') IS NOT NULL
DROP TABLE Audit.AuditTable;
GO

CREATE TABLE Audit.AuditTable
(
TableAuditID BIGINT NOT NULL IDENTITY(1, 1),
BatchID BIGINT NOT NULL,
BatchStartFlag BIT NOT NULL,
TableSchema NVARCHAR(128),
TableName NVARCHAR(128),
TableObjectID INT,
TableReservedKB FLOAT,
TableDataKB FLOAT,
TableIndexKB FLOAT,
TableUnusedKB FLOAT,
TableRows INT,
TableDataBytesPerRow INT,
CONSTRAINT PK_AUDIT_AUDITTABLE PRIMARY KEY CLUSTERED
(
TableAuditID
)
);
GO
```

To simplify our upcoming stored procedure code, we capture the table size data in a view called SummaryTableData. For speed purposes, we use the sys.partitions catalog view to grab row counts from tables:

```
IF OBJECT_ID(N'Audit.SummaryTableData') IS NOT NULL
DROP VIEW Audit.SummaryTableData;
GO

CREATE VIEW Audit.SummaryTableData
AS
WITH CTE
AS
(
SELECT OBJECT_SCHEMA_NAME(p.object_id) AS table_schema,
OBJECT_NAME(p.object_id) AS table_name,
p.object_id,
SUM(a.total_pages) AS reserved_pages,
SUM(a.used_pages) AS used_pages,
SUM(
```

```
CASE
WHEN it.internal_type IN (202, 204, 207, 211, 212, 213, 214, 215, 216, 221, 222)
THEN 0
WHEN a.type <> 1 AND p.index_id < 2 THEN a.used_pages
WHEN p.index_id < 2 THEN a.data_pages
ELSE 0
END
) AS pages,
(
SELECT SUM(p1.rows)
FROM sys.partitions p1
WHERE p1.index_id in (0,1)
AND p1.object_id = p.object_id
) AS rows
  FROM sys.partitions p
INNER JOIN sys.tables t
ON p.object_id = t.object_id
INNER JOIN sys.allocation_units a
ON p.partition_id = a.container_id
LEFT JOIN sys.internal_tables it
ON p.object_id = it.object_id
GROUP BY OBJECT_SCHEMA_NAME(p.object_id),
OBJECT_NAME(p.object_id),
p.object_id
)
SELECT table_schema,
table_name,
object_id,
reserved_pages * 8192 / 1024.0 AS reserved_kb,
pages * 8192 / 1024.0 AS data_kb,
(used_pages - pages) * 8192 / 1024.0 AS index_kb,
(reserved_pages - used_pages) * 8192 / 1024.0 AS unused_kb,
rows,
pages * 8192 / CASE rows
WHEN 0.0 THEN NULL
                    ELSE rows
END AS data_bytes_per_row
FROM CTE;
GO
```

■ **TIP:** The row counts in the `sys.partitions` catalog view are technically approximations, but the instances in which they could be incorrect are indicated to be rare. We have it on good authority that if your row count in `sys.partitions` is off considerably, you should report it to Microsoft because it may be an issue that needs to be investigated. We use it here because it is considerably faster than the `SELECT COUNT(*)` method of obtaining table row counts.

Our view calculates the space used by a table by using a method that is very similar to the legacy sp_spaceusedsystem stored procedure. Finally, we create two procedures to start and end batch auditing (StartAuditBatch and EndAuditBatch). The initial call to StartAuditBatch returns a unique batch ID number after each call and stores initial state information for the tables in the database. The EndAuditBatch procedure in the following example accepts this previouslygenerated batch ID number and closes out the batch information.

```
IF OBJECT_ID(N'Audit.StartAuditBatch') IS NOT NULL
DROP PROCEDURE Audit.StartAuditBatch;
GO

CREATE PROCEDURE Audit.StartAuditBatch @BatchID BIGINT OUTPUT
AS
BEGIN
SET NOCOUNT ON;

INSERT INTO Audit.AuditBatch
(
BatchStartTime,
BatchStatus
)
VALUES
(
SYSDATETIMEOFFSET(),
N'STARTED'
);

SET @BatchID = SCOPE_IDENTITY();

INSERT INTO Audit.AuditTable
(
BatchID,
BatchStartFlag,
TableSchema,
TableName,
TableObjectID,
TableReservedKB,
TableDataKB,
TableIndexKB,
TableUnusedKB,
TableRows,
TableDataBytesPerRow
)
SELECT @BatchID,
1,
table_schema,
table_name,
object_id,
reserved_kb,
data_kb,
index_kb,
unused_kb,
```

```
rows,
data_bytes_per_row
FROM Audit.SummaryTableData;
END;
GO

IF OBJECT_ID(N'Audit.EndAuditBatch') IS NOT NULL
DROP PROCEDURE Audit.EndAuditBatch;
GO

CREATE PROCEDURE Audit.EndAuditBatch @BatchID BIGINT
AS
BEGIN
SET NOCOUNT ON;

UPDATE Audit.AuditBatch
SET BatchStatus = N'COMPLETED',
BatchEndTime = SYSDATETIMEOFFSET()
WHERE BatchID = @BatchID;

INSERT INTO Audit.AuditTable
(
BatchID,
BatchStartFlag,
TableSchema,
TableName,
TableObjectID,
TableReservedKB,
TableDataKB,
TableIndexKB,
TableUnusedKB,
TableRows,
TableDataBytesPerRow
)
SELECT @BatchID,
0,
table_schema,
table_name,
object_id,
reserved_kb,
data_kb,
index_kb,
unused_kb,
rows,
data_bytes_per_row
FROM Audit.SummaryTableData;
END;
GO
```

Package-Level Auditing

Our *package-level auditing* functionality records package identification and execution information including an execution GUID that you can use to join back to the SSIS log table. Thisadds context to the SSIS log entries and provides additional information that can be used for troubleshootingon a per-package basis.

To store package audit information, we create an AuditPackage table, which holds package information including name, version, and a GUID that can be used to join the entries in this table to the SSIS log entries (if you use the SSIS log provider for SQL Server). Here's the code for our table:

```
IF OBJECT_ID ('Audit.AuditPackage') IS NOT NULL
DROP TABLE Audit.AuditPackage;
GO

CREATE TABLE Audit.AuditPackage
(
AuditPackageID BIGINT NOT NULL IDENTITY(1, 1),
BatchID BIGINT NOT NULL,
PackageName NVARCHAR(128),
ExecutionInstanceGUID UNIQUEIDENTIFIER,
ProductVersion NVARCHAR(20),
MachineName NVARCHAR(128),
VersionMajor INT,
VersionMinor INT,
VersionBuild INT,
LocaleID INT,
PackageStartTime DATETIMEOFFSET,
PackageEndTime DATETIMEOFFSET,
PackageElapsedTimeMS AS (DATEDIFF(MILLISECOND, PackageStartTime, PackageEndTime)),
CONSTRAINT PK_AUDIT_AUDITPACKAGE PRIMARY KEY CLUSTERED
(
AuditPackageID
  )
);
GO
```

We created two procedures for package auditing:StartAuditPackage to start the audit process, and EndAuditPackage to end the audit. The start procedure returns a unique package audit ID number after each call. That same audit ID number is passed into the end procedure to complete the audit entry. The code is as follows:

```
IF OBJECT_ID('Audit.StartAuditPackage') IS NOT NULL
DROP PROCEDURE Audit.StartAuditPackage;
GO

CREATE PROCEDURE Audit.StartAuditPackage @ExecutionInstanceGUID UNIQUEIDENTIFIER,
@ProductVersion NVARCHAR(20),
@MachineName NVARCHAR(128),
@VersionMajor INT,
@VersionMinor INT,
@VersionBuild INT,
@LocaleID INT,
@PackageName NVARCHAR(128),
```

```
@BatchID BIGINT,
@AuditPackageID BIGINT OUTPUT
AS
BEGIN
SET NOCOUNT ON;

INSERT INTO Audit.AuditPackage
(
PackageName,
BatchID,
ExecutionInstanceGUID,
ProductVersion,
MachineName,
VersionMajor,
VersionMinor,
VersionBuild,
LocaleID,
PackageStartTime
)
VALUES
(
@PackageName,
@BatchID,
@ExecutionInstanceGUID,
@ProductVersion,
@MachineName,
@VersionMajor,
@VersionMinor,
@VersionBuild,
@LocaleID,
SYSDATETIMEOFFSET()
);

SET @AuditPackageID = SCOPE_IDENTITY();
END;
GO

IF OBJECT_ID('Audit.EndAuditPackage') IS NOT NULL
DROP PROCEDURE Audit.EndAuditPackage;
GO

CREATE PROCEDURE Audit.EndAuditPackage @AuditPackageID BIGINT
AS
BEGIN
SET NOCOUNT ON;

UPDATE Audit.AuditPackage
SETPackageEndTime = SYSDATETIMEOFFSET()
WHERE AuditPackageID = @AuditPackageID;
END;
GO
```

Adding Auditing to Packages

Auditing can be added to your process by including Execute SQL tasks to call the appropriate stored procedures. In our sample package, we created two 64-bit integer (Int64) variables named User::AuditBatchID and User::AuditPackageID. We set up our sample package as shown in Figure 13-8.

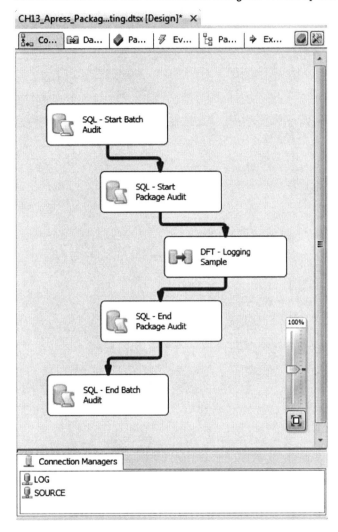

Figure 13-8. Sample package with auditing calls

The Data Flow task in this example is wrapped with start and end audit calls, in the following order:

- **SQL – Start Batch Audit** begins the batch audit process. Calls the start batch audit procedure and returns a unique batch audit ID. This is used to set the variable in the package.

- **SQL – Start Package Audit**begins the package audit process. Calls the start package audit procedure and returns a unique package audit ID, which sets the appropriate package variable. We pass several system variables to this procedure so they can be saved in the package audit table.

- **SQL – End Package Audit** ends the package audit process. This procedure closes up the auditing loop at the package level, recording audit finalization information.

- **SQL – End Batch Audit** completes the batch audit process. Calls the end batch audit procedure to finish auditing at the batch level after all packages are complete. The batch audit information recorded includes the change in table size information.

As we mentioned, the audit information you capture can be joined back to the standard SSIS log tables via the Execution Instance GUID. This GUID will give you all the log messages relevant to any given package execution, using a query such as the following.Sample results are shown in Figure 13-9.

```
SELECT au.AuditPackageID,
au.BatchID,
au.PackageName,
au.MachineName,
au.PackageStartTime,
au.PackageEndTime,
s.event,
s.source,
s.message
FROM Audit.AuditPackage au
INNER JOIN dbo.sysssislog s
ON au.ExecutionInstanceGUID = s.executionid;
GO
```

	AuditPa...	BatchID	PackageName	Machi...	PackageStartTime	PackageEndTime	event	source	message	
479	7	9	CH13_Apress_Pack...	SQL11	2011-08-24 23:38:30...	2011-08-24 23:38:32...	OnPipelinePost...	DFT - Logging Sample	Data flow engine has finished ...	
480	7	9	CH13_Apress_Pack...	SQL11	2011-08-24 23:38:30...	2011-08-24 23:38:32...	OnPipelinePre...	DFT - Logging Sample	Data flow engine is going to ca...	
481	7	9	CH13_Apress_Pack...	SQL11	2011-08-24 23:38:30...	2011-08-24 23:38:32...	OnPipelinePost...	DFT - Logging Sample	Data flow engine has finished ...	
482	7	9	CH13_Apress_Pack...	SQL11	2011-08-24 23:38:30...	2011-08-24 23:38:32...	OnPipelinePre...	DFT - Logging Sample	Data flow engine is going to ca...	
483	7	9	CH13_Apress_Pack...	SQL11	2011-08-24 23:38:30...	2011-08-24 23:38:32...	OnPipelinePost...	DFT - Logging Sample	Data flow engine has finished ...	
484	7	9	CH13_Apress_Pack...	SQL11	2011-08-24 23:38:30...	2011-08-24 23:38:32...	OnPostExecute	DFT - Logging Sample		
485	7	9	CH13_Apress_Pack...	SQL11	2011-08-24 23:38:30...	2011-08-24 23:38:32...	OnPostExecute	Sequence Container		
486	7	9	CH13_Apress_Pack...	SQL11	2011-08-24 23:38:30...	2011-08-24 23:38:32...	OnPreExecute	SQL - End Package ...		

| Query executed successfully. | | SQL11 (11.0 CTP) | SQL11\Michael (53) | SampleDatabase | 00:00:00 | 495 rows |

Figure 13-9. Sample results of audit data joined to the SSIS log table

Simple Data Lineage

One of the advantages of an auditing process as we've described it in this chapter is that you can easily extend it to include simple data lineage processes. *Data lineage* is a process by which you can trace data back to its source, essentially reverseengineering the processes by which your data arrived in its current state. In its simplest form, which we demonstrate in this section, you can use data lineage information to determine which ETL processes manipulated your data and determine the precise source from which it is derived.

■ **NOTE:** Microsoft introduced a new feature known as *Impact and Data Lineage Analysis (IAL)* in early prerelease versions of SQL Server Denali. IAL was supposed to provide enterprise data lineage features out of the box. Alas, this feature was pulled prior to Release to Market, RTM, for an "overhaul." So for now we must implement our own data lineage process until Microsoft's offering is released. The revamped IAL is expected to be released shortly after SQL Server Denali as part of Project Barcelona (more information is available at

http://blogs.msdn.com/b/project_barcelona_team_blog/).

The majority of the information we'll need to record for our simple data lineage solution is already stored in the batch and package auditing tables. This includes the start and stop times, specific package and platform identification information, and related standard log entries. All of this information can be used to reverseengineer your process, but there are a few items missing. After you've stepped backward through your process, you need to ultimately determine where your data came from, and you may in fact need additional supporting data that's not captured by the auditing solution.

For this purpose, we create a simple table that allows you to store key-value pairs related to a specific batch and package execution. Rather than limit you to a specific set of predefined entries, this design lets you store any necessary metadata at any point in your process. The table we created for this purpose is the LineageMetadata table, shown here:

```
IF OBJECT_ID(N'Audit.LineageMetadata') IS NOT NULL
DROP TABLE Audit.LineageMetadata;
GO

CREATE TABLE Audit.LineageMetadata
(
LineageMetaID int not null identity(1, 1),
BatchID int not null,
AuditPackageID int not null,
LineageKey varchar(1000) not null,
LineageValue varchar(1000),
CONSTRAINT PK_AUDIT_LINEAGEMETADATA PRIMARY KEY CLUSTERED
(
LineageMetaID
)
);
GO
```

We also provide a simple procedure to add entries to the table on demand, as shown here:

```
IF OBJECT_ID(N'Audit.AddLineageMetadata') IS NOT NULL
DROP PROCEDURE Audit.AddLineageMetadata;
GO
```

```
CREATE PROCEDURE Audit.AddLineageMetadata @BatchID int,
@AuditPackageID int,
@LineageKey varchar(1000),
@LineageValue varchar(1000)
AS
BEGIN
INSERT INTO Audit.LineageMetadata
(
BatchID,
AuditPackageID,
LineageKey,
LineageValue
)
VALUES
(
@BatchID,
@AuditPackageID,
@LineageKey,
@LineageValue
);
END;
GO
```

A sample package that implements our simple data lineage solution extends the previous auditing package to include lineage entities, such as storing the source file name, as shown in Figure 13-10.

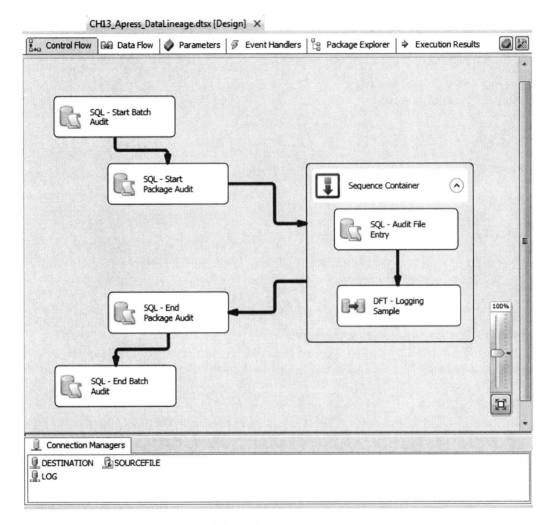

Figure 13-10. *SSIS package with additional data lineage*

To get row-level data lineage, we need to add the batch ID and package ID as columns to our data flow, and store them in the target table with the data. In our example, we've done this with a Derived Column transformation, shown in Figure 13-11.

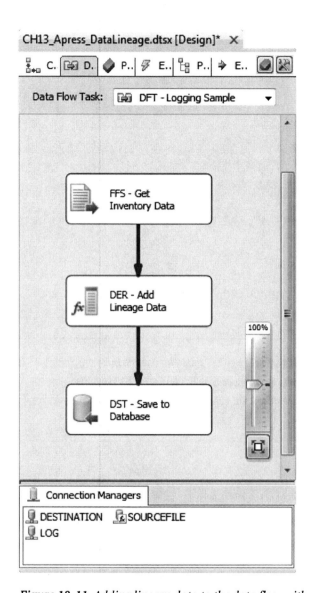

Figure 13-11. *Adding lineage data to the data flow with a Derived Column transformation*

The lineage data can be joined to the auditing data with the BatchID and AuditPackageID, as shown in the following sample query. Sample results from our test run are shown in Figure 13-12.

```
SELECT lm.BatchID,
lm.AuditPackageID,
lm.LineageKey,
lm.LineageValue,
au.PackageName,
```

```
au.PackageStartTime,
au.PackageEndTime
FROM Audit.LineageMetadata lm
INNER JOIN Audit.AuditPackage au
ON lm.BatchID = au.BatchID
AND lm.AuditPackageID = au.AuditPackageID;
GO
```

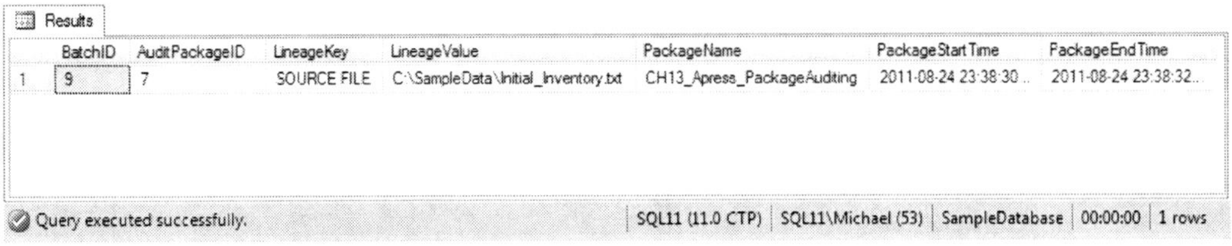

	BatchID	AuditPackageID	LineageKey	LineageValue	PackageName	PackageStartTime	PackageEndTime
1	9	7	SOURCE FILE	C:\SampleData\Initial_Inventory.txt	CH13_Apress_PackageAuditing	2011-08-24 23:38:30..	2011-08-24 23:38:32..

Query executed successfully. | SQL11 (11.0 CTP) | SQL11\Michael (53) | SampleDatabase | 00:00:00 | 1 rows

Figure 13-12. Sample lineage and audit data

As you can see in the results in Figure 13-12, we have captured enough metadata information to trace every row of data from the source file it started in, through the package that manipulated it, and finally to the destination table it ended up in.

■ **NOTE:** As we noted previously, this is a simple data lineage solution, but it can be used to build much more complex solutions. The authors have, on occasion, implemented custom data lineage solutions requiring a much finer grain of detail, such as capturing the state of individual rows and columns of data as it is processed. As you can imagine, we're enthusiastically looking forward to the release of Project Barcelona.

Summary

In many enterprise systems that are currently in production use around the world—in many industries—logging and auditing features are often overlooked. In some scenarios, lack of proper logging and auditing processes can result in countless hours of reverseengineering thousands of lines of code to uncover and fix even the simplest of errors. In the worst case, failure to implement these enterprise features could end in trouble with auditors and regulatory agencies followed by big fines and people losing their jobs. This chapter presentedSSIS's built-in logging capabilities and showed you how to extend them to add standardized auditing features to your ETL processes.

In addition, it's becoming increasingly important to store data lineage information that allows you to track data moving from one system to another as it makes its way to your data warehouses, data marts, and other data repositories. Although SSIS does not currently offer enterprise data lineage facilities out of the box, we demonstrated how to extend your auditing system to implement a basic data lineage solution that will allow you to track data at the row level back through the packages that manipulated it, all the way back to its source.

The next chapter presents ETL in a heterogeneous environment—one in which source data comes in many forms and formats.

CHAPTER 14

Heterogeneous Sources and Destinations

We want to further eliminate friction among heterogeneous architectures and applications without compromising their distinctive underlying capabilities.

—Microsoft cofounder Bill Gates

One of the key elements of a data integration tool is the ability to handle disparate sources and destinations. SQL Server Integration Services 2011 allows you to extract from any storage method and load data into just as many data storage systems. The toolset provided by Integration Services truly attempts to achieve the goal outlined by Bill Gates to allow various systems to mesh well together. As discussed in previous chapters, data integrity is a key element to success of integration projects, and SSIS provides transformations and components that allow you to handle the nonconforming data.

Data storage comes in various forms. This includes text files that cannot inherently enforce data quality (such as data types or foreign keys), other RDBMSs (including Oracle or DB2), XML files, web services, or even the Active Directory. All these systems can hold data in some structure that SSIS can unravel and integrate into one system. However, the destination is not limited to just SQL Server. Data can be loaded back into an original form if the requirements specify such a need.

This chapter covers some of the sources and destinations that SSIS can access. This chapter relies heavily on the information provided in Chapter 4 for its basis and then builds upon that foundation to provide you with examples that you can use in your everyday process.

SQL Server Sources and Destinations

The easiest of all sources and destinations for SSIS to handle is SQL Server. Reading from prior versions is relatively easy, but loading into a prior version may require some data conversions to handle newer or deprecated data types. As we mentioned in Chapter 4, the most efficient way to extract data from a SQL Server database is by using the SQL command option to write your own SQL statement. This is the recommended option to use on a SQL Server source component for several reasons. The first and foremost reason is that it allows you to limit the columns you extract to the ones you need. The SELECT * notation, used by the Table or View option, has been documented to have poor performance with SSIS source components and can cause metadata validation errors due to DDL changes. Specifying the necessary columns will keep your initial buffer lean. Another reason to write the SQL is that you can define the data types in the SQL rather than utilizing a data conversion component in the data flow. The SQL Query option also allows you to define an ORDER BY clause, which can greatly boost your performance if you need to perform a join in the data flow by using the Merge Join transformation.

■ **NOTE:** If you would like to see the performance of a SELECT * query in a source component, you can execute a package with the SQL profiler running. You should be able to compare the differences between the two implementations clearly.

The source component, shown in Figure 14-1, allows you to define your extraction set. In order to add the source component to a package, you must have a Data Flow task to add it to. We chose to utilize the SQL command option to extract the data from the source. Even though we are extracting all the columns in the table, we still enumerate all the columns rather than utilizing the * option. We utilized the query shown in Listing 14-1 as our extraction logic. One of the advantages of using the SQL command is the ability to parameterize your query.

Listing 14-1. SQL Server Source Query

```
WITH CTE
AS
(
        SELECT c.Alpha2
                ,c.CountryName
                ,c.Year
                ,c.TLD
        FROM dbo.Country c
        WHERE c.Alpha2 = ?
                AND c.Year = ?
)
SELECT Alpha2
        ,CountryName
        ,Year
        ,TLD
FROM CTE
WHERE CountryName = ?
;
```

The common table expression (CTE) can be used inside the source query to break up the logic in the query as well as to make the query readable. The parameters are qualified by placing a question mark inside the query. The parameters can also be used to add a column in the query, not just limit the rows through a WHERE clause. The parameters can be added within different sections of the query as long as they are mapped appropriately by using the Parameters button in the OLE DB Source Editor. We highly recommend that you place your parameters right next to each other so you do not end up losing track of their order when you have to map them. The provided sample could get messy because there are some parameters in the CTE as well as another parameter in the final query.

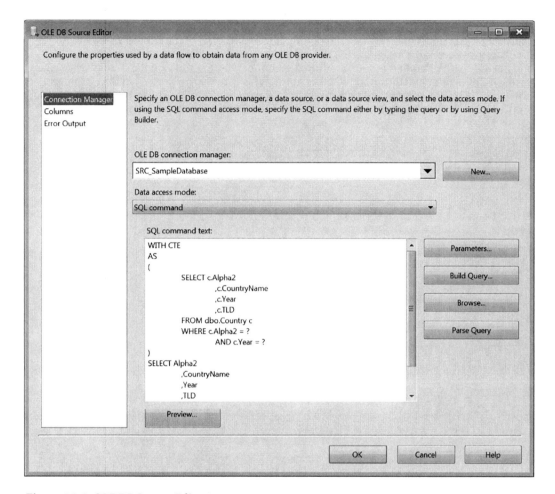

Figure 14-1. *OLE DB Source Editor*

The buttons to the right side of the SQL Command Text box allow you to modify the query in the following ways:

> **Parameters** allows you to assign a mapping to parameters listed in the query. The naming convention behind the mapping depends on the type of the connection manager. The Connection Manager chapter outlines all the mapping rules.

> **Build Query** opens a GUI that allows you to construct a SQL query.

> **Browse** allows you to import the text from a file as your query. When you click the OK button, the query will be parsed and the metadata will be verified.

> **Parse Query** parses the query that is supplied in the text field.

Figure 14-2 demonstrates the mappings that can assign variable values to the parameters defined in the SQL statement. The data types can vary depending on the data type of the context in the query. The Parameters column is crucial in assigning the values because it relies on the order of appearance of the qualifier in the query. The Param direction column determines whether the variable should be assigned a value through the statement (Output) or whether the variable is passing in a value to the statement (Input). Because the source component anticipates a tabular result set, Input is the direction that is most likely to be used. This is the reason for our recommendation of gathering the parameters as closely as possible.

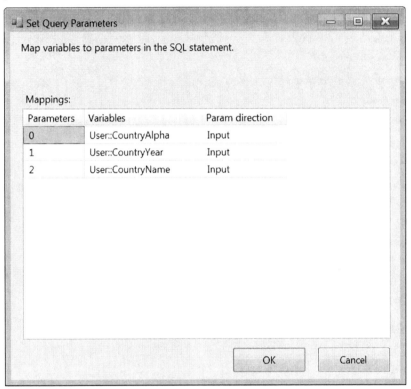

Figure 14-2. Set Query Parameters dialog box

An important aspect of the source component is the advanced properties editor. The Input and Output Properties tab, shown in Figure 14-3, in particular allows you to tweak the extracted data. A common error that appears during runtime is a string truncation error. This usually occurs when the column length exceeds the buffer allocated by SSIS. By using the Advanced Editor, you can manually modify the length of a string column or the precision and scale of a numeric column. Another key property that can be modified by using the Advanced Editor is the IsSorted property. This property informs SSIS that the data coming through is sorted. We do not recommend modifying this property unless you include an ORDER BY clause in your query. After you set the property in the OLE DB Source Output level, you can modify the SortKeyPosition property for the columns enumerated in the ORDER BY clause. The first column should have the property set to 1, the second to 2, and so on. If any of the columns are defined to be sorted in descending values, the negative value of its sort position will inform

SSIS. For example, if the second column in the `ORDER BY` clause is sorted in descending order, the appropriate value of the `SortKeyPosition` property is `-2`.

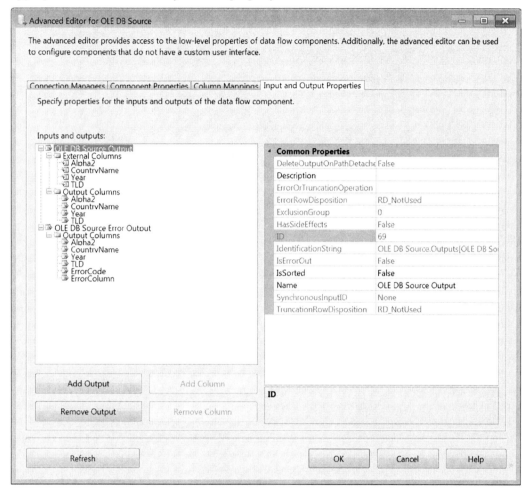

Figure 14-3. Advanced Editor for OLE DB Source—Input and Output Properties

---

■ **TIP:** For explicit data conversions, we recommend either using the `CAST()` or `CONVERT()` functions in the source query. The other option is to utilize the Data Conversion transformation.

After extracting the data from the SQL Server database, it is often the case that you will want to load the data into another SQL Server database or even the same database. SSIS provides a destination component for the SQL Server databases. For a SQL Server database, the connection manager is almost always the OLE DB Connection Manager. When loading data, the destination component for this provides the ability to create a table on the database based on the metadata of all the visible columns. The component even allows you to preview the data that already exists in the table that you are going to load the data into. Figure 14-4 shows the OLE DB Destination Editor and the options it allows.

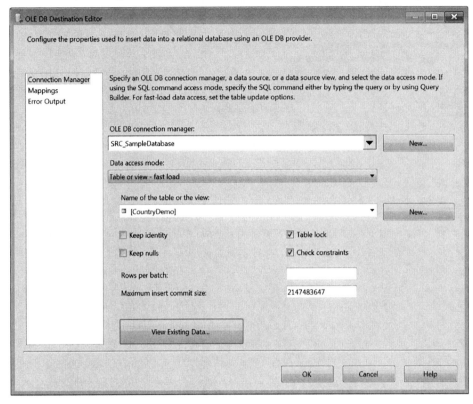

Figure 14-4. OLE DB Destination Editor

The buttons on the destination editor are there to ensure that you are using the proper destination for the dataset. The buttons perform the following functions:

New Table or View generates a create object script based on the metadata that is passed to the destination component.

View Existing Data opens a dialog box that displays 200 sample rows from the table designated as the destination.

The Fast Load option allows SSIS to bulk-load the rows as they come through the buffers. The Table or View option literally fires an INSERT statement for each individual row that reaches the destination component. The row batch size and maximum insert commit size are options that can be modified for performance gains during the data commit.

▪ **CAUTION:** If you click the New button next to the Name of the Table or the View drop-down list and then click OK on the modal window with the CREATE TABLE script, Visual Studio will attempt to create the table on the database. This relies on the user account having the proper permissions to the database.

One of the other options available with the destination component is the ability to execute SQL commands. This SQL statement will execute for every row that comes through the pipeline. It can be used for UPDATE or INSERT functionality. Depending on the data volumes, there may be other methods to optimize the loading of that data.

The Mapping page of the destination component, shown in Figure 14-5, shows you how the input columns match up with their destination column in SQL. This mapping pairs an input column, on the left, with a destination table column on the right. If there are data type or definition mismatches, you have the option of modifying the mapping to allow for different columns. This page is especially handy when dealing with Data Conversion transformations. Because the SSIS tries to automatically match based on the columns, the converted columns are usually not the ones mapped to the destination columns.

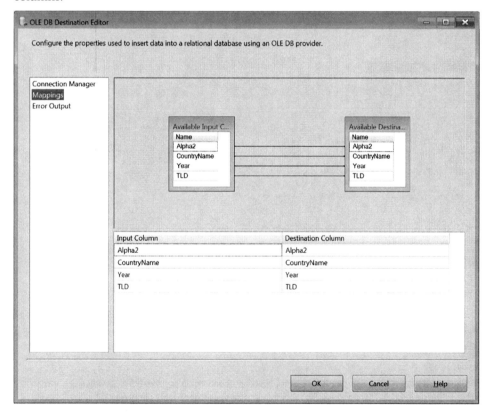

Figure 14-5. Mapping page of the OLE DB Destination Editor

In addition to the OLE DB destination, SSIS provides a SQL Server–specific bulk-load destination component, SQL Server Destination. This component bulk-loads the data into tables and views, but only if they exist on the same machine where the package is being executed. This is a huge limitation, and in the notes for the destination, Microsoft recommends using the OLE DB component instead. The editor for the component is very similar to the OLE DB destination, except it does not provide any options other than the connection manager, the table or view to load the data, and the mapping page.

Other RDBMS Sources and Destinations

For relational database management systems (RDBMSs) other than SQL Server, Microsoft provides drivers that are tuned for extracting data. For SSIS 11, the providers for these other systems have been developed by Attunity. (In prior versions, Attunity provided the drivers for Oracle connectivity.) The Source Assistant, shown in Figure 14-6, provides you with information on how to acquire providers for connectivity that do not come by default. For some of these providers, it is possible that the owner will charge you a fee for the use of their drivers.

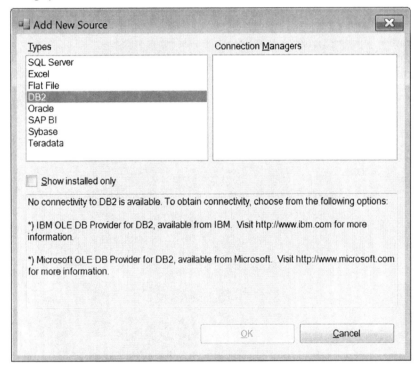

Figure 14-6. *Providers for heterogenous sources*

One of the pitfalls of using non–SQL Server connections is forgetting to ensure that the SQL variant is recognized by the provider. Some providers do not recognize the statement terminator (;), while others parse through the provided query as if it were a single line of code even though the text editor shows the new lines and formatting. In the second case, you will have to be conscious of how you comment out lines of code. You will have to use the multiline comment rather than a single-line comment.

When using different storage systems to source your data, we recommend using a Data Conversion transformation immediately after the source component. This will allow you to utilize the Union All transformation and other transformations without having to worry about data type mismatches between the datasets.

Flat File Sources and Destinations

Flat files are usually generated as an output process of a data dump. These flat files can be used as data storage, but they lack many of the advantages provided by RDBMSs. One of the appeals of keeping flat files around, however, is that security does not have to be necessarily as constricting as the database systems. They may offer quick access to the data without having an impact on the server that is hosting the data in a database system. The downsides to the flat files are that they cannot be queried, there are no means to maintain data integrity, and data quality maintenance measures do not exist. All of these advantages would have to be enforced on the database system from where the flat files are sourced, if such systems exist.

Using a flat file as a source requires the use of a Flat File Connection Manager. The connection manager is thoroughly discussed in Chapter 4. Using the properties defined in the connection manager, the source component acquires all the metadata required to extract the data. Figure 14-7 shows the options available with the Flat File Source Editor. The editor uses the configuration of the connection manager to collect the column information as well. As described in Chapter 4, the Flat File Connection Manager stores information such as the column and row delimiters, the column names, the column data type information, and some other information about the file and its data. The Preview button shows a sample of the rows that are read by using the configuration defined in the connection manager. The Retain Null Values from the Source as Null Values in the Data Flow option will preserve nulls in the pipeline. The Columns page acquires all of its information from the connection manager.

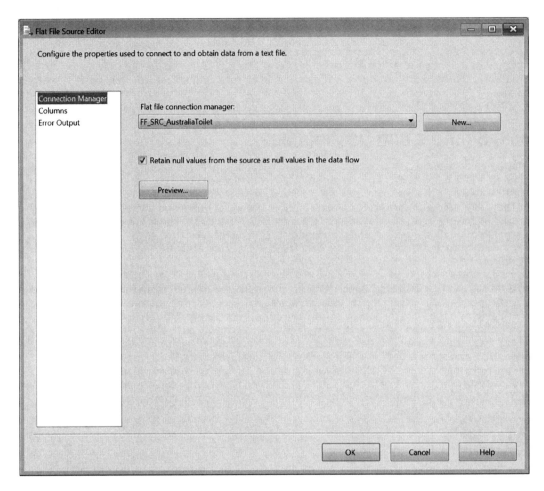

Figure 14-7. *Flat File Source Editor*

Flat file destinations, on the other hand, can operate in the opposite direction. If the flat file itself does not exist, you will have to add a new Flat File Connection Manager to configure the output file. Figure 14-8 shows the Flat File Destination Editor and how it modifies the connection manager. The New button will create a new Flat File Connection Manager. This will automatically open a dialog box, Flat File Format, which is shown in Figure 14-9. Using the option chosen in this dialog box, the connection manager is automatically configured for the most part because of the knowledge it gains from being at the end of the data flow pipeline. The Update button, however, forces you to modify the connection manager directly rather than importing the configuration through the metadata. The mappings simply map the columns in the pipeline to the columns defined in the connection manager.

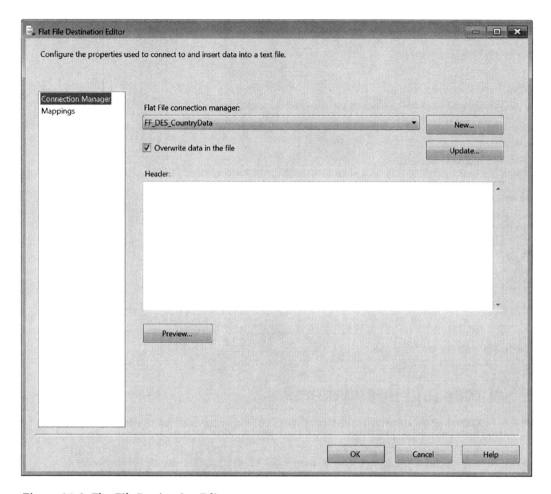

Figure 14-8. *Flat File Destination Editor*

The Flat File Format options allow you to define the layout of the flat file. Each of the options is covered in Chapter 4 for the Flat File Connection Manager section. The information for all nondelimited options is provided by the metadata stored in the pipeline.

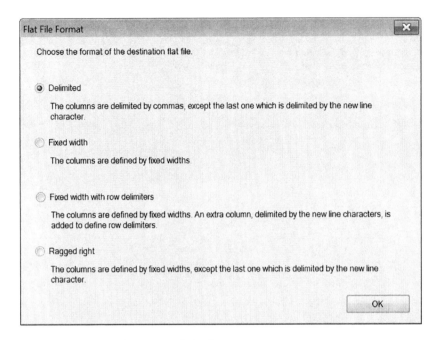

Figure 14-9. *Flat File Format dialog box*

Excel Sources and Destinations

The appeal of Microsoft Excel stems from its worksheets' similarity to database tables. Business users appreciate Excel for its ability to quickly display and modify tabular information. In the back end, Excel utilizes the Jet engine, the same engine behind Microsoft Access. This allows SSIS to execute certain SQL-like commands on the spreadsheet. The SQL interpretation of the Jet engine is nowhere as advanced as SQL Server's, but it does have some rudimentary elements that can be used for ETL processes.

■ **NOTE:** The Jet engine does not currently have a 64-bit provider. This may cause some issues as you try to manipulate spreadsheets using SSIS.

The Excel source components are similar to the flat file source components, except for the dependency on the connection manager. The connection manager for the Excel file simply defines the folder path to its location. Figure 14-10 shows the Excel source component's editor. The Connection Manager page allows you to choose the connection manager that points to the Excel file and one particular worksheet within that spreadsheet, or to provide a SQL query that will join different worksheets to return the desired data. The Jet engine does not allow the same leniency that other RDBMSs allow in terms of the data type matches on joins or null handling in data.

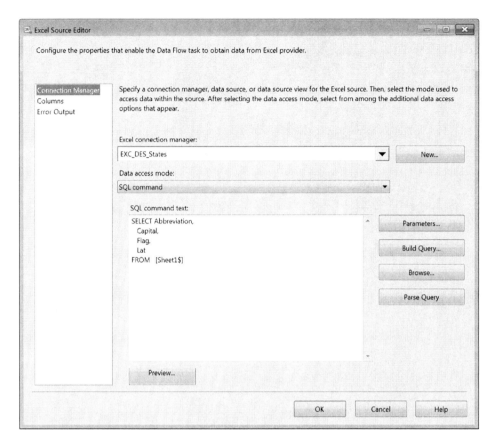

Figure 14-10. Excel Source Editor—SQL command textbox

Listing 14-2 provides the query that is used to extract the desired columns from a particular sheet. This query has the same advantages as using the SQL Command option in the OLE DB source component, in that the buffer is limited to only these four columns at the onset of the data flow. Figure 14-11 displays the Columns page, which allows you to choose the columns you wish to pass into the data flow. The difference between these two methods is that the by using the Table or View option, you are pulling all the available columns and then trimming them after SSIS has already processed the unwanted columns.

Listing 14-2. Excel Source SQL Command

```
SELECT Abbreviation,
    Capital,
    Flag,
    Lat
FROM    [Sheet1$]
```

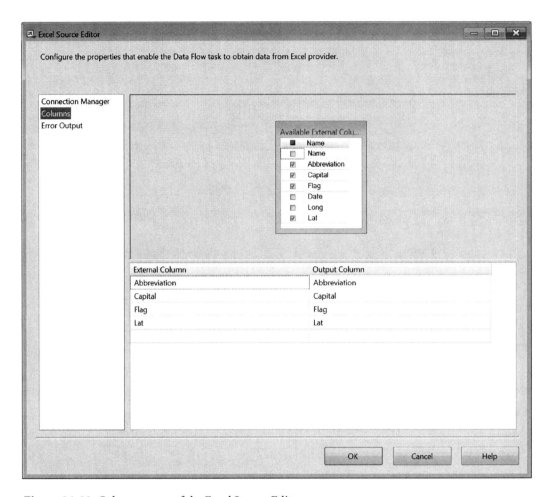

Figure 14-11. *Columns page of the Excel Source Editor*

One of the difficulties with loading data into an Excel spreadsheet is eliminating prior rows that already exist within the worksheet (table/view). SSIS loads the spreadsheets incrementally by default. In order to reload the spreadsheet, you have to use an Execute SQL task within the control flow and point it to the destination Excel Connection Manager. Figure 14-12 shows the configuration of an Execute SQL task that can achieve this end.

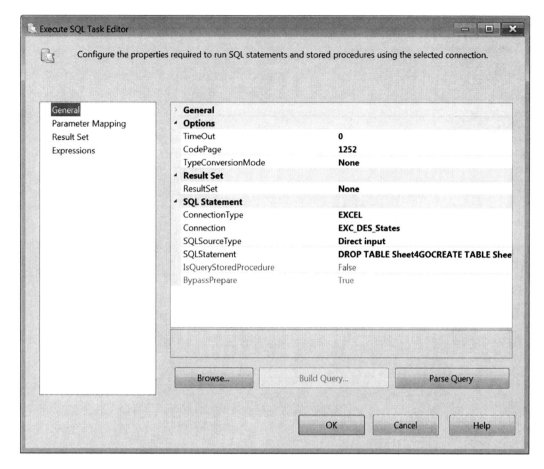

Figure 14-12. Execute SQL Task—truncate Excel worksheet

Listing 14-3 shows the actual SQL that is used to truncate an Excel worksheet. The original three spreadsheets will appear with a dollar sign ($) at the end of their names. In order to map the columns to the destination worksheet, it must exist in the file. The New button on the Excel destination component will generate the create script, just as the OLE DB destination generates a create table script. The Jet engine is extremely sensitive to keywords and will escape all the objects by placing single quotes around their names in the create script. This is similar to the OLE DB destination component escaping the objects by using square brackets around all the names.

Listing 14-3. Excel Worksheet Truncate Script

```
DROP TABLE Sheet4
GO

CREATE TABLE Sheet4(
    Abbreviation LongText,
```

```
        Capital LongText,
        Flag LongText,
        Lat Double
)
GO
```

XML Sources

A great repository for metadata is an Extensible Markup Language (XML) file. XML files can be used to describe just about anything. XML serves many purposes: SQL Server's XML functionality can output table records as XML; SSIS packages are essentially XML files that the dtexec.exe and Business Intelligence Development Studio interpret at runtime and design time, respectively; SQL Server stores extended properties of the objects in an XML, and other formats, including information not just related to ETL.

Figure 14-13 shows you the XML source editor that parses through an XML file by using an XML Schema Definition (XSD) to return the elements stored within the file. The Use inline schema will attempt to generate the XSD based on the values in the XML. However, if the XSD does not exist within the XML, the Generate XSD button will generate an XSD file for you. After the XSD is generated, it is created as its own file in the specified path. For this example, we used the upgrade log file of converting an SSIS 2008 project file to SSIS 2011 and generated an XSD for it.

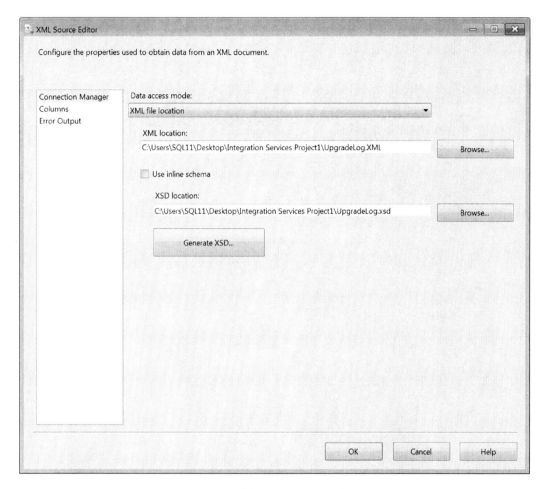

Figure 14-13. Connection Manager page of the XML Source Editor

Figure 14-14 shows the Columns page of the XML Source Editor. The interesting thing about this source component is that depending on the number of node levels of the XML, each gets its own output. The figure shows that this particular XML file has three levels: Property, Properties, and Event. The list is alphabetical and not hierarchical, so you cannot easily determine the structure just by looking at the outputs. Each output will have its column set based on the XSD.

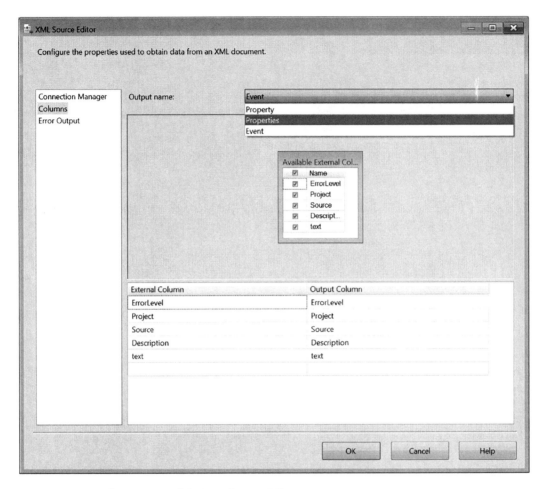

Figure 14-14. Columns page of the XML Source Editor

▓ **NOTE:** Along with an output for each of the node levels defined in the XSD, each of these outputs comes with its own error output that can be redirected as well.

Raw File Sources and Destinations

The raw file source and destinations provide an efficient method of storing data that doesn't need to keep returning to the server at every request, such as Lookup transformations using the same dataset. These files should ideally be created on the local machine that is executing the package. One of the greatest advantages that these files provide is that if a query is used to return the same dataset multiple times, the query can be executed once and the result set stored in a file. At runtime, instead of each of the Lookup transformations querying the database, the result can be acquired directly off the machine.

Figure 14-15 shows the editor of the raw file destination. This component works in a slightly different way from the other sources and destinations in that the file needs to be loaded before it can provide any metadata as a source. It also does not utilize a connection manager in order to connect to a file.

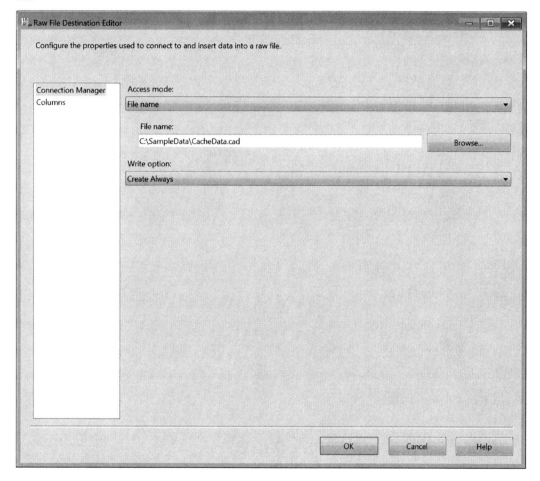

Figure 14-15. *Raw File Destination Editor*

After the data is loaded into the file, you can freely access it as a part of your process. Figure 14-16 shows the source component for the raw file. Just like the destination component, this component does not rely on a connection manager to identify the file it needs to reference. It can read the data right off the local machine and load into other destinations.

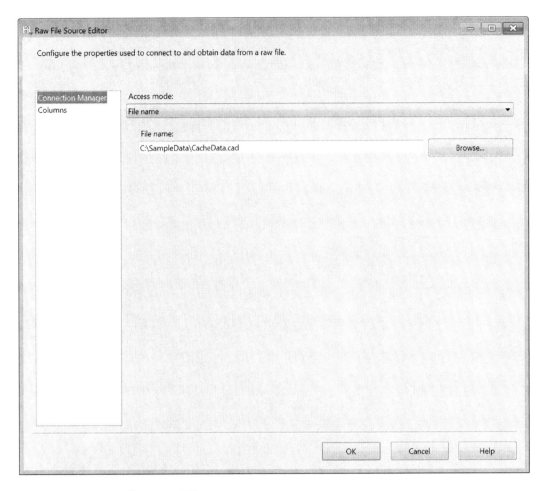

Figure 14-16. *Raw File Source Editor*

SQL Server Analysis Services Sources

Analysis Services cubes are analytical structures often used in the business intelligence field. Their greatest asset is the ability to store large numbers of aggregations so that querying might be faster. The cube itself can be queried only by using Multidimensional Expressions (MDX). The data types returned by these expressions do not always translate easily into database data types, so it is often the case that SSIS will simply cast them as character fields. There is an SSAS OLE DB provider that allows you to connect to a cube and extract certain values from the defined connection. Figure 14-17 shows the OLE DB source component that was used to query a cube.

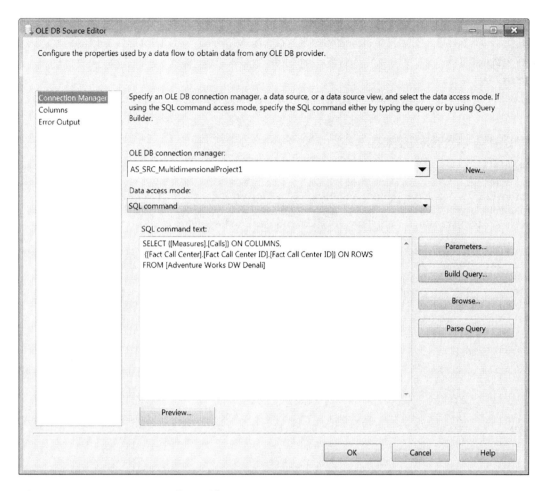

Figure 14-17. *SSAS OLE DB Editorwith MDX*

The expression in the source component, replicated as Listing 14-4, is a simple MDX query that shows the number of calls that were placed to each call center. This query does not use any filters (MDX WHERE clauses) or cross joins to slice by multiple items. This query objective is simple and can translate into a GROUP BY SQL statement with a COUNT (DISTINCT CallID) column.

Listing 14-4. *MDX Sample from an SSAS Source Component*

```
SELECT {[Measures].[Calls]} ON COLUMNS,
 {[Fact Call Center].[Fact Call Center ID].[Fact Call Center ID]} ON ROWS
FROM [Adventure Works DW Denali]
```

■ **CAUTION:** Unlike an SQL query, SSIS can get metadata from an MDX query only if it returns a dataset. If you use a filter with no data or return an empty set, SSIS will throw a metadata validation error. This can happen at design time as well as at runtime.

Recordset Destination

SSIS variables can often be used to hold data. In most cases, this data takes the form of scalar values, but in some instances an ADO.NET in-memory recordset is required. The SSIS Object type variables can be used to store tabular datasets to enumerate through the loop containers and provide additional functionality in conjunction with script components, as well as quick debugging assistants. After the recordset is stored inside the variable, the script component can be used to access the data with either C# or VB.

Figure 14-18 shows the editor of the recordset destination. The only editor for this component is the Advanced Editor. The VariableName property selects which SSIS variable will store the incoming data. The Input Columns tab is important as well because you need to identify the columns you wish to include in the variable. SSIS will not select all the columns by default. It will give you a warning until you specify the columns you require. This may sound cumbersome at first, but when used properly, it will prevent the variables from being bloated by unnecessary data.

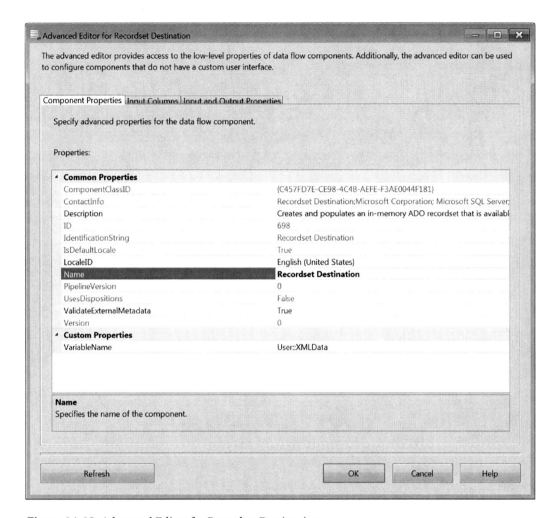

Figure 14-18. Advanced Editor for Recordset Destination

Summary

SQL Server Integration Services 11 offers the capabilities to access data that is stored in many forms. Using the different providers, you can extract your data from a wide range of RDBMSs or flat files. The providers also allow you to insert the data in just about any storage form. This chapter introduced you to the methods of storage that SSIS can extract from and load. The next chapter dives into optimizing and tuning your data flows.

Data Flow Tuning and Optimization

I feel the need, the need for speed.

—Actor Tom Cruise in *Top Gun*

Ask any given group of IT managers to name the most important aspects of an ETL process, and nine out of ten will put *raw speed* at the top of the list. Although raw throughput is important in any ETL process, the "need for speed" must be balanced against other requirements such as resource contention with other processes; correct and consistent results; and solution maintainability, manageability, and robustness.

When people hear about tuning the data flow, they often think of increasing raw speed. Processing speed is important, but the speed-only point of view is very one-dimensional. Poor ETL speed is usually the symptom and not the illness. The root cause of the slow ETL often lies in the design and implementation. In this chapter, you'll focus on optimizing your data flows to eliminate problems for which both slow speed and excessive resource usage are symptoms.

Limiting Rows at the Database

When you pull data into an SSIS data flow, especially from a SQL Server database (or other relational DBMS), you can increase your ETL processing speed by simply limiting the number of rows retrieved. On a SQL Server database or other RDBMS, this is done by adding a WHERE clause to your SELECT queries. As an example, consider a simple database table that holds daily transaction records for a large chain of department stores. The table has the design shown in Figure 15-1.

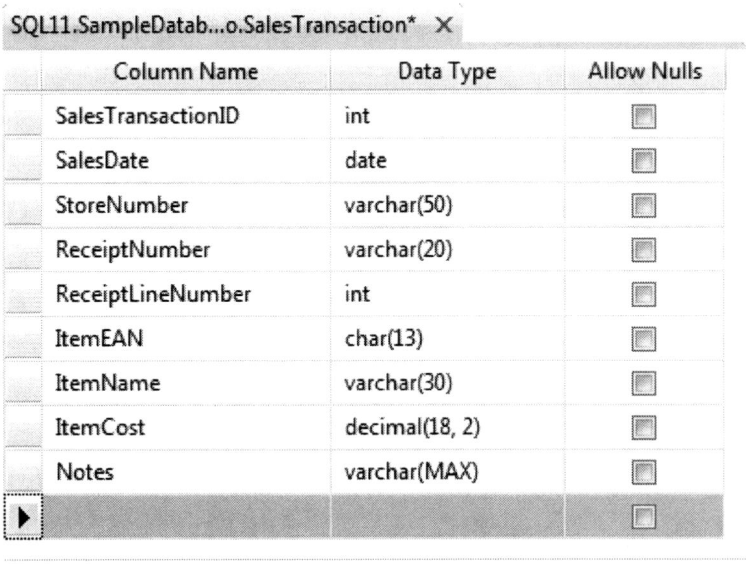

SQL11.SampleDatab...o.SalesTransaction* ✕		
Column Name	Data Type	Allow Nulls
SalesTransactionID	int	☐
SalesDate	date	☐
StoreNumber	varchar(50)	☐
ReceiptNumber	varchar(20)	☐
ReceiptLineNumber	int	☐
ItemEAN	char(13)	☐
ItemName	varchar(30)	☐
ItemCost	decimal(18, 2)	☐
Notes	varchar(MAX)	☐
▶		☐

Figure 15-1. Sales Transaction table design

Let's say this table contains 10 million rows of sales transaction data, with about 25,000 rows added to it daily. Let's consider a simple ETL process that needs to retrieve the current day's data from the table and export it to a flat file to be picked up by other processes—a common requirement when you need to feed legacy downstream systems. You have two options for identifying today's records: (1) you can limit the data in SSIS by using the Conditional Split transformation or (2) limit the data on the server. To limit the inbound data with the Conditional Split, you'll create a data flow like the one shown in Figure 15-2.

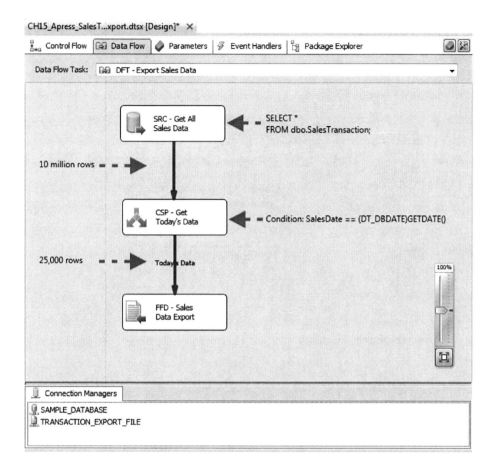

Figure 15-2. Limiting inbound data with the Conditional Split transformation

We've added annotations to highlight how this data flow works. Notice that all 10 million rows of data from our source table are pulled into the data flow by the source component. Ninety-nine percent of the rows being pulled in are unceremoniously discarded by the Conditional Split transformation to get at the 25,000 rows we actually want to export.

The alternative is to limit the rows on the server by adding the WHERE clause to your SELECT query, as shown in Figure 15-3.

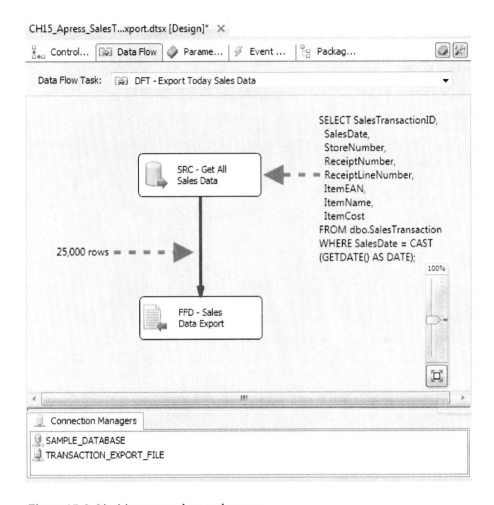

Figure 15-3. Limiting source data at the server

By limiting the data at the server in this example, you can eliminate millions of rows without pulling it all into SSIS first. If you have an index on the SalesDate column of the table, your query will be able to retrieve the data even more efficiently. The advantages of limiting the data on the server are twofold:

- You limit the number of rows being pulled into SSIS—of particular importance when you are pulling data across the network.

- You can retrieve data using fewer SSIS resources. In return, you are using more SQL Server resources, but by limiting the result set at the source, you can take advantage of many of SQL Server's set-based optimizations— particularly if you are using columns with indexes or partitions to limit the data you retrieve.

■ **TIP:** Apart from the SQL queries in the source component, SSIS data flow components cannot take advantage of SQL Server indexes.

Performing Joins in the Database

Performing joins on the server is an optimization that is closely related to the previous optimization of limiting the number of rows pulled into your data flow. Joins can help you efficiently limit the number of rows at the server. Picture the following scenario: you have 10,000 rows of data to pull into your data flow, and you have a million rows of lookup reference data. This type of imbalance is common in data warehousing applications, for instance, where a given dimension table is extremely large. You already know you won't need more than 10,000 rows of lookup reference data (at most). If it can be avoided, there's no point in pulling an extra 990,000 rows into your data flow only to discard them, as shown in Figure 15-4. This can easily be remedied by including selectivity at the data source to filter the rows that would later be discarded only after passing through the required memory buffers.

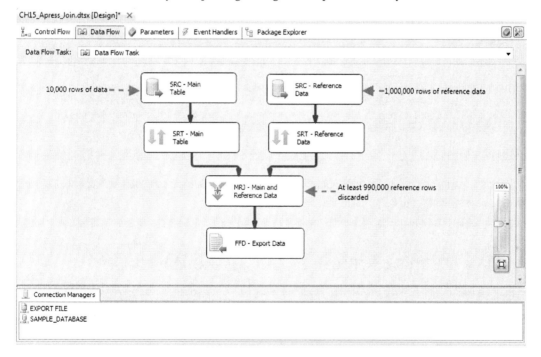

Figure 15-4. Pulling large amounts of data in Merge task

When there is a large imbalance in the size of the two data sets to be joined, it can often be done more efficiently on the server by using T-SQL join syntax. In addition to eliminating the extra network traffic that can be generated by pulling excessive data into your data flow, the SQL Server optimizer had multiple strategies it can use to fulfill a join request. SSIS can use only a *merge join*, which is basically a row-by-row scan of both data sets. The merge join works only with an equality-based join condition, and both sets of input must be presorted on the join columns. When you join on SQL Server, the query engine automatically sorts the source data as necessary, and the server will use indexes if they are defined on the join columns. SQL Server can also perform inequality joins (less than, greater than, and so forth) and supports the CROSS JOIN syntax.

■ **NOTE:** Using a Lookup transformation component eliminates the need to perform a Sort operation on the lookup reference data, but incurs the same requirement to read all the source data. The Lookup transformation provides an alternative via its partial cache and noncached modes, but these modes can cost excessive round-trips to the server and might still not be as efficient as a server-side join. Also, like the Merge Join transformation, the Lookup transformation can't use SQL indexes and table distribution statistics defined on your source tables.

Sorting in the Database

As we showed in the previous section, some of the data flow components—such as the Merge Join transformation—require sorted input. The Sort transformation in SSIS is a fully blocking component, meaning no rows can pass it until it has completed processing its entire input data set. SSIS has a single method of sorting data, whereas SQL Server has multiple strategies for fulfilling sort requests—the database can take advantage of indexes, for instance. Sorting at the database simply requires the addition of the ORDER BY clause to your SELECT query. When combined with joins and WHERE clause restrictions, sorting input at the database can significantly increase performance.

■ **TIP:** If your data is coming from a different source, such as a flat file, and if you can guarantee that the flat file is presorted, you can eliminate the Sort transformation from your data flow.

Performing Complex Preprocessing at the Database

In some cases, you may have to do multistep preprocessing on source data, before it is ready for your main ETL processing. As an example, you might need to do some server-based calculations, joins, or other steps on your data that might be done more efficiently in a set-based fashion. This is especially true of processing that requires you to serialize intermediate result sets during preprocessing (for example, pushing data into temp tables), grouping with the SQL GROUP BY clause, and partitioning data (with the SQL OVER clause). Because SQL Server can apply a number of different strategies to set-based processing problems while SSIS has essentially a single, simple row-by-row strategy for solving them, performing set-based processing tasks at the database is often more efficient.

Ensuring Security and "Read Auditing"

In some very highly secure operations, it may be a requirement to audit "read" operations against sensitive data. In these cases, it might make sense to require users and ETL processes to call stored procedures to read from critical tables. By using stored procedures as a source, you can deny direct access to tables and incorporate logic into the procedures to record all read requests being sent by users and processes.

Pulling Too Many Columns

In many cases, SSIS developers choose to do a good old-fashioned `SELECT *` query or choose the Data Access mode Table or View option on the OLE DB Source Editor. In fact, in the sample data flow in Figure 15-2, we used the query `SELECT * FROM dbo.SalesTransaction;` in the OLE DB source component. You may also have noticed that the definition for the `SalesTransaction` table contains a `varchar(max)` column named `Notes` (shown in Figure 15-1). The `varchar(max)` column can hold up to 2.1 GB of data. This column is not part of the final output to the text file, and in fact does not need to be read into the data flow at all. Using `SELECT *` or the Table or View data access mode, however, forces SSIS to read it into the data flow even though it's going to be discarded later—a potentially costly waste of resources.

▪ **TIP:** Large object (LOB) data such as `varchar(max)`, `nvarchar(max)`, and `varbinary(max)` requires special "under-the-hood" processing by SSIS to pull it into the data flow and process it. Extra overhead is associated with processing even relatively small LOB data values.

The proper method of querying source data was shown previously in Figure 15-3. In the modified sample, we've specified the column list in the source query, as shown here:

```
SELECT SalesTransactionID,
  SalesDate,
  StoreNumber,
  ReceiptNumber,
  ReceiptLineNumber,
  ItemEAN,
  ItemName,
  ItemCost
FROM dbo.SalesTransaction
WHERE SalesDate = CAST(GETDATE() AS DATE);
```

By specifying the column list, we limit the input columns to only those we actually need in the data flow.

Using Execution Trees

Whenever you execute an SSIS package, it generates an *execution tree* behind the scenes. The execution tree is used to optimize performance and to build an execution plan for your package. Consider the sample package shown in Figure 15-5. Each path shown is a branch of the execution tree.

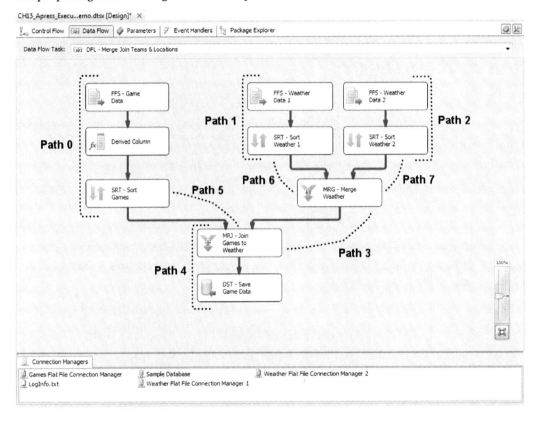

Figure 15-5. SSIS execution tree

To capture the execution tree, log the PipelineExecutionTrees event of the Data Flow task in the Logging Configuration window. You can view the execution trees in the Log Events window of BIDS when you execute the package. The execution tree shown in the preceding image is enumerated in the SSIS Log Events window as follows:

Path 0

```
Begin Path 0
    FFS - Game Data.Outputs[Flat File Source Output]; FFS - Game Data
    Derived Column.Inputs[Derived Column Input]; Derived Column
    Derived Column.Outputs[Derived Column Output]; Derived Column
```

```
    SRT - Sort Games.Inputs[Sort Input]; SRT - Sort Games

End Path 0
```

Path 0 reads in data from a flat file, adds a derived column, and pushes the result to the input of a Sort transformation. The same buffer is used to move data from the flat file source component through the Derived Column transformation and into the Sort transformation input.

Path 1

```
Begin Path 1

    FFS - Weather Data 1.Outputs[Flat File Source Output]; FFS - Weather
Data 1

    SRT - Sort Weather 1.Inputs[Sort Input]; SRT - Sort Weather 1

End Path 1
```

Path 1 reads in data from another flat file and pushes it to the input of a Sort transformation.

Path 2

```
Begin Path 2

    FFS - Weather Data 2.Outputs[Flat File Source Output]; FFS - Weather
Data 2

    SRT - Sort Weather 2.Inputs[Sort Input]; SRT - Sort Weather 2

End Path 2
```

Path 2 reads in data from a third flat file and pushes the data to another Sort transformation input.

Path 3

```
Begin Path 3

    MRG - Merge Weather.Outputs[Merge Output 1]; MRG - Merge Weather

    MRJ - Join Games to Weather.Inputs[Merge Join Right Input]; MRJ -
Join Games to Weather

End Path 3
```

Path 3 moves data from the output of the Merge transformation and into the Merge Join transformation.

Path 4

```
Begin Path 4

    MRJ - Join Games to Weather.Outputs[Merge Join Output]; MRJ - Join
Games to Weather

    DST - Save Game Data.Inputs[OLE DB Destination Input]; DST - Save
Game Data
```

```
End Path 4
```

Path 4 moves the data from the Merge Join transformation output to the OLE
DB destination component input.

Path 5

```
Begin Path 5
    SRT - Sort Games.Outputs[Sort Output]; SRT - Sort Games
    MRJ - Join Games to Weather.Inputs[Merge Join Left Input]; MRJ - Join
Games to Weather
End Path 5
```

Path 5 moves data from a Sort transformation output to the Merge Join
transformation input.

Path 6

```
Begin Path 6
    SRT - Sort Weather 1.Outputs[Sort Output]; SRT - Sort Weather 1
    MRG - Merge Weather.Inputs[Merge Input 1]; MRG - Merge Weather
End Path 6
```

Path 6 moves data from a Sort transformation output to the Merge
transformation input.

Path 7

```
Begin Path 7
    SRT - Sort Weather 2.Outputs[Sort Output]; SRT - Sort Weather 2
    MRG - Merge Weather.Inputs[Merge Input 2]; MRG - Merge Weather
End Path 7
```

Path 7 moves data from another Sort transformation output to the Merge
transformation input.

Upon reviewing the data flow execution tree, one thing that becomes readily apparent is that SSIS
generates new paths whenever it determines that new buffers are needed. This occurs essentially
whenever an asynchronous transformation is encountered. If SSIS can use the same buffer for input and
output around a component (synchronous transformations), it adds it to the existing path. If the
component uses different input and output buffers (asynchronous transformations), it finishes off the
existing path at the input and creates a new path beginning at the output. This is important in terms of
performance because asynchronous transformations must allocate new buffers and populate them,
requiring more resources and causing a performance hit. Eliminating extraneous asynchronous
transformations and the performance hit they incur can be a big performance boost. As an example, if
you can guarantee that the source data is properly sorted, you can easily eliminate the Sort
transformations to optimize our sample package.

■ **NOTE:** There are some components that seem to generate multiple copies of buffers, but in reality they don't. The Multicast, Conditional Split, and the new SQLCAT Balanced Data Distributor transformations all use "buffer magic" to seemingly move data between buffers and generate copies of data. In reality, they essentially move pointers rather than copying rows in the buffers—a much more efficient operation.

HIGHLIGHTING THE EXECUTION TREE IN BIDS

You can highlight an entire path of an execution tree by right-clicking a data flow path arrow in the BIDS designer and selecting the Resolve References option from the context menu. This pulls up the new column-mapping dialog box. If you move this dialog box out of the way, you will see that the path is highlighted, as shown in Figure 15-6. This is a handy method of checking the data flow paths visually while you're editing your package in BIDS.

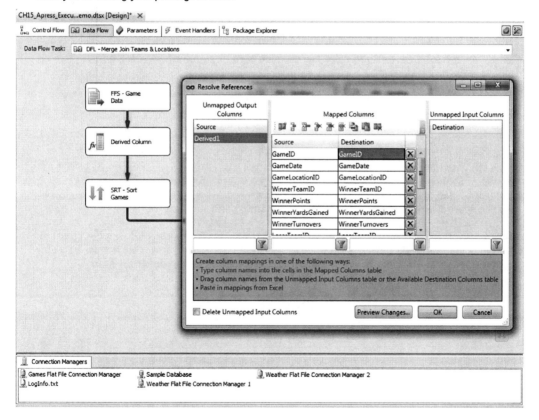

Figure 15-6. Highlighting an execution tree path in the BIDS editor

Implementing Parallelism

On multiprocessor servers, one of the biggest performance benefits you can implement is parallelism. Within a package, you can implement multiple data flows that execute in parallel, or even multiple data flow paths within the same Data Flow task. To get the most out of parallel execution, you have to plan around the resource limitations of your server.

The MaxConcurrentExecutables package setting specifies the maximum number of threads SSIS will execute in parallel in the package. The default is −1, which lets SSIS set the value dynamically to the number of logical processors plus 2. If the server you're running SSIS on has other processes running on it (SQL Server, for instance), you may want to set this property to a lower value to avoid CPU resource conflicts.

Memory is another constraint to deal with when parallelizing packages, especially when there are other processes running on the same server. SSIS automatically uses metadata to tune buffer sizes before execution begins, but during execution it is possible to run out of memory. This is particularly true if you are running multiple Data Flow tasks in parallel, pushing large amounts of data through asynchronous or blocking transformations. As an example, it's not uncommon to occasionally see packages with parallel data flows containing Lookup transformations fail because of a lack of memory when there is a large amount of reference data being cached.

■ **TIP:** Although you can influence buffer sizes by adjusting the DefaultBufferMaxRows and DefaultBufferSize settings, changing them doesn't provide much bang for the buck. SSIS automatically tunes your buffer sizes for you, and it does a good job. The other suggestions in this chapter provide much more benefit for the effort required.

Database table contention is an important consideration in your parallelization plans as well. If you want to parallelize a destination operation, for instance, consider the contention that can result against the target table and plan accordingly. We have resolved many package performance issues and outright failures over the years due to multiple Data Flow tasks trying to output to the same target table in parallel.

Finally, it's important to decide which operations to parallelize. If you are loading a data mart, for instance, you may load multiple dimension tables in parallel. If one dimension table has an extremely large number of rows, you may decide to parallelize the destinations of that data flow path.

KNOW WHEN TO SAY WHEN

When you optimize your SSIS packages, it's important to decide up front how good is good enough. At what point do you say your package is efficient enough? As in any software optimization, the Law of Diminishing Returns applies in SSIS optimization: the difficulty and complexity involved increases as you try to squeeze smaller and smaller kernels of *performance* out of your code. Notice we didn't say *speed*, but rather *performance*. Raw speed is only a single factor in overall performance, which is a much more accurate measure of efficiency that includes both speed and resource usage.

At some point, the effort involved in trying to squeeze a final 100 milliseconds out of your code is not worth the effort. Also keep the 80/20 rule in mind: focus on optimizing the 20 percent of your code that consumes 80 percent of your processing time.

Summary

This chapter has introduced several tools and methods for optimizing your SSIS packages. Many of these optimizations rely on performing operations at the source when possible and limiting the data pulled through the ETL process. This chapter also covered SSIS execution trees and some of the keys to optimizing performance through parallelism. In the next chapter, you'll consider the powerful SSIS parent-child design pattern.

Parent-Child Design Pattern

Having one child makes you a parent; having two, you are a referee.

—British journalist David Frost

With SSIS, there are several ways to introduce modular programming into your ETL processes. One of the most flexible methods is by using the parent-child design. This pattern enables you to create packages to perform very specific tasks. If these tasks should be disabled, this design pattern allows you to utilize parameter bindings to disable functionality at the package level. As the quote suggests, the more complex your ETL process becomes, the more of an organizational role the parent package plays, rather than just the role of a package that calls another.

ETL processes can become increasingly transparent when a clear design is utilized. This chapter covers some of the benefits of utilizing the parent-child design pattern and shows you how to implement it in your own processes. You will also see the different ways to implement the design pattern, allowing you to pick the one that best suits your needs.

Understanding the Parent-Child Design Pattern

The *parent-child design pattern* in a nutshell refers to any ETL process that utilizes an SSIS package to execute another package. This can be done by using the Execute Package task or even the Execute Process task by calling the dtexec.exe utility. Our recommendation is to stick with the Execute Package task because it will allow you to configure the execution of the child package much easier than the Execute Process task. Figure 16-1 shows you what a static parent package would look like. We call this a *static package* because any changes in the ETL structure or the addition and removal of packages would require a modification to this package.

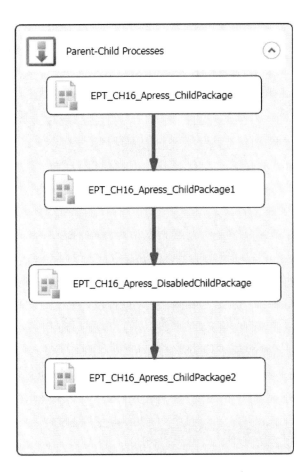

Figure 16-1. Example of a static parent package

The static package is developed with each of the tasks having their own individual settings. This implementation of the parent-child design pattern is recommended only if the execution process will not change. Maintaining and updating this implementation can be become extremely challenging very quickly. The third executable, EPT_CH16_Apress_DisabledChildPackage, has different configurations than the other three executables. In order to disable the package during execution, we pass a Boolean variable from the parent package, CH16_Apress_StaticParentPackage.dtsx, to a parameter bound to the child's Disable package property. We cover the parameter passing later in this chapter. The static implementation of the parent-child design pattern is very similar to the steps in a SQL agent job.

All the packages contain one Script task that displays a simple message to show that the package was executed. Listing 16-1 shows the C# that is contained with the nondisabled child packages. It shows a simple message that informs you of the name of the child package that was executed. As you can infer from the variable that is utilized, we listed System::PackageName as the only variable available to the ReadOnlyVariables property of the Script task.

Listing 16-1. *Child Package Script Task*

```
MessageBox.Show("The current package's name is: " +
    Dts.Variables["System::PackageName"].Value.ToString()+"\n");
```

The script for the disabled child package is slightly different, in order to alert you that this package should not be executed. This example is included to demonstrate the ease of configuring your ETL process by using a dynamic parent-child design pattern. Listing 16-2 provides the script present in the disabled child package. There is short message contained within this message box, alerting you that you should not be seeing this message.

Listing 16-2. *Disabled Child Package Script Task*

```
MessageBox.Show("The current package's name is: " +
        Dts.Variables["System::PackageName"].Value.ToString()+"\n"+
        "This package is supposed to be disabled. If you are seeing this message,
        the parameters were not assigned the proper values.");
```

The modularity behind the parent-child design packages can be described in the following terms:

> The **parent package** controls the entire ETL process. Its main duty is to execute all the necessary packages.

> **Wrapper packages** control a smaller subset of packages whose focus should be handling one particular process. Wrapper packages are either called directly by the parent package or by other wrapper packages. For example, a wrapper package can be used to execute packages that are responsible for preprocessing the sources or performing post-load processing.

> **Child packages** control the processing of the actual tasks. These packages are the workhorses of the parent-child design pattern. They are called by wrapper packages.

In the example, we combined the concept of the parent and wrapper package for simplicity. The idea behind the wrapper package is to segregate the different processes that make up your ETL requirements.

Using Parameters to Pass Values

Parameters are absolutely essential for the parent-child design pattern. In prior versions of SSIS, values were passed along by using configurations. With this version's deployment model, we encourage you to use parameters for passing values between parent and child packages. Figure 16-2 demonstrates the parameter binding we use to disable the child package. We bind a parameter that we defined in the package, DisablePackage, to the Disable package property. We can even bind parameters to task properties within the child package.

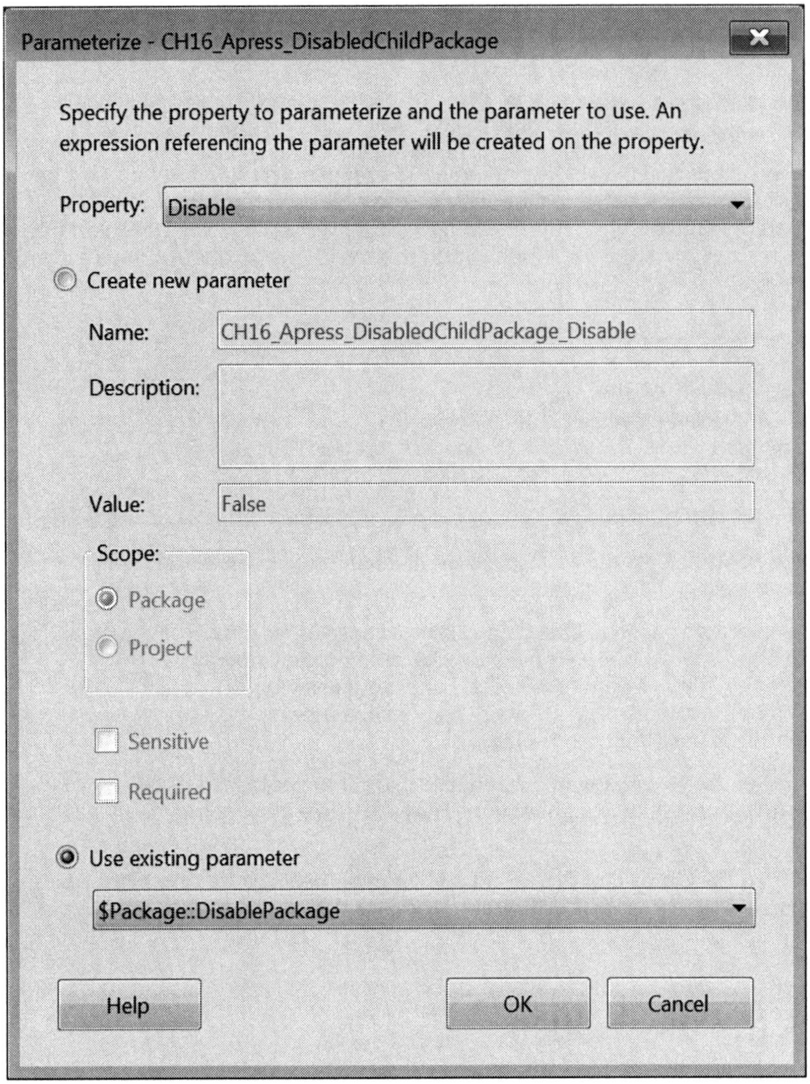

Figure 16-2. *Parameter bindings of the disabled child package*

After we parameterize the child package, any Execute Package task that is configured to execute this package will be able to identify the parameters that are defined within it. The data type of the parameter must match the property's data type. Figure 16-3 demonstrates the mapping of the parameter when using the Execute Package task.

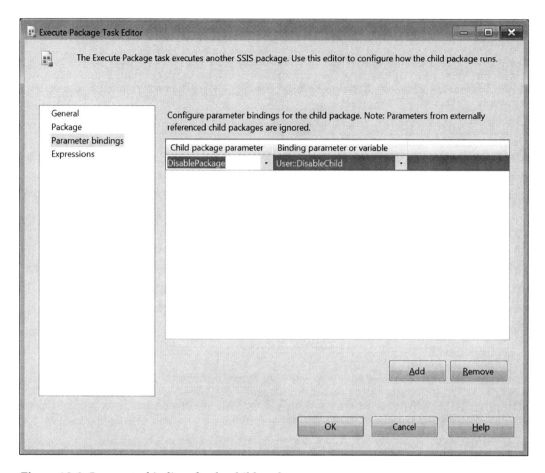

Figure 16-3. Parameter bindings for the child package

The User::DisableChild variable is a Boolean variable. It must match the data type of the parameter of the child package. Multiple bindings can be added to the package execution. We provided True as the default value of the User::DisableChild variable. This mapping is present only in packages that are not supposed to be executed.

▪ **NOTE:** Even if the package property Disable is set to True, during execution in Debug mode, Visual Studio will open the package and validate it. The package itself will not execute, but it will be opened.

Working with Shared Configuration Information

Connection managers will abound in a design pattern such as the parent-child. In order to keep the clutter to a minimum, you can utilize the project connection managers so that keeping the connection strings in sync becomes much easier. Creating a project connection manager will create the connection manager in every package within the project.

■ **CAUTION:** Deleting any project connection manager within a package will delete it from the project and all the packages within the project. If you find that you have deleted a project connection manager and cannot undo the action, you have an option to retrieve it. You first need to create the same connection manager type with the same name. After the project connection manager is created, you have to right-click it and select View Code. This opens an XML script that shows all the properties of the connection manager. The property you need to focus on is DTS:DTSID. When you open any package with a task or source component that referred to the deleted project connection manager, you will notice that the name is replaced by a GUID. You can copy that GUID and replace the DTS:DTSID of the new project connection manager with the GUID. After this, save the Code page of the project manager and close it. Reopen any of the open packages, and their contents should be able to recognize their connection manager as the newly re-created project connection manager.

Certain information can be stored within project parameters. Because parameter values can be changed only by T-SQL, parameter values are more or less read-only. Catalog views and stored procedures within the SSISDB can be used to view the values. The following objects in the SSISDB database allow you to access parameter values during execution:

catalog.execution_parameter_values is a view that displays the values that will be used during specific executions.

catalog.get_parameter_values is a stored procedure that displays and resolves parameter values of specified packages within projects stored in the Integration Services catalog.

catalog.object_parameters is a view that shows the design and server defaults for the parameters.

Overriding Properties

With the new deployment model, overriding properties by using parameters instead of configurations streamlines development. Instead of creating configurations by using variables to inherit values and then using the variable values to overwrite properties, you can now simply bind package parameters to those properties. The configurations were required by the child package in anticipation of being passed in by the parent. This often led to the issue of executing child packages on their own for testing purposes or even as a one-off in the ETL process.

Even the individual tasks and containers within a package can have their properties bound to parameters. This allows parent packages even further control of the execution of the child packages. The parent can pass information directly to the tasks, overriding the design-time property configuration. The process is the same as binding parameters to package properties. You have to right-click the object you want to parameterize and select the Parameterize option.

Logging

Logging the execution process with the parent-child design pattern can be a little tricky. The out-of-the-box package logging that is available will simply treat each message separately. The parent package messages and execution events will surround the messages and events from the child package, but there is no real way to tie their executions together other than by looking at their timing and knowing the ETL process. We discuss logging in great detail in Chapter 13.

Implementing Data-Driven ETL

One of the most flexible implementations of the parent-child design pattern is data-driven ETL. The easiest way to implement this is to store the data in a table so that it can be queried. Storing the data in a table allows you to quickly add or remove packages from your process. It also allows you to disable certain packages' execution if you do not want to permanently remove them from the process. Listing 16-3 shows the structure of a table that can be used to drive your ETL processes.

Listing 16-3. *Table CH16_Apress_PackageExecution*

```
CREATE TABLE dbo.CH16_Apress_PackageExecution
(
        Package NVARCHAR(250) NOT NULL,
        PackagePath NVARCHAR(200) NOT NULL,
        ParentPackage NVARCHAR(250) NULL,
        ExecuteOrder INT NOT NULL,
        DisablePackage BIT NOT NULL,
);
GO

CREATE CLUSTERED INDEX CIX_CH16_Apress_PackageExecution ON dbo.CH16_Apress_PackageExecution
(ParentPackage);
GO
```

This table is designed to show a hierarchical view of the ETL process. You can see the parent-child relationships and even write queries that will give you detailed information about your processes. A primary key can be defined on this table if, for instance, you do not need to execute a package multiple times. The following provides a brief explanation of what each column represents:

> Package provides the name of the child package of the current package. The wrapper package will be listed as ParentPackage, and all of the worker packages will be listed in this column. The root-level parent package will list the wrapper packages as its child packages.

> PackagePath provides the folder path of the child packages.

ParentPackage provides the name of the package that is currently being executed.

ExecuteOrder provides the order in which the packages will be executed. As tempting as it may be to keep the order neat and sequential, we recommend keeping large gaps so that you can add packages to the execution list without the headache of updating several rows.

DisablePackage determines whether the package property, Disable, will be set to True or False.

We will re-create the example we showed earlier with this dynamic approach. In order to populate the table with the proper execution information, we run the script shown in Listing 16-4. The insert statements populate the table we just created with the same type of information that was hard-coded into CH16_Apress_StaticParentPackage.

Listing 16-4. Populate dbo.CH16_Apress_PackageExecution

```
INSERT INTO dbo.CH16_Apress_PackageExecution
            (
                    Package
                    ,PackagePath
                    ,ParentPackage
                    ,ExecuteOrder
                    ,DisablePackage
            )
            VALUES
            (
                    'CH16_Apress_DynamicParentPackage'
                    ,'C:\Users\SQL11\Desktop\Integration Services Project1\
                                    Integration Services Project1'
                    ,NULL
                    ,0
                    ,0
            ),
            (
                    'CH16_Apress_ChildPackage'
                    ,'C:\Users\SQL11\Desktop\Integration Services Project1\Integration Services
Project1'
                    ,'CH16_Apress_DynamicParentPackage'
                    ,10
                    ,0
            ),
            (
                    'CH16_Apress_ChildPackage1'
                    ,'C:\Users\SQL11\Desktop\Integration Services Project1\Integration Services
Project1'
                    ,'CH16_Apress_DynamicParentPackage'
                    ,20
                    ,0
            ),
            (
```

```
                    'CH16_Apress_DisabledChildPackage'
                    ,'C:\Users\SQL11\Desktop\Integration Services Project1\Integration Services
Project1'
                    ,'CH16_Apress_DynamicParentPackage'
                    ,30
                    ,1
        ),
        (
                    'CH16_Apress_ChildPackage2'
                    ,'C:\Users\SQL11\Desktop\Integration Services Project1\Integration Services
Project1'
                    ,'CH16_Apress_DynamicParentPackage'
                    ,40
                    ,0
        );
GO
```

■ **NOTE:** The file system path is not so important if the packages are stored on the server. In that case, the process will rely on the project reference to locate the package. If your deployment strategy is to store the packages on the file system, you will have modify this example to include a Script task that will modify the connection string of the Connection Manager used to locate the child package.

As you can see, this is the same order of execution as we had in CH16_Apress_StaticParentPackage. We kept a gap of 10 between all the values of ExecuteOrder. With the data in place, we can take a look at how the dynamic package works. Figure 16-4 shows the variables we will use to control the execution process of the packages.

Name	Scope	Data type	Value	Namespace
CurrentPackage	CH16_Apress_DynamicParentPackage	String	CH16_Apress_DynamicParentPackage	Control
DisablePackage	CH16_Apress_DynamicParentPackage	Boolean	False	Control
ExecuteOrder	CH16_Apress_DynamicParentPackage	Int32	0	Control
Package	CH16_Apress_DynamicParentPackage	String	CH16_Apress_ChildPackage	Control
PackagePath	CH16_Apress_DynamicParentPackage	String		Control
Packages	CH16_Apress_DynamicParentPackage	Object	System.Object	Control

Figure 16-4. CH16_DynamicParentPackage variables

As you can see, we provided a default value for the Package variable. This is so that when we create the expression for the Execute Package task, it can validate. We basically have to provide the name of the first package that will execute. We also have a variable that contains the name of the current package as its name. This is to assist us with querying the table so that we get only the immediate child packages of the current package. Figure 16-5 shows the control flow of the dynamic version of the example.

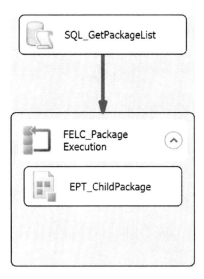

Figure 16-5. *CH16_Apress_DynamicParentPackage*

The Execute SQL task, `SQL_GetPackageList`, is used to retrieve the data from
`dbo.CH16_Apress_PackageExecution`. It contains a parameterized query that is shown in Listing 16-5. The
Foreach Loop container, `FELC_PackageExecution`, loops through the data set that is returned by the
Execute SQL task. The Execute Package task simply executes as the loop iterates through the table.

Listing 16-5. *SQL_GetPackageList query*

```
SELECT pe.Package,
       pe.PackagePath+'\'+pe.Package+'.dtsx',
       pe.ExecuteOrder,
       pe.DisablePackage
FROM dbo.CH16_Apress_PackageExecution pe
WHERE pe.ParentPackage = ?
ORDER BY pe.ExecuteOrder;
```

The `ORDER BY` clause is absolutely crucial for this process. It will ensure that the packages are
executed in the proper order. Without it, there is no guarantee that they will. Figure 16-6 shows the
parameter mapping configuration of the Execute SQL task. Note that the data type and parameter name
need to match the query supplied.

■ **NOTE:** An additional `WHERE` clause could be `pe.DisablePackage <> 1`. We did not add this in order to
demonstrate that the parameter bindings are preserved with this implementation of the parent-child design
pattern. With that clause, you would not have to worry about packages being opened and validated by Visual
Studio. They would simply be skipped over.

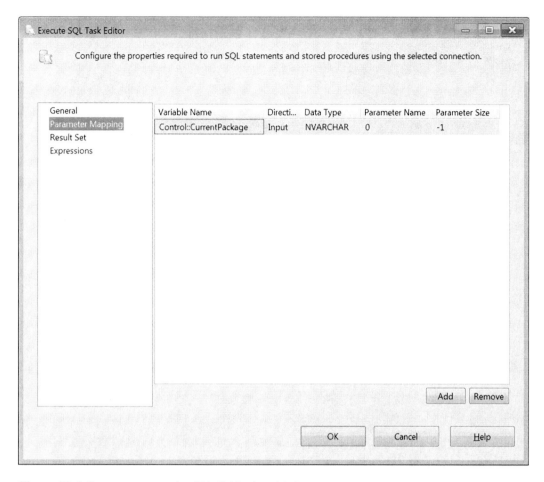

Figure 16-6. Parameter mapping SQL_GetPackageList

Figure 16-7 demonstrates the Result Set page of the SQL_GetPackageList task. The result set is stored within the Object variable that was shown earlier. With this result set, we can now supply the Foreach Loop container with the enumerator it requires.

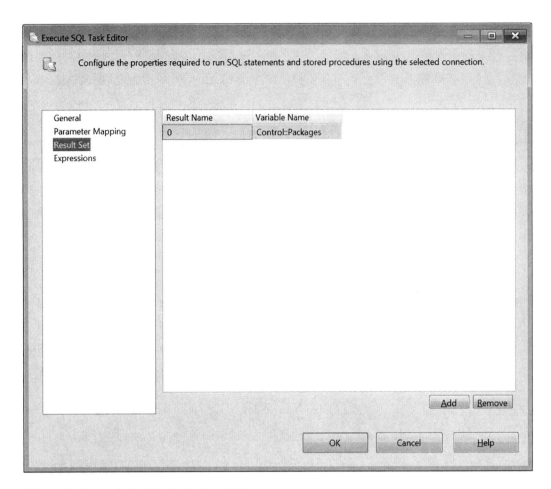

Figure 16-7. Result Set SQL_GetPackageList

Figure 16-8 shows the Collection page of FELC_PackageExecution. The Control::Packages variable is used as the ADO enumerator. It will contain the names of the packages and other vital information that can be used for the ETL processes.

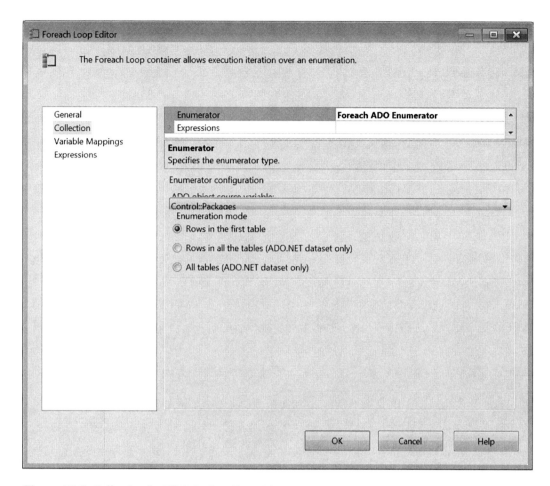

Figure 16-8. Collection for FELC_PackageExecution

Figure 16-9 demonstrates the configuration of the variables that will accept the values from each record in the table set. All five columns have been mapped to five different variables in the order that they appear in the SELECT statement. The container's configuration will not execute unless all the columns are mapped to variables of the appropriate data type.

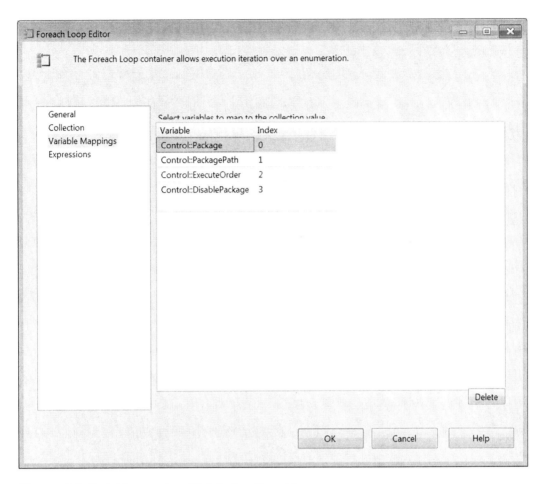

Figure 16-9. *Variable mappings* `FELC_PackageExecution`

The Execute Package task, `EPT_ChildPackage`, is configured almost identically to packages in the static example. The only difference is that all the executions will have the configurations, regardless of whether the package is to be disabled during execution or not. Figure 16-10 shows the Package page of the task. The `Password` property is left to its default because none of the packages actually have a password.

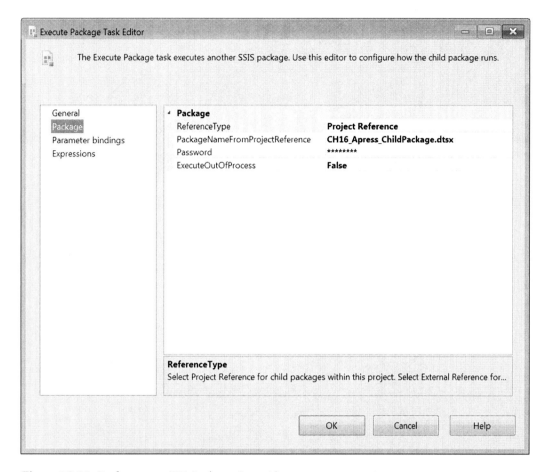

Figure 16-10. *Package page* EPT_Package Execution

The parameter bindings, shown in Figure 16-11, will be the same for all the packages. You need to ensure that the packages at least have a parameter with the same name in all of the child packages. The parameter binding to the package property also should be in place for all the child packages. This parameter mapping is the same as the one shown previously in Figure 16-2.

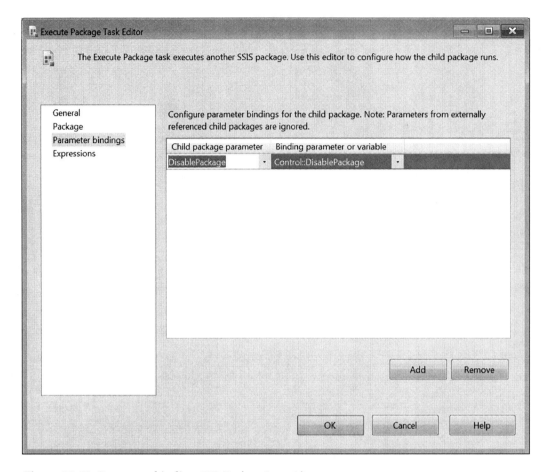

Figure 16-11. *Parameter bindings* `EPT_PackageExecution`

Figure 16-12 demonstrates the expression that really makes all this possible. The expression bound to the `PackageName` property refreshes with every iteration of the Foreach Loop container. The variable `Control::Package` is constantly updated with the values in the `Package` column from the result set of the Execute SQL task. The expression, `@[Control::Package]+".dtsx"`, performs a string concatenation that is acceptable for the property so that the appropriate package can be found within the project.

We provide a default value to the variable because the parent package needs to validate the existence of such a package. When you open the parent package within Visual Studio, it will attempt to look for a package with the name that corresponds to evaluation of the expression. Without a default value, the parent package will attempt to connect to a package named `.dtsx`. At runtime this will result in a failure during the validation phase.

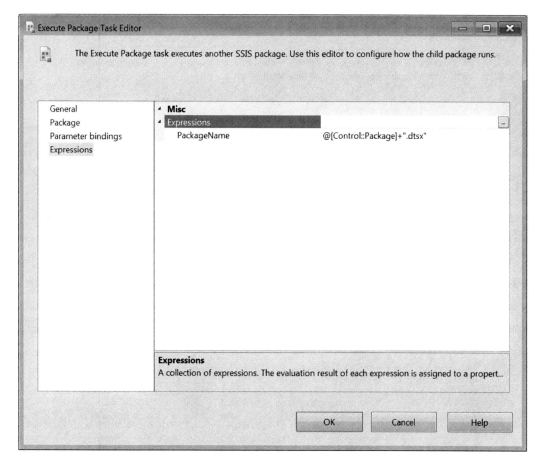

Figure 16-12. Expressions page EPT_PackageExecution

After this configuration is set up, all you need to do is to execute CH16_Apress_DynamicParentPackage. It will automatically execute the child packages just like the static example. The only difference between the two methods is that the management of the execution process and the addition of packages becomes easier. When you execute this package in Debug mode within Visual Studio, you will see message boxes similar to the one in Figure 16-13.

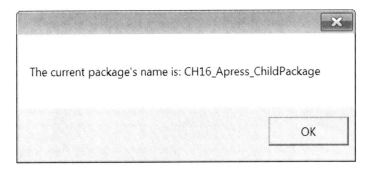

Figure 16-13. Child package message box

Summary

With designing ETL processes, it is very important to bear in mind the maintainability of the code. The parent-child design pattern offers a flexible approach that will modularize you ETL packages, allowing you to add or remove packages or executables from the process with little difficulty or code change. The static implementation will modularize your code but is not ideal if packages are constantly being developed. The dynamic parent-child implementation allows you to let the data drive your ETL processes. We used the example of a table-driven process. This concludes the design patterns section of the book. The next section covers the more advanced capabilities and functionalities of SSIS.

CHAPTER 17

Dimensional Data ETL

We are not in the eighth dimension; we are over New Jersey. Hope is not lost.

—*Adventurer Buckaroo Banzai*

In the first decade of the 21st century, the terms *data warehouse* and *data mart* were suddenly—and without warning—copied and pasted all over every database professional's résumé. Despite the apparent increased awareness in the professional community, the core components of these structures, dimension and fact tables, remained misunderstood. In this chapter, you'll look at ways to load data efficiently into your dimensional structures. You'll begin with an introduction to the terminology and concepts used throughout this chapter.

Introducing Dimensional Data

By now, most database professionals have had some level of exposure to *dimensional data*. For those who don't use it every day, this term can be a bit misleading. It doesn't really refer to any special properties of the data itself, but rather to the *dimensional model* used to store it. Specifically, dimensional data is stored in *dimensional data marts*. Data marts are relational databases that adhere to one of two logical structures: the *star schema* or the *snowflake schema*. Both of these logical structures consist of two types of tables:

> **Fact tables** contain business measure data, such as sales quantities and dollar amounts.
>
> **Dimension tables** hold attributes related to the measures stored in the fact tables, such as product colors and customer names.

A star schema features a fact table (or possibly multiple fact tables) related to denormalized dimension tables. Figure 17-1 shows a logical design for a sample star schema that holds sales receipt data for a retail store.

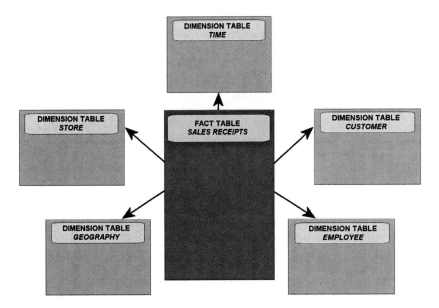

Figure 17-1. Star schema data mart

In a star schema, the dimensions are "flattened out" into denormalized tables. The snowflake schema is a logical structure similar to the star schema, but features normalized, or *snowflaked*, dimensions. Figure 17-2 features snowflaking of the Time and Geography dimensions from the previous star schema.

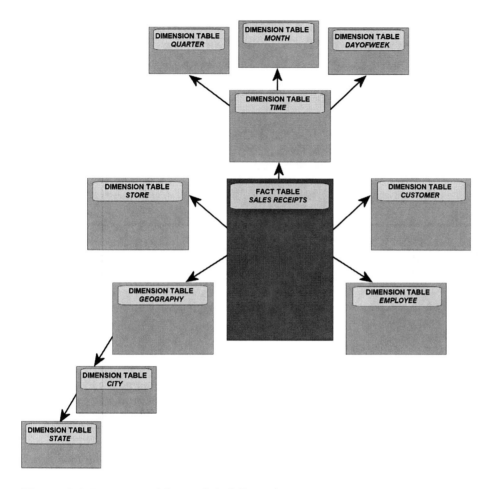

Figure 17-2. *Data mart with snowflaked dimensions*

Because of performance and complexity star schemas are more, but are not always possible to model an OLAP database in such a structure.

Data marts are usually fed by upstream systems such as normalized data warehouses and other databases. The data mart, in turn, is used to feed OLAP databases such as SQL Server Analysis Services cubes or is queried directly for reporting and analysis.

DATA WAREHOUSE, OPERATIONAL DATA STORE, AND OTHER BUZZWORDS

In addition to *data mart*, many other business intelligence–related buzzwords are out there. These include *data warehouse (DW)* and *operational data store (ODS)*, to name a couple. A data warehouse is a centralized repository of data from operational systems, specifically designed for analysis and reporting. Depending on the school of thought you subscribe to, you might build data warehouses in third normal form (the *top-down approach* espoused by Bill Inmon) or you might build several dimensional data marts with shared dimensions (the *bottom-up approach* favored by Ralph Kimball).

Data warehouses are meant to hold high-quality organization-wide historical data, often at a higher level than the lowest transactional details, and on a very long timeline. An operational data store, on the other hand, is designed to hold more-volatile operational data for shorter periods of time. An ODS is often used to feed a data warehouse.

The important aspect, in terms of dimensional data, is that an ODS and a data warehouse are generally used to feed dimensional data marts (except in the Kimball model, in which the data warehouse is the union of multiple data marts). The details of implementing data warehouses and operational data stores are out of the scope of this chapter, but you can find out more in Bill Inmon's book *Building the Data Warehouse* (John Wiley & Sons, 2005) and Ralph Kimball's book *The Data Warehouse Toolkit* (John Wiley & Sons, 2002).

Creating Quick Wins

When your boss says she wants you to optimize an ETL process (or any system for that matter), you can often translate this to mean "tweak it around the edges." With that in mind, we'll present some quick changes to give you the biggest bang for the buck.

Run in Optimized Mode

Data Flow tasks in SSIS have a setting called `RunInOptimizedMode`. Setting this property to `True` results in the data flow optimizing the task by automatically removing unused columns, outputs, and components from the data flow. In production packages, this property should always be set to `True`. This should only be set to `False` when debugging or in very specific troubleshooting scenarios. You can also set `RunInOptimizedMode` in the SSDT Project Properties. This property setting in SSDT overrides the individual Data Flow task setting when you run the package in SSDT—but only in SSDT. The default package property is `False`, enabling you to apply the Data Flow property to either `True` or `False`. Changing the project property to `True` will avoid having to update any or all data task properties. Figure 17-3 shows the property page for the Data Flow task.

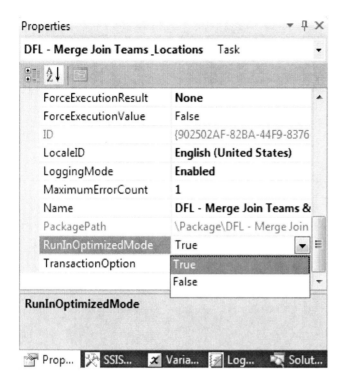

Figure 17-3. Setting the RunInOptimizedMode property to True

Remove "Dead-End" Components

When debugging SSIS components, it's common to use the Row Count component in place of a destination for error outputs. In many cases, the value returned by the Row Count is never used. Consider the sample data flow shown in Figure 17-4.

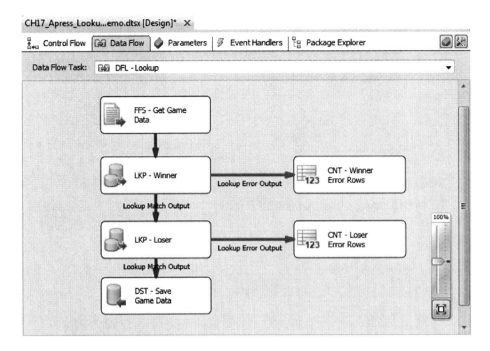

Figure 17-4. Data flow with dead-end components

In this sample data flow, we're sending the error rows from the Lookup transformations to Row Count transformations. In this case, we aren't using the values returned by the Row Counts, but SSIS still has to move the unmatched rows down that branch of the data flow and into the components. This is an unnecessary inefficiency in this data flow. Fixing this is as simple as deleting the dead-end Row Counts.

Keep Package Size Small

Owing in large part to the overhead involved in initializing a package, including allocating buffers and automated validations and optimizations, executing a large package can take considerably more time and resources than executing multiple smaller packages to get the same end result. By keeping your packages small, SSIS can execute them more efficiently. There is no hard rule on package size, but SSIS expert Andy Leonard recommends keeping individual packages to a file size of 5 MB or lower. It is also possible to identify common SSIS tasks that run in multiple packages and create smaller packages of these tasks to be used as child packages that can then be called from one or many parent packages. This helps to encapsulate logic and provide reusable components reducing development. This topic is covered in more depth in Chapter 18. Note that by keeping your SSIS packages small, you also gain the benefit of faster loading and validation in SSDT.

Optimize Lookups

There are three main methods of optimizing Lookup transformations in your data flows. The first optimization technique is to use a SQL query to populate your Lookup transformation, instead of the Table or View population mode. The Table or View mode pulls all rows and columns from a table in the database. In many cases, the Lookup transformation doesn't need all those columns. With the SQL Query mode, you can limit the results to include only a specified list of columns. There's no point in pulling megabytes (or more) of extraneous data, only to discard it immediately.

The second optimization technique for Lookup transformations involves reusing your Lookup reference data. If you have to perform multiple lookups against the same set of reference data, round-tripping to the database to pull this data two, three, or more times in a single package is a waste of resources. Instead, use the Cache transformation and load that reference data once.

Our third optimization technique for Lookup transformations is to get rid of them. You can do this by performing a join on the server side—in your source query—or by using a Merge Join transformation. Although the Lookup transformation is not technically classified as a *blocking* transformation, it can actually be *worse* for performance than a transformation in this group. The issue with the Lookup transformation is that your data flow will not even begin moving data until the Lookup finishes caching its reference data. The Merge Join transformation, which is partially blocking, allows data to move through in a more efficient fashion.

Keep Your Data Moving

The Golden Rule of ETL efficiency is "keep your data moving." Every second that data is not moving through your data flow is lost processing time that can never be reclaimed. As we discussed in Chapter 15, to keep your data moving, you should minimize the use of blocking transformations and consider performing joins, sorting, and aggregations on the server when possible.

In addition, consider using the SQL Server FAST query hint. By applying the FAST query hint to long-running source queries, SQL Server will send a burst of initial rows to SSIS, allowing your data flow to proceed. Ideally, while those initial rows are winding their way through your data flow, SQL Server will supply more rows to your source component. This hint is particularly useful for long-running queries that feed complex data flows.

▪ **TIP:** You can find out more about SQL Server query hints at http://msdn.microsoft.com/en-us/library/ms181714.aspx.

Minimize Logging

We talked about logging best practices in Chapter 13. The idea is simple: logging processing information requires resources. It takes I/O, network bandwidth, memory, and even a bit of CPU to log. Although you don't want to eliminate logging completely, you should target your production logging settings to record the minimal amount of information you need to monitor and troubleshoot your ETL processes.

Use the Fast Load Option

We discussed the fast load and bulk insert options available for OLE DB and SQL Server destination adapters in Chapter 7. When inserting rows into SQL Server tables, use these options when possible. The fast load options are much more efficient than individual, one-row-at-a-time round-trips to the server.

Understanding Slowly Changing Dimensions

Slowly changing dimensions (SCDs) are the physical implementation of the dimensions we discussed earlier in this chapter. Basically, SCDs put the *dimensional* in your dimensional data. SCDs are divided into four major types, which we discuss in the following sections.

Type 0 Dimensions

Type 0 dimensions, also known as *nonchanging dimensions* or *very slowly changing dimensions* come in two flavors:

- Dimensions with attributes that *never* change (such as a Gender dimension)

- Dimensions with attributes that *very rarely* change (such as a US States dimension)

Type 0 dimensions are generally populated one time with load scripts. The occasional update to these dimensions is usually just an operation that adds records, which can also be performed with one-off scripts. As an example, consider a Date dimension with 10 years' worth of dates in it. You might need to add another 10 years' worth of date attributes to the dimension, but this doesn't affect the existing entries. With this in mind, our best advice for Type 0 dimensions is to populate them and update them as necessary with static one-off scripts.

Type 1 Dimensions

Apart from nonchanging dimensions, *Type 1 SCDs* are the simplest type of dimension to implement—they have no requirement to store historical attribute values. When attributes in a Type 1 SCD change, you simply overwrite the old ones with the new values. A standard Type 1 SCD implementation involves storing a surrogate key (the IDENTITY column in SQL Server serves this purpose well, as will using a SEQUENCE that is introduced in SQL 2012), the business key for the inbound dimension attributes, and the dimension attribute values themselves. Consider the DimProduct Type 1 SCD table shown in Figure 17-5.

SQL11.SampleDatab...- dbo.DimProduct ×

	Column Name	Data Type	Allow Nulls
🔑	ProductID	int	☐
	UPC	char(12)	☐
	Category	varchar(25)	☐
	Manufacturer	varchar(25)	☐
	ProductName	varchar(100)	☐
	Size	varchar(10)	☐
	Color	varchar(10)	☐
	Price	numeric(10, 4)	☐

Figure 17-5. DimProduct *type 1 dimension table*

The DimProduct table holds entries describing all the products. In this example, the ProductID is the surrogate key, UPC is the business key, and the remaining columns hold the attribute values. The update pattern for the Type 1 SCD is simple, as shown in the flowchart in Figure 17-6.

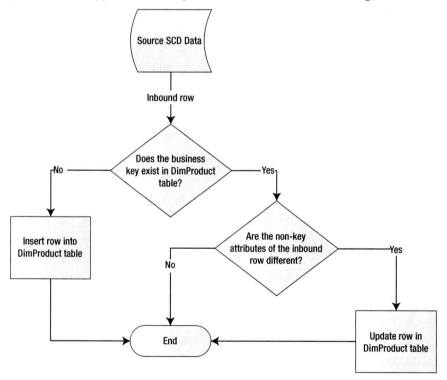

Figure 17-6. Type 1 SCD update flowchart

The process for updating the Type 1 SCD is a simple *upsert* (update-or-insert) operation based on the business key. If the business key of the inbound row exists in the dimension table, it's updated; if the key doesn't exist, it's inserted. There are several ways to implement Type 1 SCD updates:

- You can build out your own data flow by hand, which will perform the necessary comparisons and individual updates and inserts.

- You can create an SSIS custom component, or use a prebuilt custom component, to do the hard work for you.

- You can insert the raw data into a staging table and follow up with a set-based MERGE into the dimension table.

- You can use the SSIS Slowly Changing Dimension Wizard to build out your SCD update data flow.

The main question you need to answer when deciding which method to use is, where can you perform the necessary dimension member comparisons most efficiently—in the data flow or on the server? In general, the most efficient comparisons can be performed on the SQL Server side.

With that in mind, we'll skip building out a data flow by hand as it tends to be the most inefficient and error-prone method. If you're interested in pursuing this option, we recommend using the Slowly Changing Dimension Wizard instead to build out a prototype. This will give you a better understanding of how the data flow can be used to update your SCD. We'll consider the Slowly Changing Dimension Wizard later in this section.

Using a prebuilt SSIS custom component (or building your own) is another viable option, but it's outside the scope of this chapter. We recommend looking at some of the samples on CodePlex (www.codeplex.com) to understand how these components work.

Our preferred method (without custom components) is loading your dimensions into a staging table and performing the dimension updates on the server directly. Set-based updates are the most efficient method of updating dimensional data. The control flow in Figure 17-7 shows the basic layout of the Type 1 SCD set-based update.

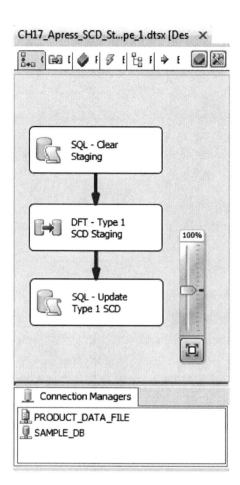

Figure 17-7. *Set-based Type 1 SCD update package*

The first step of the process is to truncate the staging table with an Execute SQL task:

```
TRUNCATE TABLE Staging.DimProduct;
```

The next step is the data flow, which simply moves the Product dimension data from the source to the staging table, as shown in Figure 17-8.

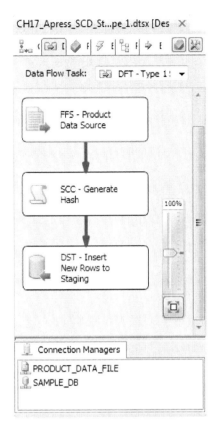

Figure 17-8. *Data flow to load the staging table*

The Flat File Source pulls the Product dimension from a flat file, and the OLE DB Destination pushes the data to the staging table. In between, there's an additional step that generates an SHA1 hash code for each row of data as it moves through the data flow.

HASH CODES

Hash codes are fixed-length "fingerprints" for data. When you push data through a one-way hash algorithm, it generates a unique code that can be used for comparison purposes. Comparisons with one-way hashes are much more efficient and easier to manage than comparisons of several columns of inbound data on an individual basis. The SHA1 hash function generates a 160-bit hash code and is considered "collision-free." This means that duplicate hash codes generated from different data are extremely rare (in fact, the odds are 1 in 2^{80}). For even lower odds of generating a collision, you can use an SHA2 family hash function, which range from 1 in 2^{128} to 1 in 2^{256}.

The .NET code we use to generate a hash code is very efficient, utilizing MemoryStream and BinaryWriter, as shown in the following code snippet.

```
public class ScriptMain : UserComponent
{

  MemoryStream ms;
  BinaryWriter bw;
  SHA1Managed sha1;

  public override void PreExecute()
  {
    base.PreExecute();
    sha1 = new SHA1Managed();
  }

  public override void PostExecute()
  {
    base.PostExecute();
  }

  public override void Input0_ProcessInputRow(Input0Buffer Row)
  {
    ms = new MemoryStream();
    bw = new BinaryWriter(ms);
    if (Row.UPC_IsNull)
    {
      bw.Write((Int32)0);
      bw.Write((byte)255);
    }
    else
    {
      bw.Write(Row.UPC.Length);
      bw.Write(Row.UPC);
    }
    bw.Write('|');

    // ...Write additional columns to BinaryWriter

    byte[] hash = sha1.ComputeHash(ms.ToArray());
    Row.Hash = hash;
    ms.Dispose();
    bw.Dispose();
  }
}
```

All the columns are written to BinaryWriter with the length of the column followed by the value. In the case of a NULL value, a length of zero is written, followed by a single byte value (this is a value that can't be generated in inbound data). Each column is followed by a vertical bar separator character. The concatenated binary string is then fed into an SHA1 generation function, and the output is assigned to the Hash column.

The final step of the Type 1 SCD update is a single update-or-insert (upsert) operation from the staging table to the dimension table. The T-SQL `MERGE` statement is perfectly suited for this job. The `MERGE` statement lets you perform `UPDATE` and `INSERT` operations in a single statement, as shown here:

```
MERGE INTO dbo.DimProduct AS Target
USING Staging.DimProduct AS Source
  ON Target.UPC = Source.UPC
WHEN MATCHED AND Target.Hash <> Source.Hash
THEN UPDATE SET Target.Category = Source.Category,
  Target.Manufacturer = Source.Manufacturer,
  Target.ProductName = Source.ProductName,
  Target.Size = Source.Size,
  Target.Price = Source.Price,
  Target.Hash = Source.Hash
WHEN NOT MATCHED
THEN INSERT (UPC, Category, Manufacturer, ProductName, Size, Price, Hash)
  VALUES (Source.UPC, Source.Category, Source.Manufacturer, Source.ProductName, Source.Size,
    Source.Price, Source.Hash);
```

■ **NOTE:** `MERGE` provides a means to incorporate `INSERT`, `UPDATE`, and `DELETE` in one statement. However, separating these steps into individual statements can improve overall performance. Compare the costs of both methods to ensure that the most efficient query is used.

The notable shortcoming of a Type 1 SCD is that historical values will be lost to an update of the current value. However, the update process is easier than a Type 2 or Type 3 SCD and also uses less space, as long-term history is not maintained.

Type 2 Dimensions

Because they maintain a long-term history of attribute values, *Type 2 dimensions* are slightly more complex to manage than Type 1 dimensions. The schema of a Type 2 SCD table differs from a Type 1 SCD in that it can contain up to three extra columns to denote a current or historic version. The additional column(s) allow the dimension table to contain the historic values rather than overwriting the affected column(s) with the current value. The dimension could contain a single column that indicates whether the row has the most current value, as displayed in Figure 17-9.

	customer_key	customer_code	state	active
1	1	COOO1jd	FL	N
2	2	COOO1jd	MT	Y

Figure 17-9. Type 2 SCD result set

While new or updated values are always inserted into Type 2 dimensions, there are additional flags on existing rows that must also be updated, such as the effective date, end date, or active column.

Adding a column to indicate only whether the row is the most current enables you to ensure that all historic changes are kept, but not to define when the specific row was active. The addition of both an active column and an end-date column would provide the means of maintaining historic values that can then be associated with the proper time frame.

The Active column denotes whether the row holds the current value, but lacks the ability to track when the value(s) were in effect. The dimension table could include a start- and end-date column, which could maintain the historic values and times, when the end date is NULL this represents the current value, or an effective date column and a column representing active or historic. The process of updating a Type 2 SCD is shown in Figure 17-10.

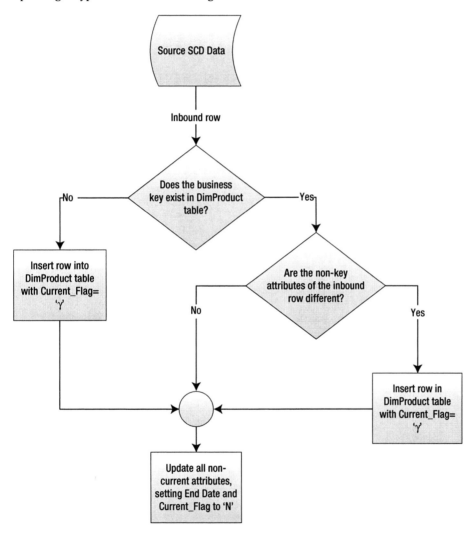

Figure 17-10. Type 2 SCD update flow

SSIS provides a Data Transformation task that can be used for both Type 1 and Type 2 SCDs. The first step in using the SCD transformation task for a Type 2 SCD is to decide whether you are going to track changes in your table by either using a simple indicator to identify current and expired records, or using effective dates. The component doesn't natively allow you to use both, although you can customize the output to do so. Figure 17-11 demonstrates using a SCD transformation task in a data flow.

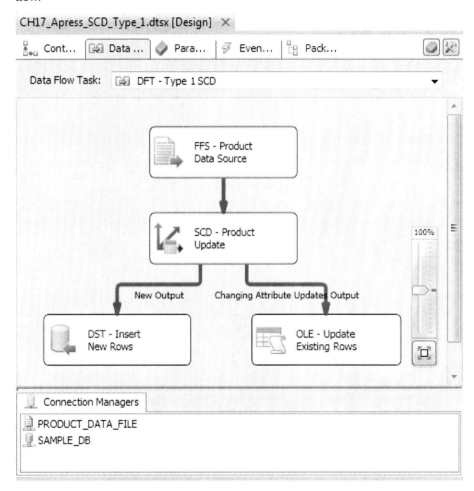

Figure 17-11. SSIS slowly changing dimension component

Type 3 Dimensions

A Type 3 SCD tracks changes by using separate columns, which limits the history to the number of columns that can be added to the dimension table. This obviously provides limitations, and the dimension table will begin to look more like a Microsoft Excel spreadsheet, as shown in Figure 17-12.

customer_key	customer_code	past_state	effective_date	current_state
1	C0001jd	FL	2012-03-27	MT

Figure 17-12. Query results of a Type 3 SCD

There are several complexities in implementing a Type 3 SCD—first and foremost modifying the table schema for each update, which make this a less than desirable means of tracking historic attributes, As a Type 3 SCD is limiting and requires changing the schema of the dimension table, it is not supported in the SCD Transformation task. It is possible to use an Execute SQL task to automate updating a Type 3 SCD, but if at any point the dimension table was referenced in a Data Flow task, it would fail the validation phase based on the schema change. The issues don't end with the processing of the dimension, but also include using the dimension in an SSAS cube or for a report, again as based on the ever-changing schema. Although utilizing a Type 3 SCD is an option, utilizing a Type 1 or 2 SCD is preferable.

Summary

This chapter introduced several tools and methods for optimizing your SSIS packages. Many of these optimizations rely on performing operations at the source when possible and limiting the data pulled through the ETL process. We also discussed the different types of dimensions and outlined ways that each dimension could be updated. In the next chapter, we'll consider the powerful SSIS parent-child design pattern.

Building Robust Solutions

The egoism which enters into our theories does not affect their sincerity; rather, the more our egoism is satisfied, the more robust is our belief.

—Novelist George Eliot

Developing an SSIS package typically focuses on the known—the data source, transformations, and destinations—and fails to address the unknown—schema changes, data type mismatches, and a changing network environment. Obviously, all development must come from a starting point—the known. However, in order to ensure that an SSIS package provides portability, stability, and resilience, it is critical to handle the unknown and to record the unidentified and inconsistent behavior. This chapter outlines the steps necessary to plan and handle the unexpected within an SSIS package.

What Makes a Solution Robust

Quite often an SSIS solution is created to fulfill an easily defined process in a specific and static environment. The source and destination schema are considered immutable and unchanging, and there is no accounting for change or error. This type of project is effortlessly created and quickly deployed, but frequently the developer fails to play *what if* in such cases and thus provides little means for the following:

- Tracking of:
  - o Performance
  - o Error information
  - o Historic metrics
- Handling variations to:
  - o Sources
  - o Connections
  - o Schema
- Portability and ease of deploying to different environments

There are several factors to be considered when attempting to create a robust solution:

Resilience: The capability of a package to proactively deal with errors, document them, and still complete

Dynamism: The capability to deal with a dynamic fluid environment based on a set of rules and not static numbers, paths, or connections

Accountability: The capability to record the behavior of steps within a package, allowing historic performance to be tracked

Portability: The capability to easily deploy a package to different environments without having to overhaul each step and connection

Taking these factors into consideration during package development can streamline troubleshooting and deployment/migration, as well as the tracking of historic performance.

Resilience

Errors can occur within an SSIS task for various reasons, and how they are handled depends on the specific task. For example, a Script task can handle errors easily and efficiently by using `try-catch-finally` blocks and can provide a means of dynamic error handling, whereas an FTP task has a limited means of proactive error handling. To ensure resiliency, tasks should provide a means of preemptive error handling and a way to reprocess tasks after an error is handled.

Data Flow Task

One of the most commonly used SSIS tasks is also one of the more difficult to incorporate error handling. A Data Flow task is the backbone of the ETL process, but lacks true structured error handling within the data flow. A prime example of this is the occurrence of a truncation error from source or transformation to destination. In this situation, there is no way to dynamically handle the error, but you can redirect the affected row to another destination, where additional evaluation can be done to ensure a successful import.

This can be easily exhibited by creating a package that contains an Execute SQL task and a Data Flow task connected by the Execute SQL tasks with an on success precedent constraint. The Execute SQL task, renamed Create People Tbl, will create a destination table in the default instance by using the AdventureWorks 2012 database with the following query:

```
IF NOT EXISTS( SELECT * FROM sys.tables WHERE name = 'People')
BEGIN
CREATE TABLE People(
FirstName      NVARCHAR(50),
MiddleName     NVARCHAR(50),
LastName       NVARCHAR(21)
)
END;
GO
```

After the Execute SQL task has been configured, change the name of the Data Flow task to **Populate People**. The control flow pane of the package should resemble Figure 18-1.

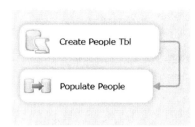

Figure 18-1. *Data flow error redirection in the control flow pane*

In the data flow pane, add an OLE DB source, OLE DB destination, Flat File destination, and a Data Conversion transformation. The OLE DB source should be renamed **AdventureWorks Person** and configured to connect to the default instance of SQL and use the AdventureWorks 2012 database. In the table selection drop-down list, select the Person schema's Person table, as shown in Figure 18-2.

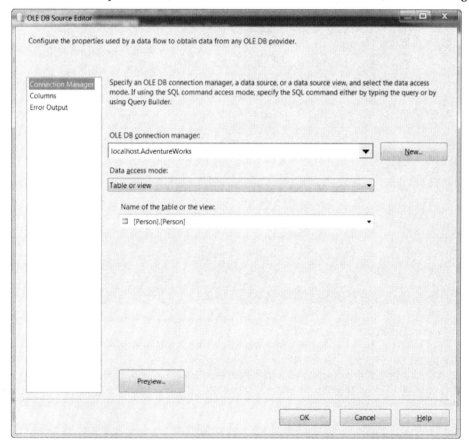

Figure 18-2. *Data flow source*

From the columns, only the FirstName, MiddleName, and LastName columns should be selected, as depicted in Figure 18-3.

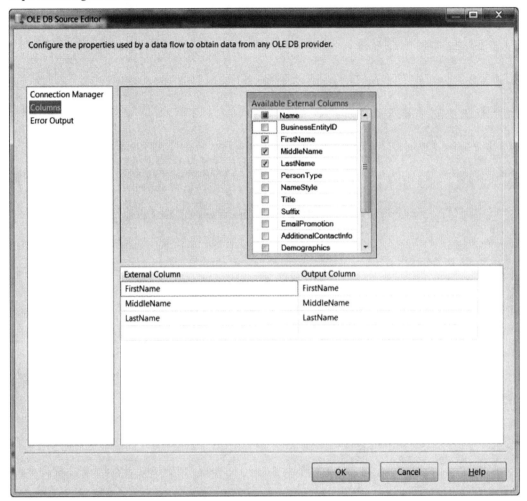

Figure 18-3. *Selecting the data flow source column*

Connect the data flow path from the OLE DB source to the data conversion task and rename the task **Convert LastName**. In the editor for the transformation task, select LastName from the available input columns and set the output alias to Coverted LastName and length to 20. This causes a single row from the source to be truncated, as shown in Figure 18-4.

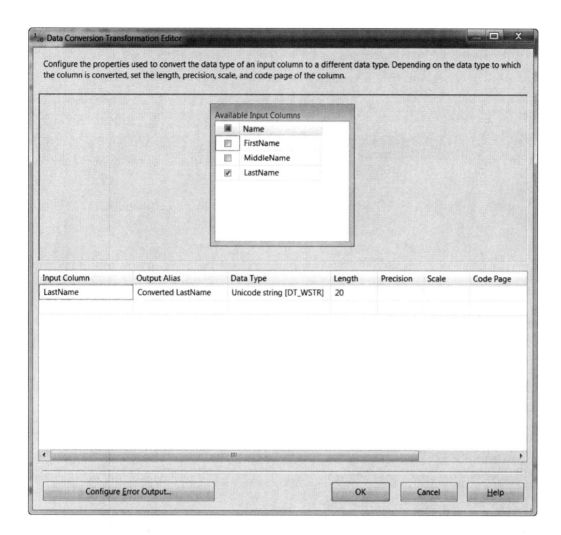

Figure 18-4. *Data transformation task*

To configure the error output, first open the editor by clicking the Configure Error Output button. of the data conversion task and change the Error and Truncation values from "Fail componenet" to "Redirect row," as shown in Figure 18-5.

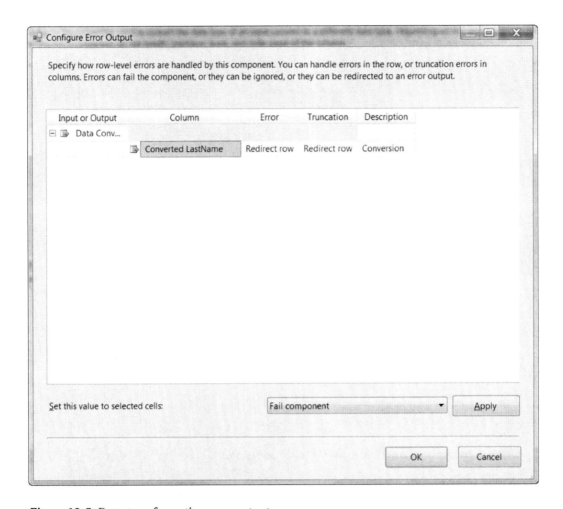

Figure 18-5. Data transformation error output

Connect the data transformation task error flow to the flat file destination and name the destination
Errors. Configure a new Flat File Connection Manager named **Errors File** to write to the path
C:\Robust\PeopleErrors.txt, as shown in Figure 18-6.

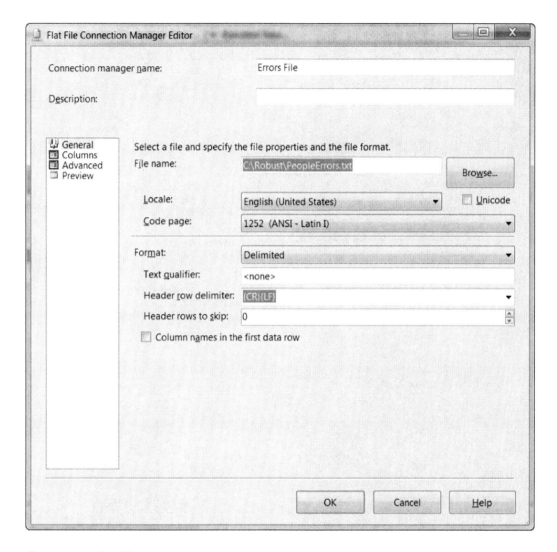

Figure 18-6. Flat File Connection Manager

In order to ensure that an error is not raised due to truncation from the transformation to the Errors file destination, select the Advanced configuration and make sure that the LastName column is set to Unicode String with a column width of 50, as shown in Figure 18-7.

▪ **NOTE:** Adjust the target filename of the destination as needed to ensure that the path is valid.

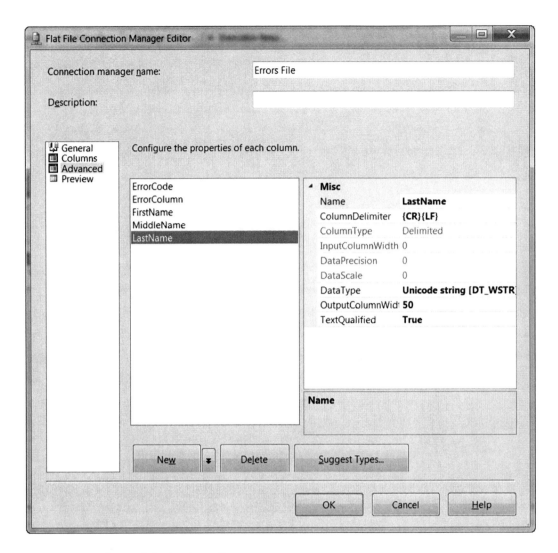

Figure 18-7. Advanced destination editor

Finally, connect the data flow from the Convert LastName transformation task to the OLE DB destination. Open the destination editor, change the name to **People Table** and select the dbo.People table as the destination table. From the mappings editor, change the LastName input mapping column to the Converted LastName column, as illustrated in Figure 18-8.

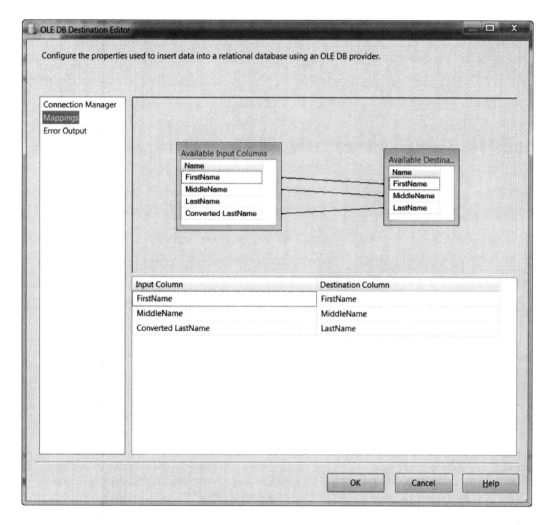

Figure 18-8. OLE DB Destination editor

The final data flow pane should resemble Figure 18-9.

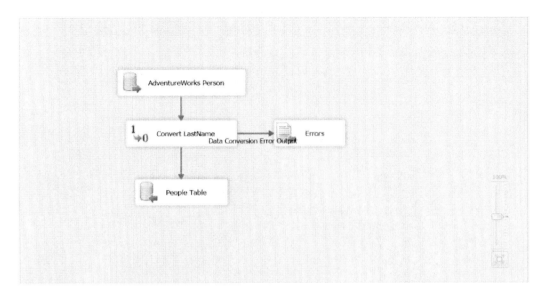

Figure 18-9. *Data flow editor pane*

When running the package, the data flow should show that 19,971 rows were successfully sent to the People Table destination, and one row to the Errors flat file destination. Instead of the Data Flow task failing due to a truncation error of a single row, the task completes and the row is still available for later processing in the flat file destination.

Although this error cannot be processed from within the Data Flow task, the fact that the redirected row contains not only the original data, but also the error code and error column in the flat file destination does provide a means of dynamic handling outside of the Data Flow task.

The ability to dynamically handle data flow errors can still be implemented, although outside of the Data Flow task, by incorporating various package components. Adding a package-level variable and using a Row Count transformation between the Convert LastName data transformation and the Error Count Data source in the Data Flow task provides the capability of utilizing a Script task to later evaluate the error flat file. Figure 18-10 displays the tasks within the Data Flow task. Figure 18-11 illustrates the control flow pane with the precedent constraint using an expression to evaluate whether the variable, Error, is greater than 0.

■ **TIP:** Make sure that the redirected rows are sent to a flexible destination. Creating a table with an identical schema as that of the intended destination will only cause the redirected row to fail again for truncation or constraint errors. In addition to the failed rows, the error description can be included in an additional column.

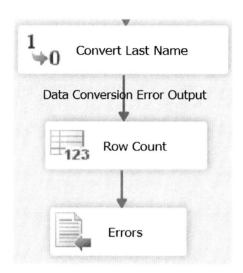

Figure 18-10. *Data flow editor pane*

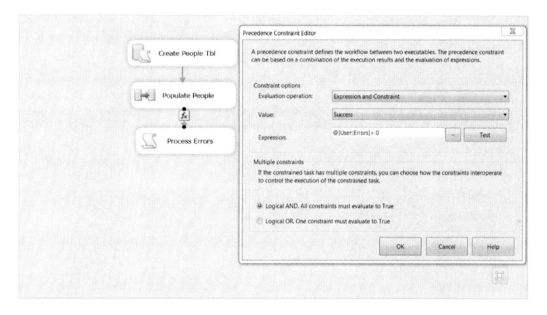

Figure 18-11. *Control flow editor pane*

As shown in Figure 18-11, the script component will be executed only if the Populate People Data Flow task completes successfully, and if the Row Count transformation incremented the Error variable. The following code illustrates how a Script task can be used to parse the redirected error rows from the text file by using the TextFieldParser class:

```
Public Sub Main()
    Dim rdr As New TextFieldParser("C:\Robust\PeopleErrors.txt")
    rdr.TextFieldType = FileIO.FieldType.Delimited
    rdr.SetDelimiters(",")
    Dim row As String()
    While Not rdr.EndOfData
        Try
            row = rdr.ReadFields()
            MessageBox.Show(row(0).ToString)

        Catch ex As Microsoft.VisualBasic.FileIO.MalformedLineException
            MsgBox("Line " & ex.Message & _
            "is not valid and will be skipped.")
        End Try
    End While


    Dts.TaskResult = ScriptResults.Success
End Sub
```

The MessageBox returns the indexed value of the error number from the row string array, which can be used to identify the specific cause. Obviously, to dynamically handle the error requires additional code, but armed with the error codes and descriptions (provided in the following Tip), a VB.NET Select Case statement can be included to iterate through the error codes, and based on the error, the appropriate action can be taken.

Event Handlers

Event handlers provide a means to proactively handle events on packages and executables and can be used to capture task-specific information for the following events:

- OnError
- OnExecStatusChange
- OnExecution
- OnPostExecute
- OnPostValidate
- OnPreExecute
- OnPreValidate
- OnQueryCancel
- OnTaskFailed
- OnVariableValueChanged
- OnWarning

An OnError event handler can be used to capture the error description and code, which can then be used to dynamically handle errors as well as record more in-depth information into the specific issue. Because event handlers are available only on executables and packages, this precludes their use from within the data flow, but can capture the failure of the data flow executable. In order for the OnError event handler to be reached, the Data Flow task must first fail, which will expel all data from the buffers, making it unavailable for later investigation.

Processing the error information within the event handler can be done most easily with a Script task passing in System:ErrorCode and System:ErrorDescription as read-only variables. Chapter 11 outlined how to create a Script task to capture error information and provided a demonstration of the OnError event bubbling up from the task level all the way to the package level. Obviously, a more complex type of logic would need to be incorporated within the script component to proactively address the specific error.

The package outlined in the preceeding sectionabove uses error redirection in the Data Flow task to prevent errors from arising and to ensure that all rows are directed to a destination. If the same package was created without redirecting the row, an OnError event handler could be used to capture the error information. Adding a Script task to the OnError event and setting the System:ErrorDescripton as a ReadOnly variable will allow the ability to capture the entire error message and provides more insight into the true cause. Using the following VB.NET code will display the message of any error that occurs within the Data Flow task:

```
MessageBox.Show(Dts.Variables(0).Value.ToString)
```

The resulting message box specifies the truncation error as well as the specific affected column. The primary difference between error redirection and the OnError event handler is that if error redirection is used, the OnError event handler will not be raised. In the preceding example, the Data Flow task stops after the truncation error occurs, and the failing row information would not be stored for later evaluation.

▦ **TIP:** SSIS error messages and numbers are outlined at http://msdn.microsoft.com/en-us/library/ms345164.aspx.

Dynamism

Beginning with SSIS 2005, configuration enabled you to make a package more portable and to easily import a package into multiple instances of SQL without requiring you to create multiple packages or to specifically configure a package for its environment. This capability has been streamlined even more in SSIS 2012 with the introduction of parameters.

Environments allow the mapping of parameters to their variables and can be used to execute a single package in multiple environments. It is common to be required to develop a package in one environment, test in another, and finally deploy to production. This kind of scenario shows the true flexibility and power of using environments in SSIS.

Parameters and environments are outlined in Chapter 19, with examples of dynamic package execution.

Accountability

After a package has been deployed and running for some time, you often have to see how each task is fairing "in the wild." I often get requests as to the total or average number of rows that are passed through a single data flow or how long a single task is taking. Although it can be easy to ascertain package run times that are scheduled within a SQL Server agent, separating task times and counts is not as simple.

Log Providers

Chapter 11 outlined configuring log providers and the saving of package execution information within a specific provider, XML, SQL, CSV, and so forth. Log providers can also be used to provide general task metrics, such as execution time. Log providers enable you to capture information that is raised by an event handler. For example, selecting the OnPreExecute and OnPostExecute events provides a means of tracking the general start and end time of tasks within a package.

Configuration of log providers is done from within the control flow pane by right-clicking and choosing Log Providers. The initial window requires defining the executable to log and in which format the log is to be written, such as XML, SQL or any supported format. After the executable and destination is configured, the event handlers can be selected, as well as the specific columns to collect. Figure 18-12 illustrates the event handlers available through the log provider.

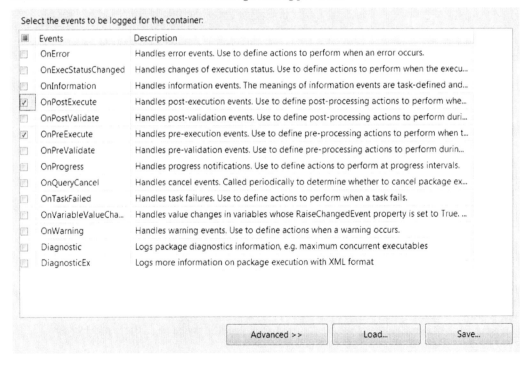

Figure 18-12. Log provider events

Using a SQL log provider for the selected events allows querying the data to find the specific task durations. Each package has its own GUID, as does each task, so utilizing a common table expression with the DATEDIFF function quickly returns the associated task's execution time. The following query uses the table created through the log shipping configuration to find the difference between the start and end time of the specific package identified by its GUID. The results are displayed in Figure 18-13.

```
WITH eventexecution
AS(
SELECT sourceid ,
            starttime
FROM sysssislog
WHERE executionid = 'B0885A09-A1BA-4638-9999-29698F357B40'
AND event = 'OnPreExecute'
)

SELECT source,
            DATEDIFF(SECOND, c.starttime, endtime) AS 'seconds'
FROM sysssislog s JOIN eventexecution c
ON s.sourceid = c.sourceid
WHERE event = 'OnPostExecute';
GO
```

source	seconds
Capture Error	2
Divide by Zero	2
Capture Error	0
Execute SQL Task	1
OnErrorEvent	3

Figure 18-13. *Task duration query results*

Custom Logging

Although log providers can capture a great deal of information in regards to package execution, some measures are missed, such as data flow row counts. Another common request is to show the total rows affected in a Data Flow task over time. Counts such as this are not included in SSIS log providers but can still be captured using custom logging.

The first step is creating a table that will hold the custom logged information, which in this example will be the package GUID, package name, task name, destination name, number of rows, and the date the task ran. For example:

```
IF NOT EXISTS(SELECT * FROM sys.tables WHERE name = 'SSISCounts')
BEGIN
CREATE TABLE SSISCounts(
ExecGUID                NVARCHAR(50),
PackageName          NVARCHAR(50),
TaskName                    NVARCHAR(50),
DestinationName          NVARCHAR(50),
NumberRows             INT,
```

```
DateImported          DATETIME2)
END;
GO
```

A package-level variable needs to be created that will hold the row count of all Data Flow tasks that is of a data type integer. Each Data Flow task should include a Row Count transformation immediately before the destination that uses the package-level variable to record imported rows.

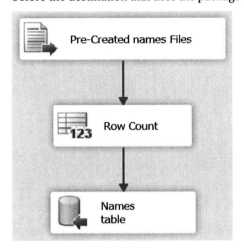

Figure 18-14. *Row count transformation*

Finally, in the PostExecute event handler of the Data Flow tasks, create an Execute SQL task that will insert the appropriate information using both system and user-defined variables. Clicking the event handlers opens the EventHandlers pane and provides two drop-downs, Executable and Event Handler, as shown in Figure 18-15. After the executable is selected, the desired event handler can be selected and the specific task can be placed on the pane.

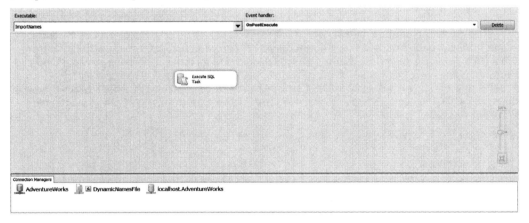

Figure 18-15. *Execute SQL task parameter configuration*

The Execute SQL task will be used to insert the count information from the Data Flow task with information that is system provided and user provided. The system-provided information is the package GUID, name, task, and the row count, and the database and time will be supplied within the query. The SQLStatement property should be set to utilize the parameters that will be defined in the task by using a question mark (?), as shown in the following code:

```
INSERT SSISCounts
VALUES(?, ?, ?, 'AdventureWorks2012DW', ?, SYSDATETIME())
```

The parameters should be organized in the same ordinal position as they appear in the query in the Execute SQL Task Editor. Figure 18-16 depicts the parameter configuration. Note that the parameter name is replaced with the index position of the variables as they appear in the insert statement.

Variable Name	Direction	Data Type	Parameter Name	Parameter Size
System::ExecutionInstanceGUID	Input	NVARCHAR	0	-1
System::PackageName	Input	NVARCHAR	1	-1
System::TaskName	Input	NVARCHAR	2	-1
User::RowCount	Input	LONG	3	-1

Figure 18-16. Execute SQL task parameter configuration

There is typically confusion in the mapping of the parameters to the ? in the SQL statement property. From the preceding figure, remember that the first parameter defined, in this case ExecutionInstanceGUID, will go where the first question mark occurs, and each parameter will follow in order. The insert statement could be rewritten, for demonstration purposes only, to better visualize this, as shown in the following code:

```
INSERT SSISCounts
VALUES(ExecutionInstanceGUID, PackageName, TaskName,
'AdventureWorks2012DW', RowCount, SYSDATETIME())
```

The preceding example demonstrates that using both system and user-defined variables in cooperation with event handlers can provide a means of custom logging. The information contained within the SSISCounts table can be used to establish a means of tracking the number of records added by the data flow and tracking the specific tasks.

Summary

This chapter presented ways to ensure durability, portability, and resiliency in SSIS packages and tasks. Many of the methods discussed in this chapter are extensions of features that are outlined throughout this book. The key concept to creating robust solutions is to do the following:

- Plan for the unknown.
- Proactively handle possible errors.
- Provide error redirection for data flow.
- Configure packages and tasks to be portable.
- Record error and metric package and task information.

Deployment Model

Program testing can be used to show the presence of bugs, but never to show their absence!

—Computer scientist Edsger Dijkstra

Version 2012 of SQL Server Integration Services introduces an entirely new way to deploy ETL processes. In prior versions, the individual package was the deployed object. With the new deployment model, the entire project becomes the deployed object. As noted in previous chapters, the inclusion of parameters and project-level connection managers facilitate this new deployment model. One of the advantages of this new model is that it enables you to create environments within SQL Server with specific values to be used for parameters. Just as Edsger Dijkstra suggests that program testing is not meant to show the absence of bugs, the ability to emulate environments with this new deployment model should greatly expedite detecting potential bugs.

This chapter guides you through deploying a project. In addition, it shows you how to upgrade your legacy SSIS projects to the new deployment model. For the execution of the ETL process, we will demonstrate how to use environments.

The Build Process

The *build process* prepares your project for deployment. It creates a deployment utility that will automate the process. The build process copies packages and objects to specified locations so that the deployment utility can identify them during the deployment process. The properties window of the project file in Visual Studio, shown in Figure 19-1, allows you to define the path for the objects to be copied. The active configuration allows you to control which output receives the build files. Each configuration creates its own folder structure within the output path.

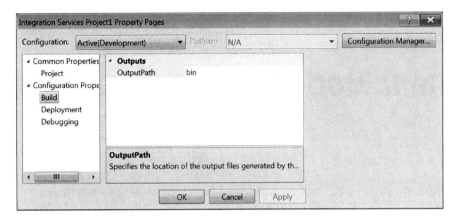

Figure 19-1. *Project Property Pages—Build properties*

The Configuration Manager button opens the Configuration Manager shown in Figure 19-2. This manager allows you to create multiple configurations to use for your build processes. Of the multiple configurations you can create, you must assign one as the default configuration for your solution. The manager also allows you to define the solution platform. In this particular example, the Development configuration is our active configuration for the solution. We base our builds on this configuration by selecting the check box in the Build column.

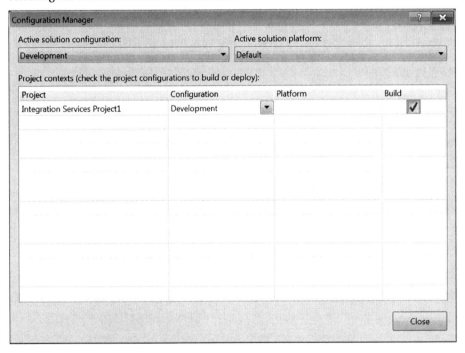

Figure 19-2. *Project Configuration Manager*

After the development is complete on all the packages, you need to use the Build utility within Visual Studio to build the project and its files. The Build utility works behind the scenes of Visual Studio and can be accessed by either right-clicking the project file in the Visual Studio Solution Explorer and selecting Build or by going to the Build menu and selecting Build *project name*. When you build a project for the first time, the directory specified as your output path will be created if it does not exist already. Inside this folder path, you will find a folder designated for the active solution configuration. This folder will contain a *project name*.ispac file, or Integration Services Project Deployment file. This file contains the deployment utility and can deploy the project to an Integration Services catalog.

In addition to the OutputPath being generated, the folder with the project file itself will create a folder path to store all the built objects. This folder, named obj, contains a subfolder for the active solution configuration. Within this folder, you will see a file for each of the packages and project parameters, the project connection managers, the project file, and the output log file.

The Deployment Process

After the project has been built, you will have the option to deploy to an Integration Services catalog on a SQL Server instance. Double-clicking the .ispac file in your active solution configuration's folder will ensure that you deploy the latest build of your objects. The other approach to deploying your project is to right-click the project file in the Visual Studio Solution Explorer and select Deploy.

Prior to deploying a project to an Integration Services catalog, you need to enable Common Language Runtime (CLR) integration on the SQL Server instance. Running the code shown in Listing 19-1 will enable CLR integration. If you do not know whether CLR is enabled, you can simply run sp_configure to see the available options.

Listing 19-1. *Enabling CLR Integration*

```
sp_configure 'clr enabled', 1;
GO
RECONFIGURE;
GO
```

After CLR integration is enabled, you can create the Integration Services catalog by right-clicking the Integration Services folder on the SQL Server instance and selecting Create Catalog. A wizard, shown in Figure 19-3, guides you through the process of creating the catalog. The default name of the database is SSISDB and cannot be renamed. If you did not run the script in Listing 19-1 enabling CLR integration, the wizard can be used to enable this feature. The catalog is created in the databases folder of the SQL Server instance.

■ **CAUTION:** In order to create the Integration Services catalog, you must provide a password. Make sure to save the password and have some process for backing up the encryption key frequently. This password is used to encrypt sensitive data that packages may contain, depending on the protection level that you choose.

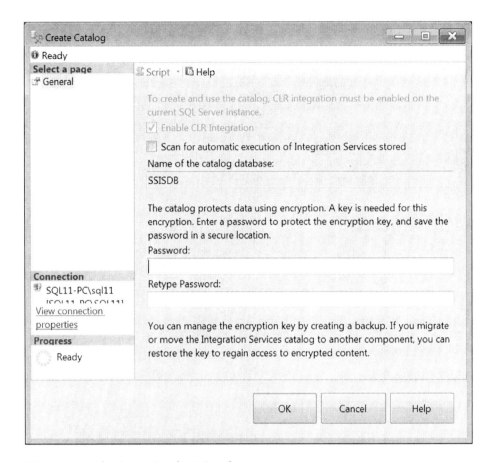

Figure 19-3. The Create Catalog Wizard

With the catalog in place, you will have to create folders within it to store the deployed projects. You can create these folders by expanding the Integration Services tree to the catalog level. On the catalog, you can right-click and select Create Folder. The Create Folder Wizard, shown in Figure 19-4, will assist you in creating each folder.

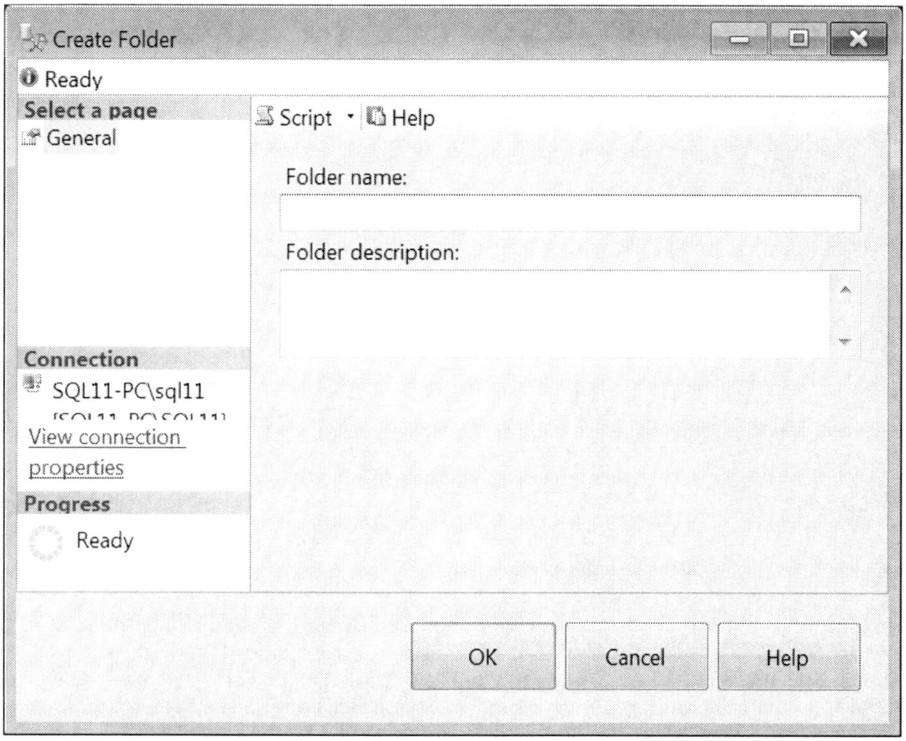

Figure 19-4. The Create Folder Wizard

After you have the folders that you need in place, your Object Explorer should look similar to Figure 19-5. The Projects and Environments subfolders are automatically created within the specified folder. All the projects that are deployed to the SSIS11 folder will be listed in the Projects subfolder. We discuss the environments later in this chapter.

Figure 19-5. *Object Explorer's Integration Services tree*

After the folder structure is in place, the Integration Services Deployment Wizard will guide you through the entire deployment process. Figure 19-6 shows the Select Source page of the wizard. This page allows you to specify the location of the project you want to deploy. The project itself is defined within either a project deployment file or Integration Services catalog. This page allows you to deploy a different project than the active project in the Solution Explorer or the selected .ispac file.

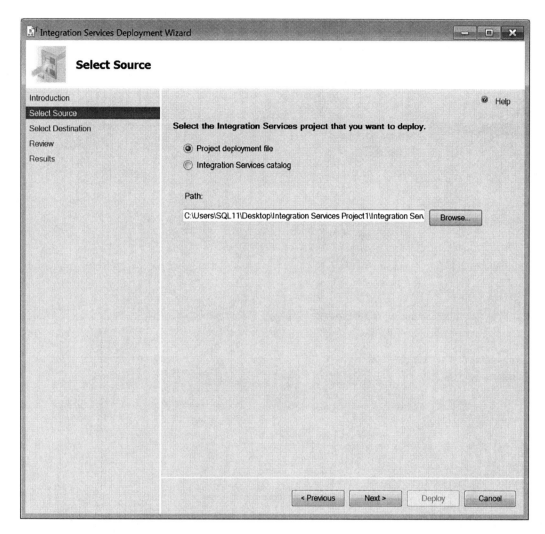

Figure 19-6. The Select Source page of the Integration Services Deployment Wizard

The Integration Services Catalog option allows you to deploy a project directly from one instance of SQL Server to another instance. The Project Deployment File option is the only option to move project objects from a file system to an Integration Services catalog. After you specify the project you want to deploy, you have to determine the destination of that project on the Select Destination page, shown in Figure 19-7.

Figure 19-7. *The Select Destination page of the Integration Services Deployment Wizard*

Unlike prior versions of Integration Services, there is no option to deploy to the file system. You need to specify a SQL Server instance with an Integration Services catalog as the destination of the project deployment. The Browse for Folder or Project dialog box allows you to navigate to the project file in the catalog that you want to associate with this deployment. The deployment wizard will give a warning if you are about to overwrite an existing project. After you have specified the destination server and folder path for the destination, you get a chance to review your configuration by using the Review page, as shown in Figure 19-8.

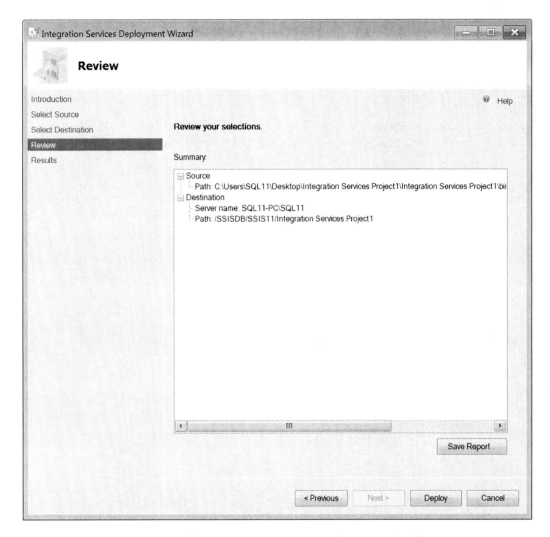

Figure 19-8. *The Review page of the Integration Services Deployment Wizard*

The Review page provides the details of the source and destination of the project deployment. Clicking the Deploy button initiates the process that installs the project to the destination. The Results page, shown in Figure 19-9, provides feedback along each step of the deployment process.

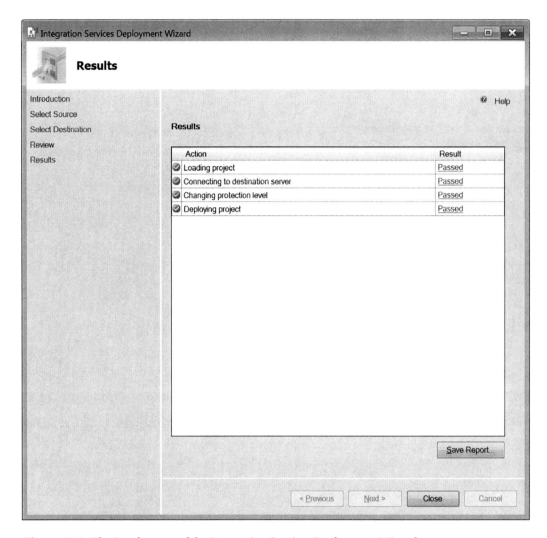

Figure 19-9. The Results page of the Integration Services Deployment Wizard

The Changing Protection Level step modifies the project protection level to use the encryption setting on the destination server. The key is created with the password you provided when creating the catalog. In order to find all the encryption keys that you have for your projects, you can query the `internal.catalog_encryption_keys` table on SSISDB.

Environments

Having deployed your project, you may want to emulate different scenarios that will execute the ETL processes. *Environments* allow you to provide values to all parameters within projects through their variables. These environment variables can also be used to configure connection managers so that data can be sourced and loaded according to the simulation you need to run.

■ **NOTE:** *Environment variable* is a misleading term that may be confused with the operating system's environment variables. The term simply applies to variables within environments the Integration Services catalog can be bound to deployed projects that exist on the catalog for execution purposes. Mappings can be created between these variables, and the different parameters can be configured for various projects.

To create an environment, navigate to the Environments subfolder where you deployed your project. Right-click the subfolder and select Create Environment. This opens a window that will allow you to create the environment. Figure 19-10 shows the Create Environment Window. This window asks for basic information such as the new environment's name and description.

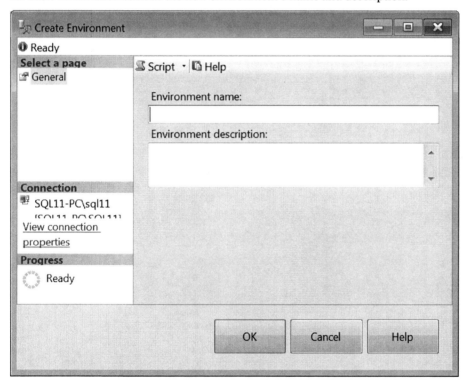

Figure 19-10. *The Create Environment Wizard*

The Script button above the text fields enables you to generate a T-SQL script that will create the environment. Listing 19-2 shows the stored procedure and its parameters that will create the Development environment.

Listing 19-2. *Creating an Environment*

```
EXECUTE SSISDB.catalog.create_environment
        @environment_name=N'Development',
        @environment_description=N'',
        @folder_name=N'SSIS11'
;
GO
```

After creating the environment, you can add variables to it. Just as with creating an environment, you can use the window shown in Figure 19-11 or the code shown in Listing 19-3 to create environment variables. To open the window, you need to right-click the environment and select Properties. The advantage of using the window is that it will allow you to define multiple environment variables.

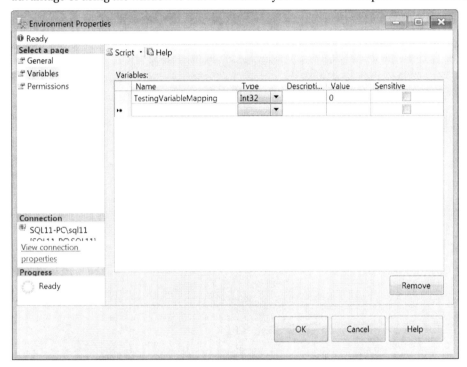

Figure 19-11. *Environment properties*

The T-SQL stored procedure for creating environment variables, catalog.create_environment_variable, uses all the columns shown in the window as parameters. The two parameters, @folder_name and @environment_name, help identify the environment where the variable will belong.

Listing 19-3. *Creating an Environment Variable*

```
EXECUTE SSISDB.catalog.create_environment_variable
        @folder_name = 'SSIS11',
        @environment_name = 'Development',
        @variable_name = 'TestingVariableMapping',
        @data_type = 'Int32',
        @sensitive = FALSE,
        @value = 0,
        @description = ''
;
GO
```

With the project, environment, and environment variables ready to go, you can configure the project to associate with the environment and its variables for specific execution simulations. The environment variables can be mapped to the different project and package parameters that are defined. You can set up these dependencies by navigating to the project in the Integration Services catalog, right-clicking it, and selecting Configure. Figure 19-12 shows the References page of the project's configuration window. This page allows you to define the different environments that can pass values to the project during execution.

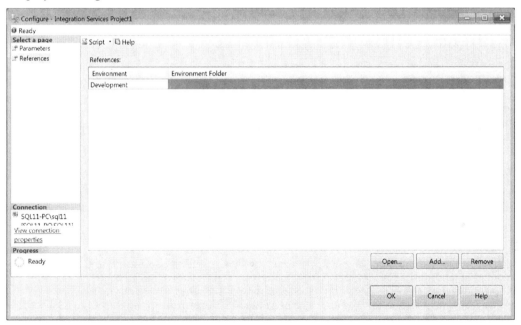

Figure 19-12. *The References page of the Configure project window*

■ **NOTE:** Environments can be referenced from locations other than the project's immediate folder structure. The environments do, however, need to be on the same SQL Server instance.

After the environment reference is set up, you can map project objects to variables within the environment. Figure 19-13 shows the Parameters page's Parameters tab of the Configure projects window. This tab allows you to map values of all the parameters contained within the project to the environment variables' values. The Scope drop-down allows you to find the parameters more easily. It can limit the parameters list to a specific package or parameter function. The tab also shows the default value defined for the parameter.

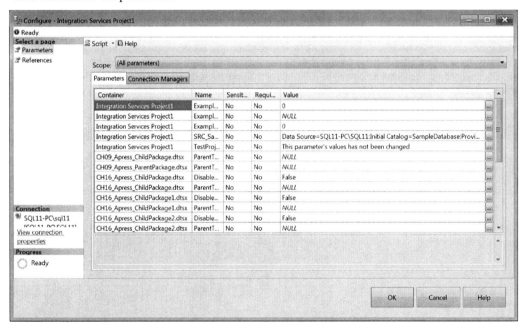

Figure 19-13. *The Parameters page and Parameters tab of the Configure project window*

The actual mapping for the parameter is generated by clicking the ellipsis button to the right of the Value field for the parameter. Clicking the button opens the window shown in Figure 19-14. The Edit Value option allows you to define a new static value for the execution regardless of the specified environment. The Use Environment Variable option will search the environments for the specified variable and map its value to the parameter. The environment variables available in the drop-down list will be those whose data types are compatible with the parameter's data type.

Figure 19-14. *The Set Parameter Value window*

■ **NOTE:** When you define multiple environment references for the projects, we recommend that you define variables with the same names and types in all the environments. The drop-down list in the Set Parameter Value window allows you to specify the variable to map to the parameter.

In addition to the parameters, the connection managers defined within the project can be mapped to environment variable values. The Connection Manager tab of the Configure project window's Parameter page, shown in Figure 19-15, allows you to create these mappings. The Scope drop-down list is similar to the list in the Parameters tab in that it will filter the connection managers defined within the project so that you can map the values easily.

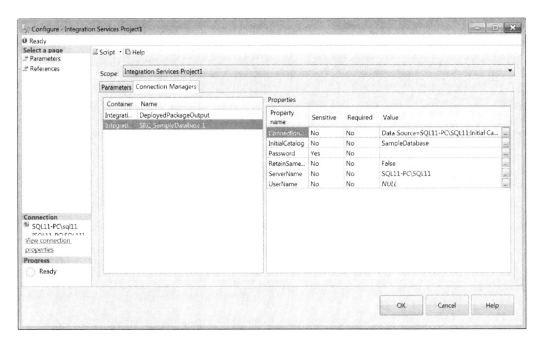

Figure 19-15. *The Parameters page and Connection Managers tab of the Configure project window*

The Set Parameter Value window allows you to map the property values of the connection managers to environment variables as well. The window, which is accessed by clicking the ellipsis button next to the Value field of the property that needs to be mapped, works the same way as the window that maps environment variables to parameters.

Execution

With the project deployed to the Integration Services catalog and configured, we can finally execute the ETL process on the server. This example demonstrates the dynamic parent-child design pattern. The versatility of this design pattern works seamlessly with the new deployment model. For more information about the parent-child design pattern, refer to Chapter 16.

In order to trace the execution of the individual packages, the packages contain a Script task that writes to a file on the file system. The file location is defined by the connection manager defined in the packages. Listing 19-4 shows the C# code that allows access to the file. The main() method calls the method appendToFile(string) in order to append the string parameter to the file. The file mode that is defined for the file stream object is Append, which allows the method to automatically add to the end of the file. The write mode allows read/write access to the file specified by the connection manager's connection string.

Listing 19-4. *Script Task Methods*

```
public void Main()
{
```

```
        // TODO: Add your code here
        string packageTime = Dts.Variables["System::StartTime"].Value.ToString() + "\n";
        string packageMessage = "The current package's name is: " +
                Dts.Variables["System::PackageName"].Value.ToString() + "\n";
        appendToFile("************************************************");

        appendToFile(packageTime);
        appendToFile(packageMessage);

        Dts.TaskResult = (int)ScriptResults.Success;
}
private void appendToFile(string appendMessage)
{
        try
        {
                FileStream fs = new
        FileStream(Dts.Connections["DeployedPackageOutput"].ConnectionString.
                ToString(), FileMode.Append, FileAccess.Write);
                StreamWriter sw = new StreamWriter(fs);

                sw.WriteLine(appendMessage);

                sw.Close();
        }
        catch (IOException ex)
        {
                ex.ToString();
        }
}
```

In order to execute a package that has been deployed as a part of a project, navigate to the package in the Integration Services catalog, right-click the package, and select Run. This pops up the Run Package window, shown in Figure 19-16, which allows you to configure the details of the execution. The first tab of the window, Parameters, allows you to configure the project-level parameters. For our demonstration, we will leave these values as the defaults from the project deployment. The execution of the packages takes place from the selected package's scope. Only the specific package's objects are configurable. In our case, the parameters and connection managers on CH19_Apress_DynamicParentPackage.dtsx are the only configurable objects.

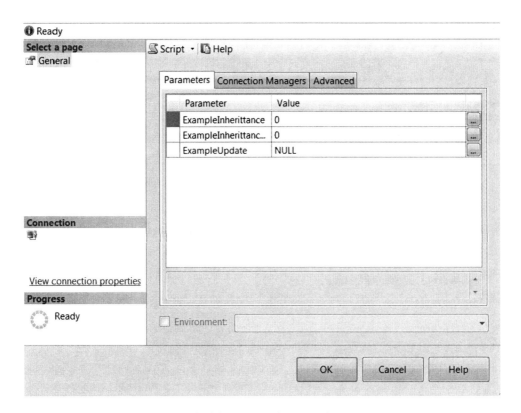

Figure 19-16. The Parameters tab of the Run Package window

The check box at the bottom allows you to use an environment that has been referenced in the project configuration. Selecting an environment will automatically apply the different object mappings that have been configured.

In order to modify the values of the parameters, the ellipsis button to the right of the Value field needs to be clicked. The Edit Literal Value for Execution window, shown in Figure 19-17, allows you to modify the value of any of the parameter values. Fill in the Value field with the value that is required for current execution. The values are used for only the current execution. If you need to reuse these values, we recommend creating an environment with the appropriate environment variables.

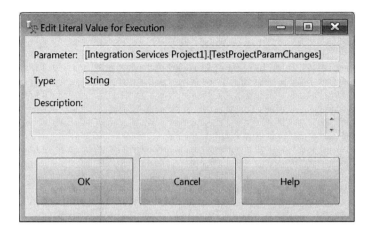

Figure 19-17. Edit Literal Value for Execution window

The Connection Managers tab, shown in Figure 19-18, shows the package's connection managers. The same Edit Literal Value for Execution window is used to modify a connection manager's property. Just like the parameter values, the value used applies only to the current execution. The value will default back to the original value that was provided when the project was deployed to the Integration Services catalog. If incorrect connection strings are passed in, the execution will fail and you will have to reconfigure all the properties. To avoid this hassle, we recommend that you design appropriate environments.

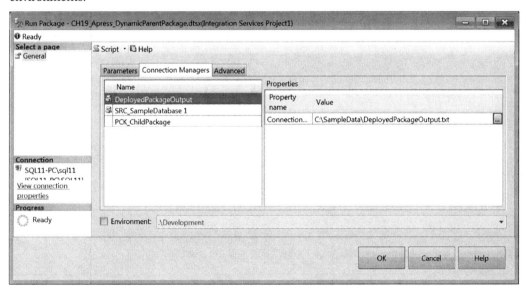

Figure 19-18. The Connection Managers tab of the Run Package window

The Advanced tab, shown in Figure 19-19, allows for the configuration of the minute details of the execution. The Property Overrides section allows you to specify the exact property that you need to modify. The Logging level lists the following execution logging options:

None disables logging for the execution. Selecting this option can provide some performance benefits, but depending on your standard operating procedures, logging may be required.

Basic logging records only error and warning messages.

Performance logging records all the events that are available.

Verbose logging records diagnostic information collected during the execution.

The Dump on Errors option allows you to create debug dump files in the case of errors during execution. The 32-Bit Runtime option allows you to run the package in 32-bit mode on a 64-bit machine. This option is vital if you are using providers that do not have a 64-bit driver, such as the Microsoft Jet Database Engine for accessing Microsoft Excel files.

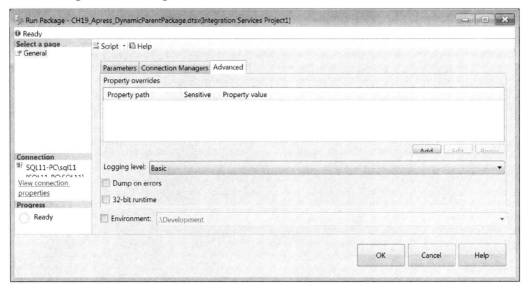

Figure 19-19. *The Advanced tab of the Run Package window*

■ **NOTE:** Even though the Environment check box appears on all of the tabs, this checkbox applies to the execution as a whole. It does not use the mappings for the context of the tabs.

Specific package object properties are configured by clicking the Add button. The Property Override window, shown in Figure 19-20, allows you to identify the property by providing the property path. This identifies a property of a particular object that is defined within the package. The Property value field allows you to provide the override value for that property.

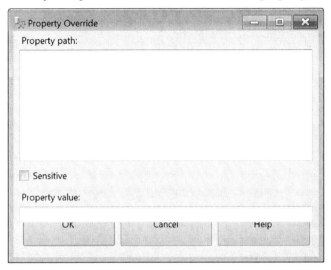

Figure 19-20. Property Override window

■ **CAUTION:** There is no check to ensure that the value provided matches the data type of the property that needs to be overwritten. You should double-check the metadata before you start overriding properties.

With the configuration of the package's execution complete, you can click the OK button to start the execution. As the execution starts, Management Studio will have a pop-up window providing you with the ID of the operation as well as the option to open the Overview Report. The Overview Report is a new addition to SQL Server 11 that provides a detailed report of SSIS package execution through the Integration Services catalog. Figure 19-21 shows the pop-up window that allows you to view the Overview Report of the execution.

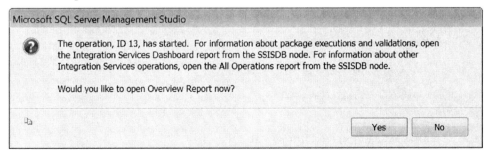

Figure 19-21. Overview Report request

Clicking the Yes button on the Overview Report request allows to you review all the details of the package execution. Figure 19-22 provides a snippet of the report, which contains information such as the start and end times of the package execution, the duration of the execution of each executable within the package, and in our particular example, the execution duration of child packages. There is a section that also reports the property overrides that were defined for the execution.

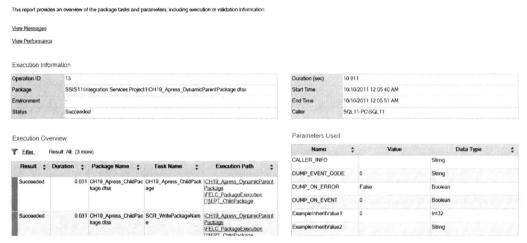

Figure 19-22. Execution Overview Report snippet

■ **NOTE:** The Overview Report itself cannot be saved, but the history of all the executions is stored within the Integration Services catalog. To view the history of executions, navigate to the folder with the project whose history you need to review, right-click the folder, and select Reports> All Executions. This will provide you with a quick overview of the different executions. If you wish to see a catalog-wide history of SSIS package executions, right-click the catalog instead of a particular folder. These reports are created by using Report Definition Language (RDL), and as such custom reports can be created and added to allow viewing from within SSMS.

With the use of File Connection Manager, the Script tasks within each package appended a string to a file that existed in a location where the server had access. Listing 19-5 shows the contents of the files after two executions of `CH19_Apress_DynamicParentPackage.dtsx`.

Listing 19-5. `CH19_Apress_DynamicParentPackage.dtsx` Result

```
**************************************************
10/1/2011 11:55:30 AM

The current package's name is: CH19_Apress_DynamicParentPackage
```

```
10/1/2011 11:55:35 AM

The current package's name is: CH19_Apress_ChildPackage

10/1/2011 11:55:38 AM

The current package's name is: CH19_Apress_ChildPackage1

10/1/2011 11:55:42 AM

The current package's name is: CH19_Apress_ChildPackage2
**************************************************
10/10/2011 12:05:46 AM

The current package's name is: CH19_Apress_DynamicParentPackage

10/10/2011 12:05:49 AM

The current package's name is: CH19_Apress_ChildPackage

10/10/2011 12:05:49 AM

The current package's name is: CH19_Apress_ChildPackage1

10/10/2011 12:05:50 AM

The current package's name is: CH19_Apress_ChildPackage2
```

▪ **NOTE:** This dynamic parent package had a similar setup to the dynamic parent package demonstrated in Chapter 16. As you can see, the disabled child package did not append a string to the file indicating that the package property value was overwritten by the parameter mapping that was configured in the parent package.

The Import Process

The *import process* refers to using the Integration Services Import Project Wizard to import an existing project into a new one. The wizard looks very similar to the deployment wizard except that it does not allow you to specify a destination for the imported project. After you import the project from its source, you can copy and paste it to the appropriate location. We discussed this process in Chapter 2.

The Migration Process

The *migration process* has been introduced with this version of SSIS to allow for legacy projects to comply with the new deployment model and features. This process is used also because prior versions of

SSIS used Visual Studio 2005 and 2008, whereas the latest version uses Visual Studio 2010. The Visual Studio Conversion Wizard is designed to make the process as painless as possible. When you attempt to open a project file from a prior version of SSIS, Visual Studio will automatically prompt you with the wizard shown in Figure 19-23. This wizard will then guide you through the steps of upgrading your project files.

Figure 19-23. Visual Studio Conversion Wizard—Introduction

Because Visual Studio already knows the project you are trying to upgrade, it will not bother asking you for the location of the project file and items that belong to the project. The next page of the wizard, shown in Figure 19-24, gives you the option of creating a backup of the files before you convert. We highly recommend that you take redundant backups before you proceed. You can always go back and clean up, but if the only copy is corrupted, it is corrupted. Having a source code versioning system can also provide some peace of mind. The second page of the wizard allows you to specify the location of the backup.

Figure 19-24. The Visual Studio Conversion Wizard's backup options

Before Visual Studio converts the files, it provides one last warning about version control. The last page of the wizard is shown in Figure 19-25. It shows a summary of the location of the project and the backup. Clicking Finish will prompt a message reporting a successful completion of the process. After you close the wizard, you will leave the project and all the items loaded in the Solution Explorer of that specific Visual Studio window.

Figure 19-25. Visual Studio Conversion Wizard—Summary

■ **CAUTION:** Visual Studio 2010 will not open project files from prior versions without upgrading the files. Ensure that you have proper backups of the legacy code before attempting to upgrade to the latest version.

Summary

With the introduction of the new deployment model in SSIS, you can now deploy your ETL processes to SQL Server without the overhead that existed in prior versions. The new environments and the environment variables remove the need for maintaining configurations for the deployment to different testing and production environments. We showed you how to build and deploy your SSIS project to SQL Server as well as how to migrate your legacy SSIS packages to the new model. The next chapter covers source control and SSIS administration and security.

Index

■ H

■ I, J, K

CPSIA information can be obtained at www.ICGtesting.com
Printed in the USA
LVOW111501050712

288896LV00004B/1/P

9 781430 236924